Philosophy — *East and West*

Edited by CHARLES A. MOORE

PRINCETON UNIVERSITY PRESS · 1946

PRINTED IN THE UNITED STATES OF AMERICA BY PRINCETON
UNIVERSITY PRESS AT PRINCETON, NEW JERSEY

TO GREGG M. SINCLAIR

President of the University of Hawaii and ardent believer in the significance of the East for the West. His enthusiasm has created in all who have met him a lasting interest in the Orient. It was he who inspired the East-West Philosophers' Conference at which this volume had its inception, and who, through his encouragement and assistance, aided materially in its preparation and publication.

Preface

This volume presents the results of the East-West Philosophers' Conference held at the University of Hawaii during the summer of 1939. At this conference, representatives of Orient and Occident were brought together to investigate, through the mediums of personal contact, discussion, and formal papers, the meaning and significance of the basic attitudes of these two major traditions. The conference was particularly concerned with the significance of the philosophy of the East for the West. The underlying purpose was to determine the possibility of a world philosophy through a synthesis of the ideas and ideals of East and West, and to reach conclusions in the form of specific suggestions concerning the most fruitful ways in which such a synthesis could be effected. These conclusions, some of which may appear to be extreme and controversial but all of which are highly provocative—and upon which the several writers do not always agree—are here presented in complete detail. Among these is the constant theme that neither Orient nor Occident is philosophically self-sufficient, each lacking that total perspective which is characteristic of philosophy. Specifically, it is held that the West needs new and wider perspectives, and that the East—in addition to its inevitable practical influence upon the West in the future—may provide inspiration as well as specific doctrines for this new Renaissance.

In general, the plan of the conference—which appears in the form and the content of this volume—called for comprehensive, though brief, descriptions of the basic systems and doctrines of the East, primarily by Oriental scholars, and analyses of these attitudes in comparison with the basic traditions of the West, by Western representatives. The constant interchange of ideas in discussion, resulting in the removal of false or inadequate interpretations of the East by Western representatives and the achievement of a greater mutual understanding, is reflected many times in this study. This aspect of the volume, and the fact that it includes personal representatives of both East and West, make it a unique chapter in the history of comparative philosophy.

For the purposes of this study, the "East" consists primarily of India, China, and Japan. Unfortunately no Indian scholar was available for the conference and so India is not personally represented here; this deficiency is mitigated, however, by the wide knowledge of Indian thought possessed by members of the conference. The volume has the advantage, however—especially in view of current developments—of a comprehensive analysis of the several phases of Japanese thought. We were especially privileged to have at the conference the outstanding Buddhist authority, Professor Junjirō Takakusu. Last-minute emergencies prevented Professors W. E. Hocking and D. T. Suzuki, who have chapters here, from attending the conference.

The style of chapter construction and documentation shows some variation throughout the book. Also, some duplication in content will be noticed in the several chapters. Suffice it to say that no ironclad rule of uniformity of style or overstrict limitation of subject matter was considered imperative. Transliteration of names and terms from the Sanskrit, Chinese, and Japanese inevitably presents difficulties. The system adopted allows for occasional variations from the basic method used for the text as a whole. In these instances, alternate spellings will be noted in the index. Chinese and Japanese names, like the transliteration of some Sanskrit terms, are made to conform to the widest usage or most familiar style. With rare exceptions, Chinese names conform to the Chinese style. Japanese names in Chapter VI follow the Japanese style; elsewhere the Western form is used. All names are listed in the index under surname.

It is a pleasure to express special appreciation to Dr. David L. Crawford, former President of the University of Hawaii, for making the Conference of 1939 possible and for his enthusiastic personal and official support of the undertaking; to Judge and Mrs. Walter F. Frear, for their generous financial assistance; to J. Leslie Dunstan, Ph.D., for exceptional assistance on the proofs and the compilation of the index; to Arthur P. Bouvier, Ph.D.; and Iwasaburo Yoshikami, for assistance on special phases of proofreading; to Mrs. Anne M. Moore, for extremely helpful clerical assistance in the arduous task of compiling the index; and to Mr. Datus C. Smith, Jr., and Miss Gladys Fornell of Princeton University Press for their generous assistance throughout the process of publication and their unusual patience and kindness in view of delays and numerous other difficulties encountered in the course of dealing under wartime conditions with an editor 6,000 miles distant.

I should like to add my deep personal appreciation for the great assistance rendered by Dr. Chan Wing-tsit throughout the long period from the very inception of the plans for a Philosophers' Conference to the completion of the manuscript for publication.

Appreciation is hereby expressed to the following publishers for permission to use quotations from their publications: George Allen and Unwin, Ltd., London; The Buddhist Society, London; University of California Press, Berkeley; University Press, Cambridge, England; Crown Publishers, New York; E. P. Dutton & Co., New York; Longmans Green & Co., London; Harvard University Press, Cambridge, Mass.; Japan Society, London; Luzac and Co., London; The Macmillan Co., New York; John Murray, London; Open Court, La Salle, Ill.; Kegan Paul, Trench, Trübner & Co., London; Arthur Probsthain, London; Random House, New York; and Charles Scribner's Sons, New York. Acknowledgment is also made of the use of quotations from books of publishers in the Orient, from whom permission was not obtained because of present unusual circumstances.

C.A.M.

Honolulu, T.H.
July 1944

CONTENTS

CHAPTER I

Value of the Comparative Study
of Philosophy

By William Ernest Hocking

The Western world is beginning to take the Orient seriously. It has for perhaps two centuries held a scholarly interest in the Orient as a place of various interesting developments of civilization. It has during these two centuries mastered languages, and edited and translated many classical Oriental texts. It has added immensely to our knowledge of Oriental history. In all of this scholarly work, there has been very little assumption that the philosophies of the Orient have something important for us. With the outstanding exception of Schopenhauer, no Western philosopher of the first rank has incorporated major Oriental ideas into his system of thought.

This scholarly objectivity has gone hand in hand with political objectivity. The Orient has been there to be dealt with and to be used as a source of supply, and as a great market, but without a fundamental fraternity.

Today there is a new spirit of respect: the element of fraternity begins to enter. The Orient speaks our languages, and we begin to speak its languages. A hundred bridges are being built across these diverse ways of living, partly through the agencies of new political cooperation, and partly through the work of science and of art. In science we still retain the leadership in respect to the volume and importance of discovery and adventure, although Oriental scientists are beginning to contribute to the growing volume of a truth which is above race and nation. But in the fine arts we have become aware that in many points the Oriental sensitivity is incomparably greater than our own. In the field of color, for example, we have done well with the contrast and harmony of two colors. It is only in China that the corresponding harmony and balance of three colors has been successfully achieved.

2

One cause of this change of attitude is, of course, our far more adequate means of knowledge of the Orient, but a second cause is practical. We are having more and more to do with the Orient in every respect, and we need to know what it is with which we have to do. Commercial and political dealings are never mere exchanges of goods and services; there is always a psychological element. There are ways of selling which are not successful. Things which appeal to the Western buyer do not always appeal to the Oriental buyer. It is not merely that knives and forks have a poor market in a country which uses chopsticks, but that the whole sense of what constitutes a comfortable and satisfactory life is different. The emotional reactions of people have to be taken into account in diplomatic and commercial dealings. The offended customer is one who will not buy, even if he wants to, and we are dealing everywhere with what we may designate as the emotional basis of life.

Now the *philosophies of the Orient and the religions of the Orient are the avowal of this emotional basis.* We are accustomed to say that the Orient is inscrutable, another way of saying that we do not understand its emotions. That is because we look in the wrong place for the source of these emotions. If you look into the eyes of a person, you may be puzzled to know how he feels or why he feels as he does. But if you wish to know the background of consciousness out of which emotions spring, you will find it is the traditions which have made him. The record of Oriental religions and philosophies is the self-expression of the Oriental reaction to life. It is the key to the Oriental character. The most concrete of our practical interests will require a closer acquaintance with these sources of Oriental feeling, even at the moment when these traditions are being turned away from by the Orientals themselves. No such changes can be sufficiently deep to make over in a short time that quality of civilization, which for several thousand years has transmitted itself with extraordinary faithfulness.

3

Studies of Oriental thought have all of the usual value of the comparison of civilizations. They show how much akin the minds of men are under all circumstances. Just as arithmetic is the same the world over, so is science in its simple beginnings in the observation of the sky, the earth, and living things. But they show also, and sometimes with startling contrast, differences in the very bases of our world views—the data of sense, of observation, and of our primary evaluations. We are accustomed to think that science runs along a linear track, and that there is a definite higher and lower stage of knowledge. But even in the progress of the sciences there is great advantage in beginning over again on a different tack, and using a different eye. The Indians have seen things about animal life which have completely eluded us. Chinese perception of natural forms and qualities has many novelties for duller gaze. The Japanese sense of harmony and illusion in landscape opens a new gamut of original perception in the stories and fancies about living things. The possibilities in the textures of hand-wrought jade and emerald, gold and iron, are a sort of elementary physical revelation. These peculiar powers of perception have not hitherto been developed by the Orient into new phases of science. The scheme of scientific development has been lacking. China devised gunpowder, and used the compass long before it was known in the West, but has written no systematic treatise on physics or chemistry. But now that the form is theirs, having been transmitted from the West, these powers of observation will perform their own unique function, and show new sides of nature, as in the studies of plant physiology by Bose of Calcutta.

What is true of science is true also of metaphysics and of ethics. There are universal principles, as in logic and metaphysics. There is indeed some tendency to assume that the "categories of thought" are different in East and West. It has recently been maintained that the subject-predicate structure of Greek language, which has imposed an Aristotelian subject-attribute cast on all Western thinking, is escaped in Chinese thought, because the verb "to be" has no exact Chinese equivalent: "shih" as a general term of affirmation has no infinitive form. It may be true that Chinese thought is more naturally relational. But it is a question of emphasis. The basic categories both of being and of value are the same everywhere. If it were not so, there would be no hope of an international understanding nor of international order. Nor could scholars write about these differences articles which would be understood in both hemispheres.

This being granted, the importance of comparative studies depends on the fact that there are emphases within the body of truth which are racial, just as there is a racial psychology. Indeed, what we mean by a racial psychology is chiefly a characteristic difference in moral emphasis. These differences are frequently causes of alienation or antipathy. Racial prejudice is very largely a judgment that the ethical or aesthetic sense of another people is constitutionally defective somewhere. Now this opinion may be true without constituting either a superiority on the part of the judge or a moral gulf. For it is quite likely to be true of the critic that his moral judgments also are defective somewhere! The real question is whether each is *capable of recognizing* that his moral judgments are defective; for if so, he is judging his judgments by a standard more nearly universal, and common ground can be reached. If, then, any racial psychology is based upon peculiarities of moral judgment, or let us say, value judgment, this is a fact of the utmost importance, but not necessarily a final fact; for the discovery that this is the case is an agent for changing it. Differences of racial perception in ethics and in aesthetics are an enrichment to the total magazine of human experience. The influx of new knowledge about Oriental philosophy ought to be a powerful means of reaching for ourselves a better grasp of universal principles in these fields.

4

It must be remembered that the Orient is more consciously philosophical than the West. That is to say, it is usual in Oriental countries that life is governed by conscious reference to general principles of philosophy or religion. These general principles find their way more naturally into conversation. To many a Western mind this is an oddity. It seems to the hardheaded realist that the Oriental mind is very much engaged with unrealities.

In this point it is clearly the realist who is naive. Generally speaking, the pragmatic and realistic temper of the West takes the things of experience at their face value as real. It treats its physical objects and its commercial credits as realities in the full sense of the word. It believes that its "progress" is largely due to this realism. It does indeed remind itself occasionally that these things are not final, and that there is a mystery behind the overt facts; but having recognized the existence of a mystery, perhaps once a week, it then proceeds to treat the world as though this mystery were of no practical importance.

It ignores the fact that its own codes of conduct have emerged from a state of mind—an Oriental religion—in which these very mysteries were supremely real. As a consequence, just on its practical side, the Western consciousness is divided and confused. It is vaguely religious without knowing why. It accepts ethical guidance without adequate powers of criticism because it has forgotten how it came by it. If you ask the average Westerner what life means, he is dumb. He is satisfied to live, and to let somebody else think about it.

The Oriental is wiser; his philosophy is always at work. He has no philosophy and no religion which is not at work. His reflections are kept in close connection with his actions. We have to learn from the Orient the practical significance of metaphysics. A race of people who could beget so jejune a scheme of thought as logical positivism, which declares metaphysical problems meaningless, has every reason to listen quietly to the mind of the Orient.

5

In so doing we are, of course, simply reverting to our own origins. To become acquainted with the Orient on the side of its philosophy —and religion—is to become acquainted with our ancient selves. The history of the Orient is like all history, at the bottom a history of facts, but it is still more fundamentally a history of ideas; and this history has yet to be written.

6

One who delves in the rich mine of Oriental thought will come upon many points in which he is ready to acknowledge the superiority of Oriental genius. The poverty of the Orient, the widespread misery of the rural population, is an economic fact which deserves, like all such facts, to be measured and recorded. But we ought to record at the same time, that under these appalling conditions the Orient has maintained an extraordinary level of inner human dignity. There are glaring evils patent on the surface of Oriental life, and the necessity of change is apparent, not only to the West but to the East. Our era will be known as the era of social awakening in Asia; but with the evil there has gone a partial solution. No one who studies the "problem of evil" can afford to neglect the inward history of the common man of China and India, to discover if possible how under these conditions he has maintained so high a human level.

We often think of Confucianism as a static system of social forms. China itself is inclined to identify Confucianism with an outmoded family life, shackles which the present age has to cast off. But there is a spirit in Confucianism which no one can encounter without recognizing its essential immortality. Confucius no doubt believed in forms, but he did not believe in forms without meaning. There could be no greater appeal to sincerity than his which prized so highly the art of "giving things their right names." When we consider that Western hypocrisy in politics and elsewhere consists in giving things more decorous names than they deserve, we appreciate the scope of this searching maxim that things shall be given their right names. And even in the detail of living we can learn the Confucian standard of the "princely man." Confucius praised one of his disciples, attributing to him two outstanding merits—first, he did not have to learn over again what he had learned once. Second, he did not "transfer his feelings," meaning thereby that one does not, because he is annoyed by one episode, carry his annoyance into the next one, nor because he is amused at one moment carry an unfit hilarity into the next. The ideal man is emotionally adequate to each occasion. The nicety of justice in this ideal is a simple instance of the fineness of ethical observation which we find throughout the rich repertoire of Oriental reflection.

7

To come now from these general observations to questions of principle, let us ask what sort of significant insight may be expected of the comparative study of Eastern and Western philosophies.

If philosophy were a simple deductive science, both Western and Eastern philosophy could regard themselves self-sufficient and in no absolute need of light from any other quarter of the globe. The original premises ought to agree, and the inferences from them would constitute a body of truth indifferent to time and place. The increased number of workers which might accrue if Western philosophy and Eastern philosophy were to join hands would indeed, as in the case of science, facilitate the progress of philosophy; but we could expect no qualitatively different insight.

But philosophy is primarily a matter of *what a person sees*, and then of his capacity to make a rational connection between what he sees and what he otherwise knows; his premises are his original observations about the world. Hence people who can add something to our vision are the most important aids to progress in philosophy. The very fact that the Orient has *different modes of intuition*—which is sometimes put in the misleading form that there is a gulf between the mentalities of East and West—is the fact which makes their contributions to philosophy so important to us, and ours to them. It is fortunate from this point of view that Oriental and Western philosophies have grown for so long a time in separation. They have become established in their ways of looking at things. Each has become the charter of a civilization more or less durable. If the test of a philosophy were the durability of the civilization which is based on it, the Orient would unquestionably have the greater warrant. When Sarendranath Dasgupta spoke at the opening of the new Buddhist temple at Sarnath, on November 11, 1931, he pointedly declared that European civilization, though professing a religion of peace, had signally failed to keep its house in an order of good will, whereas Buddhism had actually promoted peace, had never progressed by aid of political pressure; and he welcomed what he referred to as the Hindu-Buddhist civilization of the future in Asia. The considerations which underlay this remarkable utterance deserve our most serious thought.

The supplementation of philosophies takes place even in the abstract branches of logic; but it is most conspicuous in metaphysics, ethics, and the foundations of social life. Let us consider, for example, two matters in which our own philosophy is in difficulties, and in which the Orient has something distinctive to say: the question of individualism versus corporate social life, and the question of otherworldliness (or mysticism) versus realistic humanism.

8

Individualism is, or has been, with us a shibboleth. We have regarded it as an ideal more or less incorporated into our legal system. We cannot say that we do in fact hold the individual sacred, but we establish our laws on the assumption that individuals have equal rights in the sight of the law, and from this point we deduce our systems of civil rights and our democracy. But the basis of equal rights is equal worth; and can we say that we do in fact attribute equal (and "sacred") worth to all human individuals?

A Chinese writer recently accused our civilization of hypocrisy on precisely this ground. We go to the Orient and talk about the sacred rights of the individual, but, as he pointed out, street car companies in America which kill a statistical number of individuals per year have been known to decline to install safety-fenders, on the ground that the cost of the fenders would be greater than the annual indemnities for lost lives and lost limbs. In practice we think of life in terms of dollars and cents, so the Chinese critic argued: "sacredness" is a sentiment, not a principle.

Nor, again, do we find in practice that to treat the individual as the absolute unit of social life, the seat of all rights and powers, answers to the social facts. Group and corporate existence has its rights also, and its claims upon its membership. Not to recognize this is to weaken the organic life of the state.

More particularly, individualism has in practice tended to destroy the capacity of our democracies to achieve unity of action and feeling: the claim of rights has eaten up the awareness of common duty. And the totalitarian reaction expresses a distrust of the moral bases of democracy. We cannot meet the totalitarian case by simply reasserting our confidence in democracy. We have to reconsider the philosophical basis of democracy and the meaning of such individualism as we shall continue to hold. In this respect, the Orient is likely to be very instructive to us.

9

The Orient has never proposed individualism as a primary principle, nor the sacredness of personality. Western critics have maintained that its philosophies tend to regard the world of experience as illusory, and individual differences likewise. Buddhism regards as the root of all suffering the craving for individual separateness. For Hinduism in its classic form, the great realization is to the effect that we are identical with Brahman, and therefore identical with each other. This is not the only form of Hindu philosophy and it is unjust to Indian thought to identify Hinduism with this doctrine; but it has nevertheless a wide influence. And in so far as this is the case, it is evident that no individualism could be based upon it, except as a tentative working maxim for an inferior order of reality. Perhaps Indian thought, which has been busied of late in repudiating the habit of Westerners to characterize its outlook in terms of Advaita Vedānta, may return to take a certain satisfaction in that aspect of Vedānta which corrects a Western fallacy, the fallacy of personal separation.

In any case, the stability of Oriental society is due in part to a healthy indisposition to exaggerate the importance of difference in social function and status, which its philosophies record and sustain. The indigenous philosophies of the Far East almost universally attribute a religious significance to the family, as an overindividual entity within which diversity of function is the rule. The family, in turn, provides and cares for all, creating a domesticity in which all share without an artificial profession of equality. The spirit of the family has until recently pervaded the wider groups, leading to a relative acquiescence in social difference, and an indisposition to insist on invidious social comparisons. Caste or occupational type are allowed to outline a career: has not Manu said that the confusion of castes is the greatest of all misfortunes? The relative lack of that stridency in personal ambition which shows itself in the determination to "rise," and so a certain freedom from the restlessness and insistence on rights which so fills our Western societies with complaint, struggle, and class war, is at least in part an element of social strength. We might perhaps say that it is characteristic of Oriental philosophy to regard social "justice," when justice is defined in terms of individual claim to material goods and position, as a matter of minor importance. And in so far as this is the case, there goes with the natural inequality among men a disposition to endure without complaint a degree of social hardship. This power of endurance and of acquiescence is aided in some parts of the Orient by the doctrine of *karma*, which represents the actual circumstances of the individual as having a meaning in terms of his eternal destiny, a meaning not fixed by his own present efforts, nor by those of society.

Now under the first impressions of Western observers, all of this acquiescence is pernicious, and a factor in social stagnation. We have tried to instill into the Orient a disposition to fight injustice, and to reform its institutions in the interest of individual freedom of action; we have recommended a disposition to rebel, to help oneself, to forget *karma*, to take social and individual fortunes into one's own hands; we want to inspire the Oriental with a discontent which we like to qualify as "divine." And the modern Orient, more than half convinced of this program, finds the germ of individual, aggressive effort in its own philosophies, and fans these into a new life.

Allowing that this trend is right, may I raise the question whether it is more than half right? Perhaps the ability of the Orient to endure is at least in some measure a virtue which we lack and hardly understand. In my judgment, we shall have no just estimate of our own social order until we have understood the philosophical bases of this Oriental outlook, in which the lot of the individual is not immersed in, but entwined with, the fortunes of a corporate group or groups, whether the family, the occupational group, or the nation.

10

This brings me to the second character of Oriental philosophy about which I wish to speak, otherworldliness. The feeling that the visible world is not the whole world has certainly had a role to play in the imagination of millions of persons whose lives are humdrum and difficult beyond anything that we in the West know. The average Oriental farmer lives in a world of incessant toil, but also in a world of vivid imagination, in so far as he thinks of his relation to the departed members of his own clan. His dealings with these spirits in his family worship are likely to be superstitious. He attributes to them an influence on his worldly fortunes which they do not have. When he becomes critical and intellectual, he is likely to discard the whole outlook. The traditional philosophy attempts to maintain the two worlds in comparative insulation one from the other. We think that these two phases of the world fall too far apart in the Orient, that its philosophy tends too much to be a cult of a transcendent reality which has nothing to do with this world. The intelligentsia of the new Orient falls in with this judgment: its otherworldliness disappears in a pragmatic or humanistic secularism.

The great value to the Orient of the pragmatic criticism of metaphysical ideas is not to be discounted; it has still a large work to do. This may be taken as a contribution from Western to Oriental thought, so far as the present incentive goes; though again it has had the effect of reanimating pragmatic roots existing in the traditions of the Eastern philosophies themselves, especially in China. But there is a difference between criticism and construction; and since pragmatism in the West has shown itself singularly incapable of building a positive world view, it behooves both East and West to consider the sources of those bold structures of faith which have for so long served as the matrices of culture.

If we are to retain for civilization a working difference from a sordidly practical and material outlook on the world, if we are to achieve a genuine humanism, we shall have to reconsider the bases of former otherworldliness. And in this reconsidering we shall do well to examine the types of mystical conviction not yet lost to the Orient which are so near the sources of our own historic faith. No metaphysic retains today its full traditional force; and yet no traditional metaphysic has lost its contemporary importance.

II

I have mentioned two points in which the comparison of philosophies promises to add to our resources for sound judgment. These may serve as illustrations of the general principles that each philosophy we are dealing with is a variety of vision; that in the philosophic task, never so urgent as today, we need not only two eyes but many eyes; and those very differences which constitute the felt strangeness of the Orient are precisely the differences which make its thought indispensable for us. To summarize:

There are three historic attitudes in dealing with what is beyond our own circle of ideas. First, "This is strange and alien—avoid it." Second, "This is strange and alien—investigate it." Third, "This appears strange and alien—but it is human; it is therefore kindred to me and potentially my own—learn from it." Until two centuries ago, we were for the most part acting upon the first maxim. For another two centuries, the eighteenth to the twentieth, we have acted on the second: we have been concerned with an objective study of the East. The two centuries ahead of us must be devoted to the third, an attempt to pass beyond scholarly objectivity to a working human association and the common pursuit of universal truth.

CHAPTER II

An Outline of Indian Philosophy[1]

By George P. Conger

An OUTLINE of Indian philosophy may in the present connection be restricted almost entirely to various stages in the development of Hinduism. The great systems of Buddhism are to be discussed elsewhere in this volume by one of the world's most famous scholars. Of the other important non-Hindu systems, some, like Islam, are not of Indian origin, and others, like Jainism, may—in the present limitations of space—be treated briefly.

HINDUISM

For Hinduism we have to consider at least six bodies of literature: (1) the *Vedic hymns,* (2) the *Brāhmaṇas,* (3) the *Upanishads,* (4) the *Sūtras,* with commentaries, etc., (5) the *Laws of Manu,* (6) the *Bhagavad Gītā.* For our present purpose these documents are like a jungle of intertwining trunks and branches. Problems of priority and mutual influence are often complex, but here they are of relatively small importance.

The usual view is that the Hindus were an Aryan people, racially akin to the Greeks and other European stocks, and that they came into northwest India sometime in the second millennium B.C., conquering the aboriginal inhabitants of that region and gradually extending their sway to the east and south. Some of the aborigines were won over to the new culture and were the ancestors of the later low caste *śūdras*; others who were not absorbed remained without caste and were the ancestors of the present-day "untouchables."

[1] The great amount of scholarly literature available on Indian philosophy made it unnecessary to include here an extensive exposition—as was felt to be advisable in the cases of Chinese philosophy and Buddhism. Professor Conger wishes the editor of this volume to state that at the Conference he undertook the work on Indian philosophy only after unsuccessful efforts had been made to secure a Hindu scholar.—Editor's Note.

1. The Vedic hymns (chants, sacrificial formulas) in the main represent an early and relatively prosperous stage of the Hindu invasion. They are original expressions of primitive polytheism, addressed to deities who appear to be personifications of natural forces and national aspirations. Particularly in the *Rig Veda*, one feels the vigor and freshness of the morning of mankind. The other collections (*Sāma Veda, Yajur Veda, Atharva Veda*) are secondary. Philosophically the Vedic polytheism belongs among the dualisms and supernaturalisms, although it should be noted that the deities are not so clearly or highly personified as are the Olympian gods of the Greeks. Books I and X of the *Rig Veda* are later than the other portions, and contain rudiments of ideas which later were of prime importance—that the universe is structured like man's body (RV, X, 90) and that the ultimate Reality is one (RV, I, 164, 46; X, 129).

As the invasion penetrated to new territories and conditions became less favorable, the Hindus appealed to their gods with more and more reliance upon elaborate sacrifices and ceremonies. These procedures were recorded and defended in the Brāhmaṇas, priestly commentaries on the Vedas, designed to show the connections between Vedic passages and details of the sacrificial rituals and to confirm the rituals because of their supposed point-by-point correspondence to the basic structures of man and also of the universe. The Brāhmaṇas are fantastic defenses of an impossible system, but they are important in Hindu philosophy as affording a transition to, and in a way a basis for, later ideas.

2. The Brahmanic speculations with all their audacity could hardly expect to attain efficacy or to retain faith. Something else was necessary; in the search for it certain *rishis* or seers withdrew to the northern forests, where their meditations eventually gave to the world the incomparable Upanishads. These documents, the records of conversations of those who came to "sit near" the *rishis*, in the course of centuries accumulated in various collections, to a number usually given as one hundred and eight, with twelve or thirteen of them selected as of chief importance.

3. With all their variations, the Upanishads are essentially esoteric teachings, developed by more or less secluded groups far away from the world of increasing difficulties with which Brahmanic methods could not cope. They are for the most part anonymous,

though occasionally names are mentioned—among others that of a
certain Yājñavalkya, who must be said to belong high in the history
of philosophy. In many passages the Upanishads mark little or no
advance on the Brāhmaṇas; they are mixtures of magic and mythol-
ogy, with strange interpretations of rituals, fantastic etymologies
and allusions, and inconsistencies enough to give point to many
later controversies. But the general trend is plain. The old Brahmanic ritual and the Vedic pantheon alike are increasingly supplanted
by a technique of meditations designed to solve life's problems
(a) by developing the view that not merely man's body but also
his mind is in structural correspondence with the universe, and
(b) by realizing much more fully that the ultimate Reality is one.
The former doctrine can, according to the Upanishads, be demonstrated; the latter may be adumbrated by illustration and description, but at last must be apprehended intuitively. As adumbrated in
thought, it may be expressed as a combination or fusion of three doctrines which when taken one by one are familiar in the West:

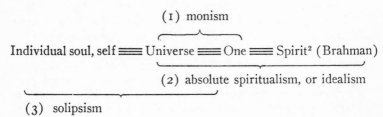

(1) monism

Individual soul, self ══ Universe ══ One ══ Spirit[2] (Brahman)

(2) absolute spiritualism, or idealism

(3) solipsism

The doctrines of (a) and (b) may be combined to say that according to the Upanishads the individual soul is analogous to and
ultimately identical with the universal spiritual Reality. This Reality at the last is to be immediately experienced by the individual
as the reality of his own self, and thus as essentially indescribable;
but as helps toward realizing it many partial and proximate descriptions are offered in terms of being, life, breath, thought, bliss, and
so on. To attain this realization of one's own identity with the absolute Brahman is to gain release or, as we might say, salvation.
Along with pronounced tendencies to monism there are in some

[2] The word "Spirit" is not an exact rendering of "Brahman," but is to be
understood as an approximation. Brahman, one might say, is "Something
quasi-psychological."

of the later Upanishads statements which justify at least a proximate dualism much like that familiar to us in the distinction between
spirit and matter.

Even the Upanishads did not at first altogether dominate Indian
thought. There are traditions of a once-flourishing crude materialism, the so-called Chārvāka system, which poured contempt upon
priests and in other matters was so positivistic that it would not
even admit the validity of inference to supplement our perceptions.
But at our distance this system disappears from Indian thought as
mysteriously as it comes into view. The field is left to others, whose
discussions, carried on for fifteen hundred years or more, crystallized in the six "orthodox" systems and those of their opponents,
the Jains and the Buddhists. All these developments are intertwined
in complicated ways; every document we possess must be said to
presuppose long unrecorded or unrecovered traditions of discussion
and controversy.

4. The six systems reflect differences of interpretation and emphasis among those who sought to follow the teachings of the Upanishads, keeping with those texts and with the Vedas a thread of
connection which, although sometimes dubious, suffices to label the
systems as "orthodox." For their primary formulations, the systems
go back to the so-called *Sūtras*, short cryptic and mnemonic sentences or phrases, so obscure that they have required successive
generations of commentators. The six systems differ somewhat in
their metaphysics, but agree in their ultimate aim. They are all concerned with the attainment of release from the necessity of rebirth
through the realization of some basic truth about the soul and the
world. They may be studied in three pairs, in each of which the
two member systems are mutually complementary: thus we have
the Nyāya-Vaiśeshika, the Sāṅkhya-Yoga, and the Pūrva Mīmāṁsā
(Mīmāṅsā)-Vedānta systems.

The word "Nyāya" connotes interpretation, or that by means of
which one is led to a conclusion. The *Nyāya Sūtras* are ascribed to
a certain Akshapāda or Gautama (not to be identified with the
founder of Buddhism); in the course of centuries there were important commentaries by Vātsyāyana, Uddyotakara, and Vācaspati
Miśra.

The system furnishes a technique of argumentation designed to
remove false knowledge and to provide the true knowledge requisite

for salvation. Such knowledge may be obtained by perception, by inference, by comparison (i.e., recognition of similarities or analogies) and by testimony. The Nyāya is empirical, realistic, and pluralistic. Among the twelve recognized *prameyas* or objects of knowledge are the self, the body, sense objects, various mental functions, rebirth, and emancipation. There are discussions of fallacies in logic and argumentation, which deserve comparison with Aristotle's *Topica* and *Sophistici Elenchi.* There is a famous "five-membered syllogism," but examination of it shows that the members which would have been strange to Aristotle are added for psychological and rhetorical, rather than for logical reasons.

Where the Nyāya emphasizes methods of knowing, its companion, the Vaiśeshika, emphasizes content. The word comes from that which means "particularity"; the system aims to present a catalogue of particular things or objects of knowledge. The *sūtras* are attributed to Kaṇāda, with later commentaries by Praśastapāda, Udayana, and others.

The *padārthas* or categories are substances, qualities, actions (or motions), generality, particularity, inherence, and, according to some, absence or privation. The nine substances are the four elements, ether (*ākāśa*), time, space, soul, and mind. Among the qualities (with their relations to various substances carefully specified) we find color, taste, smell, touch, sound, number, measure, knowledge, happiness, and sorrow. Under "actions" various forms of motion are enumerated. Generality, particularity, and inherence are treated realistically, as essentially independent of the objects which manifest them. Whatever the ramifications of such a catalogue, the interest in knowing it is always that of securing salvation.

More important than either of the foregoing systems is the Sāṅkhya, named from the word meaning "enumeration" and based on *sūtras* attributed to Kapila, with an important commentary by Vijñāna Bhikshu. The Sāṅkhya is virtually a dualism of spirit and matter, developed in accordance with Upanishadic passages which allow such interpretation. On the one hand, the Sāṅkhya combats the absolute monism of the main Upanishadic tradition, as this was being developed in the Vedānta; on the other hand, the Sāṅkhya is opposed to the nihilism of the Buddhists, and possibly also directed against the materialism of the Chārvākas. Thus subtleties are met by fresh subtleties. Like the Vaiśeshika, the Sāṅkhya catalogues the objects of knowledge or characteristics of the world, this time in a list of twenty-five *tattvas* or truths. Of these, two are primal and also ultimate—*purusha* (let us say, pure awareness), and *prakriti* (let us say, a material principle). The *purushas* are plural; they are at least the rudiments of what we know as individual souls. *Prakriti* has three *guṇas*, or components—*sattva, rajas,* and *tamas,* roughly describable as brightness or clearness, energy or activity, and heaviness or obstruction. An individual *purusha* touches off the world process—i.e., its own individual version of it—by concerning itself with *prakriti*; this "stirs up" *prakriti* and upsets the primal equilibrium of its three *gunas.* According as one or another *guna* preponderates in the series of disturbances or rearrangements which follow, the world as we know it is gradually evolved. It is quite proper to speak of the Sāṅkhya as an evolutionism; the evolution proceeds by successive integrations of component *guṇas* and thus at the same time by successive differentiations within *prakriti*.

First there is a principle of intelligence, the scope of which is sometimes cosmic (*mahat*) and again subjective (*buddhi*). In it *sattva* predominates to such a degree that it is hard to tell the difference between it and the original *purusha*. It becomes more definitely individualized in the next stage, *ahaṅkāra* or egohood. Then, by fresh combinations of component *guṇas*, there follows the development of five sense organs and *manas* or mind which coordinates them; five "organs of activity"; five *tanmātras* or potential subtle elements (roughly comparable in some respects to electrons, positrons, etc.); and finally the familiar five elements of ordinary gross matter. When all these *tattvas* are known the way is clear for the dissociation of the *purusha* from *buddhi* and the attainment of that utter detachment from the world, that disinterestedness which is release. The primal *prakriti* is neither absorbed nor dissolved; it is simply abandoned by each *purusha* as its release is attained.

For the attainment of this detachment certain disciplines are needed; these are supplied to the Sāṅkhya by its complement, the Yoga system. The word is akin to our "yoke," but the sense is better conveyed by our verb than by our noun. The *Yoga Sūtras* are attributed to Patañjali, with an important commentary by Vyāsa. In its authentic form the system is a discipline of concentration and control of mind, in which strict observance of the personal virtues is a means of obtaining right knowledge. In aid of concentration various bodily exercises or postures are recommended; some of them are such that students are warned not to attempt them without a teacher. Perhaps it was as nothing more than an object of meditation, but Yoga, unlike Sānkhya, made a place for a personal deity. To the utterly faithful devotee the *sūtras* promised supernatural powers almost without limit, and many stories strange to the West have grown up in and around the traditions. It is hardly necessary to add that the word "yoga" has been frequently misused in recent years, until what passes as Yoga has become the most widely discussed, if not the most widely discredited, of Indian systems.

The Vedānta, or "end of the Vedas" develops the main line of Upanishadic tradition, arguing for absolute spiritual monism and attempting to show that all Upanishadic passages when properly interpreted teach this doctrine. The *Vedānta Sūtras* are ascribed to Bādarāyana, but they are eclipsed by famous commentaries, first by Gaudapāda and then above all by Śankara and Rāmānuja. Śankara with elaborate arguments maintains the *advaita* (nondualist) view that the ultimate Reality, the individual self identical with Brahman, is "one without a second." Our ordinary convictions about the world are declared to be the result of *avidyā*, ignorance, and *māyā*, illusion, and must be resolved in an ultimate intuition of an identity such that nothing is left for the self except "self-shiningness." The qualified nondualistic view of Rāmānuja finds Reality to be not a bare identity but a synthetic whole with internal differences and personal qualities.

The Vedānta is complemented by the Pūrva Mīmāṁsā, with *sūtras* ascribed to Jaimini and interpreted in commentaries, for example by Kumārila and Prabhākara. The system contains some discussions about knowledge, but is chiefly an interpretation of Hindu ritual in ways which were believed to help in attaining the Vedānta ideal of identification with Brahman and thus release.

5. The Laws of Manu, a slowly accumulated code ascribed to Manu as a kind of Hindu Moses or Lycurgus, supply a framework of social and ethical principles which are presupposed as the matrix and expression of the more abstract metaphysical doctrines which we have considered. The West needs to understand that, seen in the setting where he belongs, the Hindu with all his absolute monism is very far from being ethically neutral or indifferent. To

call him "unethical" is a travesty. His four twenty-year stages of life (student, family man, contemplative, and wandering holy man) and even his overcrystallized caste system hold him to strict account, and at the same time turn the edge of accusations of pessimism and otherworldliness which the West has all too easily made. The fact that many men fail to meet the requirements of the Hindu system should not blind us to its true character; if failures are to be counted as definitive, all systems stand indicted together.

6. The *Bhagavad Gītā*, even though for us in somewhat inconsistent fashion, combines many of the foregoing doctrines with that of avatars or successive incarnations of the Supreme Being. The avatars come periodically, whenever the world needs to be rescued, and, for example in Krishna, elicit a personal loyalty and devotion comparable to those of Buddhism or other faiths for their central figures.

The inclusiveness of the *Bhagavad Gītā*, and of Hindu philosophy in general, is well illustrated by its words "Whatsoever deity any man wishes to worship with faith, to him I render that faith steady." Hinduism appears strangely inchoate and disorganized to Western minds, first because its really rigid social framework is forgotten and then because, with that framework presupposed, so much in the way of doctrine is left to the individual's choice. In Hinduism from the midst of a structured society each man seeks in his own way either to apprehend or avoid the universe in one spiritual experience.

NON-HINDU SYSTEMS

Long before all these developments in Hinduism were completed, Jainism and Buddhism had arisen in India and the latter had begun to make its way around the world. Little informal groups or *ashrams*, where students come to live with a teacher, have been formed in India without number, ever since the days of the Upanishads. Jainism and Buddhism grew from two such groups, which introduced variations capable of spreading and surviving. Jainism was primarily a system of asceticism, traced to a certain Mahāvīra, who is supposed to have lived in the sixth century B.C. It survives to this day in India as a minor religion, numbering one or two million adherents. In its long history it has retained a belief in the

soul as distinct from matter, and has developed a few logical subtleties, but it has been altogether surpassed in world importance by
the other slightly younger group, the followers of Gautama (or
Gotama) the Buddha. Buddhism gained an amazing hold upon
India, developed great monastic communities, universities, and
systems of philosophy while it was spreading to Ceylon, to Burma,
to Siam, to China, to Korea, and eventually to Japan. The discussion of Buddhism in this volume is left to a colleague honored
and loved, so that no attempt is made here to do justice to these
developments even within the Indian picture.

Several interesting developments in contemporary Indian philosophy, some of them with possibilities of fruitful contact with
Western thought, are outside the scope of this chapter. They could
be covered in large measure by a summary of the volume entitled
Contemporary Indian Philosophy, edited by Professor S. Radhakrishnan (London: Allen & Unwin, 1936), to which reference
should by all means be made.

Three questions which are often asked may be touched briefly
in conclusion. What is the place of Indian philosophy in history?
Why has Indian philosophy so evidently suffered from arrested
development? What can Indian philosophy teach the West or contribute to a planetary culture?

The place of Indian philosophy in the history of thought is original and permanent. The *Rig Veda* is older than the Old Testament,
and the earlier Upanishads antedate Plato. India was the birthplace
and the homeland of Buddhism; after undergoing profound changes
in its own land, Buddhism spread through the East on the whole
with fewer modifications than Christianity experienced when it
was cast in the molds of Greek and later European thought. It now
seems unlikely that Indian Brahmanism was of much influence on
Taoism in China; some of the texts, especially in clumsy translations, can be made to show similarities, but the genius of Taoism is
more naturalistic and less speculative. It is more likely that Indian
thought spread to the West and even that it influenced pre-Alex-
andrian Greece. This is a subject which with the progress of archeo-
logical and historical research needs continually to be reexamined.

At any rate the way was open, particularly through the Persian Empire, and there are many evidences of similarity if not of kinship.

Why has Indian philosophy, at least until recently, suffered from arrested development? Any attempt to answer this question must be very cautious; the history of Indian philosophy is at best only imperfectly known, and Western knowledge of it is notoriously defective. The whole story cannot be told until more sources are available. In the meantime reasons for the decline of several systems may perhaps be found in the Indian characteristic of extreme veneration for teachers and traditions which gradually wear out from exhaustion and inbreeding without receiving fresh ideas from outside; or again, in the discouragements incident upon repeated invasions, conquests, and oppressions; or more recently in loss of confidence when confronted by vigorously championed Western critical and empirical methods. But whatever be the case with Hindu philosophy, Hinduism as a religion has never stopped. It has in fact shown amazing absorptive and productive power—a power which accounts for many otherwise strange occurrences in Indian history, from the disappearance of Buddhism there to the influence of Christianity upon Gandhi. Within Hinduism, the Vedānta philosophy is still of wide influence and prime importance. And Indian thought is like the banyan tree; it is capable of spreading out to new ground and taking fresh root.

What can Indian philosophy contribute to the West, or to the new planetary culture which is just beginning to take shape? One's answer depends almost entirely upon one's estimate of the philosophies of supernaturalism and idealism. Western supernaturalism has tended to be self-sufficient, and officially its monotheisms would spurn any contribution from any polytheism, although India's picturesque and sometimes blithe polytheism might soften many a line where monotheism has been rigid and severe. For idealism the way is more open; in fact the Upanishads, the Vedānta, Spinoza, Hegel, and all their followers are so close together that when seen from a little distance their differences disappear. All of them agree that the primary and ultimate Reality is Spirit, God, or Mind; if this philosophy is to be taken seriously then India can contribute the rich experience of a hundred generations to strengthen the wavering idealisms of the West, and the problem

of a planetary philosophy may not be much more than a clearing
up of details—perhaps no more than a clearing up of details of
vocabulary.

But if in the West, in spite of current reaffirmations, supernaturalism collapses and idealism evaporates, and if both are succeeded
by naturalism, the contribution of India must be quite different. It
may be merely prolonged insistence, in the face of overwhelming
odds; sometimes it seems as if India's mission were to teach us that,
if we are willing to pay the price, we may still maintain our dream-
world of the spirit as we want it to be. Or, India's contribution
may lie along the line of abstraction and extrapolation; the West
is concerned with the multiplicity of things which are near, where
India, in common with other philosophies of the East, has concentrated more intently upon a unity of things much more remote.
The West has been explicit, analytical; India has been on the whole
more mystical, recognizing that its best thought falls short of the
ineffable. It may be that the weight of Western naturalism will find
a kind of compensation in an Eastern indefiniteness, in an ultimate
in which our strident differences and sharp distinctions are dissolved. This may all come to pass, although for Western problems
it is not a solution but a dissolution. It is a fair question whether
Western thought even if it could be led by India to a reality indefinite and indescribable, would be better off than it is now.

If we cannot evade naturalism, another procedure would be to
face it, to look straight into the data of the sciences for empirical
indications of kinship between man and nature. Here India, like
most other cultures, can bear witness to one or another version
of the old macrocosm-microcosm formula, although for anything
approaching an adequate modern investigation India could furnish
neither method nor content.

With or without supernaturalisms and idealisms, the abiding contribution of India to Western thought is more subtle and pervasive:
it abides in example rather than in precept. India presents to the
centuries a culture which has had time to ripen and acquire maturity; the West will appreciate it whenever the West comes to appreciate the need for some slowing of the tempo. With all the abuses
and limitations of the caste system, India shows to a Western
world which is half engulfed in the flux of its own progress the
strength of a structured society and the importance of recognizing

the fact that society has a structure. An individual, after all, must have status as well as drive. To a Western world too often entangled and stifled by its possessions and its conquests, India shows the deep resources of contentment with little. Perhaps in importance beyond all these things, India at its best demonstrates that men through centuries can be profoundly and sublimely religious without insisting as do the Semitic faiths that the Object of religious devotion must be personal. In all these matters the question here is not so much whether India can contribute, as whether the West is ready to receive.

CHAPTER III

The Story of Chinese Philosophy

By Chan Wing-tsit

CHINESE philosophy is an intellectual symphony in three movements. The first movement, from the sixth to the second century B.C., was essentially a period of development of the three major themes of Confucianism, Taoism, and Mohism, and the four minor ones of Sophism, Neo-Mohism, Legalism, and Yin Yang Interactionism, all with their contrasts and harmonies, to the accompaniment of the others of the "Hundred Schools." The second movement was characterized by the intermingling of the different motives which resolved into the dominant chord of medieval Chinese philosophy, while the note of Buddhism was introduced from India to give it the effect of counterpoint. In the third movement, the longest of all, from the eleventh century to the present day, the characteristic notes of Chinese philosophy were synthesized to transform the persistent chord of Confucianism into the long and unique melody which is Neo-Confucianism.

This analogy immediately suggests that there is consonance as well as dissonance among the main systems of Chinese thought, a significant fact to note particularly in the case of ancient schools. The opposition between humanistic Confucianism and naturalistic Taoism is, at first sight, almost irreconcilable. But any complete distinction inevitably distorts the picture. Early Taoism is nearer to Confucianism than is generally understood, especially in its philosophy of life. Contrary to the popular belief that Lao Tzǔ taught the renunciation of life and society, his ethical doctrine was more akin to that of the world-wise Confucius than to Hinduism or Buddhism. This opinion is neither new nor personal, but a general one among native historians of Chinese philosophy. Both Dr. Hu Shih in his *The Development of the Logical Method in Ancient China*[1] and Professor Fung Yu-lan in his *The History*

[1] The New China Book Co., Shanghai (1917), 1922.

of Chinese Philosophy[2] interpreted Lao Tzŭ in a way quite different from that to which the West is accustomed. The main interest of Taoism and Confucianism is life, the chief difference being that in Taoism the preservation of life comes with following nature, whereas in Confucianism the fulfillment of life comes with the full development of man.

EARLY CONFUCIANISM: CONFUCIUS, MENCIUS, HSÜN TZŬ AND THE CHUNG YUNG

The movement of humanism began with Confucius (551-479 B.C.). It gained momentum in Mencius and Hsün Tzŭ, and finally reached the climax in Neo-Confucianism. It is a story of more than two thousand years. It is the story of Chinese life and thought. From the time of Confucius to the present day, the chief spiritual and moral inspiration of the Chinese has been the Confucian saying that "It is man that can make truth great, and not truth that can make man great."[3]

To say that Confucius was humanistic is not to deny that the sage showed a reasonable interest in religion. Confucius was, on the one hand, a reformer, a pioneer in universal education for all those who cared to come[4] and for people of all classes,[5] a man who traveled for fourteen years over many states in search of an opportunity to serve the rulers in order that the Moral Law (*tao,* the Way)[6] might prevail. He was, on the other hand, a conformist, a man who was "faithful to and fond of the ancients,"[7] a man who

[2] Pt. I, 1930; Pt. II, 1933. Pt. I, translated by D. Bodde, Henri Vetch, Peiping, 1937.

[3] Confucius, *Lun Yü (Analects),* Bk. XV, Ch. 28 (cf. English translations by James Legge, *The Analects,* in *The Chinese Classics,* London, 1861-1897, Vol. I, 1872, and also in *The Four Books,* Honan, 1871, new ed., The Chinese Book Co., Shanghai, 1932; by W. E. Soothill, *The Analects of Confucius,* Yokohama, 1910, new ed., Oxford University Press, 1937; and by Arthur Waley, *The Analects of Confucius,* Allen & Unwin, London, 1938).

[4] VII, 7. Translations in this chapter, unless otherwise noted, are mine.

[5] XV, 38.

[6] Literally, the Way. The same word is used by both Confucianists and Taoists, but with radically different meanings.

[7] *Lun Yü,* VII, 1.

attempted to uphold the culture of Chou[8] of which the worship of Heaven and ancestors was an integral part. Consequently he said that "The superior man stands in awe of . . . the decree of Heaven."[9] He believed that "If the Moral Law is to prevail, it is the decree of Heaven."[10] He himself offered sacrifices to his ancestors and "felt as if his ancestors were actually present," saying, "If I am not present at the sacrifice, it is as if I did not sacrifice at all."[11] Nevertheless, he frankly put the welfare of men before religion. His reluctance to discuss Heaven caused his pupils to say that his view of the way of Heaven "could not be heard."[12] He "never discussed strange phenomena, physical exploit, disorders, or spirits."[13] When his pupil asked about serving the spirits and about death, he replied, "We do not yet know how to serve men; how can we know how to serve the spirits? . . . We do not yet know about life; how can we know about death?"[14]

From these it is evident that Confucius was a humanist even in religious matters; he was not a priest, much less the founder of the religion bearing his name. Man, and man alone, engaged his primary attention. This can be seen from the following passage which is his entire system in a nutshell:

"The ancients who wished to make manifest the clear character of the people of the world, would first set about ordering their national life. Those who wished to order their national life, would first set about regulating their family life. Those who wished to regulate their family life, would first set about cultivating their personal life. Those who wished to cultivate their personal lives, would first set about setting their hearts right. Those who wished to set their hearts right, would first set about making their wills sincere. Those who wished to make their wills sincere, would first set about extending their knowledge. The extending of knowledge depends upon the investigation of things. When things are investigated, then knowledge is extended; when knowledge is extended, then the will becomes sincere; when the will is sincere, then the heart is set right; when the heart is set right, then the personal life is cultivated; when the personal life is cultivated, then the family life is regulated; when the family life is regulated, then the

---

[8] III, 9, 14; XVII, 5; VII, 5.
[9] XVI, 8. [10] XIV, 38. [11] III, 12.
[12] V, 12. [13] VII, 20. [14] XI, 11.

national life is orderly; and when the national life is orderly, then there is peace in this world."[15]

This is a comprehensive program, but may be summed up in one word, namely, *jên*, or true manhood. This is the central idea in the Confucian system, around which the whole Confucian movement developed. Confucius neither defined nor analyzed *jên*. It is even recorded in the *Lun Yü* (*The Analects*) that he "seldom" talked about it.[16] Although 55 out of the 498 chapters of the *Lun Yü* are devoted to the discussion of true manhood, the Master viewed the matter with such high seriousness that he gave the impression of having seldom discussed the subject.

The statement nearest to a definition of *jên* is that it "consists in mastering oneself and restoring the moral order (*li*)."[17] This practically amounts to the entire Confucian philosophy, since *jên*, so defined, involves the realization of the self and the creation of a social order. Specifically, true manhood consists in "being respectful in dealing with oneself, being earnest in handling affairs, and being loyal in one's associations with people."[18] A man of "strong, resolute, simple, and modest character" is "near" to true manhood.[19] Again, "One who can practice five things wherever he may be, is a true man . . . namely, earnestness, broadness, truthfulness, diligence, and generosity."[20] "The true man," Confucius said, "wishing to establish his own character, also seeks to establish the character of others. Wishing to succeed, he also seeks to help others succeed."[21] In a word, to be a true man is to "love all men."[22]

Such a true man is what Confucius called the "superior man," who is the combination of "the good man who has no sorrow, the wise man who has no perplexities, and the courageous man who has no fear."[23] He makes righteousness "the substance of his being," propriety "the basis of his conduct," modesty his "starting point," and honesty his "goal."[24] He "restrains himself in matters of sex when his blood and vital force are strong. When he reaches maturity and his blood and vital force are full of vigor, he restrains himself in matters of strife. When he reaches old age and his blood and

---

[15] *Ta Hsüeh* (*The Great Learning*), Introduction; cf. translation by Lin Yutang, in his *The Wisdom of Confucius*, pp. 139-140.
[16] *Lun Yü*, IX, 1. [17] XII, 1. [18] XIII, 19.
[19] XIII, 27. [20] XVII, 6. [21] VI, 28.
[22] XII, 22. [23] XIV, 30. [24] XV, 17.

vital force have already weakened, he restrains himself in matters of acquisition."[25] He aims at nine things. "In the use of his eyes, his object is to see clearly. In the use of his ears, his object is to listen distinctly. In expression, his object is to be gracious. In manners, his object is to be respectful. In speech, his object is to be sincere. In business, his object is to be earnest. In doubt, he seeks clarification. In anger, he thinks of consequences. In the face of gain, he thinks of righteousness."[26] He does not do anything contrary to the principle of propriety,[27] wants to be slow in word but diligent in deed,[28] and thinks of truth instead of profit.[29] He enjoys the pleasure derived from the due ordering of rituals and music, from talking about the good points of others, and from friendship with many virtuous men.[30] He would give up wealth and rank but endure poverty and mean position for the sake of moral principles.[31] He does not do to others what he does not want others to do to him,[32] "repays evil with justice (uprightness) and repays kindness with kindness."[33] He exercises filial loyalty to his parents, to the point of never disobeying but adhering strictly to the principle of propriety in serving them when they are alive and in burying them and sacrificing to them when they are dead.[34] He is respectful to his superiors.[35] In short, he is a perfect man.

This emphasis on humanism in Confucius is supreme. It underlies all his political, educational, aesthetic, and even his logical doctrines. People are to be ruled by the good examples of the rulers, guided by virtue, and regulated by the principles of propriety,[36] and the object of government is to bring wealth and education to the people and security to the state.[37] Knowledge is "to know men."[38] The superior man "studies in order to apply his moral principles."[39] Poems are "to stimulate your emotions, to broaden your observation, to enlarge your fellowship, and to express your grievances." "They help you in your immediate duties to your parents and in your more remote duties to your prince. They widen

[25] XVI, 7.   [26] XVI, 10.   [27] XII, 1.
[28] IV, 24.   [29] XV, 31; IV, 12, 16.   [30] XVI, 5.
[31] IV, 5.   [32] XV, 23.   [33] XIV, 36.
[34] II, 5.   [35] I, 2.
[36] II, 1, 3; XII, 17, 19; XIII, 4; XI, 25.
[37] XIII, 9; XVI, 1.   [38] XII, 22.   [39] XIX, 7.

your acquaintance with the names of birds, animals, and plants."[40]
Even the "rectification of names," the nearest Confucian approach
to logic, is to be carried out along humanistic lines. For example,
music does not mean merely bells and drums,[41] for names, when
rectified, have a practical flavor. So to rectify names in a state
means to "Let the prince *be* a prince, the minister *be* a minister,
the father *be* a father, and the son *be* a son."[42]

This humanism is complete. But what is its logical foundation?
Confucius said that "there is a central principle running through
my entire doctrine."[43] This central principle is generally accepted
to mean "none other than being true to oneself and reciprocity."[44]
If this interpretation is correct, then we are forced to conclude
that the foundation of the Confucian system lies in the moral realm,
that is, in human experience itself. The principle is also generally
taken to be identical with the Confucian doctrine of Central Harmony (*chung yung*, golden mean). Indeed, this doctrine is of supreme importance in Chinese philosophy; it is not only the back-
bone of Confucianism, both ancient and modern, but also of Chinese
philosophy as a whole. Confucius said that "to find the central
clue (*chung*) of our moral being and to be harmonious (*yung*)
with the universe" is the supreme attainment in our moral life.[45]
This seems to suggest that Confucius had as the basis of his ethics
something psychological or metaphysical. This was not developed,
however, until two centuries later. For Confucius, *chung yung*
definitely meant the golden mean, as indicated by the saying "To
go too far is the same as not to go far enough."[46] The psychological
foundation is to be provided by Mencius and Hsün Tzŭ, and the
metaphysical by the book known as the *Chung Yung* (or *The Doctrine of the Mean*).

Confucius was mainly interested in a practical world and therefore taught us how to do good without going into the problem of
why we should do good. To Mencius (371-289 B.C.), however, we
do good not only because we *should*, but because we *must*, for "Human nature follows the good just as water seeks the lower level."[47]

[40] XVII, 9.   [41] XVII, 11.   [42] XII, 11.   [43] IV, 15.
[44] IV, 15.   [45] VI, 27.   [46] XI, 15.

[47] *Mêng Tzŭ (The Works of Mencius)*, VI, I, 2 (cf. English translation by
James Legge, *The Works of Mencius*, in *The Chinese Classics, op. cit.*, Vol. II
and in *The Four Books, op. cit.*).

"If men become evil, that is not the fault of their natural endow-
ment."[48] All men originally have the sense of mercy, the sense of
shame, the sense of respect, and the sense of right and wrong, and
these are what we call the "four fundamentals" of benevolence,
righteousness, propriety, and wisdom.[49] This moral consciousness
is rooted in the heart of a perfect man,[50] which can be demonstrated
by the facts that children all know how to love their parents,[51] and
that when men suddenly see a child about to fall into a well, a sense
of mercy and alarm is inevitably aroused in their hearts.[52]

This native feeling for the good is "inborn ability," which we
possess without the necessity of learning, and is also "inborn
knowledge," which we possess without the necessity of thought.[53]
Thus "all things are already complete in the self. There is no greater
delight than to return to the self with sincerity."[54] For "sincerity
is the way of Heaven, whereas to think how to be sincere is the
way of man."[55] The guiding principle of human conduct is therefore "the full exercise of one's mind." "To exercise our minds
fully is to know our nature, and to know our nature is to know
Heaven. To preserve our minds and to nourish our nature is the
way to serve Heaven. To maintain the singleness of mind whether
we suffer premature death or enjoy long life, and to cultivate our
personal character and let things take their course, is the way to
establish our destiny."[56] Thus the prerequisites of a harmonious
moral order are all complete in us. Instead of looking to nature in
order to know ourselves, we look within ourselves in order to know
nature. We don't even have to look to the sage, because he "belongs
to the same species as ourselves."[57] The clue to the centrality and
harmony of the universe as well as ourselves is therefore not far to
seek. It lies within our nature. To develop our nature is to realize
the virtues intrinsic in it, which Mencius first reduced to the "four
fundamentals," and further to benevolence, which is "man's mind,"
and righteousness, which is "man's path."[58] The former is the
ethical basis of society while the latter is the foundation of politics.
The term "benevolence" (*jên*) must be understood in its more

---

[48] *Ibid.*, VI, I, 6.   [49] *Ibid.*, VI, I, 6; II, I, 6.
[50] *Ibid.*, VII, I, 21; VII, II, 24; VI, I, 10; VII, I, 21.
[51] *Ibid.*, VII, I, 15.   [52] *Ibid.*, II, I, 6.   [53] *Ibid.*, VII, I, 15.
[54] *Ibid.*, VII, I, 4.   [55] *Ibid.*, IV, I, 12.   [56] *Ibid.*, VII, I, 1.
[57] *Ibid.*, VI, I, 7.   [58] *Ibid.*, VI, I, 11; VI, I, 1.

fundamental meaning of true manhood, for "*Jên* is that by which
a man is to be a man. Generally speaking, it is the moral principle."[59]
The moral man does nothing which is not according to true manhood.[60] In fact, he loves all men.[61] The most natural demonstration
of true manhood is loyalty to parents, which to Mencius was the
greatest of all virtues.[62] "Of all which a filial son can attain to,
there is nothing greater than honoring his parents."[63] Filial piety,
then, is the foundation of the five human relationships. "Between
father and son, there should be affection; between sovereign and
minister, righteousness; between husband and wife, attention to
their separate functions; between old and young, a proper order;
and between friends, fidelity."[64] When these are demonstrated, a
harmonious social order will prevail.

This attempt to provide a psychological foundation for humanism
is a significant development in the Confucian school, not only because it marks a great advance, but also because it exerted tremendous influence upon the whole school of Neo-Confucianism, especially from the fourteenth century to the present day.

The psychological development in Hsün Tzŭ (c. 355-c. 288 B.C.),
however, took almost the opposite direction. Not that the humanistic spirit is any weaker in him; on the contrary, it is much stronger. The Moral Law (*tao*) is "not the way of Heaven, nor the way
of Earth, but the way followed by man, the way followed by the
superior man,"[65] and more specifically, "Tao is the way to rule
a state," or in other words, "to organize the people."[66] Consequently he vigorously advocated the control of nature:

> You glorify Nature and meditate on her:
> Why not domesticate her and regulate her?
> You obey Nature and sing her praise:
> Why not control her course and use it?
> You look on the seasons with reverence and await them:
> Why not respond to them by seasonal activities?
> You depend on things and marvel at them:

[59] *Ibid.*, VII, II, 16.　　　　　[60] *Ibid.*, IV, II, 28; VI, I, 10.
[61] *Ibid.*, IV, II, 28.　　　　　　[62] *Ibid.*, IV, I, 27.
[63] *Ibid.*, V, I, 4.　　　　　　　[64] *Ibid.*, III, I, 4.
[65] *Hsün Tzŭ*, Ch. VIII (cf. English translation by H. H. Dubs, *The Works
of Hsüntze*, Probsthain, London, 1928, p. 96).
[66] *Ibid.*, Ch. XII.

Why not unfold your own ability and transform them?
You meditate on what makes a thing a thing:
Why not so order things that you may not waste them?
You vainly seek the cause of things:
Why not appropriate and enjoy what they produce?
Therefore, I say, To neglect man and speculate about Nature
Is to misunderstand the facts of the universe.[67]

Hsün Tzŭ believed the control of nature to be necessary because he found that human nature is sharply different from what Mencius pictured it to be. To Hsün Tzŭ, "The nature of man is evil; his goodness is acquired (through training)."[68] The motive here is obviously to emphasize education, an emphasis that made him the outstanding philosopher of education in ancient China. As the original nature of man is evil, he "needs to undergo the instruction of teachers and laws."[69] Thus virtue is not inborn, but is to be "accumulated," just as mountains are formed by accumulation of earth.[70] The guiding principle of accumulation for the individual is *li* or propriety;[71] that for society is the "rectification of names,"[72] and that for the government is "modeling after the latter-day sage kings."[73] When virtue is "accumulated" to a sufficient degree, man then can "form a triad with Heaven and Earth."[74]

By the end of the fourth century B.C., Confucianism took another step forward. There was an attempt to provide a metaphysical foundation for its humanism, as we can see from the book called *Chung Yung*,[75] or *The Doctrine of the Mean*. According to this book, our central self or moral being is conceived to be "the great basis of existence," and harmony or moral order is "the universal law in the world. When our true central self and harmony are

[67] Ch. XVII (translation by Hu Shih, in his *The Development of the Logical Method in Ancient China*, p. 152).

[68] Ch. XXIII (cf. Dubs, p. 301).   [69] *Ibid.* (cf. Dubs, p. 302).

[70] Ch. VIII (cf. Dubs, p. 115).   [71] Ch. XIX (cf. Dubs, p. 213).

[72] Ch. XXII (cf. Dubs, p. 284).   [73] Ch. XXI (cf. Dubs, p. 277).

[74] Ch. XVII (cf. Dubs, p. 174).

[75] Traditionally ascribed to Tzŭ Ssŭ (492-431 B.C.), grandson of Confucius. It is a chapter of the *Li Chi* (*Li Ki*, or *The Book of Rites*). Translation by Ku Hung-ming: *The Conduct of Life*, The Wisdom of the East Series (London: John Murray, 1906), revised by Lin Yutang, in his *The Wisdom of Confucius*, The Modern Library (New York: 1938), pp. 104-134, and in his *The Wisdom of China and India* (New York: Random House, 1942), pp. 843-864.

realized, the universe then becomes a cosmos and all things attain their full growth and development."[76] Thus "the life of the moral man is an exemplification of the universal moral order."[77]

The *Chung Yung* further states that being true to oneself (*ch'êng*, sincerity) is "the law of Heaven," and to try to be true to oneself is "the law of man."[78] This truth is "absolute," "indestructible," "eternal," "self-existent," "infinite," "vast and deep," "transcendental and intelligent."[79] It contains and embraces all existence; it fulfills and perfects all existence. "Such being the nature of absolute truth, it manifests itself without being seen; it produces effects without motion; it accomplishes its ends without action."[80] Only those who are "their absolute true selves" can "fulfill their own nature," can "fulfill the nature of others," can "fulfill the nature of things," can "help Mother Nature in growing and sustaining life," and can be "the equals of Heaven and Earth."[81] How original this metaphysical tendency was in Confucius is uncertain, but it became an extremely significant factor in later Confucianism, particularly in the Neo-Confucianism of the eleventh and fifteenth centuries.

EARLY TAOISM: YANG CHU AND LAO TZŬ

While this movement of Confucian humanism was progressing, naturalistic Taoism developed in parallel, with different ways but similar aims of life. As the goal of Confucianism is the fully developed life, that of Taoism is simple and harmonious life. Although the term "Taoism" (*tao chia*) was not used until the first century B.C., in the *Shih Chi* (Historical Records) by Ssŭ-ma Ch'ien (145-86 B.C.), the Taoist movement must have been going on for some centuries. But whether Yang Chu or Lao Tzŭ was the first leader of the movement is a controversial matter.[82] In the case of Yang

---

[76] *Ibid.*, Ch. I.   [77] Ch. II.   [78] Ch. XX.
[79] Ch. XXVI.   [80] *Ibid.*   [81] Ch. XXII.

[82] Lao Tzŭ is traditionally dated at c. 570 B.C. In the last two decades, the theory of Wang Chung (1744-1794) that Lao Tzŭ and the *Tao-tê Ching* belonged to the fourth century B.C. has been revived and accepted by many Chinese and Western scholars. The former include Liang Ch'i-ch'ao, Ku Chieh-kang, Fung Yu-lan (*The History of Chinese Philosophy*; Bodde's tr., p. 170 ff.), Ch'ien Mu, etc. The latter include Arthur Waley (*The Way and Its Power*, 1934, pp. 101-108), Homer H. Dubs ("The Date and Circumstances

Chu (c. 440-c. 366 B.C.) the spirit is certainly that of simplicity and harmony. He was not a hedonist who urged all men to "enjoy life" and to be satisfied with "a comfortable house, fine clothes, good food, and pretty women," as the spurious *Lieh Tzŭ* of the third century A.D. represents him,[83] or an egoist "who would not have plucked out one single hair though he might have benefited the whole world by doing so," as Mencius purposely made him appear to be.[84] He was rather a follower of nature who was mainly interested in "preserving life and keeping the essence of our being intact, and not injuring our material existence with things,"[85] "a man who would not enter an endangered city, join the army, or even exchange a single hair for the profits of the entire world."[86] Even in the chapter entitled "Yang Chu" in *Lieh Tzŭ*, the main emphasis is to "let life run its course freely,"[87] and to ignore not only riches and fame, but also life and death. It was this naturalistic emphasis that made him the representative Taoist of his time.

In the case of Lao Tzŭ, the keynote in his *Tao-tê Ching* is "simplicity," a central idea by which other apparently strange concepts must be understood. A "simple" life is a life of plainness in which profit is discarded, cleverness abandoned, selfishness minimized, and desires reduced.[88] It is the life of "perfection which seems to be incomplete," of "fullness which seems to be empty," of "ab-

---

of the Philosopher Lao-dz," *Journal of the American Oriental Society*, Vol. LXI, No. 4, Dec. 1941, pp. 215-221; "The Identification of the Lao-Dz," *ibid.*, Vol. LXII, No. 4, Dec. 1942, pp. 300-304), etc. Although Dr. Hu Shih does not rule out the possibility of this theory, he feels that evidences are insufficient to justify it ("A Criticism of Some Recent Methods Used in Dating Lao Tzŭ," 1933, tr. in *Harvard Journal of Asiatic Studies*, Vol. II, Nos. 3 and 4, Dec. 1937).

[83] *Lieh Tzŭ*, Ch. VII. See below, p. 51.

[84] *The Works of Mencius*, Bk. VII, Pt. I, Ch. 26.

[85] *Huai-nan Tzŭ*, Ch. XIII (cf. E. Morgan, *Tao, the Great Luminant*, p. 155).

[86] *The Works of Han Fei Tzŭ*, Ch. L.

[87] *Lieh Tzŭ*, Ch. VII. See English translation of the chapter by A. Forke, *Yang Chu's Garden of Pleasure*, Murray, London, 1912.

[88] *Tao-tê Ching (Tao Teh King)*, Chs. XIX, XII. Well-known translations of the *Tao-tê Ching* are: *The Canon of Reason and Virtue*, by Paul Carus, The Open Court Co., Chicago, 1913; *The Way and Its Power*, by Arthur Waley, Allen & Unwin, London, 1934. Lin Yutang's translation, "The Book of Tao," in his *The Wisdom of China and India*, is good.

solute straightness which seems to be crooked," of "skill which seems to be clumsy," and of "eloquence which seems to stutter." It is the life of "producing and rearing things without taking possession of them," of "doing work but not taking pride in it," and of "ruling over things but not dominating them."[89] It is the life which is "as pointed as a square but does not pierce, as acute as a knife but does not cut, as straight as an unbent line but does not extend, and as bright as light but does not dazzle."[90]

Other fantastic ideas of Taoism have developed and died, but this is the living factor that has made Taoism a strong fiber of Chinese ethics even today. It is the point of agreement with the most powerful intellectual system of China, namely, Confucianism.

It is true that Lao Tzŭ was extremely critical of the existing order, even to the point of crying that "When the Great Way (Tao) was obliterated, benevolence and righteousness arose. When wisdom and knowledge appeared, there emerged hypocrisy."[91] But he denounced civilization in the same spirit as he attacked war, taxation, and punishment,[92] essentially because of their excessive and destructive character. Lao Tzŭ was no deserter of civilization. According to authentic historical records, he was a small governmental official. Dr. Hu Shih suggests that he and Confucius were both ju, literati of the priest-teacher type who bore the torch of civilization; that Lao Tzŭ was an orthodox ju, a "ju of the meek" who clung to the culture of the conquered people of Yin, which was characterized by nonresistance, contentment, etc., whereas Confucius, in spite of the fact that he was a descendant of Yin, was a ju of a new type, a "ju of the strong," who advocated the replacement of the degenerating Yin culture by the growing culture of the ruling people of Chou.[93] Thus we must look at Lao Tzŭ as a teacher of simple living rather than as a forsaker of life.

It is also true that Lao Tzŭ taught the strange doctrine of wu wei, generally interpreted as "inaction." But it is a mistake to think of wu wei as anything suggesting complete inactivity, renunciation, or

[89] Ibid., Chs. XLV, X, LI, XII, XXIV.   [90] Ch. LVIII.
[91] Chs. XVIII, II, XII, XIX, XXXVIII.
[92] Chs. XXX, XXXI, LXVIII, LXXIII, LIII, LXXV, LVII, LXXIV, LXXV.
[93] Hu Shih, Shuo Ju, 1934, now included in Hu Shih Lun-hsüeh Chin-chu, First Series, Commercial Press, Shanghai, 1935, pp. 3-81.

the cult of unconsciousness. It is rather a peculiar way, or more exactly, the natural way, of behavior. "The sage manages his affairs without assertion, and spreads his doctrines without words."[94] The natural way is to "support all things in their natural state" and thus allow them to "transform spontaneously."[95] In this manner, "The Way undertakes no activity, and yet there is nothing left undone."[96] "The sage ruler does things without assertion, and thus nothing remains unregulated."[97] From this it is quite clear that the way of *wu wei* is the way of spontaneity, to be contrasted with the artificial way, the way of cleverness and superficial morality. It was the life of artificiality that drew Lao Tzǔ's vigorous attack and led him to glorify the reality of the nonexistent, the utility of the useless, and the strength of the weak.[98]

This represents no effort to replace being with nonbeing, nor the strong with the weak. It is rather an affirmation of the importance of both of them. The "eternal nonbeing" and the "eternal being" "came from the same source but appear in different names."[99] The truly weak is identical with the truly strong. As Lao Tzǔ said, "What is most perfect seems to be incomplete," and "What is most full seems to be empty."[100] In these utterances, Lao Tzǔ was even a step nearer to the golden mean. On the surface, he seems to be the champion of the female as the fundamental principle of life and infancy as the ideal state of being.[101] He also seems to advocate emptiness and quietude.[102] At bottom, however, his ethical position comes much nearer to the center than to the extreme. "Since much talk always fails in due course, it is better to adhere to the principle of centrality."[103]

The main difference between Lao Tzǔ and Confucius lies in the fact that while with Confucius the measure of all things is man, with Lao Tzǔ it is nature. Simplicity, *wu wei*, and other ethical ideals are all moral lessons drawn from nature, which is the standard for Heaven and Earth as well as for man.[104] It is the Way, or Tao, the universal principle of existence. It is "the source of Heaven and

[94] *Tao-tê Ching*, Ch. II. [95] Chs. LXIV, XXXVII.
[96] Ch. XXXVII. [97] Chs. III, LVII.
[98] Chs. XL, XI, LXXVIII, XLIII, LXXVI.
[99] Ch. I. [100] Ch. XLV.
[101] Chs. VI, XX, XXVIII, LXI, X, XLIX, LV.
[102] Ch. XVL. [103] Ch. V. [104] Ch. XXV.

Earth" and "the mother of all things."[105] It is eternal, one, all-pervasive, and absolute.[106] Above all, it is natural.[107]

As reality is natural, so must our life be. To be natural is to live like water, which is "similar to the highest good" and "almost identical with Tao."[108] Water "occupies places which people detest," but "it benefits all things without making any demand."[109] "There is nothing softer and weaker than water, and yet there is nothing better for attacking hard and strong things."[110] The idealization of infancy is nothing more than the idealization of the natural state. It is not the state of ignorance and incapability. It is rather a state of quietude, harmony, and insight. Above all, it is the state of life.

"Tao produced the one. The one produced the two. The two produced the three. The three produced all things. All things possess *yin* (the passive or female principle) and contain *yang* (the active or male principle), and the blending of the vital force (*ch'i*) produces harmony."[111] To know this harmony is called "the Eternal," and to know the Eternal is called "Insight."[112] Lao Tzŭ said:

> Attain complete emptiness.
> Maintain steadfast quietude.
> All things come into being, and I see thereby their return.
> All things flourish, but each one returns to its root.
> This return to its root is called quiescence;
> It signifies its return according to its Fate.
> To return according to Fate is called the Eternal.
> To know the Eternal is called Insight.
> Not to know the Eternal and to act blindly is disastrous.
> To know the Eternal is to be liberal.
> To be liberal is to be without prejudice.
> To be without prejudice is to be comprehensive.
> To be comprehensive is to be great.
> To be great is to be like Tao (the Way).
> To be like Tao is to (possess it) forever and not to fail throughout one's lifetime.[113]

This is perhaps the most comprehensive passage in the *Tao-tê Ching*. We must note that the climax of the whole procedure is

[105] Chs. I, IV, XXV.   [106] Chs. I, XIV, XLII, XXV, XXXIV, XXI.
[107] Ch. XXV.   [108] Ch. VIII.   [109] Ch. VIII.   [110] Ch. LXXVIII.
[111] Ch. XLII.   [112] Ch. LV.   [113] Ch. XVI.

"not to fail throughout one's lifetime." Here we have the humanistic flavor of naturalism. Life is not to be abandoned but to be made secure and valuable. The greatness of Tao is perfect primarily because it never considers itself great.[114] "He who knows contentment suffers no humiliation. He who knows when to stop suffers no disaster. There he can be safe and secure."[115] It is "only those who are not anxious about life that excel in making life valuable."[116] In short, the philosophy of Lao Tzŭ can be summed up by his phrase "the way of long life and lasting vision."[117]

When this emphasis on a simple and harmonious life in Taoism is understood, we are in a position to see why this naturalistic and atheistic philosophy should have been made the foundation of a superstitious religion notorious for its practice of alchemy and belief in immortals in medieval China. The simple reason is that the primary motive of the corrupt Taoist religion was to search for longevity. The effect of the movement was that man took more and more to a negative philosophy, losing confidence in himself as well as in a progressive social order. Such an attitude was diametrically opposed not only by Confucianism but by Mohism as well.

MOHISM, SOPHISM, AND NEO-MOHISM

As in Confucianism, the main interest of Mohism is man. Instead of the general and vague "true manhood," however, Mo Tzŭ (between 500 and 396 B.C.) advocated the welfare of men. "Promote general welfare and remove evil" became the motto of the whole Mohist movement.[118] Mo Tzŭ was so much opposed to the Confucian empty talk of "rituals and music" that he entirely rejected them in favor of "benefits" in terms of population and wealth. "Ancient kings and princes," he said, "in the administration of their states all aimed at wealth for the country and a great population."[119] Consequently he insisted that "men should marry at twenty and women at fifteen,"[120] and it was on the ground of population that he denounced war. Military expeditions, he said, break up family

[114] Ch. XXXIV.   [115] Ch. XLIV.   [116] Ch. LXXV.   [117] Ch. LIX.
[118] *Mo Tzŭ*, Ch. XVI (cf. English translation by Mei Yi-pao, *The Ethical and Political Works of Motse*, Probsthain, London, 1929, p. 87).
[119] Ch. XXXV (cf. Mei, p. 182).   [120] Ch. XX (cf. Mei, p. 118).

life and result in the decrease of population.[121] He strongly advocated economy of expenditure.[122] He attacked funerals and music, not on the basis of morality or decorum, as Confucius would, but on a strictly utilitarian basis. "The practice of elaborate funerals and extended mourning inevitably results in poverty for the nation, in reduction of population, and in disorder of government."[123] By the same token, music enjoyed by the rulers leads to heavy taxes, interferes with farming and other productive enterprises by taking musicians away from their occupations, and wastes the time of government officials.[124]

Our practical philosopher arrived at this utilitarian humanism not merely as a reaction against the formalistic tendency of Confucius, but also as a result of his scientific method. "For any doctrine," he said, "some standard of judgment must be established. . . . Therefore for a doctrine there must be three tests. . . . There must be a basis; there must be examination; and there must be practical application. On what should it be based? It should be based on the activities of the ancient sage-kings. How should it be examined? It should be examined by verifying it with what the people actually see and hear. How to apply it? Put it into law and governmental policies, and see whether or not it is beneficial to the state and the people."[125]

Instead of attempting to direct and regulate experience by a central principle such as the "central harmony" of Confucius or the Tao of Lao Tzŭ, this utilitarian philosopher chose to arrive at a general principle through a comprehensive survey of actual experience. Whether there is fate or not, for example, must be determined by the actual experience of the eyes and ears of the people. "If people have seen or heard it, I shall say that there is fate. If none has seen or heard it, I shall say that there is no fate."[126] Although this positivism sounds crude, the practical and objective character of Mo Tzŭ's philosophy is unmistakable.

This practical character carries with it a pragmatic flavor, because utility and choice are held to be the guiding principles for value and conduct and even for truth. "The reason why Mo Tzŭ censures music is not because the sound of bells, drums, harps, and flutes is

[121] Ch. XX (cf. Mei, p. 119).   [122] Chs. XX and XXI.
[123] Ch. XXV (cf. Mei, p. 127).   [124] Ch. XXXII (cf. Mei, pp. 175-180).
[125] Ch. XXXV (cf. Mei, pp. 182-183).   [126] Ch. XXXVI (cf. Mei, p. 189).

unpleasant . . . but because it does not contribute to the promotion of general welfare and the removal of evil."[127] By the same token, "All activities that are beneficial to Heaven, the spirits, and men" are to be fostered as "heavenly virtues," whereas "all words and deeds that are harmful to them" are to be looked upon as an "enemy."[128] There can be nothing that is good but not useful.[129] The value of such virtues as loyalty and filial piety is their "great benefit" to all people.[130]

Thus value in Mohism is limited to "benefits," and every value is to be appraised in terms of its ability to "promote welfare and remove evil." A good life and a well-ordered society depend primarily on a right choice of such values. "A blind man cannot distinguish black and white, not because he is ignorant of their definitions, but because he cannot choose between them." Similarly, "the superior men of the world do not know what benevolence really is, not because they do not know its definition, but because of their failure to choose what is really benevolent."[131]

To test the utility of a value, it must be put to application to see whether it actually contributes to the "promotion of welfare and removal of evil." The fundamental principle of this application is the famous Mohist doctrine of Universal Love, which aims at the greatest amount of happiness for the greatest number of people through people's "loving one another and benefiting one another."[132] "This is," Mo Tzŭ declared, "the principle of the ancient sage-kings and of the general welfare of men."[133] Lack of it is the cause of social disorder.[134] So let everyone "treat other countries as his own, treat other families as his own, and treat other people as he treats himself."[135] It is interesting to note that even this principle is not free from utilitarian flavor, for at least one of the reasons for this benevolent doctrine is a utilitarian one, namely, "Those who love others will be loved."[136]

It is obvious that the foundation of such a utilitarian philosophy cannot be sought in any internal sanction. Instead, it is to be sought

127 Ch. XXXII (cf. Mei, pp. 175-177).
128 Ch. XXVIII (cf. Mei, p. 155).   129 Ch. XVI (cf. Mei, p. 89).
130 Ch. XVI (cf. Mei, p. 97).   131 Ch. XLVII (cf. Mei, p. 225).
132 Ch. XV (cf. Mei, p. 83).   133 Ch. XVI (cf. Mei, p. 97).
134 Ch. XIV (cf. Mei, p. 78).   135 Ch. XV (cf. Mei, p. 82).
136 Ch. XV (cf. Mei, p. 83).

STORY OF CHINESE PHILOSOPHY 41

in "the experience of the wisest men of the past." This reverence for the past in no way undermines the practical spirit of the Mohist philosophy. It rather enhances it for, according to Mo Tzŭ, "The governmental measures of the ancient sage-kings were designed to revere Heaven, to serve the spirits, and to love men."[137]

Another sanction, the religious one, also sounds the note of practical interests. "If everybody believes in the power of the spirits to bless the good and condemn evil, there will be no disorder."[138] This belief, when applied to the state and the people, "becomes a principle of restoring order to the state and promoting the welfare of the people."[139] It was because of this practical efficacy of religion that Mo Tzŭ became its chief defender in ancient China, more so even than Confucius. One may not accept the theory that Mo Tzŭ founded a religion, and that his followers organized a religious order of some sort. One cannot deny, however, that Mo Tzŭ went further than Confucius in the attempt to preserve a religious system. While Lao Tzŭ definitely tended toward the left and Confucius adhered to the "golden mean" in the belief in the supernatural, Mo Tzŭ unmistakably represented the right. We may safely say, however, that the criterion of the Mohist religious belief was again human interest, for Mo Tzŭ said, "I do whatever Heaven wishes me to do; and Heaven does whatever I wish Him to do."[140]

Just how the Mohist school developed after Mo Tzŭ is still a matter of controversy. There is some evidence that it became a religious order. But another aspect of its development, its logical tendency, known as Neo-Mohism, is of more interest to us. The Neo-Mohists, who flourished in the third and fourth centuries B.C., sought to establish their practical philosophy on a logical foundation, and in doing so, they found it necessary to refute the sophistry of Hui Shih (390-305 B.C.), Kung-sun Lung (c. 400-c. 300 B.C.), and other Sophists. The former expressed his ideas in such paradoxes as "The greatest has nothing beyond itself: it is called the Great Unit. The smallest has nothing within itself: it is called the Little Unit"; "The sun begins to set at noon; a thing begins to die at birth"; and "I go to Yüeh today and arrived there yesterday."[141]

---

[137] Ch. XXVII (cf. Mei, p. 138).
[138] Ch. XXXI (cf. Mei, p. 160).
[139] Ch. XXXI (cf. Mei, p. 170).
[140] Ch. XXVI (cf. Mei, p. 136).
[141] *Chuang Tzŭ*, Ch. XXXIII.

Kung-sun Lung and his group were even more sophistical, and claimed that "The egg has feathers"; that "A fowl has three legs"; that "Wheels do not touch the ground"; that "The shadow of a flying bird never moves"; that "A swiftly fleeting arrow sometimes does not move and sometimes does not rest"; that "A brown horse and a dark ox make three"; and that "If a rod one foot in length is cut short every day by one half of its length, it can never be exhausted even after ten thousand generations."[142] Kung-sun Lung further asserted that "A white horse is not a horse" because "the word 'horse' denotes shape and the word 'white' denotes color." "A horse is not conditioned by any color, and therefore both a yellow horse and a black one may answer. A white horse, however, is conditioned by color. . . ."[143] He propounded the theory that all things are "marks," designations or predicates,[144] and that the qualities of solidity and whiteness are independent of the substance of the stone.[145] The main interest of the Sophists lay in such concepts as space and time, potentiality and actuality, motion and rest, the general and the particular, and substance and quality. In short, the whole movement of the Sophists represented an interest in knowledge for its own sake, an interest not at all in harmony with the keen interest in life in Taoism, Confucianism, and Mohism alike. It is no wonder that Sophism became the target of attack by all of them.[146]

But the Neo-Mohists, in order to maintain their practical interest in the face of the intellectualism of the Sophists, had to make their own logical system strong enough to defend their utilitarian philosophy. Consequently they wrote *The Six Books of Neo-Mohism* in the form of definitions, propositions, notes, and proofs, now incorporated in *The Works of Mo Tzŭ.*[147] In them they developed seven methods of argumentation, namely, the methods of "possibility," "hypothesis," "imitation," "comparison," "parallel," "analogy," and "induction."[148] They classified names in three classes,

[142] *Ibid.*

[143] *Kung-sun Lung Tzŭ*, Ch. II (cf. English translation by A. Forke, "The Chinese Sophists," *Journal of the North China Branch of the Royal Asiatic Society*, Vol. XXXIV, 1901-1902, pp. 61-82).

[144] *Ibid.*, Ch. III.   [145] *Ibid.*, Ch. V.

[146] *Chuang Tzŭ*, Ch. II; *Hsün Tzŭ*, Ch. XXI.

[147] *Mo Tzŭ*, Chs. XL-XLV.   [148] *Ibid.*, Ch. XLV.

"general, generic, and private."[149] They discovered the "method of agreement," which includes "identity, generic relationship, coexistence, and partial resemblance"; the "method of difference," which includes "duality, absence of generic relationship, separateness, and dissimilarity"; and the "joint method of differences and similarities."[150] "Identity means that two substances have one name, while generic relationship means inclusion in the same whole. Both being in the same room is a case of coexistence, whereas partial resemblance means having some points of resemblance. . . . Duality means that two things necessarily differ. Absence of generic relationship means to have no connection. Separateness means that things do not occupy the same space. Dissimilarity means having nothing in common."[151] They defined a model as "That according to which something becomes,"[152] and explained that "the concept of a circle, the compass, and the actual circle . . . all may be used as a model."[153] They rejected the theory of the Sophists that solidity and whiteness and stone are three. On the contrary, they maintained that solidity and whiteness are in the stone,[154] and that the two qualities are not mutually exclusive.[155]

While it is significant that the Neo-Mohists refused to tolerate distinctions such as that of quality and substance, an equally important point to note is that knowledge is power. To the Neo-Mohists, knowing means "to meet."[156] Whether it takes the form of "understanding,"[157] "learning," "inference," or "searching,"[158] its end is conduct.[159] The function of knowledge is to guide man in his behavior, especially in the intelligent "choice" between pleasure and pain. "If a man wants to cut off his finger, and his knowing faculty is not aware of its harmful consequences, it is the fault of his knowing faculty. If he knows the harmful consequences and is careful about it, he will not be injured. But if he still wants to cut off his finger, then he will suffer."[160] But "when one cuts off a finger to preserve the hand, that is to choose the greater benefit and to choose the lesser harm."[161] By such intelligent "choice," the

[149] Ch. XL.
[150] Ch. XL.
[151] Ch. XLII.
[152] Ch. XL.
[153] Ch. XLII.
[154] Ch. XLIII.
[155] Chs. XL, XLII.
[156] Ch. XL.
[157] Ibid.
[158] Ibid.
[159] Ibid.
[160] Ch. XLII.
[161] Ch. XLIV.

Mohist "promotion of general welfare and removal of evil" may be carried out.

It is unfortunate that this logical movement died almost in its infancy, and thus deprived China of a disinterested, analytical, and scientific system of logic on which metaphysics and epistemology might have been built. However, the overwhelming interest in human affairs was not the only factor that prevented the growth of intellectualism. There was a strong anti-intellectual movement in China in the fourth century B.C., the best representative of which was Chuang Tzŭ.

CHUANG TZŬ; THE YIN YANG SCHOOL

In both the moralistic humanism of the Confucian school and the utilitarian humanism of the Mohists, the intellect enjoyed a rightful place. It is true that Lao Tzŭ condemned knowledge in no uncertain terms, but "insight" in the Tao-tê Ching is contrasted with cleverness and deceit. By the time of Chuang Tzŭ (between 399 and 295 B.C.), it was developed to the point of almost complete unconsciousness. In Chuang Tzŭ's own language, true knowledge is "great knowledge," and great knowledge is "wide and comprehensive."[162] By this he meant that the mind "makes no distinctions, entertains no subjectivity, but abides by the universal."[163]

The underlying principle for this doctrine of pure unity is that Tao produced all things,[164] is the ground for all things,[165] and is in all things, even in such lowly things as the ant, the tare, the potsherd, and ordure.[166] From the point of view of Tao, therefore, "all things are equal," a theme to which the entire second chapter of Chuang Tzŭ is devoted. "Take the beam and the pillar, or take a sickly looking woman and Hsi Shih (famous beauty), or take greatness, monstrosity, delusion, and strangeness. Tao identifies them as one. Separation is the same as construction; construction is the same as destruction."[167] Generally speaking, "the 'this' is also

---

[162] Chuang Tzŭ, Ch. II (cf. English translations by Fung Yu-lan, Chuang Tzŭ [Ch s. I-VII], Commercial Press, Shanghai, 1931, p. 45; and by H. A. Giles, Chuang Tzŭ: Mystic, Moralist, and Social Reformer, Kelly & Walsh, Shanghai, 1926, p. 14).

[163] Ch. II (cf. Fung, p. 52).

[164] Ch. VI (cf. Fung, p. 117).   [165] Ch. VI (cf. Fung, p. 118).

[166] Ch. XXII (cf. Giles, pp. 285-286).   [167] Ch. II (cf. Fung, p. 52).

the 'that,' and the 'that' is also the 'this.' "[168] From the standpoint of "mutual causation," the " 'that' is produced by the 'this' and the 'this' is caused by the 'that.' "[169] This is to say that "Birth comes from death and death comes from birth"; that "Where there is possibility, there is impossibility"; that "the right comes from the wrong and the wrong comes from the right."[170] By the standard of Tao, too, "There is nothing under the canopy of heaven greater than the tip of an autumn hair, and the huge mountain T'ai is a small thing."[171]

This doctrine of "equality of things" or "identity of contraries" cannot be pushed any further. Its glorification of unity, identity, and synthesis may be regarded as a virtue, but its condemnation of the particular, the concrete, and the specific must be viewed as a defect. If absolutely no distinction could be made, not only logic, but morality also, would be impossible. Indeed, in the eyes of Chuang Tzŭ, civilization is not a blessing, but a curse. "The sage, therefore, . . . considers knowledge as a curse. . . . He needs no morality . . . he is nourished by nature. To be nourished by nature is to be fed by nature. Since he is fed by nature, what is the use of man's effort?"[172] All benevolence and righteousness, rites and music, must be "forgotten."[173]

This is primitivism to the last degree. Nowhere else in Chinese philosophy do we find such extreme primitivism. Chuang Tzŭ's naturalistic philosophy of life exerted tremendous influence on the fatalistic libertines of the fifth and sixth centuries, while his naturalistic metaphysical doctrines became points of contact between Taoism and Buddhism. His emphasis on incessant, spontaneous transformation and the "equality of things," has affected almost all Chinese philosophers in the last fifteen centuries. As a glorifier of nature, he still is today, as he has been for the last fifteen centuries, the main fountain of inspiration and imagination to Chinese artists, particularly landscape painters.

The greatness and importance of Chuang Tzŭ lie primarily in his exaltation of nature. Humanism to him lost all meaning, because man in the world is nothing more than "the tip of a hair upon a

[168] Ch. II (cf. Fung, p. 50).
[169] *Ibid.*
[170] *Ibid.*
[171] Ch. II (cf. Fung, p. 56).
[172] Ch. V (cf. Fung, p. 106).
[173] Ch. VI (cf. Fung, pp. 128-129).

horse's skin."[174] This being the case, "those inwardly upright"
want to be "companions of nature"[175] and "followers of nature."[176]
They do not want to "assist Heaven with man."[177] That is to say,
as long as "horses and oxen have four feet," do not "put a halter
on a horse's head or a string through a bullock's nose."[178] Not to
assist Heaven with man is Chuang Tzŭ's version of *wu wei*, in
which alone can happiness be found. "Perfect happiness and preservation of life are to be achieved through spontaneity."[179] "Do not
be the owner of fame. Do not be a reservoir of plans. Do not be
burdened with work. Do not be a master of knowledge. Identify
yourself with the Infinite and wander freely in the unfathomable.
Exercise fully what you have received from nature without any
subjectivity. In one word, be empty."[180]

When one reaches this state, one becomes a "pure man," one who
"did not know what it was to love life or to hate death. He did not
rejoice in birth, nor resist death. Spontaneously he went; spontaneously he came; that was all. He did not forget whence he came;
nor did he seek to know where he would end. He accepted things
gladly, and returned them to nature without reminiscence. This is
not to violate Tao with the human heart, nor to assist Heaven with
man. . . . Being such, his mind was free from all thoughts. . . . He
was in harmony with all things, and thus on to Infinity."[181]

To achieve this end, we must "have no self," "have no achievement," and "have no fame."[182] We must "let our mind be at ease
in abiding with the nature of things. Cultivate our spirit by following what is necessary and inevitable." "For our external life, there
is nothing better than adaptation and conformation. For our internal
life, there is nothing better than peace and harmony."[183] Here we
have primitivism, mysticism, quietism, fatalism, and pessimism in
a nutshell.

The tone of fatalism and pessimism was made intense by the
fact that both reality and the life of men are ever changing. "The
life of a thing passes by like a galloping horse. In no activity is it
not in the state of change; at no time is it not in the state of flux.

[174] Ch. XVI (cf. Giles, p. 202).
[175] Ch. IV (cf. Fung, p. 78).
[176] Ch. VI (cf. Fung, p. 115).
[177] Ch. VI (cf. Fung, p. 113).
[178] Ch. XVII (cf. Giles, p. 211).
[179] Ch. XVIII (cf. Giles, p. 222).
[180] Ch. VII (cf. Fung, p. 141).
[181] Ch. VI (cf. Fung, p. 113).
[182] Ch. I (cf. Fung, p. 34).
[183] Ch. IV (cf. Fung, pp. 85-86).

What is it to do? What is it not to do? Verily, it can only let its spontaneous transformation go on."[184] Existence is transitory, the life of man being just as momentary as that of things. "They come in and go out of existence; their maturity is impermanent. In the succession of growth and decay, they are ceaselessly changing form. Past years cannot be recalled; time cannot be arrested. The succession of states is endless; and every end is followed by a new beginning."[185] In this fleeting universe, the only way for man to have peace is to let nature take its own course. He should not question "whether there is a mechanical arrangement which makes the movement of heavenly bodies inevitable," or "whether the rotation of heavenly bodies is beyond their own control."[186] Perhaps there is an Overlord of all, but "if there were really a sovereign, the clue to his existence is wanting."[187] The only thing we are sure of is that "All things spring from germs and become germs again." "All species come from germs. Certain germs, falling upon water, become duckweed . . . become *lichen* . . . become the dog-tooth violet . . . produce the horse, which produces man. When man gets old, he becomes germs again."[188] In passages like these we cannot help being attracted by Chuang Tzǔ's poetic imagination and his evolutionary thought. But we are also impressed with the inevitable "spontaneous transformation" and transitory existence. In the face of these irreducible facts, the pure man "harmonizes all things with the equality of nature and leaves them alone in the process of natural transformation. This is the way to complete our lifetime. . . . We forget the distinctions of life and death and of right and wrong. We find contentment in the realm of the Infinite and we therefore stop there."[189]

We should not forget, of course, that in spite of the idea of escape in Chuang Tzǔ, his main interest was still the "preservation of life." He devoted an entire chapter to "the fundamentals for the cultivation of life."[190] In this he joined the chorus of the "Hundred Schools" that flourished in the fourth and third centuries B.C. in China. They were all seekers after a good life, each having a unique doctrine of its own. In no other period in Chinese history, or in

[184] Ch. XVII (cf. Giles, p. 209).   [185] *Ibid.*
[186] Ch. XIV (cf. Giles, p. 173).   [187] Ch. II (cf. Fung, p. 46).
[188] Ch. XVII (cf. Giles, p. 228).   [189] Ch. II (cf. Fung, p. 63).
[190] Ch. III.

the history of any country, was there more freedom of thought and more profuse intellectual development.

Running through this multiple development was one strong intellectual current the origin of which can be traced to the remote past, when divination was the only form of intellectual activity. This is the theory of *yin* and *yang*, or the passive or female and active or male universal principles, which, according to the *Tao-tê Ching*, made the harmony of the world possible. In the Confucian classic *I Ching*[191] we learn that "In the beginning there is the Great Ultimate (*T'ai Chi*) which generates the Two Primary Modes. The Two Primary Modes produce the Four Forms. The Four Forms give rise to the Eight Elements. These Elements determine all good and evil and the great complexity of life." The date of the *I Ching* is still surrounded by an atmosphere of uncertainty, but the fundamental ideas, that the universe is a dynamic system of incessant change from the simple to the complex, and that the Two Primary Modes (*yin* and *yang*) are the agents of the change, must have antedated the compilation of the book by centuries.

No student of Chinese history should underestimate this idea of *yin* and *yang*, not only because it largely conditioned the Chinese outlook toward reality, but also because it provided the common ground for the intermingling of the divergent philosophical schools. The movement was so strong that by the fourth century B.C. it became an independent school. Eventually it identified itself in the second century B.C. with the common and powerful movement under the name of Huang Ti as well as the prevailing philosophy of Lao Tzŭ, and assumed the name "Huang-Lao." At the same time, the *yin yang* idea of the *I Ching* became the most important aspect of Confucianism. Indeed the note of *yin yang* is the dominant note in the second movement of China's intellectual symphony, namely, medieval Chinese philosophy.

EARLIER MEDIEVAL PHILOSOPHY

It was around the doctrine of *yin yang* that earlier medieval Chinese philosophy developed, in various directions. In both Huai-nan Tzŭ the Taoist and Tung Chung-shu the Confucianist, it led to a microcosm-macrocosm philosophy, while in Wang Ch'ung it led

[191] *The Book of Changes.*

to naturalism in direct opposition to the correspondence theory. Huai-nan Tzŭ (d. 122 B.C.) attempted to develop a more rational cosmology than his predecessors. He suggested that "There was a Beginning," a "beginning of an Anteriority to this Beginning," and a "beginning of an Anteriority even before the beginning of this Anteriority,"[192] and that the Great Beginning produces in succession space, the universe, the primary vital force, the *yin* and *yang*, and finally the material form.[193] But these are merely the unfolding of Tao.[194] Furthermore, although insects, fish, birds, and animals "differ in their nature and destiny," "they all come from the same Great Beginning," "with reference to which the pure man makes no distinction."[195] So far, Huai-nan Tzŭ does not depart from ancient Chinese philosophy. But the *yin yang* idea in him adds a new note to Taoism. "Heaven has the Four Seasons and the Five Elements. . . . These find a correspondence in man's four limbs and five viscera . . ."[196] for they are merely different manifestations of the same principles of *yin* and *yang*.

The spirit of correspondence assumes an even more important aspect in Tung Chung-shu (177-104 B.C.) who was instrumental in making Confucianism a state cult. To him, "All things have their complements of *yin* and *yang*. . . . The underlying principles of prince and minister, father and son, husband and wife, are all derived from the way of *yin* and *yang*. The prince is *yang*, and the minister is *yin*. The father is *yang,* and the son is *yin*. The husband is *yang*, and the wife is *yin*."[197] In short, everything conceivable can be reduced to these two universal principles. These two principles express themselves through the medium of the Five Agents with which all things in the world correspond. The Five Agents have their correspondence in the five tones, five tastes, five colors, the various directions, the seasons, and the moral virtues.[198]

This scheme of correspondence must have had unusual fascination for the medieval Chinese, for it dominated Chinese thought

[192] *Huai-nan Tzŭ*, Ch. II (cf. English translation by E. Morgan, *Tao, the Great Luminant*, Kelly & Walsh, Shanghai, 1933, p. 31).

[193] *Ibid.*, Ch. III (cf. Morgan, p. 58).

[194] *Ibid.*, Ch. VII (cf. Morgan, p. 59).

[195] *Ibid.*, Chs. XIV, VIII, XIX.   [196] *Ibid.*, Ch. VII (cf. Morgan, p. 60).

[197] Tung Chung-shu, *Ch'un-ch'iu Fan-lu*, Ch. LIII. See E. R. Hughes, *Chinese Philosophy in Classical Times*, London, Dent, 1942, pp. 293-308.

[198] *Ibid.*, Chs. XXXVIII, XLII.

for no less than five centuries. Both the Taoists and Confucianists found it congenial because it was a systematized expression of the idea of harmony, an idea close to their hearts. But the real spirit of harmony, whether the central harmony of Confucianism or the inner harmony of the Taoists, or the harmony between man and nature as taught by both schools, was lost. The movement of correspondence became a matter of intellectual sport, a game of puzzles, and finally a superstition. Volume after volume of "Complementary Texts" was written to aid the interpretation of the *I Ching*. This body of literature became so huge and so influential that many important state policies were decided upon by strange confirmations from these superstition-infested books. Chinese philosophy had entered upon a dark age, an age in which Confucianism developed into a state cult rather than a rational philosophy, and Taoism degenerated and identified itself with the lowest forms of religious worship. It was natural that there should arise strong reaction against such a state of affairs. Gradually the critical spirit made itself felt, until it reached such a high pitch from the third to the fifth century that it gave rise to a strong movement of textual criticism and an equally strong movement of free political thought.

The outstanding representative of this critical spirit was Wang Ch'ung (27-c. 100 A.D.). Perhaps no other Chinese philosopher could rival him in rational thinking and critical spirit. He attacked all kinds of erroneous beliefs, beliefs in ghosts,[199] in thunder as the sound of Heaven's growling,[200] in calamities as visitations of Heaven,[201] in the past as superior to the present,[202] and many other false beliefs. He held that "all things are produced spontaneously by the fusion of the vital forces of Heaven and Earth (*yin* and *yang*)."[203] These spontaneous creations are not for the sake of man, because the opinion that Heaven produces grain for the purpose of feeding mankind is tantamount to making Heaven the farmer of man.[204] Furthermore, "If Heaven had produced its creatures on pur-

---

[199] Wang Ch'ung, *Lun Hêng*, Ch. XX (cf. A. Forke's translation, *Mittelungen des seminars für orientalische sprachen*, Vol. IX, pp. 371-376).

[200] *Ibid.*, Ch. VI (cf. *Mittelungen*, Vol. X, pp. 66-76).

[201] *Ibid.*, Ch. XIV (cf. *Mittelungen*, Vol. IX, pp. 299-300).

[202] *Ibid.*, Ch. XVIII (cf. *Mittelungen*, Vol. XI, pp. 84-85).

[203] *Ibid.*, Ch. XVIII (cf. *Mittelungen*, Vol. IX, p. 272).

[204] *Ibid.*, XVIII (cf. *Mittelungen*, Vol. IX, p. 272).

pose, it ought to have taught them to love each other and not to prey upon and destroy one another."[205] We have here the most thoroughgoing naturalism in Chinese philosophy.

LATER MEDIEVAL PHILOSOPHY

Wang Ch'ung was fighting to reinstate naturalism on a rational ground by appealing to reason and experience. Had Chinese philosophy developed along this line, its story would have been different. Unfortunately, Taoism as a philosophy hardly developed, except in the case of the book called *Lieh Tzŭ* (c. 300 A.D.) where the idea of Tao is carried to the point of fatalistic mechanism,[206] and in the philosopher Ko Hung (Pao-p'o Tzŭ, c. 268-c. 334 A.D.) in whom the Taoist philosophy was made the philosophical basis for alchemy and the search for longevity. In Kuo Hsiang (c. 312 A.D.) alone was the true spirit of Taoism revived. He restored and developed the Taoist doctrines of naturalism and spontaneous transformation to a position of dignity.

In Confucianism, the only notable development was in Han Yü (767-834 A.D.), the success of whose theory of three grades of human nature and whose defense of Confucianism were due more to his beautiful literary style than to his reasoning. The really constructive phase of Chinese philosophy in the period was the introduction and development of Buddhist philosophy.

BUDDHISM

The story of Buddhism is told in two other chapters by eminent authorities. It is necessary here only to point out what was really Chinese in the development of Buddhism in China.

All the Buddhist schools were introduced, preserved, and developed in China, but only those consonant with the Chinese temper lasted. Neither the Hīnayāna school of *ens*, the realistic Abhidharmakośa school (Chü-shê, Kusha, c. 600-c. 800 A.D.) which held that "All exists," nor the Hīnayāna school of *non-ens*, the nihilistic Satyasiddhi school (Ch'êng-shih, Jōjitsu, 412-c. 700 A.D.) which

---

205 *Ibid.*, Ch. III (cf. *Mittelungen*, Vol. IX, p. 284).

206 *Lieh Tzŭ*, English translation by L. Giles, *Taoist Teachings from the Book of Lieh Tzŭ*, Murray, London, 1912.

insisted that "Neither the self nor the *dharmas* (elements of existence) are real," had a long history in China. Also, neither the
Mahāyāna school of *ens*, the idealistic Vijñaptimātratā school
(Yogācāra, Fa-hsiang, Wei-shih, Hossō, c. 600-1100 A.D.) which
asserted that "All is mere ideation," nor the Mahāyāna school of
non-ens, the negativistic or, rather, absolutistic Mādhyamika school
(San-lun, Sanron, c. 500-1100 A.D.) which regarded reality as
"Void," flourished in China for long. Clinging to either the *ens* or
non-ens position, they existed in China as essentially Indian systems,
without being assimilated into Chinese thought. Those Buddhist
schools that combined the *ens* and the *non-ens* tendencies, however,
continue to live up to this day.

The tendency to combine different and even opposing elements
into a synthetic whole is characteristic of Chinese thought. We will
recall that in Lao Tzŭ, Tao is conceived as both "is" and "is not,"
a point further developed in Chuang Tzŭ to become his famous
theory of the identity of contraries. We will also recall that in Confucius the Mean was held to be the highest ideal, to the rejection of
anything one-sided or extreme. We will recall, too, that in Neo-
Mohism the distinction of substance and predicates, of the universal
and the particular, etc., was severely criticized. The Yin Yang tradition was, through and through, a tradition of synthesis of opposites. The whole movement of medieval Chinese philosophy
was not only a continuation of the central emphasis on synthesis
of the ancient schools, but was itself a synthesis of the opposing
philosophies of Confucianism and Taoism. This synthetic tendency,
which affected practically all indigenous Chinese philosophies, also
affected Buddhism in China.

Roughly speaking, just as Abhidharmakośa, Satyasiddhi, Vijñaptimātratā and Mādhyamika were hardly more than Indian Buddhism
on Chinese soil, the five Buddhist schools which are the most prominent in China today whether in amount of influence or in length of
time, are typically Chinese. They are typically Chinese, not only
because they still exist in China, but also because of their synthetic
character. They all discarded their original extreme position of *ens*
or *non-ens* in favor of a synthetic position of the "Middle Doctrine." The Avataṅsaka school (Hua-yen, Kegon, c. 600 A.D.-   )
started with the theory of causation by mere ideation, developed
the theory of "Universal causation of *Dharmadhātu*," or universal

causation of Elements of the Principle, and culminated in what Professor Takakusu calls Totalism. It originated the "Ten Metaphysical Propositions" to the effect that all elements are perfect and real, that the elements reflect one another, and that all of them are at the same time simple and complex, one and many, exoteric and esoteric, pure and varied, etc., so that the universe is a "grand harmony without any obstacle." Thus we see that this school, originating in India but chiefly developed in China, represents a culmination of the "both-and" spirit of Buddhism.

The other school which shifted from the *ens* position to the both-*ens*-and-*non-ens* position is the Mystical school (Mantra, Trueword, Shingon, c. 300 A.D.-   ), which is a mystical religion rather than a philosophical system. Yet even here the synthetic mode of thought is evident. It is an Indian religion baptized and tranformed by Chinese ethical ideals. This school treats the universe as the spiritual body, or the Body of Law, of the Buddha, which manifests itself as the "Realm of Diamond Element," that is, the static world, and the "Realm of Matrix Repository," that is, the dynamic world. These two phases, however, are but different manifestations of the same Buddha. "They are two and yet not two."

The same shift from an extreme position to the "Middle Doctrine" is even more evident in the other three schools which were formed in China and are therefore typically Chinese. While both the Avataṅsaka and the Mystical schools started from the position of *ens*, the T'ien-t'ai (Tendai, c. 580 A.D.-   ) started from the position of *non-ens*. Beginning with the negativistic doctrine of the Void, this school finally arrived at the "Perfectly Harmonious Triple Truth" of the Void (Things have no reality), Temporariness (But they have temporary existence), and the Mean (They are at the same time the True State). These three are identical, and Suchness, or the True State, involves both phenomenon and noumenon. Consequently it calls itself the Round Doctrine. This synthetic spirit must strongly appeal to the imagination of the Chinese, for T'ien-t'ai is still the strong Buddhist sect in China today.

As to the Meditation (Ch'an, Zen, c. 450 A.D.-   ) and the Pure Land (Ching-t'u, Jōdo, c. 300 A.D.-   ) schools, they are essentially Chinese creations, although certain sources can be traced to India. The Pure Land Sect is a creed of faith, the least philosophical of all the schools we have mentioned. Its fundamental beliefs, however, such as salvation for all and salvation by faith, are based on the idea of "One in all and all in one." It accepts the idea that Nirvāṇa has neither space nor time, neither life nor death. But it interprets this as nothing other than the land of the Buddha of Infinite Light and Infinite Life, that is, the Pure Land.

The most significant of all the Buddhist schools, so far as Chinese thought is concerned, is Zen (Ch'an in Chinese). Zen is basically a method, not a method of writing or words, which the school rejects, but a method of "direct intuition into the heart to find Buddhanature." Nevertheless this method is based, on the one hand, on the assumption of the eightfold negation of production and extinction, annihilation and permanence, unity and diversity, and coming and departing, and, on the other hand, on the affirmation of the reality of the Buddha-nature in all things. The Zen method of "direct intuition," together with its "abrupt enlightenment," gave the Chinese mind a way of ready and complete release, and for this reason had a peculiar charm to them. Above all, its sole reliance on meditation imposed on the Chinese mind a severe mental and spiritual discipline which was invigorating, and quickened the Chinese imagination which the glorious poetry and landscape painting of the T'ang dynasty had already awakened.

But such quietism was fundamentally out of harmony with the practical and humanistic Chinese. The zenith of Zen was soon reached and its decline began. With this, Chinese medieval philosophy came to a close. Thus the second movement of the intellectual symphony of China concluded with a song without words. There was harmony, but harmony in silence.

NEO-CONFUCIANISM

Ever since the advent of Buddhism in China, Chinese philosophers had been very critical of it. The fatal attack was delivered by the Neo-Confucianists whom we are now about to study. They felt that there was nothing "substantial" in Buddhism, and that the Buddhists' fear of birth and death was motivated by selfish interest.[207] They considered the Buddhist theory of renunciation untenable because they insisted that even though a man might desert his

[207] *Ch'êng-shih I-shu* (Posthumous Writings of the Ch'êng Brothers), Chs. XIII, XV.

family, he could never escape from society so long as he sets his feet on earth.[208] They believed that things were always in the process of transformation, and consequently, the Buddhist doctrine of formation, duration, deterioration, and extinction was unsound.[209] They criticized the Buddhists for mistaking concrete reality for emptiness, because the Buddhists regarded all things, including clothing and food, as void, and yet they lived on those things every day.[210] They found that the Buddhist Void was really founded on the failure to understand the Reason of things.[211] They showed that even the Buddhists could not get away from human relationships because, while they severed their kinship with their parents, they organized themselves in a society of masters and pupils.[212] They condemned the Buddhists as unjust and cowardly, because they worked for their own interest and avoided social responsibility.[213]

From these criticisms we can see the spirit of Neo-Confucianism. The story of Neo-Confucianism is virtually the story of modern Chinese philosophy. It has not only dominated Chinese thought for the last millennium but also dominated Japanese thought for many centuries. In China, it developed in three phases, namely, the Reason school in the Sung period (960-1279), the Mind school in the Ming period (1368-1644), and the Empirical school in the Ch'ing period (1644-1911). In Japan, it was represented by the Shushi school (Chu Hsi) and the Oyomei school (Wang Yang-ming).[214]

[208] *Ibid.*, Ch. XVIII.   [209] *Ibid.*, Ch. XVIII.
[210] Chu Hsi, *Yü Lei* (Sayings Arranged by Topics), Ch. CXXVI.
[211] *Ibid.*   [212] *Ibid.*
[213] Wang Yang-ming, *Ch'üan-hsi Lu*; cf. F. G. Henke, *The Philosophy of Wang Yang-ming*, p. 159. Also *Ch'êng-shih I-shu*, Ch. XIII.
[214] The term "Neo-Confucianism" is used in the West to designate the Confucian philosophy in the Sung, Ming, and Ch'ing dynasties (960-1911). For the sake of convenience, I am using it in this sense. However, the term is not a direct translation of any Chinese appellation. Since Confucian philosophy during these periods changed radically, the Chinese have no general name for it. They distinguish the philosophy of each dynasty by the name of that dynasty. Thus the philosophy of the Sung period (960-1279) is called Sung Hsüeh (Philosophy of Sung). It is also called Li Hsüeh (Rational Philosophy or Reason School), Hsing-li Hsüeh (Philosophy of Nature and Reason), and Tao Hsüeh (Philosophy of the Way or Moral Law), because Reason, Nature, and Moral Law were the basic concepts of the time. Like-

The Reason School: The Ch'êng Brothers and Chu Hsi

The central idea of the movement is focused on the Great Ultimate (*T'ai Chi*). "The Great Ultimate moves and generates the active principle, *yang*. When its activity reaches its limit, it becomes tranquil, engendering the passive principle, *yin*. When the Great Ultimate becomes completely tranquil, it begins to move again. Thus movement and tranquillity alternate and become the occasion of each other. . . . By the transformation of *yang* and its union with *yin*, the Five Agents of Water, Fire, Wood, Metal, and Earth arise. When these five vital forces (*ch'i*) are distributed in harmonious order, the four seasons run their course."[215] "These Five Agents are the basis of their differentiation while the two Primary Modes constitute their substance. The two Modes are really two aspects of the same thing. Consequently, the Many is ultimately One and the One is differentiated in the Many. The One and the Many each has its own proper state of being. The great and the small each has its determinate nature."[216] A vivid example of the One-in-Many and Many-in-One relationship is that of the moon. "The Great Ultimate is really one. But as each of the myriad things is differently endowed, each has a Great Ultimate, unique and complete. For example, the moon up in the sky is one. But the moon

wise, the philosophy of the Ming period (1368-1644) is called Ming Hsüeh (Philosophy of Ming). It is also called Hsin Hsüeh (Philosophy of Mind) because the outstanding philosophy of the period was Idealism, although Rationalism continued to exist. Inasmuch as the Idealists also concentrated on the problems of Reason, Nature, and the Moral Law, their system is also called Li Hsüeh, Hsing-li Hsüeh, and Tao Hsüeh. The philosophy of the Ch'ing period (1644-1911) has no general name other than Ch'ing Hsüeh (Philosophy of Ch'ing), since there were many philosophical currents, including Rationalism and Idealism. The predominating philosophy, however, was an empiricism which developed as a reaction against both of them. The Chinese call this empirical system P'o Hsüeh (Concrete Philosophy) and Han Hsüeh (Philosophy based on the Han—206 B.C.-220 A.D.—Criticism of Ancient Texts). I use the term "Empirical School" for this system because it is more descriptive than the two Chinese terms.

215 Chou Lien-hsi, *T'ai-chi T'u-shuo* (Explanation of the Diagram of the Great Ultimate).

216 Chou Lien-hsi, *I T'ung-shu* (Explanation of *The Book of Changes*), Ch. XXII.

can be seen everywhere as its light covers rivers and lakes. We cannot say that in this case the moon is broken to pieces."[217]

Thus reality is a progressively evolved and a well-coordinated system. But it is not the only coherent order. Everything is a unified system, a Great Ultimate in itself. "With reference to the entire universe, there is in it one Great Ultimate. With reference to the myriad things, there is a Great Ultimate in each of them."[218] For instance, "Heaven and Earth are one great system of yin and yang. The year, the month, and the day, all have their own systems of yin and yang."[219]

This philosophy of One-in-All and All-in-One was a direct product of the Confucian metaphysics of change. But it is quite probable that its development was inspired by the totalistic philosophy of Buddhism. If that is so, we have here a fundamental distinction between the two systems. While the Buddhist philosophy was based on the Void, which is the denial of the particular, the Neo-Confucian philosophy was based on Reason, which is an affirmation of it. Reason (Li, Law) is the keynote of the Neo-Confucian system. In the words of the Ch'êng brothers (I-ch'uan, 1033-1107, and Ming-tao, 1032-1086), "We say that all things are one reality because all things have the same Reason in them."[220] They all have Reason because things "must have their principles of being."[221] As Reason is the universal principle, "The Reason of a thing is one with the Reason of all things."[222]

This Reason needs an agency through which to operate and also needs to be embodied. It must, therefore, be supplemented by a substantiating and particularizing principle. This is ch'i, or vital force, which, working through its own avenues of the Five Agents and in the forms of yin and yang, differentiates the One into the Many so that each of the Many has its own "determinate nature." "When yin and yang are equal, form and substance are present. When these two original principles are not equal, the dormant nature and manifest nature of things are differentiated."[223] The

---

[217] Chu Hsi, Yü Lei (Sayings Arranged by Topics), Ch. XCIV.

[218] Chu Hsi, ibid., Ch. I.   [219] Ibid.

[220] Ch'êng-shih I-shu (Posthumous Writings of the Ch'êng Brothers), Ch. II.

[221] Ibid., Ch. XVIII.   [222] Ibid., Ch. II.

[223] Shao K'ang-chieh, Huang-chi Ching shih (Supreme Principles for the State and for Society).

vital force is indispensable to reality, because "Without the vital force, Reason would have nothing to adhere to,"[224] and would degenerate into the state of the Buddhist Void. To the Neo-Confucianists, the Buddhist Void, to be valid at all must be substantiated with the vital force. This was exactly what happened in one of the early Neo-Confucianists. "The Ultimate Vacuity of necessity has vital force." "The Ultimate Vacuity . . . is the being of the universal vital force. Its concentration in one place and its extension to all places are but objectifications caused by change. . . . The void is nothing but vital force."[225]

While Reason and vital force function differently, it was never the intention of the Neo-Confucianists to contrast them sharply. Basically there is no distinction between them, because "There is no Reason independent of the vital force, and there is no vital force independent of Reason."[226] "The Great Ultimate is Reason, whereas activity and tranquillity are the vital force. As the vital force operates, Reason operates. The two are mutually dependent and are never separated. The Great Ultimate may be compared to a man, and activity and tranquillity may be compared to a horse. The horse carries the man and the man rides on the horse. As the horse comes and goes, so does the man."[227] The main difference between them is that "Reason is above corporeality." From the point of view of incorporeity, therefore, we may say that Reason is prior to the vital force.[228] This distinction is made, however, merely from "a certain point of view." They are really two phases of the same thing, each working for the realization of the other.

It is this cooperative functioning of Reason and the vital force that makes the universe a cosmos and the fullest realization of "central harmony." "The universal principles of *yin* and *yang* and the Five Agents manifest themselves in all directions and in all degrees, but there is perfect order in them."[229] This order is demonstrated in the production and coexistence of things. "The sequence of creation is the sequence of being. The coexistence of the great and small, and the high and low, is the order of being. There is a

---

[224] Chu Hsi, *Yü Lei*, Ch. I.

[225] *Chang Hêng-ch'ü Hsien-shêng Ch'üan-chi* (Complete Works of Chang Hêng-ch'ü), Bk. II, Ch. I.

[226] Chu Hsi, *Yü Lei*, Ch. I.   [227] *Ibid.*, Ch. CXIV.

[228] *Ibid.*, Ch. I.   [229] *Ibid.*, Ch. I.

sequence in the production of things, and there is an order in their existence."[230] Thus the universe, with all its myriad things, is a harmonious system. "Centrality is the order of the universe, and harmony is its unalterable law."[231] As such, the cosmos is a moral order. This is the main reason why the greatest of the Neo-Confucianists, Chu Hsi (1130-1200), said that "the Great Ultimate is nothing but the Reason of ultimate goodness."[232]

A moral order means a social order. Therefore, just as man is a social being, so is a thing a social entity. The Neo-Confucianists stressed emphatically the fact that no thing can be isolated from the others. "It's absurd to say that anything can stand by itself," because "Unless there are similarities and differences, expansions and contractions, beginnings and endings, to reveal its characteristics," the individuality cannot "stand out," and the thing is therefore not really a thing.[233] That is to say, unless there is community, there cannot be individuality.

This leads to a new and interesting emphasis in Neo-Confucianism, namely, that everything has its opposite. "Through virtue of their Reason, Heaven and Earth and all things do not exist in isolation but necessarily have their opposites."[234] "As there are forms, there are contraries."[235] This is true because the underlying principles of being cannot stand by themselves. "*Yang* cannot exist by itself; it can exist only when it is allied with *yin*. Similarly, *yin* cannot alone manifest itself; it can manifest itself only when accompanied by *yang*."[236] Consequently "No two of the productions of creation are alike."[237]

This being the case, Chuang Tzŭ's doctrine of "the equality of things" and the Buddhist denial of birth and extinction must be totally rejected. "It is the nature of things to be unequal,"[238] the Neo-Confucianists reiterated. "Although there is nothing in the world which is purely *yin* or purely *yang*, as *yin* and *yang* always interact, yet the distinction between rising and falling, and between birth and extinction, should not be ignored."[239] "In the operation

[230] Chang, Bk. II, Ch. V.
[231] Ch'êng, Ch. VII.
[232] Chu Hsi, *Yü Lei*, Ch. CXIV.
[233] Chang, Bk. II, Ch. V.
[234] Ch'êng, Ch. XI.
[235] Chang, Bk. II, Ch. I.
[236] Shao, *op. cit.*
[237] Chang, Bk. II, Ch. I.
[238] *The Works of Mencius*, Bk. III, Pt. I, Ch. 4.
[239] Ch'êng, Ch. II.

of *yin* and *yang*, and Heaven and Earth, there is not a single moment of rest in their rise and fall, and in their zenith and nadir. . . . These two tendencies cause the differences of things and an infinite number of transformations take place. This is why it is said that it is the nature of things to be unequal."[240]

The constant succession of zenith and nadir may suggest that "appearance and disappearance follow a cycle."[241] But this cycle does not mean a cycle in the Buddhist sense. Things do not return to their origin, as the Buddhists and Taoists claim, because "when a thing disintegrates, the vital force is at an end. It is absurd to say that the vital force returns to its origin. . . . What is the need of such an exhausted vital force in the creative processes of the universe? It goes without saying that the force used in creation is vital and fresh."[242] Every creation is therefore a new creation, and the universe is perpetually new.

All these characteristics of the universe are but its Reason. It is the duty of man to comprehend this Reason in order to appreciate fully the meaning of his existence. We must "investigate things to the utmost." As the Ch'êng brothers said, "A thing is an event. A perfect understanding of an event can be obtained by investigating to the utmost the Reason underlying it."[243] This does not mean "to investigate the Reason of all things to the utmost or to investigate the Reason of only one thing to the utmost. As one investigates more and more, one will come to understand Reason."[244] We do not even have to go far for such investigation, for "Reason . . . lies before our very eye."[245] It makes no difference whether the investigation is directed to the nature of fire and water or the relationship between father and son, nor does it make any difference whether it is done by reading about and discussing truth and principles or by handling affairs and dealing with people in the proper way.[246] When sufficient effort is made, understanding naturally comes. When this takes place, our nature will be realized and our destiny will be fulfilled, because "the complete realization of the Reason of things, the full development of one's nature, and the establishment of destiny are simultaneous."[247]

[240] Ch'êng, *Ts'ui Yen* (Sayings).
[241] Chang, Bk. II, Ch. I.
[242] Ch'êng, Ch. XV.
[243] Ch'êng, Ch. XV.
[244] Ch'êng, Ch. XV.
[245] Chu Hsi, *Yü Lei*, Ch. XCIV.
[246] Ch'êng, Chs. XIX and XVIII.
[247] Ch'êng, Ch. II.

This is inevitable because if we investigate things thoroughly and understand their Reason, we will find that "All people are my brothers and sisters, and all things are my companions,"[248] because all men have the same Reason in them. Consequently we should not entertain any distinction between things and the ego.[249] We must love universally. It is only in fully developing the nature of other people and things that one's own nature can be developed.[250] This is the foundation of Neo-Confucian ethics, the ethics of *jên*, true manhood, benevolence, or love. Thus ethics has a firm basis in metaphysics, because love is "the source of all laws," and "the foundation of all phenomena."[251] The fact of universal production is a concrete evidence of *jên* or love.[252]

To achieve the end of full understanding of Reason and a life of *jên*, the human mind must go through severe discipline. The mind must be sincere (*ch'êng*) and serious (*ching*). As Chu Hsi defined them, "Seriousness is apprehension, as if there were something feared. Sincerity is truth and the utter absence of anything false."[253] They are the "way of Heaven" and the "essence of human affairs."[254] Specifically, sincerity means "to have no depraved thought," and seriousness means "to maintain unity of mind, that is, absolute equanimity and absolute steadfastness."[255]

The emphasis on seriousness, especially in the Ch'êng brothers and Chu Hsi, soon assumed almost religious significance. Some of their followers frankly explained it in terms of Buddhist meditation. As a matter of fact, the dual formula of the Neo-Confucianists of the Reason school, that is, extension of knowledge and the practice of seriousness, might have some correspondence with the *dhyāna* and *prajñā*, or meditation and insight, of medieval Buddhism.[256] The Neo-Confucian movement became an inward movement, the mind gradually assuming importance. With the ascendancy

---

[248] Chang, Ch. I.   [249] Shao, *op. cit.*   [250] Chang, Bk. II, Ch. VI.
[251] Chu Hsi, *Ch'üan-shu* (Complete Works), Ch. LXVII (cf. English translation by J. P. Bruce, *The Philosophy of Human Nature by Chu Hsi*, Probsthain, London, 1922, p. 317).
[252] Chou, Ch. XI.
[253] Chu Hsi, *Ch'üan-shu*, Ch. XLVIII.
[254] Ch'êng, Ch. XI.   [255] Ch'êng, *Ts'ui Yen.*
[256] Hu Shih, "Religion and Philosophy in Chinese History," in *Symposium on Chinese Culture*, ed. by Sophia Zen, Shanghai, 1931, p. 57.

of the role of the mind, Neo-Confucianism passed on from its first
phase to the second, from the Reason school to the Mind school.

The Mind School: Lu Hsiang-shan and Wang Yang-ming

The philosophy of the Mind school already took definite form
in Lu Hsiang-shan (1139-1193), who said that "The universe is
identical with my mind, and my mind is identical with the universe."[257] This is because both the mind and the universe are conceived as expressions of the Moral Law. "There is no Moral Law
beyond events, and there are no events beyond the Moral Law."[258]
But "any event within the universe is my affair, and any affair of
mine is an event in the universe."[259] There is no suggestion of
solipsism in these utterances, for "My mind, my friend's mind, the
mind of the sages generations ago, and the mind of the sages of
generations to come are all one."[260]

This idealistic tendency developed until it reached its climax in
Wang Yang-ming (1473-1529), to whom the mind and Reason are
one and the same thing. "The mind itself is identical with Reason.
Is there any event or any Reason in the universe," he asked, "that
exists independent of the mind?"[261] Take, for example, the matter
of filial piety. The principle of filial piety lies, not in one's parents,
but in one's own mind. "If I seek the Reason of filial piety in my
parents, is it, then, really in my own mind or is it in the person of
my parents? If it is in the person of my parents, is it true that after
my parents pass away my mind in consequence lacks the Reason
of filial piety? . . . What holds here is true with reference to the
Reason of all affairs and all things."[262] "The controlling power of
the body is in the mind. The mind originates the idea, and the nature of the idea is knowledge. Wherever the idea is, we have a thing.
For instance, when the idea rests on serving one's parents, then
serving one's parents is a 'thing,' . . . Therefore I say that there is
neither Reason nor thing apart from the mind."[263] If we say that

[257] *Lu Hsiang-shan Ch'üan-chi* (Complete Works).
[258] *Ibid.*   [259] *Ibid.*   [260] *Ibid.*
[261] *Wang Yang-ming Ch'üan-chi* (Complete Works), Bk. I (cf. English
translation by F. G. Henke, *The Philosophy of Wang Yang-ming*, Open Court,
Chicago, 1916, p. 50).
[262] *Ibid.*, Bk. II (cf. Henke, pp. 303-304).
[263] *Ibid.*, Bk. I (cf. Henke, p. 59).

Heaven and Earth and things exist, it is due to our consciousness of them. "If Heaven is deprived of my intelligence, who is to respect its eminence? . . . When Heaven, Earth, spirits, and the myriad things are separated from my intelligence, there are no longer Heaven, Earth, spirits, and the myriad things. If my intelligence is separated from Heaven, Earth, spirits, and the myriad things, it also ceases to exist."[264] As to the relationship between the mind and external objects, Wang Yang-ming argued that these objects are really not external to the mind. We do see flowers blossom and drop on the high mountains seemingly without connection with the mind. But as our philosopher observed, "Before you see these flowers, they and your mind were both in the state of calmness. As soon as you look at them, however, their colors at once become clear. From this you can know that these flowers are not external to your mind."[265]

Since the mind is the embodiment of Reason, it follows that if one would truly comprehend truth, he must discover it from his own mind. He must "fully exercise his mind." "The original nature of the mind is perfectly good. When this original nature is affected by deviation from the Mean, there is evil."[266] The emergence of evil is, therefore, to be explained by a disturbed condition of the mind which is originally good. "The mind may be compared to a mirror. The mind of the sage is like a bright mirror, the mind of the ordinary man is like a dull mirror. . . . When, after effort has been made to polish the mirror, it is bright, the power of reflecting has not been lost."[267] In short, evil is due to the loss of the "original nature" of the mind.[268]

To return to the original nature of the mind, any disturbance must be avoided. The mind must be left in a state of "tranquil repose," in which alone is the highest good attained.[269] When the mind is clear as the result of tranquil repose, it will naturally know what is true and what is good. In other words, knowledge of the good is inborn in us. "The mind has the native ability to know. If

264 *Ibid.*, Bk. III (cf. Henke, p. 184).
265 *Ibid.*, Bk. III (cf. Henke, p. 169).
266 *Ibid.*, Bk. III (cf. Henke, p. 156).
267 *Ibid.*, Bk. I (cf. Henke, p. 94).
268 *Ibid.*, Bk. I (cf. Henke, p. 82).
269 *Ibid.*, Bk. XXVI (cf. Henke, p. 210).

one follows his (pure) mind, he naturally is able to know. When
he sees his parents, he naturally knows what filial piety is; when
he perceives his elder brothers, he naturally knows what respect-
fulness is; when he sees a child fall into a well, he naturally knows
what commiseration is. This is inborn knowledge of the good,
without any necessity of going beyond the mind itself."[270]

Not only is knowledge of the good inborn, but practicing the
good is also native, because knowledge and conduct are identical.
This theory of the unity of knowledge and conduct is characteristic of Wang Yang-ming, although Neo-Confucianists of the
Reason school had suggested it. If man fails to treat his parents
with filial piety or his elder brother with respect, it "is due to the
obstruction of selfish desires and does not represent the original
character of knowledge and practice. There has been no one who
really has knowledge and yet fails to practice it. . . . Smelling a
bad odor involves knowledge; hating the odor involves action.
Nevertheless, as soon as one perceives the bad odor, one already
hates it."[271]

Since man is born with the capacity to know and practice the
good, the chief duty of man is to "make clear one's pure character." "Making clear one's pure character consists in loving the
people. . . . When one's heaven-endowed nature becomes pure and
reaches a condition of the highest good, his intelligence becomes
clear and not darkened. This is a manifestation of the highest good.
It is the essence of pure character; it is also what we call the inborn knowledge of the good." "When the highest good manifests
itself, right is right and wrong is wrong."[272]

Making clear one's pure character consists in love (*jên*) because
the mind of man and the mind of things have a common structure.[273]
This is to say that "Heaven and Earth and I are a unity."[274] An
ideal man "considers Heaven, Earth, and the myriad things as one
unity." Consequently, he "views the earth as one family and his
country as one man."[275] His love is extended even to plants and
animals, because when he hears the pitiful cry and sees the fright-

---

[270] *Ibid.*, Bk. I (cf. Henke, p. 60).   [271] *Ibid.*, Bk. I (cf. Henke, p. 53).
[272] *Ibid.*, Bk. XXVI (cf. Henke, pp. 204-205).
[273] *Ibid.*, Bk. III (cf. Henke, p. 183).
[274] *Ibid.*, Bk. III (cf. Henke, p. 184).
[275] *Ibid.*, Bk. XXVI (cf. Henke, p. 204).

ened appearance of a bird or an animal that is about to be slaughtered, a sense of commiseration instinctively arises in his mind.

In a metaphysical and ethical system such as this, the importance of the mind is supreme. Although Wang Yang-ming based his idealistic philosophy on the doctrine of the "rectification of the mind" of *the Great Learning* and the doctrine of the "preservation of the mind" of Mencius, one can easily detect the influence of Zen. The emphasis on tranquil repose definitely proves such influence. At any rate, no Confucianist, whether in medieval or modern times, had ever gone to such an extreme position and thereby departed from the golden mean of Confucius.

The Empirical School: Tai Tung-yüan

Reaction against such extreme idealism, even in the camp of Neo-Confucianism itself, was inevitable. The third phase of Neo-Confucianism, that of the Ch'ing period (1644-1911), may be said to be such a reaction. In rejecting the philosophy of the Mind school in favor of an empirical philosophy, however, the last stage of Neo-Confucianism was more than merely a reaction. It represented an effort to retain all that is good in ancient, medieval, and modern Confucianism, and to return to the central harmony of Confucius and Mencius.

Thus to say that the Neo-Confucianism of the Empirical school was really an anticlimax of the Neo-Confucianism of the Reason and Mind schools does the Neo-Confucianists of the Ch'ing dynasty great injustice. There were no names in this period so great as those in the Sung and Ming dynasties, to be sure. Neither were there as many novel theories. But if Tai Tung-yüan (1723-1777), the greatest philosopher of the Empirical school, can be taken as representative, there was an earnest attempt to reestablish Confucianism on a more balanced basis. The Neo-Confucianists of the Reason school had contrasted Reason and the vital force, considering the former above corporeity, pure, refined, and universal, and the latter corporeal, mixed, crude, and particular. Tai Tung-yüan vigorously criticized this bifurcation of reality. To him, "The distinction of what is corporeal and what is above corporeity refers to the operation of the vital force. . . . What is corporeal is that which has taken a definite form, and what is above corporeity is that which has not taken a definite form. . . . Thus corporeity means the transfiguration of things and not the vital force."[276] The vital force, together with its Five Agents and the two universal forces of activity and passivity, is not anything inferior to Reason. To Chu Hsi and his circle, Reason is the Moral Law (*tao*) which is above the vital force. To Tai Tung-yüan, on the other hand, the Moral Law means nothing but the operation of the vital force. There is no distinction, then, between Reason and the Moral Law on the one hand, and the vital force on the other. Both Reason and the vital force are the Moral Law.

"The Moral Law refers to the incessant transformation, whereas Reason refers to the complete fullness of the Moral Law. . . . That which produces life is the source of transformation, and that which produces life in a systematic order is the flow of transformation. . . . As there is growth, there is repose, and as there is repose, there is growth. This is how the universe keeps on forming and transforming. That which produces life is called *jên* (love or goodness), and that which is responsible for the orderliness of life is called propriety and righteousness."[277]

Thus the Moral Law finds expression in constant and orderly transformation, the realization of which is Reason. This name can apply to all that is in harmony with the characteristics of the universe. "With reference to its naturalness, it is called harmony. With reference to its necessity, it is called constance."[278] Consequently, only "those who can comprehend the harmony of the universe are qualified to discuss the Moral Law."[279]

With harmony as the keynote, the philosophers of the Empirical school advocated the harmony of human nature, which they, following most of the Confucianists before them, held to be good. In the discussion of Reason from the eleventh to the sixteenth century, the general opinion had been that good action proceeds from Reason whereas evil action proceeds from desire, thus sharply contrasting Reason and desire. To later Neo-Confucianists like Tai

---

[276] Tai Tung-yüan, *Mêng-tzŭ Tzŭ-i Su-chêng* (Commentary on *The Works of Mencius*), Pt. II, No. 17.

[277] Tai Tung-yüan, *Yüan Shan* (An Inquiry into Goodness), I.

[278] Tai Tung-yüan, *Tu I Hsi-tzŭ Lun-hsin* (On the Discussions of Human Nature in Appendix I of *The Book of Changes*).

[279] *Ibid.*

Tung-yüan, however, this opinion was erroneous, because "Men and creatures all have desires, and desires are the functions of their nature. Men and creatures all have feelings, and feelings are the operations of their nature."[280] Since they are inborn, they "should not be violated."[281] The problem is, therefore, not how to suppress desires and feeling, but how to harmonize them with Reason. If their functionings "do not err," they are in harmony with Heaven and Earth.[282] The general formula seems to be that "we should not be without desires, but that we should minimize them."[283]

Modern Neo-Confucianists came to the defense of desires and feeling, not only because they are inborn, but also because desire and Reason are inseparable. "Desire refers to a thing, whereas Reason refers to its principle."[284] "A thing is an event. In speaking of an event, we cannot go beyond daily matters such as drinking and eating. If we cast aside all daily matters and say that herein lies Reason, that is not what the ancient sages recognized Reason to be."[285] Furthermore, feeling, which engenders desires, does not violate Reason. On the contrary, "Reason never obtains where feeling does not. . . . When feeling is expressed neither too much nor too little, it is called Reason."[286] When we harmonize feeling and desires with Reason, we will then come into harmony with the universe. When all men and things are in harmony with the universe, there will be the fulfillment of the Moral Law.

In emphasizing the harmony of Reason and "daily events," the Neo-Confucianists in the last three hundred years were demanding a return from the speculative to the empirical, from the universal to the particular, from the abstract metaphysics of Chu Hsi and Wang Yang-ming to the socio-political interest of Confucius and Mencius. In short, they insisted on "practical application." This practical emphasis ultimately culminated in K'ang Yu-wei (1858-1927) and T'an Ssŭ-t'ung (1865-1898) who made *jên* the basis of their doctrine of "practical application" and political reform. For the guidance of social and political reform, however, modern China found her traditional philosophies inadequate. She looked to the West for the solution of her problems. Stimulated by the Renaissance led by Dr. Hu Shih, Western philosophies became

---

[280] *Ibid.*   [281] *Yüan Shan*, I.   [282] *Tu I*, etc.

[283] *Mêng-tzŭ Tzŭ-i Su-chêng*, Pt. I, No. 10.

[284] *Ibid.*   [285] *Ibid.*, Pt. I, No. 3.   [286] *Ibid.*

dominant in twentieth century China. Western pragmatism, materialism, Neo-Realism, Vitalism, and New Idealism almost dealt indigenous philosophies a fatal blow. Nevertheless Chinese philosophies have survived, because their ideals are still the ideals of China.[287]

These ideals have been examined throughout Chinese history and have been found valuable, and no philosophical system that hopes to enjoy a permanent place in China is likely to reject them. We refer particularly to the ideals of central harmony, of cordial relationship between nature and man, of the "both-and" attitude, of the golden mean, of humanism, of the preservation of one's life and the full realization of one's nature, of mental tranquillity, of incessant transformation and spontaneous creation, of the interaction of the active and passive universal principles, of the harmony of the One and the Many, and of the goodness of human nature. Because of impact with Western philosophies, a change of tone is already noticeable in Chinese philosophy.[288] There can be no doubt that Chinese philosophy will be baptized by Western science, logic, and epistemology. In the next movement of the philosophical symphony of China, therefore, there will be new notes and new chords, combining those of traditional China into a new harmony.

[287] For a summary of philosophy in contemporary China, see my chapter "Philosophies of China," in *Twentieth Century Philosophy*, ed. D. D. Runes, Philosophical Library, New York, 1943, pp. 541-571.

[288] Fung Yu-lan's "New Rational Philosophy," for example, is the Rationalism of the Ch'êng brothers and Chu Hsi modified by Western Objectivism. See *ibid.*, pp. 561-567.

CHAPTER IV

Buddhism as a Philosophy of "Thusness"[1]

By Junjirō Takakusu

A PRELIMINARY REMARK

BRAHMANISM, as it was represented in the Upanishads, was a philosophy of "Thatness" (*Tattva*) and was based on the theory of the reality of Being. The chief concern was, therefore, the immortality of Ātman (Self) as an individual principle and the eternity of Brahman, which was also conceived as *Mahātman* (Great Self), as the universal principle. The highest principle, Brahman, which words were inadequate to describe, was rarely defined. Sometimes, no definition would be admitted, as exemplified in the famous words of Yājñavalkya, "*neti, neti*" ("not, not"). At other times some appropriate definitions, such as *saccidānandam,* to which we shall return soon, were given and seriously discussed.

Buddhism, on the other hand, was a philosophy of "Thusness" (*Tathatā*) and started with the theory of becoming, admitting no *ātman,* individual or universal, and no eternalism whatever. The staying reality of Being is, according to Buddhism, only for one instant. Things come into being and pass on; nothing remains the same for two consecutive moments. The universe is thus a never-ceasing conflux of Life-waves (*Saṁsāra* [*Saṅsāra*]). Even in Buddhist realism, a reality will be conceived in momentary existence or in the continuum of transitoriness.

[1] There is much in this chapter which is strange and difficult to the Western reader. Some preliminary knowledge of Buddhism is almost imperative. The difficulty is due in part to the necessary condensation of so much material into the short space of a single chapter. The difficulty was increased by the fact that the chapter treats only of the fundamental principles, and not the well-known and popular phases, of Buddhist philosophy. The language and capitalization provided further difficulty, but editing was kept to a minimum so as to avoid any possibility of distortion of meaning. These difficulties do not lessen the value of this study, however, for, as Professor Conger says in Chapter IX, "If we are to understand the Buddhist systems, we must not be deterred by ordinary difficulties."—EDITOR'S NOTE.

The fundamental principles of Buddhism were summed up by the Buddha in the three items of negation: 1. All elements have no self (*sarvadharma anātmatā*). 2. All component things are impermanent (*sarvasaṃskāra anityatā*). 3. All is suffering (*sarvam duḥkham*), or, to use Stcherbatsky's wording, no substance, no duration and no bliss.

Even the ultimate principle, Nirvāṇa, which was said to be Bliss, was literally the "state of fire blown out," i.e., the state in which life-conditions were negated, a noncreated state.

Buddhism was thus from the outset based on the theory of negation by which the principle of "Thusness" was established. Accordingly, all the Buddhist schools which rested chiefly on some dialectic arguments could be designated as those of negative Rationalism, the static nature of "Thusness" being only negatively arrived at as the remainder.

Before we proceed to see the far-reaching contrast of Buddhism with Brahmanism we must note that within the sphere of Buddhism one finds no story of Creation, no Creator, no God, no First Cause, no monotheistic idea. Nor do we have any trace of materialism, hedonism, or extreme asceticism.

Saccidānandam

(Brahman)

The indefinable "Brahman" (n.) was "defined" in the Upanishads as *saccidānandam*. Let us proceed with these words. The name "Brahman" was not without a meaning. The word $\sqrt{Brih}$ means "to grow," "to increase." Probably the source of strength in matter and mind was the purport. Whatever it was, it was the name of the "highest principle" (n.), the "manifested God" (m.), and sometimes it meant "prayer." It existed from the beginning, one without a second, the real, the true. Its attribute was *saccidānandam*.

sat	cit	ānandam
Being	Thinking	Joy
Existence	Thought	Bliss
self-existent	all-knowing	Blissful
the real	the intellectual	the valuable

In the Upanishads a pantheistic idea was already ripe and the universal principle was conceived also to be immanent in an individual. The Self (Ātman) gradually became the individual principle. The Supreme God which the Upanishadic philosophers objectively sought and found was now discovered subjectively in their own person. It was an Intellectual Reality, the Lord of Cognition, the Internal Guide, the Light of Mind, the True Light, the Highest Splendor. Where there is no sun, no moon, no star, no lamp, Ātman alone shines in darkness, from whom all beings partake of the light. It was finally identified with the universal Self, which was also called *Mahāpurusha* (Great Person) or *Mahātman* (Great Self). Finally the mysticism of identity was realized: *"Tat tvam asi"* ("Thou art that"), and *"Aham Brahman asmi"* ("I am Brahman").

The theory of "Thatness" was thus completed and it was the conclusion of the Upanishad philosophy. Now we come to the Six Systems of India. The trend of thought seems to have been divided into two, though they were always interdependent.

For convenience, let us suppose that Buddhism arose with those six schools of Indian philosophy, although in reality those schools were all *systematized* after Buddhism. Some primary forms of the schools, at least special tenets of each, must have existed at the Buddha's time.

The Buddha denied the existence of the universal principle and the individual principle (*ātman*) of the Vedānta and proposed self-lessness (*anātman*). In contrast to the Mīmāṁsā the Buddha rejected the eternity not only of voice but of everything else, and proposed impermanence (*anitya*). In this way the idea of *sat* was removed. Then *cit* was denied too and the theory of ignorance (*avidyā*) was set forth. Not only *sat-cit* but also *ānandam* (joy) was removed and the proposal of the theory that all is suffering (*duḥkha*) was brought forward.

Besides, the Vedic authorities were denied and the sacrifice of animals was denounced. Even the charms and sorceries of the *Atharva Veda* were strictly forbidden. The caste system, based on racial distinction, was rejected in his community. He called it the "community of one caste" (*saṅgha*), and the "saṅgha of the noble" (*Aryas*), notwithstanding the fact that the *Arya* and the *Anarya* (non-*Arya*) races came together. He often protested, saying: "It is not of races altogether, but of persons individually, that we can

SIX INDIAN SYSTEMS OF PHILOSOPHY
IN RELATION TO BUDDHISM

Sat (Being)		*Cit* (Knowledge)
Action section (*Karmakanda*) (Realistic)	Buddha	Knowledge section (*Jñānakanda*) (Idealistic)
I *Mīmāṁsā school* (Realistic Ritualistic Monism) Theory of eternity of voice Six sources of knowledge Five-membered syllogism	566-486 B.C.	**IV** *Vedānta school* (Idealistic Pantheistic Monism) Theory of reality and identity of Ātman and Braham, the individual and universal principles
II *Vaiśeshika school* (Atomic Pluralism) Indivisibility and eternity of atom Polarity and neutrality of atom Theory of effect not inherent in cause Six categories (later 7 or 10) of reality (substance, attribute, function, sameness, variousness, unity)	Buddhism 500 years of its metaphysical and dialectical development	**V** *Sāṅkhya school* (Evolutional Dualism) Immortality of *ātman* and eternity of *prakriti*, the natural principle Threefold suffering Theory of effect inherent in cause Theory of the world's periodic destruction Three sources of knowledge
III *Nyāya school* (Logical Realism) Theory of noneternity of voice Sixteen categories of argument Four sources of knowledge Five- or three-membered syllogism Fifty-four fallacies or causes of defeat	Nāgārjuna about 125 A.D. Four methods of argument Two truths Eight negations	**VI** *Yoga school* (Dualistic meditative Intuitionism) Eight methods of restraint in meditation Three sources of knowledge Four immeasurable meditations
Dignāga (about 500 A.D.) Buddhist Logic Two sources of knowledge Three-membered syllogism Thirty-three fallacies		Asaṅga-Vasubandhu (about 410-500 A.D.) Buddhist Yogācāra meditation Three sources of knowledge Four immeasurable meditations
Hsüan-tsang and Chi (about 650 A.D.) in China Last Systematization of Logic		Bodhidharma and Hui-k'o in China (c. 530 A.D.) Foundation of Zen

speak as the noble (*arya*) or ignoble (*anarya*) because there will be some ignobles among the *Aryas* or some nobles among the *Anaryas*." The highest stage of cultivation was, in Buddhism, an "*Arya pudgala*," a noble person.

The Buddha's rejection of the Brahmanistic principles was thus complete. We can say that all the Brahmanistic elements were wiped out and completely eliminated from Buddhism. He was not antagonistic toward the other systems, however. With Sāṅkhya he shared the theory of periodic destruction of the world-system (*kalpa*) and the prohibition of animal sacrifice; with Yoga, the meditative doctrine of immeasurability (*apramāṇa*) and other rules of concentration; and with Vaiśeshika and Nyāya, the pluralistic ideas and the logical method of argument.

The Buddha's system was the philosophy of self-creation. What method did he use and what view did he take for the realization of life? The Buddha's view of human existence was very peculiar. According to his idea, the generation-move of beings was different from the intellection-move. The generation-move was again *sat*-move, i.e., the real particles moving on, while the intellection-move was *cit*-move, i.e., the active energy moving on. These two motions when combined form our life-flux.

One's intellection way will be different from that of father and mother. Every man is created by himself and is creating himself, each taking his own way and completing the wave-length of his generation-move. "Intellection-move" means that even when we are born in an hereditary life and inherit our father's and mother's particles, we have our own accumulation of intellection energy latent in us. In Buddhism this is called innate intellect or *a priori* knowledge. It is something like "subconscious intellect." All intellect that can be acquired after our birth is called post-natal intellect or *a posteriori* knowledge. According to Buddhism, education ought to be carried on so as to draw out and not distort the prenatal intellect. To perfect one's personality means to perfect one's intellect, i.e., to attain Perfect Enlightenment.

Buddhism is personal and individual to the end. One holds fast to one's own personality until one's final beatitude is attained. One does not come down from a highest principle, for such does not exist. One will attain his own highest principle. That is Nirvāṇa, "perfect freedom," totally nonconditional and nondeterminant. One is perfectly free, even to condition and to determine. Even one's realm is not definite or conditioned. It is the Nirvāṇa of No-Abode.

FUNDAMENTAL PRINCIPLES OF BUDDHIST PHILOSOPHY

Following the usual procedure, I shall try to set forth the general principles which are to be regarded as a common denominator of all the schools of Buddhism. At present I shall bring out six such principles:

(1) The Principle of Causation.
(2) The Principle of True Reality (Thusness).
(3) The Principle of Totalism.
(4) The Principle of Indetermination.
(5) The Principle of Reciprocal Identification.
(6) The Principle of Perfect Freedom or Nirvāṇa.

The Principle of Causation

According to Buddhist thought, human beings and all living things are self-created or self-creating. The universe is not homocentric; it is a co-creation of all beings. Even if the universe is not homocentric, as long as all beings have common purposes, it is natural that there should be groups of similar types of beings. Buddhism does not believe in the idea that all things came out of one cause, but holds that everything is inevitably created out of two or more causes.

The creations, or becomings, out of antecedent causes continue in series in point of time—past, present, and future—like a chain. This chain is divided into twelve divisions, called the Twelve Cycles of Causations and Becomings. And because these cycles are interdependent on one another, they are called Dependent Production or Chain of Causation.

The formula of this theory is as follows: From the existence of *this, that* becomes; from the happening of *this, that* happens. From the nonexistence of *this, that* does not become; from the nonhappening of *this, that* does not happen.

a. CAUSATION BY ACTION-INFLUENCE

There is law and order in the progress of cause and effect. This is the theory of Causal Sequence.

In the Twelve Cycles of Causations and Becomings, it is impossible to point out which one is the first cause, because the twelve make a continuous circle which we call the Wheel of Life. It is customary to represent the Wheel of Life in the following manner:

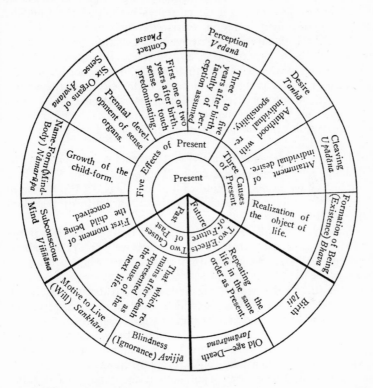

Modern people generally regard time as progressing in a straight line from the infinite past through present to infinite future. In Buddhism, however, time is regarded as a circle with no beginning or end. Time is relative.

The death of a living being is not the end; at once another life begins to go through a similar process of birth and death, and thus to repeat the round of life over and over again. Thus a living being, when regarded in relation to time, forms an endless continuum.

It is impossible to define what a living being is, for it is always changing and progressing through the cycles of life. The whole series of cycles must be taken in their entirety as representing the one individual being. So, a living being, when regarded in relation to space, forms a complex in the shape of a ring. The Wheel of Life—in the diagram—is a clever representation of the Buddhist conception of a living being in relation to both space and time.

The Wheel of Life is a circle with no beginning, but it is customary to begin its exposition at Blindness. Blindness is only a continuation of Death. At death the body is abandoned, but the Blindness remains as the crystallization of the effects of the actions performed during the life. This Blindness is often termed Ignorance, but this Ignorance ought not to be thought of as the antonym of knowing; it must include in its meaning both knowing and not knowing—Blindness or blind mind.

Blindness produces blind activity. The "energy" or the effect of this blind activity is the next cycle, Motive to Live, or Will. This Motive to Live is not the kind of will which is used in the term "free will"; it is rather a blind motive toward life or the blind desire to live.

Blindness and Motive to Live are called the Two Causes of the Past. They are causes when regarded subjectively from the present, but, regarded objectively, the life in the past is a whole life just as much as the life of the present is.

In the life of the present the first stage is Subconscious Mind. This is the first stage of an individual existence and corresponds, in the actual life, to the first moment of the conception of a child. There is no consciousness yet; there is only the subconscious mind or the blind motive toward life. When this Subconscious Mind advances one step and takes on a form, we have the second cycle of the present, Name-form. The Name is the mind, because mind is something we know by name and cannot grasp. Name-form is the stage of prenatal growth when the mind and body are combined.

In the third cycle a more complex form is assumed and the six organs of sense are recognized. They are the eyes, ears, nose, tongue, body, and mind.

The fourth cycle corresponds to the first one or two years after the birth of the child. The six organs of sense reach the state of activity, but the sense of touch predominates. The living being begins to come into contact with the outside world.

Now that the living being is able to manifest its consciousness, it begins to take in the phenomena of the outside world consciously. This is the fifth cycle, called Perception, representing the period of growth of a child three to five years old. Here the individuality of the living being is definitely recognized; in other words, the status of the present life has been completed.

The above five cycles are called the Five Effects of the Present. In these cycles the individual is formed, but the individual is not entirely responsible for its own formation, because the causes of the past have pushed the development of these cycles. From here on, the individual begins to create causes on his own responsibility, or, in other words, enters the true sphere of self-creation.

The first of the Three Causes of the Present is Desire. Through Perception the individual experiences sorrow, pleasure, suffering, enjoyment, or neutral feeling. When the experience is sorrow, suffering or neutral feeling, nothing much will happen. But when it is pleasure or enjoyment, the individual will endeavor to make it his own. This effort is Desire. It produces attachment. The first step of this attachment is the next cycle, Cleaving, the effort·to retain the object of Desire. The last state of this attachment is Formation of Being. The term Existence is often used for this cycle, but as it is a link between the present and future, and the preliminary step for Birth, I believe "Formation of Being" is a more fitting term.

Desire, Cleaving, and Formation of Being represent the three stages of the activities of an adult, and together they constitute the Three Causes of the Present. While an individual is enjoying the effects of the past, he is forming the causes for the future. While the plum fruit is ripening on the tree, the core in the fruit is being formed. By the time the fruit is ripe and falls to the ground, the core too is ready to bring forth a new tree of its own to bear more fruit in the future.

In the Future two cycles are listed—Birth and Old-age-Death, or, in short, Birth and Death. When viewed from the Three Causes of the Present, Birth and Death may be termed the effects. But when viewed in the light of the continuous Wheel of Life, we may regard the future as the time when the causes of the present open out and close. Also, the Effects of the Future contain in themselves causes for the life still further in the future.

The present is one whole life and so is the future. Past, Present, and Future are each an independent whole life. Past, Present, and Future are relative terms, however. Objectively, there is no Future or Past. There is Present only. A living being does nothing but repeat the life in the Present.

It is clear that the Causation Theory of Buddhism is not like the Theory of Causality of modern physical science for the latter is a fixed theory. In Buddhism every cycle is a cause when viewed from its effect. When viewed from the antecedent cause, it is an effect. Also it may be said that there is a cause in the effect, and an effect in the cause. There is nothing fixed in this theory. The Theory of Causality of physical science may be disproved, but the Causation Theory of Buddhism is never to be disproved.

Blindness, which remains after the death of a living being, is the crystallization of the actions (*karma*) which the living being performed during its life, or, using other words, the "energy" or influence of the actions that remain. Action[2] is the dynamic manifestation of mental and physical energy. The crystallized or stilled form of this energy may be called Action-influence or potential energy. Action-influence remains after the action ceases, and this is what makes the Wheel of Life move. As long as there is energy it has to work, and the cycles of causation and becoming will inevitably—blindly—go on forever.

In other words, a living being determines its own nature and existence by its own actions. Therefore we may say it is self-created. The act of self-creation has continued in the past for thousands and millions of lives, and the living being has gone around the circle of Twelve Cycles over and over again. And, according to the nature of the preceding Action, the next Wheel of Life may be of a higher order or of a lower order. That is, a living being may assume any form of life—human form, *Deva's* form, or animal form. The incessant transformation of life is called undulation of life (*saṅsāra*).

Often *Saṅsāra* (Constant flow) is translated as "Transmigration

[2] The word "action" is used throughout as the most suitable translation of "karma."

of Soul," but that is a very misleading translation, for the idea is not that a soul lives after the death of the body and moves into another body. *Saṅsāra* means the creation of a new life by the influence of the actions of the former living being. In the first place, Buddhism denies the existence of soul. Life is like the waves on the water; the vibration of one particle causes the vibration of the next particle, and thus the waves are transmitted a long distance. One wave is one life, and the series of lives is *Saṅsāra*. In the Buddhist theory the series of lives does not go on infinitely as in a straight line. They turn in a circle and repeat the circle over and over again. The Wheel of Life is a small circle of one life, while the great circle (the series of the Wheel of Life) is *Saṅsāra*.

Since this self-creation is regulated by the Action of the individual being, it does not depend upon the authority of another—for instance, a God. Nor is it affected by the Action-influence of different individuals. "Self-acted, self-rewarded," and "For a good cause, a good result; for an evil cause, an evil result"—these are the rules.

In Action-influence there are Individual Action-influence and Common Action-influence. Individual Action-influence creates the individual being. Common Action-influence creates universality and the worlds where living beings exist. In this connection the words "Individual Effect" and "Common Effect" are used.

From another point of view Action may be classified into three kinds: Good Action, Evil Action, and Neutral Action. Also, according to the way its retribution is received, Action may be classified into four kinds, as follows: Action to receive retribution immediately, Action to receive retribution in the present life, Action to receive retribution in the life to come, Action to receive retribution in one of the lives following the next.

There are two ways of viewing the process of becoming. The order of cause and effect is usually regarded as arising in sequence in relation to time. However, when all the factors of the Twelve Cycles of Causation are considered as belonging to one being, we see that it possesses all at the same time. (For example, one does not abandon the Six Organs of Sense to gain Contact.) Therefore, we may regard all factors as mutually dependent, none being purely a cause nor purely an effect, but all developing simultaneously.

Buddhism regards all things in the universe as "existence depending upon series of causes." Only when there is cause, is there existence. Without cause there can be no existence. No existence is permanent or conclusive. In Buddhist terminology, such an existence is called "Conditional Existence." Such a way of regarding all things is called "Knowing and perceiving the reality as such." To regard all things in the universe as dynamic becoming is the characteristic of Buddhism.

Delusion is the illness of the mind, while Action is its physical manifestation, and the result is Suffering. For instance: one may be angry in mind and act accordingly, striking or killing, and later suffer retribution. From this suffering of retribution one will acquire more delusions and consequent actions and suffering, thus repeating the same wandering ever and anon. Such is the Chain of Causation by Action.

Who or what is responsible for the progression of the Chain of Causation by Action? To explain this question clearly we must study the theory of Causation by the Ideation-store.

b. CAUSATION BY THE IDEATION-STORE *(Ālayavijñāna)*

Actions *(karma)* are divided into three groups, i.e., those of the body, those of speech, and those of volition. When one makes up one's mind to do something, one is responsible for it and is liable to retribution, because the volition is a mind-action even if it is not expressed in speech or manifested in physical action. But the mind being the inmost recess of all actions, the causation ought to be attributed to the mind-store or Ideation-store.

The Buddhist Ideation Theory divides the mind into eight faculties: the eye-sense, the ear-sense, the tongue-sense, the nose-sense, the body-sense, the sense-center (the sixth, *manovijñāna*), the individualizing center of egotism (the seventh, *manas*), and the storing center of ideation (the eighth, *ālayavijñāna*—Ideation-store or mass).

Of these eight faculties, the seventh and eighth require some explanation. The individualizing Center of Egotism is the center where all selfish ideas, egotistic opinions, arrogance, self-love, and illusions are fermented and is the source of all delusions. The Storing Center of Ideation is the center where the seeds of all manifestations (i.e., ideas behind all actions) are deposited. Buddhism holds that the origin of all things is the effect of ideation. Let it suffice at present to say that the Storing Center of Ideation is the "seed bed" of all that exists. Every seed (i.e., every idea or mental impression) lies in the storing center, and when it sprouts out into the object-world (as an action), a reflection returns as a new seed (idea or impression upon the mind). That is, the mind reaches out into the outer world and, perceiving objects, puts new ideas into the mind-store. And again, this new seed sprouts out to reflect a still newer seed. Thus the seeds accumulate and all are stored there together. When they are latent, they are called seeds, but when they are active they are called manifestations. The old seeds, the manifestations, and the new seeds are mutually dependent, forming a ring which forever repeats the same process. This is called the "Chain of Causation by Ideation."

That which makes the seeds sprout out is the manifestation of the seed itself. That is, the motive force which makes the chain of causation move is nothing but the ideation. It is easy to see from this theory of Causation by Ideation that Delusion, Action and Suffering originate from mind-action, or ideation.

The Storing Center of Ideation is carried across rebirth to determine what the next form of life should be. This Storing Center might be regarded somewhat as the soul is looked upon in other philosophies and religions. According to the Buddhist idea, however, what is reborn is not the soul, but is simply the result (in the form of ideational effects) of the actions performed in the preceding life. In Buddhism the existence of soul is denied.

One should ask where this Storing Center of Ideation comes from. To explain that we must study the theory of Causation by "Thusness."

c. CAUSATION BY THUSNESS *(Tathatā* or *Tathāgatāgarbha)*

"Thusness," or "Suchness," is the only term that can be used to express the ultimate indefinable, the unnamable reality. It is otherwise called the "Matrix of Thus-come."

"Thus-come" is a designation of the Buddha employed by himself instead of "I" or "we," but not without a special meaning. After he had attained Enlightenment, he met the five ascetics with whom he formerly shared his forest life. These five ascetics addressed him saying, "Friend, Gautama." The Buddha admonished them, saying that they ought not to treat Thus-come as their friend and their equal, because he was now the Enlightened One, the Victorious, All-wise One. When he had "thus come" in his present capacity as the instructor of all men and even of *Devas*, they should treat him as the Blessed One, not as an old friend.

Again, when the Buddha went back to Kapilavastu, his former home, he did not go to the palace of his father, but lived in the Banyan grove outside the town, and as usual went out for daily begging. Śuddhodana, his King-father, could not bear the idea of his own son, the prince, begging on the streets of Kapilavastu. So he visited the Buddha in the grove and entreated him to return to the palace. The Buddha answered in the following words: "If I were still your heir, I should return to the palace to share your comfort with you, but my lineage has changed. I am now a successor to the Buddhas of the past, all of whom have 'thus gone' as I am doing at present, living in the woods and begging. Accordingly, your majesty must excuse me." The king understood the words perfectly and became a pupil of the Buddha at once.

Now, "Thusness" or the matrix of "Thus Come" or "Thus Gone" means the true state of all things in the universe, the source of an enlightened one, *the basis of enlightenment*. When static, it is enlightenment itself (with no relation to time or space), but when dynamic, it is in human form assuming an ordinary way and feature of life. "Thusness" and the "Matrix of Thus Come" are practically one and the same—the ultimate truth. In Mahāyāna the ultimate truth is called "Thusness."

Now we are in position to explain the "Causation Theory of Thusness." Thusness in its static sense is spaceless, timeless, undifferentiated, without beginning or end, formless, and colorless, because Thusness itself without its manifestation cannot be sensed or described. Thusness in its dynamic sense can assume any form. When driven by a pure cause it takes a lofty form; when driven by a tainted cause it takes a depraved form. Thusness, therefore, is of two states. The one is Thusness itself, the other is its manifestation, its state of Life and Death.

There are, therefore, three series of causations to be considered: (a) Causation by Action-influence as depicted in the Wheel of Life; (b) The origin of action, Causation by Ideation-store; (c) The origin of the Ideation-store, Causation by Thusness. One must not

ask where Thusness or the Matrix of Thus-come originates, because it is the noumenon, the ultimate Thusness.

d. Causation by the Universal Principle *(Dharmadhātu)*

We have thoroughly examined the origin of causation, but it is
still necessary to consider the mutual relationship of the becomings
of all things, and, therefore, we pass on to the principle of universal
causation.

The Universe, or all things, is the dynamic manifestation of
Thusness. All things are mutually dependent, mutually permeating
without any hindrance to one another.

"Dharmadhātu" means "the element of the principle," and has
two aspects: (1) the state of "Thusness" or noumenon, and (2) the
world of phenomenal manifestation. In this Causation Theory it
is usually used in the latter sense, but, in speaking of the ideal
world as realized, the former sense is to be applied.

Buddhism holds that nothing was created singly or individually.
All things in the universe—matter and mind—arose simultaneously,
all things in it depending upon one another, the influence of all
mutually permeating each, thereby making a universal symphony of
spiritual totality. One item lacking, the universe is not complete;
without the rest, one item cannot be.

When the whole cosmos arrives at a harmony of perfection, it
is called the "Universe One and True," or the "Lotus Store"
("wreath"). In this ideal universe all beings will be in perfect
harmony, each finding no obstruction in the existence and activity
of another.

Although the idea of the interdependence and the simultaneous
rise of all things is called the Theory of Universal Causation, the
nature of the rise being universal, it is rather a philosophy of the
Totality of All Existence than a philosophy of Origination.

According to this theory, four states of the universe can be conceived: (1) the real, or the world of actual life; (2) the ideal, or
the world of principle; (3) the ideal realized, or the world in which
the principle is applied in actual life, or the fact and the principle
harmonized; (4) the real harmonized, or the world in which the
actuality attains harmony in itself.

The first, second, and third states are easily understood, for those
are the ideas often discussed by thinking men. But the fourth may

be somewhat difficult to understand, because in these individualistic modern times it is usually thought that one individual is inevitably opposed to another, that classes in a society are opposed among themselves, that a business concern is in competition with another. A similar thought is often held in physical science also—no more than one object can occupy one position, and, therefore, all objects are opposed among themselves. Even in the world of learning, philosophy, for instance, stands by itself; so do religion and politics. According to some, even art should have an independent existence, as art for art's sake. Such independent existence of all the branches of learning is in fact a dissolution of civilization. But the unification of the divergent branches will be a difficult task, for dissolution is the natural outcome in a world of individualistic tendencies.

The Principle of Totality, on the other hand, demonstrates that all things in the real world ought to have harmony among themselves, and it advances the following reasons: (1) Because of the simultaneous rise of all things; (2) Because of the mutual permeation of the influence of all things; (3) Because of the necessity of mutual identification between all beings (mutual self-negation to agree with each other) for the realization of harmony; (4) Because of the necessity of unity, or harmony, between the leaders and the followers for the attainment of a purpose; (5) Because all things have their origin in ideation—therefore a similar ideal ought to be expected of all; (6) Because all things are the result of causation and, therefore, are mutually dependent; (7) Because all things are indeterminate and mutually complementary—therefore harmony should be established among all things without hindrance; (8) Because of the fact that all beings have the nature of Buddha dormant in themselves; (9) Because of the fact that all beings from the highest to the lowest are parts of one and the same *maṇḍāla* (circle); (10) Because of mutual reflection of all activities—as in a room surrounded by mirrors, the movement of one image causes the movement of the thousand reflections. Buddhist writers enumerate twenty reasons, but for our purpose these ten will be quite sufficient.

The Principle of True Reality (Tathatā)

Many of the problems concerning "Thus-come," "Thus-gone," "Thusness," or "Suchness" have just been studied in connection with the Causation theory. Thusness, however, is the ultimate foundation of Buddhist thought concerning the real state of all that exists, and therefore, deserves further treatment in itself.

It is natural for people first to seek the innermost essence among the outward appearances of all things or to seek an unchanging fact among changing things. Failing in this, people try to distinguish the unknowable from the knowable, the real from the apparent, or the thing-in-itself from the thing-for-us. This effort, too, ends in failure, for what they select as the real or the thing-in-itself is utterly beyond human knowledge. Such efforts may be called the search for the world-principle or for the life-principle. The method of search is also various. Some are monistic or pantheistic, while others are dualistic or pluralistic.

Against all these views Buddhism stands aloof by itself. Buddhism is atheistic—there is no doubt about it. When questioned about the first cause or principle, the Buddha always remained reticent. The Buddha was, after all, a man, but a man with perfect enlightenment. As a man he taught men to become men like himself. Though people are apt to regard him as a superman, he did not regard himself as such. He was simply a perfected man. The Buddha did not deny the existence of gods (*Devas*), but he considered them only as the higher grade of living beings, also to be taught by him.

As to the life-principle, he denied the existence of ego or soul or any kind of thing which one may call the real self—as we have seen before. To see the true nature or the true state of all things is not to find one in many or one before many, nor is it to distinguish unity from diversity or static from dynamic. The true state or the true reality is the state without any specific characteristic. It is very difficult for the human mind to understand this idea of a reality in which there is no "sub-stance" at all.

The idea of an abiding substance with changing qualities is very deeply rooted in our habits of thought. Buddhist schools, no matter what they are, Hīnayāna or Mahāyāna, realistic or idealistic, are utterly free from such a habit of thought, and all maintain the theory of pure change without substratum. So when *any* Buddhist speaks of the true state of reality he means the state without a specific nature. The state without any specific characteristic or special condition is Nirvāṇa, according to the general views of the

Hīnayāna schools, because Nirvāṇa is the state of perfect freedom from bondage. The Realistic school (the Sarvāstivāda), belonging to the Hīnayāna, goes a step further and assumes that selflessness, impermanence, and flamelessness are the true state of all things. The Nihilistic school (the Satyasiddhi) holds that all things, matter and mind, are void or unreal and that nothing exists even in Nirvāṇa.

The Mahāyāna school teaches, on the one hand, that the truth can be discovered only by negative views of becoming (the school of negativism, the Mādhyamika), and on the other hand, it holds that true perfection can be realized negatively by denial of the illusory and causal nature of existence (the school of idealism, the Vijñaptimātra). The "Wreath" school (the school of totalism, the Avataṅsaka) of the Mahāyāna thinks that the ideal world, or the World One and True, is without any independent individuals. The "Lotus" school (the phenomenological school, the Puṇḍarīka) considers the manifested state to be the true entity immanent-in-nature.

On the whole, to see only the fact that a flower is falling is, after all, a one-sided view, according to the theory of impermanence. We ought to see that immanent in the fact of a flower's falling there lies the fact of a flower's blooming, also that immanent in the blooming of the flower there is the fact of its falling. Thus, the antithesis of falling (extinction) and blooming (becoming) being synthesized, we form the view of mutual identification which is an unbiased view of the mean, or Middle Path.

We have to admit the saying that in any color or smell of a flower we see the manifestation of the true mean. This amounts to saying that we see inaction in action and action in inaction, immotion in motion and motion in immotion, calm in wave and wave in calm. We thus arrive at the true state of all things: i.e., the Middle Path. And this is Thusness or Suchness. This view of the true state of things is somewhat like the phenomenological view which holds that noumenon can be seen only through phenomenon.

When the view is negatively expressed it is the true negation or void, because any special state of things is denied altogether. Such is considered to be the ultimate basis of Buddhist thought. When the ultimate principle is viewed from the universal point of view it is called "the principle- or law-element" (*Dharmadhātu*), but when it is viewed from the personal point of view it is named "the Matrix of Thus-come or Thus-gone" (*Tathāgatāgarbha*), the Nature of Principle, the Buddha Nature, and the spiritual or Law-body. These are all practically synonymous. Without knowing the principle of Thusness or Void in the highest sense of the word, one can in no way understand the Mahāyāna doctrine. The word "void" in its highest sense does not indicate "nothingness"; it means "devoid of special conditions," "unconditioned," "indeterminate."

As a summary: The ultimate indefinable, when defined, the nameless, when named, can only be expressed in a word like "Thusness." It is *Dharma*-nature in things in general and is Buddha-nature in living beings. It is Nirvāṇa (Perfect Freedom) as the ultimate principle of life, when all earthly conditions have been blown out. Strictly as the Buddha's personality, it is *Dharmakāya* (ideal body), but when "Thusness" refers to the universe, it is *Dharmadhātu* (principle- or law-element). Another name for "Thusness" is the "Matrix of the Thus-come" (*Tathāgatāgarbha*). These synonyms are all intuitively given names and are to be considered as interpretations of the indeterminateness of Nirvāṇa.

The Principle of Totalism (Dharmadhātu)

This principle—which has been discussed somewhat more fully above[3]—is based upon the universal causation of *Dharmadhātu* (element of law or principle) which we may regard as the self-creation of the universe itself. One ought not to forget that it is nothing but a causation by the common Action-influence of all beings, and that the principle is also based upon a synthesis of two conflicting ideas, Self and Selflessness, i.e., the world of one-all.

The Principle of Indetermination

Buddhism has nothing to do with fatalism, for it does not admit the existence of anything like destiny or the decree of fate. According to Buddhist doctrine, all living beings have assumed the present life as the result of self-creation, and they are, even at present, in the midst of creating themselves, or, in other words, every being is a stage of dynamic becoming. Though the grade and form of life vary in each birth, one ought not to think of the strict distinction

[3] See "The Principle of Causation," sec. d.

of time as past or future. In truth there is present only. That is to
say, we have a long continuity of existence, birth and death being
simply the rise and fall of the waves in the ocean of life. Birth and
death are not the predestined fate of a living being, but a "corollary
of action (*karma*)," as it was called by some. One who acts must
sooner or later reap the effect; while enjoying an effect, one is sow-
ing the seeds anew, thus causing the next wave of life to be high
or low according to circumstances. There is no idea of the transmigration of soul in the ordinary sense of the term.

Now, by way of contrast, let us examine other Eastern schools
of thought. Confucianism is a determinism in the sense that Heaven
is considered the basic principle of human life. The same is true of
Taoism as it holds Tao, or the vivifying principle, to be the source
of the universe. With Brahmanism in India, too, Brahman is made
the creative principle or a personified god. Very similar ideas of determinism can be found among many of the Western schools of
thought.

Buddhism, on the other hand, has quite a different method of
approach. While practically all other schools of thought begin with
a static first principle, Buddhism begins with the actual, dynamic
world, and on the basis of the principle of self-cultivation strives to
realize the ideal. *Sansāra* (the Rise and Fall of Life) is not an
onward flow, but a waving circle, each wave being a cycle of life
appearing on the great orbit of *Sansāra*. It has no beginning or
end; one cannot point out the beginning of a circle. There is, therefore, no place in Buddhism for the idea of a first cause or creation.
In the *Dhammapada* (Book of Religious Verse) the idea is described as follows: "All that we are is the result of what we have
thought; it is founded on our thoughts; it is made up of our
thoughts." We must remember, however, that though the volition is
free or undetermined in the human world, it may appear as abstract
energy-instinct or animal desire among the beasts and lower forms
of life which are the lesser waves in the continuity of self-creation.

It is the motion of the mind-action which defines the form of an
individual life. All things, matter and mind, have no substratum,
no soul, no reality, no such thing as absolute self or ego. What
appears to be real is a temporary existence, a causal sequence, one
ripple in the long line of waves, the effect of two or more causes
combined.

As long as you do not insist on the existence of a central principle or absolute ego, you may define yourself in any way you please. Generally speaking, it is satisfactory to say that you exist and to describe yourself. But in minutely definite and exact language, it is impossible to define your own self or to describe yourself. However, there will be no danger of losing yourself, for no one can extinguish the influence of your action or latent energy. A particular manifestation of that energy in human form is yourself and the whole of you.

By virtue of your own action you will get your next life and so on along the endless line of lives. Having no permanent center, a living being changes itself as time goes on, sometimes for better, sometimes for worse. Your self does not exist apart from the changing manifestations, but the cycle of the changing manifestations as a whole *is* yourself. There is, therefore, no possibility of the disappearance of your identity.

The idea of indetermination in the world of differentiation is expressed by many terms: "having no special nature" or "having no definite nature"; "all things are emptiness" or "having no special state"; "all are of temporary existence" or "all are existence by combination of causes." "No substance, no duration" is the root idea of Buddhism.

A real and permanent thing and a real and permanent self do not exist in the world of becoming. "Without change no life," as Bergson asserts. Buddhism has been teaching the Principle of Indetermination of matter and mind for over 2500 years, but no anxiety or inconvenience has been caused by it as some modern physicists fear over the spread of the idea of the Uncertainty Principle of physical science.

The Principle of Reciprocal Identification

Identification here means synthetic unification. An identification may be found in the union of two different materials, just as two different metals mixed make an alloy. Another kind of identification may be assumed when the same entity appears different according to viewpoint. The statement "Ignorant will is identical with perfect enlightenment" sounds very strange, but it is the same mind or person, tied down by ignorant will in illusion, who becomes enlightened when his wisdom is perfected. Still another identification is established in the case of the whole entity's being one and the same thing, like water and wave. If one does not understand the principle of reciprocal identification one cannot understand Mahā-yāna Buddhism.

The Hīnayāna school is generally satisfied with analysis and is rarely inclined to synthesis. The Mahāyāna school, on the other hand, is generally inclined to synthetic identification of two conflicting ideas. If one party adheres to its own idea while the other party insists on its own, a separation will be the natural result. And this is what happens in the Hīnayāna school. The Mahāyāna school teaches that one ought to put one's own idea aside for a moment and identify oneself with the position of the other party, thus mutually synthesizing the opposed positions. Then both parties will find themselves perfectly united. This is really a process of self-denial which is minutely taught in the dialectic method of the school of Negativism.

This mutual identification by mutual self-negation, when realized, has a great practical value in smoothing out conflicting opinions or in creating a sympathy among opposing parties. In this way diversity can be brought to unity, the world is identified with a paradise, and illusory existence is synthesized with the enlightened life. Such ideas as seeing noumenon in phenomenon, regarding motion as calm or calm as motion, identifying action and inaction, purity and impurity, perfection and imperfection, one and many, the particular and the general, permanence and impermanence, all are attainable on this theory. It is one of the most important ideas of the Mahāyāna and it is indispensable to a clear understanding of the Buddhist doctrine as taught in this school.

The Principle of Perfect Freedom (Nirvāṇa)

The year 486 B.C. or thereabouts saw the conclusion of the Buddha's activity as teacher in India. The death of the Buddha is called, as is well known, Nirvāṇa—"the state of a fire blown out." When a fire is blown out, nothing remains to be seen. So the Buddha was considered to have entered into an invisible state which can in no way be depicted in word or in form.

In spite of thoughtful instructions by the Buddha, some of his disciples were expressing a dissenting ideal on the subject of Nir-vāṇa even before his funeral. So we ought to assume that there were some who had an idealistic and free-thinking tendency. This free-thinking group, whom many consider the forerunners of the Mahāyāna school, took great liberty in their interpretation of Nir-vāṇa, because the Buddha did not speak much of it during his life-time. Whenever he was asked by a questioner whether he was to live after death or what sort of world he was to enter after Nirvāṇa, he always remained silent. But we cannot say that, because of his silence, he denied the existence of the Nirvāṇa world. Whenever the Buddha remained silent to a question requiring an answer of "yes" or "no," his silence meant assent. His silence to the question concerning Nirvāṇa was due to the fact that his listeners could not understand the profound philosophy involved. The Buddha advised people to become his disciples without wasting time on problems which were too profound to be understood by an ordinary man—probably after a long cultivation as a disciple of the Buddha, they might come to understand. It is quite natural, therefore, that after his departure all the metaphysical discussions and speculations should center around the subject of Nirvāṇa.

The main problem of Buddhism, either formalistic or idealistic, concerned the extinction of human passion, because this distorted state of mind is considered to be the source of all evils of human life. Human passion can be extinguished even during one's lifetime. Therefore liberation from disorder of mind is the chief object of Buddhist culture; and the extinction of passion, of desire, of sense, of mind, and even of individual consciousness is also mentioned.

Nirvāṇa did not involve any idea of deification of the Buddha. It simply meant the eternal continuation of his personality in the highest sense of the word. It meant returning to his original state of Buddha-nature, which is his *Dharma*-body but not his scripture-body as the formalists take it to be. *Dharma* means the *"ideal"* itself which the Buddha conceived in his perfect Enlightenment. The idealists hold that the Buddha has the *Dharma*-body, the body identi-cal with that ideal, i.e., the spiritual body. The ideal was expressed in the Buddha's preachings but those preachings were always re-stricted by the language and the occasion and the listeners. There-fore the idealists hold that the scripture is not the Buddha's ideal itself. This ideal body without any restricting conditions whatever is Nirvāṇa.

The formalists, on the other hand, hold that the scripture is the perfect representation of the ideal of the Buddha. Hence their opinion is that the Buddha lives forever in the scripture-body, Nirvāṇa being entire annihilation and extinction.

Now, let me illustrate the principle of Nirvāṇa in the light of space and time. It was an illusion on the part of philosophers, especially some of the Indian philosophers, to believe that space and time were infinite. Buddhism, however, has never treated space and time as infinite, for Buddhism takes them to be physical matters. Space is made one of the five elements—earth, water, fire, air, and space—and it is sometimes represented to be of round shape as if to anticipate the modern theory of the curvature of space. The atoms are said to be so fine that they are almost empty. Time is treated as real in some schools while in other schools it is treated as unreal. But it is to be particularly noted that time has never been considered to exist apart from space. Space and time are always correlative.

The theory that space is curved, set forth by modern physicists, has considerably facilitated the elucidation of the doctrine of Nirvāna. The universe, or the *Dharmadhātu* (principle-element) as it is technically called, is the region which is occupied by space and time, and where are controlled all the waves of existences. So, in practice, the space-time world is the ocean of the waves of life and death. It is the sphere of *Saṅsāra* (Flowing cycles of life), the world of creation, of energy, of action, of causation and ideation, of self-creation, and of dynamic becoming. It is the sphere of desire, form, and mind.

In opposition to such a world we can presume theoretically that there must be a sphere spaceless and timeless, of no creation, with no causation, and not disturbed by the waves of life and death. There will be no *Dharmadhātu* (principle-element) in the dynamic sense of the word, i.e., the world of manifestation. But there will be the *Dharmadhātu* in the static sense of the word: i.e., as it is in itself, namely, Thusness or Suchness, the ultimate state of Nirvāṇa.

Dharmadhātu, or the actual world, is an encircled and restricted world which may be represented as follows:

The sphere of matter-mind
The sphere of space-time
Of life-death, action, causation
creation, becoming
Of *Saṁsāra* (life flux)
The world of desire, form, mind
Of Action-influence
Nirvāṇa with the life conditions
remaining
The realm of phenomena

Outside of the *Dharmadhātu* there must be the unrestricted world to be described as follows:

Spaceless-timeless

Nirvāṇa without the life-conditions

Lifeless-deathless

No creation, no causation, no becoming

Perfect Enlightenment, perfect
freedom

Thusness, Suchness, the state of
Thus-come, Thus-gone

Among the Buddhist texts which have come down to us we do not find passages expressly indicating these points. However, we have one text—though its Indian original has not as yet been discovered—which contains the idea much as I have expressed it here.

It says: "In the *Dharmadhātu* (real) there are three worlds—desire, form, and mind. All created things or beings, noble and ignoble, both cause and effect, are within the *Dharmadhātu.* The Buddha alone is outside the *Dharmadhātu.*" The idea in this text is practically identical with the diagram given above.

The Mahāyāna text of the *Mahāparinirvāṇa Sūtra,* not being satisfied with the negative elucidations, explains Nirvāṇa in affirmative words such as: permanency (in contrast to worldly impermanence), as bliss (against human suffering), as self (against the selflessness of all beings), and as purity (against the pollution of human life). However, as they are all transcendental qualities of the Buddha, these terms ought not to be taken in the ordinary sense of the words. For instance, one must not picture to oneself a special location, a world of Nirvāṇa, where the Buddha lives in peace and joy, for the Buddha's Nirvāṇa is the Nirvāṇa-of-No-Abode, the state of Perfect Freedom.

An ordinary *Arhat* (Saint) will cut off all obstructions caused by passion or desire, thereby attaining his purpose of annihilation. He finds a satisfaction in the destruction of his intellectual life, because he thinks that the source of distinction, opposition or differentiation in things lies in consciousness. He thinks his state of annihilation is the ideal Nirvāṇa. In truth, however, he has returned to the original blindness (*avidyā*—ignorance) in leaving the obstruction of intellect. He himself may be thinking that he has done away with the blindness, too, but blindness is the basic principle of existence which cannot be simply cut off, just as darkness cannot be destroyed without a light. The only way to eliminate darkness is to bring a light into the room. By virtue of enlightenment the darkness that bars intellect will be destroyed.

Technically speaking the extinction of human passion is called the "Nirvāṇa with the condition of 'being' still remaining" or, in a more literal expression, "the Nirvāṇa with the *upādhi* remnant," *upādhi* being the material and immaterial condition of being. Plainly, this means becoming a person without passion while yet alive. It can be termed "conditional Nirvāṇa."

Then the next question will be: What is the Nirvāṇa without this *upādhi* remnant? It is the total extinction of the conditions of being as well as passion, or one may call it the annihilation of being. This is the Nirvāṇa exemplified by "Perfect Quiescence."

The formalistic view of the Buddha here comes to an end with the annihilation of being. But the speculative views of the idealistic standpoint have a fresh start with the passing of the visible Buddha into the invisible state. Even in his lifetime the Buddha had perfect freedom in intellectual activity, and, while he was a person, he had been superpersonally enlightened. How much more free must he have been when he passed into the thoroughly unconditioned state of Nirvāṇa! He had now returned to his "Spiritual" body, i.e., Ideal-body. It is called the Body of His Own Nature, "self-natured Body," in contradistinction to the "Body Manifested for All Beings" ("Body for Things or Beings"). All the incarnation theories entertained in later years have their origin in this interpretation of Nirvāṇa.

The Buddha in Nirvāṇa has perfect freedom to live anywhere he pleases; he can act in whatever way he wishes, and on that account he has no fixed abode, and his Nirvāṇa is called the Nirvāṇa-of-No-Abode. The Blessed One may reappear in this world when he feels the necessity of saving all beings as Śākyamuni did. Therefore, the Buddha, according to the idealistic view, does not live in the world of life and death, since he is not bound by causation. However, at the same time he does not rest at ease in Nirvāṇa, because he is the sufferer of others' suffering.

Methods of Attaining the State of Perfect Freedom (Nirvāṇa)

To reach that state of perfect freedom Buddhism sets forth two methods. One is by a dialectical ladder, the other by an introspective (meditative) plan. Which to choose is a matter of taste but it depends on one's preparation.

Method of Dialectic

The spiritual inheritance of the Buddha, handed down to the present world, was threefold: the way-of-Life-view (darśana-mārga), the way-of-Life-culture (bhāvanamārga), and the way-of-Life-ideal (aśaikshamārga). The last, negatively expressed as "the way of no more learning," is most significant.

The Buddha regarded the world as the emanation of ignorance. With the Buddha ignorance is the cause of practically all of the dynamic becomings of life. To begin with, ignorance covers the blind motive to live, the conscious ignorance of childhood, illusory

ideas or earthly desires of manhood, erroneous assertions, false doctrines, superstitions, hallucinations, epistemological mistakes, and
the incapability of escaping from a perplexed life. It is, in fact, the
ignorant activity of will. However, there is no definite entity called
ignorance because it is merely the state of being without knowledge.
Buddhism aims at the undoing of ignorance. It is foolish to think
of getting light by destroying darkness. Bring a light, then darkness will be no more. Buddhism, therefore, begins with the search
for knowledge.

People who join the Buddhist Community are first taught the
"threefold learning": higher conduct, higher thought or meditation,
and higher wisdom. "Knowledge and views resulting from deliverance from ignorance" or "knowledge and views according to truth
as it ought to be," are results of the "threefold learning." In case
one is well prepared for progress, the way-of-Life-view is carefully
taught. The central principle is the Eightfold Path. At length, when
the noble aspirant attains the position of a would-be-Buddha he is
further trained in the Six Perfections of which the "perfection
of knowledge and wisdom" is considered most important. The
completion of knowledge and wisdom is Perfect Enlightenment
(*Bodhi*). It follows naturally that the perfection of knowledge
and wisdom is perfection of personality. Such a personage is called
"Buddha," the "Enlightened." And one who has become perfectly
enlightened is one who has the power of enlightening all others.

(1) THE THEORY OF THE DOUBLE TRUTH:
COMMON-SENSE TRUTH AND HIGHER-SENSE TRUTH

Now, let us see how the Buddhist philosophers applied the original principle of knowledge and wisdom to the problem of life in
order to clarify or illumine the world of ignorance.

It was Nāgārjuna, the greatest and foremost philosopher India
has ever produced, who solved the problem successfully. He was a
talented speculator of the Nāga tribe of south India, and flourished
about 125 A.D. at the time of King Kanishka. He first proposed the
theory of double truth: common-sense truth and higher-sense truth.
On one side, he would admit a popular common-sense argument
as a truth, but, at the same time, would lead the people to a higher
truth based on, say, a scientific investigation. Gradually, the common-sense truth would absorb that higher truth. The formerly con-

flicting truths, being united, would now become a new common-sense truth. This common-sense truth would confront another still higher truth based on a thorough investigation. Both would be admitted as truths. Now the people would all begin to live on the basis of scientific results. Science would become a common-sense truth. However, a still more advanced scientist would come forth ˀnd declare the assumption of old scientists untenable. If modern scientists go hand in hand with philosophers, there will perhaps be a time when philosophers will represent the common-sense truth of the world. (These examples may be too modern, of course.) An illustration would be:

A	common-sense truth
B	higher truth
AB	common-sense truth
C	higher truth
ABC	Common-sense truth
D	higher truth

and so on until we reach the highest truth, that of "Thusness," negatively by denying all special, one-sided, or biased common-sense truths.

During Nāgārjuna's time the problem was that of *ens* or *non-ens*. The Buddha once said: "All exists." At other times he said, "All is void," "Nothing exists." Self was denied, individual self (Ātman) and universal self (Brahman). "No substance, no soul, no permanence, no duration" was the Buddha's idea. Therefore, a nihilistic as well as a realistic tendency of thought might have existed side by side even during the Buddha's time.

After the Buddha's Nirvāṇa, there was a period of great confusion in Buddhist thought for some centuries. Sarvāstivāda (all-exists school), the Realistic school, seems to have been the first to systematize its ideas. These thinkers compiled a great literature of the *Abhidharmaka* (higher *dharma*) philosophy. This Realistic school was called *Vaibhāshika* (optionalist). Against this Realism, Harivarman's (250 A.D.) Nihilistic school was systematized. When the realistic *ens* (*sat*) is common-sense truth, the nihilistic *non-ens* (*a-sat*) is higher-sense truth. When, however, both together become common-sense truth, the negation of both will be the higher-sense truth. This is Nāgārjuna's philosophy of "middle view" (*mādhya-mika*). The theory of repeatedly leaving behind the common truth involves the assumption of transcendental truth and is at the same time a gradual denial of common truth ever enriched intensively.

(2) THE EIGHTFOLD NEGATION OF BECOMING

Nāgārjuna then proposed another wholesale denial of the world of phenomena: neither birth nor death, neither permanence nor extinction, neither unity nor diversity, neither coming nor going. This Eightfold Negation (in four pairs) is the basis of his negativistic philosophy. This theory of Eightfold Negation is the extensive denial of all dynamic becomings. The denial of phenomena means that the state of being is not real but that it is a causal wave, a relative existence, only temporary, transitory and nominal. The thought that phenomena exist is illusory and erroneous. If you hold to one view or the other, either to *ens* or to *non-ens*, or to a conditional *ens* or to a conditional *non-ens*, you get only a biased idea, a one-sided view, and the real Middle Path can never be realized. The theory of Middle-Path-Ideal can be reached only by the wholesale denial of both *ens* and *non-ens*. Negation is the only way to attain the highest truth. The "Middle-Path-Ideal" of Nāgārjuna is identical with the highest truth.

(3) THE FOURFOLD BASIS OF DIALECTIC ARGUMENT

The third theory of Nāgārjuna is the establishment of Four Bases of Argument. The fourfold argument, e.g., as to cause, are: 1. self-caused (as self-existent) ; 2. caused by another; 3. caused by both together; and 4. caused by neither (e.g., in the materialistic school which admits no cause). These are all negated: "not caused by self," "not caused by another," "not caused by both together," "not caused by neither." These negations seem to have been directed against some tenets then prevalent. But when the fourfold method of argument was made applicable to any problem expecting an answer of "yes" or "no," we have: 1. "yes"; 2. "no"; 3. either "yes" or "no" depending upon conditions; 4. neither "yes" nor "no." Thus we get *ens, non-ens,* either *ens* or *non-ens* (conditional), and neither *ens* nor *non-ens*. An argument cannot have any forms other than these four. Without investigation of these four aspects no problem can be satisfactorily solved. People often judge from the opposite points of "yes" or "no," and do not think of the case of "either yes or no, according to conditions offered." The fourth point, "neither 'yes' nor 'no,'" may have a double meaning. It may mean "the question has nothing to do with me" or "I stand over and above 'yes' and 'no.'" From the standpoint of the fourth argument Nāgārjuna denied reality in the four manifestations as explained in the Eightfold Negation. Life-wave is void; that is, all elements are void because they become devoid of all specific features. This is the all-transcending truth, the ultimate principle, because all pluralistic ideas are done away with. This is the Middle Path, the Golden Mean, because all inclinations one way or the other, and all one-sided views are eliminated. It is the absolute śūnyatā (void). Thus we are led to the highest ideal, that of the Middle Path. "Thusness" is hereby arrived at negatively as the remainder.

(4) THE THEORY OF THE MIDDLE-PATH-IDEAL

The highest truth—or you may call it the true Real—is the Middle Path, the Golden Mean. With Nāgārjuna, the Middle Path is simply the middle view (mādhyamika) and it is synonymous with the "Highest Truth," "the view that has no inclination, no bias, no attachment and no specific feature." Now let us call this Middle Path the Ideal. The Ideal of the ens school (realism) is the middle path between hedonistic inclination and pessimistic tendency. The Ideal of the non-ens school (nihilism) is the middle path, that is, the truth attainable by admission of the nonreality of all things or beings: no self, no permanence, nonreality of all elements (dharma) and nonconditioned Nirvāṇa (extinction). The Ideal of the either-ens-or-non-ens school (idealism) is the middle path between ens and non-ens, but it is, in one way, the school of conditional neither-ens-nor-non-ens. It is "neither ens," because the ens of the outer world (matter and form) is entirely denied, and it is also "nor non-ens" because the non-ens of the inner world (mind) is negated. That is, the ens of the mind-world is affirmed. The idealists, therefore, call their Ideal the middle path of neither-ens-nor-non-ens. As a matter of fact, however, the Mādhyamika is really the school of neither-ens-nor-non-ens, for it denies both ens and non-ens.

(5) THE THEORY OF THE RECIPROCAL IDENTIFICATION OF ANY TWO OPPOSED IDEAS

Another phase of the method of dialectic is the theory of a Reciprocal Identification of any two opposed ideas, which has been treated above.

Method of Meditation

All the basic principles of Buddhism at once melt into the way-of-Life-culture which, in reality, is the application of the life-view to the practical life. As to the realization of the life-ideal, the theory of perfect freedom (Nirvāṇa) speaks for itself. It is a state, spaceless, timeless, of no condition, of no abode, of no limitation whatever. Negatively, Nirvāṇa is "extinction," "total negation," "undifferentiated indetermination"; but positively, it is perfect freedom. It is identical with Perfect Enlightenment (*Bodhi*). Nirvāṇa may be attained by meditation and contemplation, if the negation theory of the method of dialectic still proves unsatisfactory to anyone. Buddhism is pansophism.

If I say that Buddhism as rationalism is negative and as intuitionism is passive, it may seem to some to have nothing to do with actual life. On the contrary it is a philosophy of self-creation and teaches the way-of-Life-view, the way-of-Life-culture, and the way of realization of the Life-ideal. Since Buddhism takes the integration of consciousness seriously, the method used ought to be exhaustive and negative to wipe out all possibilities of errors and perplexities. If the fullness of insight, that is, the perfection of knowledge and wisdom, is aimed at, one should not linger in the world of transitoriness or be entangled in the wire of attachment. For without self-discipline there will be no equipoised mental activities; without poise, no insight. The Buddha, therefore, teaches the threefold learning: higher discipline, higher thought or meditation, and higher insight. These three are inseparable. The ideal of the would-be-Buddha is the Sixfold Perfection: charity (for others), discipline (for oneself), resignation (in toil), bravery (in effort), contemplation (meditation), and wisdom (insight). Insight cannot be attained without the preceding five, especially meditation.

The Buddha contemplated under the *bodhi* tree on the twelve cycles of causation, first in order, then in reverse, "this is, therefore that is; this is not, therefore that is not," all being interdependent.

When he became perfectly enlightened, and was about to preach his ideal, he further meditated 49 days as to how, where, whom, to teach his ideal. When he began to teach, he taught about the actual life of suffering which was easy to demonstrate or intuit. "Aging, ailing, and dying are suffering. Birth is not joy, because it ends in death, union is not joy, if it ends in separation." When people began to realize the hardship of life, he taught them not to be deceived by the guise of joy but to face the suffering as suffering. His Four Noble Truths to be believed by the noble are: 1. Suffering; 2. Cause of suffering; 3. Extinction of suffering; 4. The way to the extinction of suffering. The Truths 1 and 2 are real, and 3 and 4 are ideal. What these are should be known by the first round of learning (investigation) according to the way-of-Life-view. Next, the Truth of suffering should be fully realized. The cause of suffering should be cut off. The extinction of suffering fully experienced (or intuited) and the way leading to extinction of suffering should be cultivated (or practiced). These should be pursued by the second round of learning (realization) according to the way-of-Life-culture. Thirdly, the Truth of suffering has been known, the cause has been cut off, the extinction has been attained, and the way leading to the extinction of suffering has been cultivated. These constitute the third round of learning (perfection), the stage of no-more-learning.

The way to extinction of suffering is the well-known Eightfold Path of the noble, i.e., right view; right thought; right speech; right action; right remembrance; right effort; right livelihood; right contemplation. These are principles of ethics, but at the same time a religion by which perfection of personality is attained and self-creation is fulfilled.

Though the highest principle is reached chiefly and ultimately by meditation, we must realize that Buddhists use other methods of self-culture in order to attain the ideal end. The Buddhist schools which use chiefly the method of meditation (*dhyāna*) can be called the schools of intuitionism, in which Thusness is intuited in differentiations, noumenon and phenomenon being inseparable.

The method of meditation is twofold: (1) *Tathāgata* meditation and (2) Patriarchal meditation. The former was taught by the Buddha along with the other teachings, while the latter was transmitted only in Japan, the founder patriarch being Bodhidharma, an

Indian who came to China in 520 A.D. What we call Zen at present is this second method.

(1) TATHĀGATA MEDITATION (*Nyorai Zen*)

As we have seen, the existence of the higher meditation of the Three Learnings, the contemplation of the Six Perfections, and the right meditation of the Eightfold Path of Life-view show that meditation is one of the most important factors in the teaching of Buddhism. Meditation is the "basis of action." The object of meditation with the Buddha seems to have been to attain, first, tranquillity or calmness of mind and, then, activity of insight.

(a) Calmness (*Śamatha*)

A fivefold restraint of mind is to be practiced:

1. Meditation on impurity of the worldly life, to adjust the mind with regard to passion and avarice. (individual)
2. Meditation on mercy, to cultivate the idea of sympathy to others and to stop the tendency to anger. (universal)
3. Meditation on causation, to get rid of ignorance. (individual)
4. Meditation on diversity of realms, to see the difference of standpoints and to get rid of a selfish view. (universal)
5. Meditation on breaths, to aid concentration and to cure the tendency of mental dispersion. (individual)
   When one's faulty mind has been adjusted and calmness has been obtained, one proceeds to the next.

(b) Insight (*Vipaśyanā*)

Fourfold retention of mind

1. The impurity of body is meditated upon and fully realized.
2. The evils of sensations are meditated upon and fully realized.
3. The evanescence or impermanence of mind and thoughts is meditated upon and fully realized.
4. The transiency of all elements or selflessness is meditated upon and fully realized.

These practices are called "bases of action," which is one of the modes of analytical meditation. Forty such meditations with the corresponding subjects of meditation, are given in the *Visuddhi-magga*. They are: the ten universals, the ten impurities, the ten reflections (reflection on the Buddha, on the Doctrine, etc.), the four sublime states (friendliness, compassion, etc.), the four formless states (the infinity of space, of consciousness, etc.), the one perception (of the loathsomeness of nutriment), and the one analysis (into the four elements).

The ordinary way of meditation is as follows:

Arrange your seat properly, sitting erect, legs crossed, having your eyes not quite closed, not quite open, looking 10 or 20 feet ahead.

You may sit properly but your body may move on account of your breaths. Count your in-breath and out-breath as one and slowly count as far as 10, never beyond.

Now your body may seem upright and calm but your thought may move about. You have to meditate on the impurity of the human being in illness, death, and after death.

When you are well prepared to contemplate, you will begin to train yourself in concentration by meditating upon the ten universals.

It is a meditative unification of diverse phenomena into one of the ten universals, that is, blue, yellow, red, white, earth, water, fire, air, space, consciousness. In this you will meditate on the universe until it becomes to your eyes one wash of a color or one aspect of an element.

If you meditate on water, the world around you will become only running water.

Such a process of meditation is common to Hīnayāna as well as Mahāyāna, and is the feature of the *Tathāgata* meditation.

(2) PATRIARCHAL MEDITATION (*Soshi Zen*)

The history of the Zen is mythical. It is said that one day, Brahmā came to the Buddha who was living at the Vulture peak, offered a *kumbhalā* flower and requested him to preach the law. The Buddha ascended the Lion seat and taking the flower, touched it with his fingers without saying a word. No one in the assembly could understand the meaning. The venerable Mahākāśyapa alone smiled with joy. The world-honored One said: "The *piṭaka* (collection of writings) of the Eye of the True Law here is entrusted to you, oh Mahākāśyapa! Accept it and hand it down to posterity." Once Ānanda asked him what the Buddha's transmission was. Mahākāśyapa said: "Go and take the Banner-stick down!"[4] Ānanda understood him at once. Thus the mind-sign was handed down successively. The 28th patriarch from the Buddha was Bodhidharma who came to China in 520 A.D.

Later Bodhidharma went to Mount Wut'ai, where he remained nine years, and, facing a cliff behind the edifice, meditated in silence. Bodhidharma transmitted his idea to Hui-k'o (Eka) who in turn transmitted it to later Zen teachers in China and Japan.

Zen has much philosophy in it, but it is not a philosophy in the ordinary sense. Zen is the most religious school of all, yet it is not a religion in the ordinary sense of the word. It has no scripture of the Buddha, nor does it follow any discipline set forth by the Buddha.

Unless it has a *sūtra* or a *vinaya* (discipline) text, no school or sect would seem to be Buddhistic. According to the ideas of Zen, however, those who stick to words, letters, or rules that have been set forth can never get into the speaker's true idea. The ideal or truth conceived by the Buddha should be different from that preached by him, because the preaching is necessarily conditioned by the language he uses, by the hearers whom he is addressing, or by the environment in which the speaker and hearers are placed. What Zen aims at is the Buddha's ideal, pure and unconditioned. The school is otherwise called "the school of the Buddha's mind" (*Busshin Shū*). The Buddha's mind is after all a human mind. An introspection of the human mind alone can bring an aspirant to perfect enlightenment. But how?

The general purport of Buddhism is to let one see rightly and to walk rightly. The way of viewing is different from the way of walking. People walk often without seeing the way. Religions generally lay importance on practice, that is, how to walk, but neglect intellectual activity to find the right way, that is, how to see. To judge whether the path we are going to take is right or not, first of all, science is important, and all branches of science are welcomed

----

[4] A Banner-stick is the sign to indicate that preaching is going on at that place.

by Buddhism. But as we go on, we shall discover that philosophy is much more important than anything else. Buddhism is a philosophy in the widest sense of the word. In case science and philosophy do not give a satisfactory result we have to resort to the meditative method of Zen to get insight into any given problem. First, find your way and begin to walk in it. Steps acquired by meditation can carry you across the wave-flux of human life, or over and above the airy region of the heavenly world (Form and Formless) and can finally make you perfect and enlightened like the Buddha. Contemplation is the eye to give insight and, at the same time, feet to procure a proper walk. Zen (meditation and concentration) is the lens on which diverse objects outside will be concentrated and again dispersed and impressed on the surface of the negative plates inside. The concentration on the lens itself is *samādhi* (concentration) and the deeper the concentration is, the quicker the awakening of intuitive intellect and wisdom. The further impression on the negative film is *prajñā* (wisdom), and this is the basis of intellectual activity. Through the light of "insight" or wisdom, we see in review the outer world of diversity once again so as to function or act appropriately toward actual life.

The meditation of the Patriarchal Zen, therefore, is not an analytical method like science, nor is it a synthetic method like philosophy. It is a method of thinking without ordinary thinking, transcending all methods of logical argument. To think without any method of thinking is to provide an opportunity for the awakening of intuitional intellect or wisdom. Other methods of meditation, as taught by Hīnayāna, by Yogācāra of pseudo-Mahāyāna, by the abrupt method of "calm and insight" of the Tendai school, or by the mystical Yogācāra of the Shingon school can be used if an aspirant likes, but are in no way necessary.

A summary of the ideas peculiar to Zen is as follows: "from mind to mind it was transmitted"; "not expressed in words or written in letters"; "it was a special transmission apart from the sacred teaching"; "look directly into the human mind, comprehend its nature and become an enlightened Buddha"; and "the very body or the very mind is the Buddha." The idea was very well expressed in Hakuin's hymn on sitting and meditating (*za-zen*): "All beings are originally Buddhas; it is like ice and water: without water there will be no ice. This very earth is the lotus-land and this body is Buddha."

Generally the Zen expressions and statements are very witty and often paradoxical, but the basic idea is the identity of *ens* and *non-ens*. For example, the "true state is no (special) state"; "the gate of *Dharma* is no gate"; "holy knowledge is no knowledge." The mutual identification of two opposed ideas, such as black and white, good and evil, pure and impure, or the like, results from deep meditation. "The ideal body has no form, yet any form may come out of it." "The golden mouth has no word yet any word may come out of it." Many ideas of like nature are often encountered.

There is, however, a peculiar process in Zen. To concentrate one's mind in silent meditation, a *kōan* (public theme) is given to an aspirant to test his qualification toward enlightenment. On receiving a *kōan* one sits in silence in the Zen hall. One has to sit at ease, cross-legged and well-poised with upright body, with his hands in the meditating sign, and with his eyes neither quite open nor quite closed. It is called *za-zen* (sitting and meditating), which may go on for several days and nights. The daily life, lodging, eating, sleeping, swimming or bathing, should be regulated properly. First of all, the threefold silence is strictly required and kept, that is, while meditating, dining or bathing, no word should be uttered and no noise should be made. In the Zen hall a superintending priest with a large flat stick strolls around now and then, and if any sleep, yawn, or show a neglectful attitude he is rewarded with a number of slaps. Sometimes a public dialogue called a *mondō* (question and answer) takes place and the traveling students ask questions of the teacher who gives answers, hints, or scoldings. When a student or any aspirant thinks that he is prepared in the problem, he pays a private visit to the teacher's retreat and explains what he understands and proposes to resolve the question. When the teacher is satisfied he will give sanction; if not, the candidate must continue to meditate.

The Zen, which is generally practiced in a forest retreat, seems to be far away from the real world but the general trend of mind of the Zen people is toward a strict observance of rules and a minute accomplishment of discipline. Their ideals are immediately expressed in their daily life and in personal experiences. They are generally very practical. The famous words of the Zen patriarchs, such as "no work, no food," "one day without work, one day without food," "every day, good day," "daily mind the way," "the living, the teaching," "going, staying, sitting, or lying are the sacred teaching," exemplify their practical application of ideals. We can say without hesitation that it requires training to hear a voice in silence, to find action in inaction, motion in immotion, or to have preparedness in peace, and fearlessness in death. Such a tendency must have appealed to the warrior class, thus eventually producing the way of knightly behavior (bushidō).

Besides, when we see the Zen influence so conspicuously discernible in Japan, in literature, drama, painting, architecture, industrial arts, and the social life (tea ceremony, vegetable cookery, flower-arrangement, decorations of rooms), and at present, in the educational training of Japan, the Zen ideas can be regarded as almost inseparable from the national life of all Japan. Probably the national ideal of simplicity, purity, and sincerity can find its expression most appropriately in the Zen practice of Buddhism.

CONCLUSION

In Buddhist systems, investigation by oneself and argument with others, meditation by oneself and teaching to others, all go together. When the Life-view is formed it is at once applied to Life-culture, aiming at a realization of the Life-ideal. Accordingly, it is philosophy but it is at the same time religion; there is, in fact, no distinction between the two. One ought not to think that these two are not as yet differentiated in Buddhism, because Buddhism holds that these two should not be divided. Otherwise it will end either in a philosophical amusement or a superstitious belief. Some Buddhist ideas may seem to be purely theoretical, but no Buddhist theory, however negative or passive, will be without an application to actual life.

So, with Buddhism, philosophy will be at once an ethics. For example, the theory of selflessness will at once melt into the denial of all egocentric ideas; one will become nonindividualistic, not thinking of self-interest, unselfish, nonegoistic. A negation of all becoming in the real world may appear dreadful at first sight, but when it is applied to actual life, it becomes self-denial, a negation of all biased ideas, or of all one-sided views, a wiping-out of all attachments, a preparedness for the final fullness of insight, the state of Nirvāṇa, perfect freedom, an unconditioned, nondeterminate Thusness. In this way no negative principle or passive view will remain negative or passive when it is applied to Life-culture All tends toward the realization of the Life-ideal.

CHAPTER V

An Interpretation of Zen-Experience

By Daisetz Teitarō Suzuki

THE philosophy of Zen Buddhism is that of Mahāyāna Buddhism, for it is no more than a development of the latter. But the development took place among a people whose psychology or mentality widely varies from the Indian mind whose product Buddhism is. As I view it, Buddhism, after Nāgārjuna and Vasubandhu and their immediate followers, could not continue its healthy growth any longer in its original soïl; it had to be transplanted if it were to develop a most important aspect which had hitherto been altogether neglected—and because of this neglect its vitality was steadily being impaired. The most important aspect of Mahāyāna Buddhism which unfolded itself in the mental climate of China was Zen. While China failed to perfect the Kegon (or Avataṅsaka) or the Tendai system of Mahāyāna thought, she produced Zen. This was really a unique contribution of the Chinese genius to the history of mental culture generally, and it was due to the Japanese that the true spirit of Zen has been scrupulously kept alive and that its technique has been completed.

When it is asked what Zen is, it is very difficult to give an answer satisfactory to the ordinary questioner. For instance, when you ask whether Zen is a philosophy or a religious faith, we cannot say it is either, as far as we understand these two terms in their usual sense. Zen has no thought-system of its own; it liberally uses Mahāyāna terminology; it refuses to commit itself to any specified pattern of thinking. Nor is it a faith, for it does not urge us to accept any dogma or creed or an object of worship. It is true that it has temples and monasteries where images of the Buddhas and Bodhisattvas (would-be Buddhas) are enshrined in some specially sanctified quarters, but they do not hesitate to treat them unceremoniously when they find it more useful for the elucidation of their subject matter. What the Zen masters stress most is a certain kind of experience, and this experience is to express itself in ways most characteristic of Zen. Those ways, they consider, constitute the essential features of Zen as differentiated from the other schools of Buddhism as well as from any religious or philosophical thought-systems of the world. What modern students of Zen have to do is to make a thorough examination of Zen-experience itself and of the ways in which the experience has expressed itself in history.

2

To study Zen means to have Zen-experience, for without the experience there is no Zen one can study. But mere experience means to be able to communicate it to others; the experience ceases to be vital unless it is adequately expressible. A dumb experience is not human. To experience is to be self-conscious. Zen-experience is complete only when it is backed by Zen-consciousness and finds expression in one way or another. In the following I will attempt to give a clue to the understanding of Zen-consciousness.

Daian (died 883), the Zen master of Dai-i San, once gave this to his congregation: "(The conception of) being and nonbeing is like the wistaria winding around the tree."

Sozan, hearing this, lost no time in undertaking a long journey, for he wished to find out the meaning of Daian's most enigmatic statement. Seeing the master engaged in making a mud-wall, he approached and asked, "(The conception of) being and nonbeing is like the wistaria winding around the tree; did you really say that?"

The master said, "Yes, my friend."

Sozan queried, "When the tree is suddenly broken down and the wistaria withers, what happens?"

The master threw up his mud-carrying board and laughing loudly walked away toward his living quarters. Sozan followed and protested: "O Master, I come from a remote district three thousand *li* away, I have sold my clothing to pay for the traveling expenses, and this for no other purpose than to get enlightened on this subject. Why do you make fun of me?"

The master felt pity for the poor monk and told his attendant to gather up money enough for his return trip. He then turned toward Sozan, saying, "Some day you may happen to see a master who is known as 'One-eyed Dragon' and he will make you see into the matter."

Later, Sozan came to Myōshō and told him about the interview he had with Daian of Dai-i San. Myōshō said, "Daian is all right through and through, only he misses one who really understands his mind." Sozan now proposed the same question to Myōshō, saying, "What happens when the tree is broken down and the wistaria withers?" Myōshō said, "You make Daian renew his laughter!" This made Sozan at once comprehend the meaning of the whole affair, and he exclaimed, "After all there is a dagger in Daian's laughter." He reverentially bowed in the direction of Dai-i San.

3

In this citation, what strikes one most is the disparity between the question and the answer, for as far as our common sense or logic allows us to see, no connection whatever exists between the statement concerning being and nonbeing and the master's laughter or, as is given later on, Yengo's repetition of his own master. The question in regard to being and nonbeing is a philosophical one dealing with abstract ideas. All our thoughts start from the opposition between being and nonbeing; without this antithesis no reasoning can be carried on, and therefore the question is a fundamental one: "What will become of our thought-system when the conception of being and nonbeing is wiped out?" When the tree dies, naturally the wistaria withers. Being is possible only with nonbeing, and conversely. This world of particulars is comprehensible only when we recognize the fundamental antithesis of being and nonbeing. Where shall we be when this is no more? An absolute nothingness? This too is inconceivable. Is it an error then to speak at all of the antithesis? But it faces us; we cannot get rid of this world of birth-and-death, which, however, in its present state, is quite unsatisfactory to our moral and spiritual nature. We always have the craving to go beyond the antithesis which somehow does not seem to be final; it points to something higher and deeper, and this we wish to take hold of. The mutual conditioning of antitheses must be transcended, but how? This is in fact the question raised by Sozan.

As long as we stay with the mutual conditioning of opposites, i.e., in the world of antitheses, we never feel complete; we are always haunted with a feeling of uneasiness. Sozan must have been deeply stirred with the question of being and nonbeing, of birth and death, or, speaking more like a Christian, with the problem of immortality. When he heard of Daian of Dai-i San making the statement about it, he thought that here was the master who could solve the riddle and give him spiritual rest. He sold his scanty possessions and with what little he could realize he managed to travel a long way up to Dai-i San. Seeing the master engaged in making the mud-wall, he approached him precipitously and wished to be enlightened on the subject: "What will become of us, of human souls, of their immortality, when the world with all its multitudinous contents is reduced to ashes at the end of the present *kalpa*?"

The question is metaphysical as well as religious. It is religious as long as it does not attempt to develop its significance along the purely intellectual line; it is metaphysical inasmuch as its approach is by means of abstract concepts. This is a feature peculiar to Zen Buddhism. If we choose, we can call it a kind of practical philosophy, and this practicalness may well be illustrated by the laughter given by Daian of Dai-i San as an answer to Sozan's question. Sozan was metaphysically minded enough to resort to such an abstraction as being and nonbeing, while his practical mindedness is shown by transforming this abstraction into the relation between concrete objects such as the wistaria and the pine tree. Even this practical mindedness of Sozan was thoroughly upset by Daian's ultrapracticalness: the throwing up of the mud carrier, and the laughter, and the hurried departure for his room. Daian was all action while Sozan was still on the plane of word symbolism; that is, he was still on the conceptual level, away from life itself.

4

As long as we are gregarious animals and therefore social and rational, everything we experience, be it an idea, an event, or a feeling, we desire to communicate to one another, and this is possible only through a medium. We have developed various mediums of communication, and those who can command them at will are leaders of humankind: philosophers, poets, artists of all kinds, writers, orators, religionists, and others. But these mediums must be substantiated, that is, must be backed by real personal experiences. Without the latter, mediums are merely utilized and will never vibrate with vitality.

Some mediums are more readily counterfeited than others, being subject to all devices of ingenious simulation. Language as one such medium lends itself most easily to misrepresentation, intentional or otherwise. The highest and most fundamental experiences are best communicated without words; in the face of such experiences we become speechless and stand almost aghast.

Another consideration we make about means of communication is that however eloquent a medium may be it will not have the desired effect on the one who never had an experience somewhat similar in kind or one fainter in intensity. Like a pearl thrown before the swine, the eloquence is wasted. On the other hand, if two people have had an experience of the same nature, the lifting of a finger will set the whole spiritual mechanism in vibration, and each can read the other's inner thought.

The Zen master is an adept in the use of a medium, either verbal or actional, which directly points to his Zen-experience and by which the questioner, if he is mentally ripe, will at once grasp the master's intention. The medium of this kind functions "directly" and "at once," as if it were the experience itself—as when deep calls to deep. This direct functioning is compared to one brightly burnished mirror reflecting another brightly burnished one which stands facing the first with nothing between.

5

In the case of Daian and Sozan, the latter was still a captive in the prison of words and concepts, and not capable of grasping reality at first hand. His mind was filled with ideas of being and nonbeing, of trees and wistarias, of birth and death, of the absolute and the conditioned, of cause and effect, of *karma* and Nirvāṇa; he had no direct, nonmediated understanding of reality; and this was indeed the reason why he brought himself before the amateur mason, after traveling over a distance of several thousand *li*. The mason master was a master indeed in every sense of the word. He never argued with the logician who was entangled like the wistaria around the problem of being and nonbeing. He did not talk about the ab-

solute; he never resorted to a dialectic of contradiction; he never
referred to a fundamental assumption lying behind the antithesis of
being and nonbeing. What he did was simply to throw down his
mud carrier, give a hearty laugh, and hurry to his private quarters.

Now let us ask: Was there anything funny about Sozan's question? We human beings are always worried over the disruption of
things we see, especially about the dissolution of this carnal existence, and about the life to come after it, if there should be one.
This seems to be quite a natural feeling with us all and why should
this excite the Zen master's laughter? Merely laughing was not
enough, he even threw down his instrument of work, stopped his
wall making, and made for his quiet retreat. Does he mean by this,
that it is far better to ask nothing, to enjoy life as it goes on, to
take things as they display themselves before us, to laugh when
laughable objects are presented, to weep when events excite this
feeling, in short, to accept all things and be cheerful about them?
Or did he mean that when the world should come to an end, he
wanted to enjoy the ending with the world? Or did he mean that
there is no such thing as the ending of anything—things are eternal
as they are, a world of relativity is mere appearance—and, therefore, that there is in reality no breaking down, no withering, thus
barring all conceptual guessings based on the notion of relativity and
appearance? Or did he laugh at the questioner's stupidity, which
showed that the latter had failed to realize the working of something
in himself quite apart from or rather along with his deep concern
for the breaking down of the tree and the withering of the wistaria?
Such a variety of meaning may be read into Daian's behavior. But
what is desired here from the Zen point of view is to experience the
meaning itself and to leave its intellectual interpretation to the elaboration later on of your Zen-consciousness, which inevitably rises
out of the experience.

In any event Sozan could not take in Daian's laughter, or, as we
would say, he could not grasp the idea that was behind it or in it.
He next visited Myōshō, "the One-eyed Dragon," wishing to be
enlightened about the whole situation, in which he found himself all
the more involved. Myōshō, however, did not give him any plausible
intellectual explanation which might satisfy a philosophical inquirer;
he simply remarked that this questioning on the part of Sozan would
end in renewing Daian's laughter. This was really an enigmatical

confirmation of the predecessor, but, miraculously enough, it helped Sozan to dive into the significance of Daian's puzzle. The whole thing was clarified now and the only step he could take was to bow reverentially in the direction where Daian was and to express his heartfelt appreciation.

6

Through the whole course of this incident, there are no metaphysical discussions of any form; nor are there any devotional proceedings such as confession, repentance, or mortification; again there are no references to sin, God, prayer, shrinking from an everlasting fire, or asking for forgiveness. It starts with a kind of philosophical inquiry concerning being and nonbeing, which is likened to the wistaria winding itself around the tree; but the solution given is not at all along the line suggested by the question —it is absolutely beyond what the ordinary-minded people can expect on such occasions. In the whole history of human thought there is really nothing comparable to this extraordinary Zen transaction. And what is still more extraordinary and incomprehensible is the fact that Sozan, the inquirer, finally grasps the meaning of the strange behavior of the master, which evidently solves the antithetical entanglements of being and nonbeing.

7

Somewhat similar to this Zen-incident was the experience of Rinzai (Lin-chi), whose case is given in one of my *Essays in Zen Buddhism,* and I quote it:[1]

Rinzai (died 867) was a disciple of Obaku and the founder of the school that bears his name. His Zen-experience shows some interesting features which may be considered in a way typically orthodox in those days when the *kōan* system of Zen discipline was not yet in vogue. He had been studying Zen for some years under Obaku when the head monk asked:

"How long have you been here?"

"Three years, sir."

"Have you ever seen the master?"

"No, sir."

---

[1] *Essays in Zen Buddhism,* II (London: Luzac & Co., 1933), pp. 33-35.

"Why don't you?"

"Because I do not know what question to ask."

The head monk then told Rinzai: "You go and see the master and ask: 'What is the principle of Buddhism?'"

Rinzai saw the master as he was told and asked, "What is the principle of Buddhism?" Even before he could finish the question, Obaku gave him several blows.

When the head monk saw him coming back from the master, he inquired about the result of the interview. Said Rinzai sorrowfully, "I asked as you told me and he struck me several times." The monk told him not to be discouraged but to go again to the master. Rinzai saw Obaku three times and each time the same treatment was accorded him, and poor Rinzai was not any the wiser.

Finally, Rinzai thought it best to see another master and the head monk agreed. The master directed him to go to Daigu. When Rinzai came to Daigu, the latter asked, "Where do you come from?"

"From Obaku."

"What instruction did he give you?"

"I asked him three times about the ultimate principle of Buddhism and each time he gave me several blows without any instruction. I wish you would tell me what fault I committed."

Daigu said: "No one could be more thoroughly kindhearted than that dotard master, and yet you want to know where you were faulty."

Thus reprimanded, Rinzai's eye was opened to the meaning of Obaku's apparently unkind treatment. He exclaimed: "After all, there is not much in Obaku's Buddhism!"

Daigu at once seized Rinzai's collar and said: "A while ago you said you could not understand and now you declare that there is not much in Obaku's Buddhism. What do you mean by that?"

Rinzai without saying a word probed Daigu's ribs three times with his fist. Daigu loosened his hold on Rinzai and remarked, "Your teacher is Obaku; I am not at all concerned with your business."

Rinzai returned to Obaku who asked him, "How is it that you are back so soon?"

"Because your kindness is much too grandmotherly!"

Obaku said, "When I see that fellow Daigu, I will give him twenty blows."

"Don't wait for that," said Rinzai, "have them now!" So saying he gave the old master a hearty slap.

The old master laughed a hearty laugh.

8

In Rinzai's case the answer was given, not in the form of laughter, but in a more forbidding manner, for he was given so many blows by the master. In fact, however, whether it is a blow or a laugh or a kick or a slap, it does not make much difference so long as it comes directly from an experience on the part of the master. Rinzai too failed to comprehend Obaku and had to run to Daigu for elucidation. And the elucidation came in the form of a good-natured comment: "Obaku was indeed grandmotherly!" The dealing of the hard blows was a kindhearted treatment to wake up the spirit-weary Rinzai.

From these citations we can readily see what a remarkable experience Zen is. Is it a philosophy? Or is it a religion? What kind of spiritual discipline is it after all? Zen-experience is an absolutely unique one in the whole history of human culture.

To make this point clearer, I will add another Zen-incident in relation to the antithesis of being and nonbeing.

The same problem came up later between Yengo and Daiye, of the Sung dynasty. Yengo wanted Daiye, his disciple, to give his view on the statement aforementioned regarding the tree and the wistaria. Whenever Daiye tried to express himself, the master invariably interrupted him, saying, "Not that, not that." About half a year passed, when Daiye one day asked Yengo, "When you were with your master Goso Hoyen, I understand you approached him with the same problem, and I wish to know what Goso's response was." When Yengo hesitated, Daiye insisted, "Your asking at the time took place before an open congregation, and I do not think there is any harm in your giving me Goso's answer now." Yengo could no more refuse him and said, "When I asked my teacher, Goso, about the statement concerning the conception of being and nonbeing, his answer was, 'No paintings, no delineations can do justice to it!' When I further asked, 'What happens when the tree is suddenly broken down and the wistaria withers?' Goso said, 'You are caught in your own trap!'"

The reiteration on the part of Yengo revealed at once the whole secret before his disciple's mind, for Daiye now thoroughly understood what it was, and this fact made Yengo say, "You now see by yourself that I have never deceived you."

9

The statement that "(this antithetical world of) being and nonbeing is like the wistaria winding around the tree," in fact aptly describes the state of affairs about us. Intellectually speaking, we cannot go beyond this. The philosophers attempt to make it logically comprehensible—this fundamental contradiction lying at the bottom of this life—and they succeed in varied degrees only to be superseded by those who follow. Some day they may develop perfect logic or dialectic which will be the final word to our ratiocination. But people not so intellectually gifted as professional philosophers, yes, even the philosophers themselves as human beings endowed with feelings for the most fundamental experience, have an insatiable longing for a spiritual rest which may not necessarily yield to logical treatment. In other words, we cannot wait for a perfect thought-system which will solve most satisfactorily all the mysteries of life and the world; we impatiently aspire for something more practical and of immediate utility. Religion talks of faith, teaching that God somehow takes care of us, all the intellectual difficulties notwithstanding. Let the antithesis of being and nonbeing remain as it is; for what is beyond our intellectual comprehension may best be left in the hands of God. The faith that things are all well somehow or other with God, in whom we have our being, delivers us from doubts and worries.

The Zen way of deliverance, however, is not that of religion; to be free from doubts and worries, Zen appeals to a certain inner experience and not to a blind acceptance of dogmas. Zen expects us to experience within ourselves that the suchness of things—the antithesis of being and nonbeing—is beyond the ken of intellectual painting or dialectical delineation, and that no amount of words can succeed in describing, that is, reasoning out, the what and why of life and the world. This may sound negative and may not be of positive use to our spiritual life. But the real trouble with us whenever we try to talk about things beyond intellection is that we always make our start from intellection itself, although this may be natural and inevitable; therefore, when Zen-experience and other such things are talked about they sound empty as if they had no positive value. But Zen proposes that we effect a complete *volte-face* and take our stand first on Zen-experience itself and then observe things—the world of being and nonbeing—from the point of view of the experience itself. This is what may be designated as an absolute standpoint. The usual order of things is hereby reversed: what was positive becomes negative and what was negative becomes positive. "Emptiness" is reality and "reality" is emptiness. Flowers are no longer red, and the willow leaves are no longer green. We are no longer a plaything of *karma*, of "cause and effect," of birth and death; values of the changing world are no longer permanent ones; what we consider good or bad from the worldly point of view is neither good nor bad, for it has only a relative value. Logically too, the antithesis of being and nonbeing holds good only for our relative knowledge, for our discursive understanding. After the Zen-experience, an entirely new order of things takes place, a complete change of front is effected, and the result is that a relative world of changes and multiplicities is contemplated *sub specie æternitatis*. This in a way may be considered the meaning of "No paintings, no delineations can do justice to it."

10

Can we say then that Zen teaches a kind of mystical contemplation of life and the world? Before this is answered, let me make a further remark about Yengo and Goso, who also had a great deal to do, as we saw, with the problem of being and nonbeing.

When Yengo asked Goso concerning the breaking down of the tree and the withering of the wistaria, Goso emphatically declared, "You are caught in your own trap." The truth is that the Zen-experience by itself is not enough; it must be elaborated by means of Zen-consciousness or Zen-dialectic, if it is to be articulate and communicable not only to others but to oneself. The experience needs to be rationalized, as it were; it wants to speak out. It wants to assert itself, to be conscious of itself; and to do this, Zen has its own way, has opened up quite a unique one—absolutely unique we may say. Where no paintings, no drawings can portray a perfect world of Zen-experience, how can we speak of being and nonbeing, of tree and wistaria, of birth and death, of synthesis and antithesis, of immanence and transcendence, of destruction and construction, of breaking down and withering and being reduced to nothingness? All these ideas and categories are so many instruments we have devised for our own convenience in this world of action and work; but unless we know how to make use of them as occasion requires, they turn against us and trap us; that is, we are ensnared and enslaved by them. When the Zen-experience is not properly made articulate it becomes an instrument of mischief. The experience is a double-edged sword, requiring careful handling, and in this handling Zen follows its own tradition, which first originated in the philosophy of Mahāyāna Buddhism and later managed to follow up the channel of Chinese psychology.

II

I am not certain whether Zen can be identified with mysticism. Mysticism as it is understood in the West starts generally with an antithesis and ends with its unification or identification. But in Zen there is no antithesis, therefore no synthesis or unification. If there is an antithesis, Zen accepts it as it is, and makes no attempts to unify it. Instead of starting with dualism or pluralism, Zen wants us to have a Zen-experience, and with this experience it surveys a world of suchness. It has adopted Mahāyāna terminology, it is true, but it has the tendency to resort to concrete objects and happenings. It does not reduce them to oneness—which is an abstraction. When all things are reduced to oneness, it asks to what this One is reducible. If all comes from God, lives in God, and returns to God, Zen wants to know where this God is or lives. If the whole world with all its multiplicities is absorbed into Brahman, Zen asks us to point out the whereabouts of Brahman. If the soul survives the body, Zen demands that you locate the soul or bring it out before us.

A master was asked where he might be found after his death, and he said, "Lying on my back in the wilderness, my limbs pointing straight up to the sky!" When another master was asked about the immutability of Nirvāṇa, he replied, "The fallen leaves follow the running stream while the autumnal moon rises above the solitary peak." Another appeared in the pulpit apparently ready to give a sermon, but as soon as he mounted it, he declared that his discourse was over, saying, "Fare well!" After a while he resumed, "If there is any who has no understanding yet, let him come out." A monk made an advance toward the master and bowed down reverentially whereupon the master, raising his voice, said, "How painful!" The monk stood up and was about to propose a question, but the master cried, "Ho!" and drove him out. When another monk approached, saying, "What is the most wonderful word (expressing the highest truth)?" the master merely remarked, "What say you?" Going carefully over all these *mondō* (dialogues), where do we find traces of mysticism in Zen? The masters give no hints whatever as to the annihilation or absorption of the self in the absolute, or the casting of the world into the abyss of Nirvāṇa.

12

Mystics, I believe, generally agree with this characterization of God: "God is not an 'object' for human understanding. He utterly transcends knowledge, and everything one says of Him is untrue. 'Be still,' Eckhart says in a sermon, 'and prate not of God (i.e., the Godhead), for whatever you prate in words about Him is a lie and is sinful.' 'If I say God is good, it is not true; for what is good can grow better; what can grow better can grow best. Now these three things (good, better, best) are far from God, for He is above all,' i.e., all such distinctions. No word that voices distinctions or characteristics, then, may be spoken of the Godhead. Eckhart's favorite names are: 'the Wordless Godhead'; 'the Nameless Nothing'; 'the Naked Godhead'; 'the Immovable Rest'; 'the Still Wilderness, where no one is at home.' "[2]

However mystical one may be, he cannot avoid using the term "God" or "Godhead" or some concept corresponding to it. But this is not so with Zen. Zen avoids, not necessarily deliberately but unavoidably I believe, abstract terms. When the question arises concerning such terms, the Zen master turns them down, making the questioner realize the fact that they have no direct hold on life. Zuigan Shigen asked Ganto (829-887 A.D.), "What is the original eternal reason?"

---

[2] Rufus Jones, *Studies in Mystical Religion* (London, 1909), pp. 225-226. By permission of The Macmillan Co., Publishers.

Ganto: "Moving!"

Zuigan: "What about it when moving?"

Ganto: "It is no more the original eternal reason."

This made Zuigan reflect for some time over the matter.

Ganto continued, "When you assert, you are still in the world of senses; when you do not assert, you sink into the ocean of birth and death!"

Ganto does not wish to see his disciple stay with the original eternal reason, nor does he want him to lose the sight of it. He knows that Zen is neither to assert nor to deny, that Zen is the suchness of things. The Zen masters are not mystics and their philosophy is not mysticism.

13

In this respect, Kwasan's answer, which he gave uniformly to the various questions regarding Buddha, Mind, and Truth, is significant.

Kwasan (died 960) used to quote the passage from Sōjō's work, *The Sacred Treasure*: "Learning-and-disciplining is called (the stage of) Hearing; nonlearning, (the stage of) Approximation; and when these two (stages) are transcended, we pass on to (the stage of) Truth."

A monk came up and asked: "What is the stage of Truth?"

The master said, "I know how to beat the drum."

Another time a monk asked, "What is the first principle?"

"I know how to beat the drum."

The master's response was the same when he was asked by still another monk: "I do not ask you about 'Mind is Buddha,' but I wish to know what is meant by 'Not Mind, Not Buddha.' "

"I know how to beat the drum," quickly came from the master.

On another occasion, a monk asked, "How would you treat him if a man of the highest attainment should come?"

Still the master would not give up his favorite expression: "I know how to beat the drum."

Let me note here that Kwasan was probably once a drum beater in his career as a monk, and it is likely not only that he said "I know how to beat the drum," but that, so saying, he actually beat the drum, or at least he went through the whole process, keeping time "Do-ko-dong, do-ko-dong!"

When you say "this" or "that," however abstract and universal it may be, you are singling the particular "that" or "this" out of multiplicities, thus making it one of them. We cannot help this as long as we are what we are, so many "that's" or so many "this's." The only way to escape this infinite regression is actually to beat the drum, or to dance up and down with a rice-bowl, or to sing out loudly "La-la-la!"

14

A nun called Ryūtetsuma one day came to see Isan (died 853), the veteran master. ("Isan" is believed to be the posthumous name of Reiyu who founded a Chinese sub-sect of Zen at Dai-i-San or Isan.) The master, seeing her approach, said, "Old Cow, are you come?" This is as if to say, "It is best for an old lady like you to stay home comfortably and enjoy these long spring days. What makes you leave your quiet peaceful hut? An altogether unnecessary tottering out!" The nun, however, announced: "To-morrow they are going to have a great religious function at Taisan; I wonder if you are going to attend it yourself." This is a mere story, for Taisan in the north is many thousand *li* away from Isan, which is situated in South China, and so, how could the nun know of the event and how could Isan fly to such distance? The nun seems to mean that she herself was going to be present at the function even across the great continent and that her coming over here was nothing. However old and doddering, she is mistress of herself, just as the sun rises in the East at dawn or as the cat leaps up in the garden to catch a butterfly. Can you too perform this miracle? But Isan had his own way of asserting his mastership. He threw himself down on the floor. What did he mean by this? Did he prefer a quiet nap to the active exercise of traveling so many miles? Did he mean that lying quiet is just as much a miracle as to be busily engaged in the practical affairs of life? Did he mean that the absolute is active in lying down as well as in being up and doing? What was the nun's response to this? Without saying anything or doing anything, she just left Isan alone, and made for her own retreat.

What is the significance of the whole proceeding? Probably I have read too much of Zen-like thought into it. Instead of that, we may take it just as an episode in our daily life. A visitor appeared; she was welcomed and they—visitor and host—had a pleasant conversation about various things of life, among them a big feast given at a certain monastery. The old master enjoyed the visit, but, getting tired, he fell asleep, and she left without further ceremony—this is what takes place between old friends. When the event is over, we have a pleasant memory of friendship, and the matter happily comes to an end.

Shall I make a more general statement of this Isan-and-Ryūtetsuma incident? We are born to this world of many incidents and accidents, we go through them doing our best, and when the time comes we say good-by to them all. If we are bound for the Pure Land, very well; if otherwise, also very well. We are perfectly passive in this respect, or perfectly active—all depends on the point of view we like to take. Zen has added nothing to the sum-total of reality, nor has it subtracted an iota of it. Zen is radical realism rather than mysticism.

We must remember here, however, that Zen does not mean to ignore our moral thoughts, aspirations, and feelings which determine the value of life while on earth. Zen is essentially concerned with the thing most fundamental and most primary, and as to what relates to our worldly lives it leaves that where it properly belongs. Everything that exclusively belongs, as it were, to the dualistic sphere of existence is taken up by moral philosophy, religion, political science, and other fields of human consciousness, while Zen aims at taking hold of what underlies all these phenomenological activities of the Mind.

15

Rudolf Otto, while referring to Fichte's mysticism together with Eckhart's, which he differentiates from Śaṅkara's, writes: "Thus the true relationship of the man who is saved is for Fichte, as it was for Eckhart: To know that he is one with the One, life with the Life, not united but absolutely unified, and *at the same time*, to stand in this world of multiplicity and division, not straining after its dissolution, but with Eckhart, working righteousness in it, and with Fichte, completing in it the living deed of ethical culture, and thus with both teachers bringing into this very world of nonbeing and of death, Being and Life. He must do this in such a way that his transcendental possession is itself the very source of power and the impelling force to moral and cultural activity."[3]

Even with Eckhart and Fichte, we observe that the basis of their philosophy lies in the dualism of being and nonbeing, of life and death, oneness and multiplicity. At times, it is true, they seem to go beyond the antithesis, but as their thought primarily revolves around the dualistic axis, they always return to it after they have made a so-called mystical excursion into the field of identity. Zen, on the other hand, always keeps itself in the suchness of things, where this world of multiplicity and discrimination is at once the transcendental world of emptiness (*śūnyatā*) and nondiscrimination (*avikalpa*). Zen, therefore, tries to guard most jealously against our consciousness getting tipped to one side or to the other. This is not a deliberate balancing. In the beginning of Zen-life there may be something of the sort, but the object of its discipline is to transcend all such artificialities and to have the principle of suchness work out its own activity.

16

When Hofuku (died 928) and Chōkei (853-932) took a walk in the mountain, Hofuku pointed at it and said, "Look here, this is no other than the Holy Peak itself!" Chōkei replied, "Fine, just as you say, but what a pity!" Zen is loath to see its experience lopsided, for it is sure to end in a lame Zen-consciousness. Chōkei's remark points to this.

Hyakujo (754-814) was asked, "What is the most wonderful fact in the world?" He answered, "I sit here all by myself on the top of Mount Daiyu." The monk bowed to him, and Hyakujo struck the monk. This striking is significant, betraying the spirit of Zen, for Zen aspires to independence, self-mastery, freedom from every form of one-sidedness which means restraint and conditionality.

When Baso (died 788) was asked, "What is the first principle of Buddhism?" he struck the monk, saying, "If I did not strike you thus, all the world would be laughing at me." When another monk came to him with this: "What is the idea of Bodhidharma coming

[3] *Mysticism, East and West*, trans. by Bertah L. Bracey and Richarda C. Payne (New York, 1932), p. 230. By permission of The Macmillan Co., Publishers.

from the West?" Baso told him to come forward and he would let him know. The monk as he was told stepped forward. Baso lost no time in giving him a slap over his ear and said, "The secret's already out."

When these Zen incidents are observed from the point of view of relativity and dualism, they appear to have no sense whatever; but when looked at from the inside as it were, there looms up the big character, "Zen," which is the key to all the "mysteries" so far cited. What Zen dislikes most is mediation, deliberation, wordiness, and the weighing of advantages. Immediacy is impossible as long as we are onlookers, contemplators, critics, idea-mongers, word-manipulators, dualists, or monists. All these faults are corrected and Zen is revealed when we abandon our so-called common-sense or logical attitude and effect a complete about-face, when we plunge right into the working of things as they move on before and behind our senses. It is only when this experience takes place that we can talk intelligently about Zen-consciousness from which the Zen-incidents or Zen-dialogues making up the annals of Zen are produced.

17

Zen therefore is not mysticism although there may be something in it reminding one of the latter. Zen does not teach absorption, identification, or union, for all these ideas are derived from a dualistic conception of life and the world. In Zen there is a wholeness of things, which refuses to be analyzed or separated into antitheses of all kinds. As they say, it is like an iron bar with no holes or handles to swing it about. You have no way to take hold of it; in other words, it cannot be subsumed under any categories. Thus, Zen must be said to be a unique discipline in the history of human culture, religious and philosophical.

Zen often speaks of a flash of lightning as if it valued an instantaneous or instinctive action in dealing with the fundamental problems of life. When somebody asks you about Buddhahood or Godhead, you strike the questioner, saying, "What a blockheaded fellow of a monk!" There is no time lost between asking and striking, and you may think this is an immediacy, which is Zen. But the fact is far from it. Zen has nothing to do with rapidity or immediacy in the sense of being quick. A flash of lightning refers to the nonmediating nature of Zen-experience.

Zen-experience, one may say, is a kind of intuition which is the basis of mysticism. We have to be careful, however, about the use of the term "intuition." If we make it presuppose the existence of an antithesis of some form, Zen is not this kind of intuition, which we may designate as static or contemplative. If Zen-experience is an act of intuition, it must be distinguished from the static form, and let us call it dynamic or actional. The following Zen-incidents may, I hope, help one to understand what I mean by dynamic intuition which is Zen-experience.

18

So, some more Zen-incidents are given here, in order to indicate which way Zen-consciousness tends. They are culled at random from a Zen work known as *The Transmission of the Lamp*. When these incidents are perused thoughtfully and without bias one may be able to come in touch with an invisible thread running through them.

1. An officer once visited Gensha (834-908) who treated him to a dish of cake. The officer asked, "They speak of our not knowing it while using it all the time. What is this 'it'?" Gensha looked as if he were not paying attention to the questioner, for he innocently picked up a piece of cake and offered it to the officer to eat. The latter finished it and repeated the question. The master said, "There you are! It is daily made use of and yet they know it not!"

2. One day Chōsa had all his monks work in the field to gather wood. The master said, "You all partake of my power." "If so, why do we all have to work in the field?"—This came from the monks at work. Chōsa reprimanded them, saying, "If you did not all work, how can we gather enough wood for our kitchen?"

3. When Nansai visited Seppo (822-908), the latter made him see Gensha. Gensha said, "Says an ancient master: 'This is the matter I alone have the knowledge of.' What do you say to that?" Nansai replied, "You should know that there is one who does not seek being known." Gensha concluded, "What is the use of your going through so many hardships then?"

4. A monk asked Gensha, "What is my Self?" Replied Gensha, "What do you want to do with your Self?"

5. A monk came to Gensha and wished to know how he was discoursing on the principle of Zen. Said Gensha, "I have very few listeners." Monk: "I wish to have your direct instruction." "You are not deaf?" came straightway from the master.

6. When Seppo with all his monks was working on the farm, he happened to notice a snake. Lifting it up with a stick, the master called the attention of the whole gathering, "Look, look!" He then slashed it in two with a knife. Gensha came forward, and picking up the slain snake threw it away behind them. He then went on working as if nothing had happened. The whole party was taken aback. Said Seppo, "How brisk!"

7. One day Gensha entered the pulpit, and for a while he sat quietly without saying a word. He then began, "All the kindheartedness I have is given out to you without reserve. Do you understand?" A monk ventured the question: "What is the meaning of a perfect silence?" The master said, "No talking in sleep!" Monk: "Please tell, O master, about what concerns us most in Zen." "No use dreaming!" "I may be dreaming, but how about you?" Said the master, "How could you be so senseless as not to know what's what?"

19

Any reader who goes carefully over all the Zen incidents cited in this chapter will see that there is something in Zen which we never meet anywhere else in the history of human thought and culture. It certainly begins with enough rationalism since it deals, as we have already noticed, with such religio-philosophical concepts as being and nonbeing, truth and falsehood, Buddha and Nirvāna; but after the beginning is once made, the matter is strangely switched off in a most unexpected direction, ending sometimes in what seems to be a comedy or farce or even a quarrel. Indeed, the history of Zen is filled with such records. To judge them by the ordinary standard of reasoning is altogether out of place, for the standard is simply inapplicable here. Superficial people, however, are likely to insist upon trying what ought not to be tried here; their world of vision is very limited, and they fail to realize that there is a much wider world than theirs, which is beyond their mentality. The fact alone that Zen has been thriving in the Far East ever since the days of Bodhidharma and Yeno (Hui-nêng) and Rinzai, and that those masters and their followers, monks and otherwise, have contributed considerably to the widening of the spiritual horizon and to the enhancement of human ideals, is enough to prove the practical value and usefulness, not to say anything about the validity, of Zen-experience. The only thing, let me repeat, we can state here about Zen is that it is an altogether unique product of the Oriental mind, refusing to be classified under any known heading, as either a philosophy, or a religion, or a form of mysticism as it is generally understood in the West. Zen must be studied and analyzed from a point of view which is still unknown among Western philosophers, and I am sure the study will give us a rich yield, not only in philosophy and the science of religion, but also in psychology and allied studies.

CHAPTER VI

Shintō: Japanese Ethnocentrism

By Shunzō Sakamaki

An adequate comprehension of the major ramifications of Japanese nationalist ideology postulates familiarity with the general outlines of the history and philosophy of the national cult, Shintō (The Way of the Gods). The history of Shintō is quite as old as that of institutional Christianity, and in this necessarily sketchy summary of its major movements attention is paid mainly to philosophical tenets propounded by its most articulate protagonists prior to the present period.

Before the arrival of Buddhism from the continent in the sixth century A.D., there was but little metaphysical speculation in Japan. There was no body of literature, no school of philosophy, no intellectual stimulus to encourage or maintain sustained inquiries into the invisible imponderables of the universe. Intellectual flights of fancy were closely circumscribed by the limits of the physical environment. There was no word for Nature, as something apart and distinct from man, something that might be contemplated by man, the "thinking reed." Man was treated as an integral part of a whole, closely associated and identified with the elements and forces of the world about him.

The physical universe was regarded as tripartite—the ethereal firmament above, the world on the surface of the earth, and the shadowy nether regions in the bowels of the earth. In this universe there were divinities beyond number, "800 myriads" of them. They were indiscriminately denominated *kami*, which literally means "above" or "superior" in rank or position and which is a Japanese counterpart of the Melanesian *mana*. A classic definition of the term *kami* is that of Motoöri Norinaga (1730-1801), renowned scholar of Japanese antiquity:

"The term *kami* is applied in the first place to the various deities of Heaven and Earth who are mentioned in the ancient records, as well as their spirits (*mitama*), which reside in the shrines where they are worshipped. Moreover, not only human beings, but birds, beasts, plants and trees, seas and mountains and all other things whatsoever which deserve to be dreaded and revered for the extraordinary and preëminent powers which they possess are called *kami*.

"They need not be eminent for surpassing nobleness, goodness, or serviceableness alone. Malignant and uncanny beings are also called *kami*, if only they are the objects of general dread.

"Among *kami* who are human beings I need hardly mention Mikados. . . . Among others there are the thunder, the dragon, the echo, and the fox, who are called *kami* by reason of their uncanny and fearful natures. The term *kami* is applied in the *Nihongi* and the *Manyōshū*, an anthology of ancient poetry, to the tiger and the wolf. Izanagi gave to the fruit of the peach, and to the jewels round his neck, names which implied that they were *kami*. . . . There are many cases of seas and mountains being called *kami*. It is not their spirits which are meant. The word was applied directly to the seas or mountains themselves, as being very awesome things."[1]

The more important of the *kami* were in greater or less degree affiliated with the natural phenomena of birth, growth, change, and death. Among these divinities were those populating the Plain of High Heaven (*Takamagahara*), these *kami* being both anthropomorphous and anthropopathic. They lived, moved, and had their being in quite the same manner as their human counterparts, with whom many of them also shared the attribute of mortality.

From the divine hosts inhabiting the Plain of High Heaven there eventually emerged two deities, Izanagi and Izanami, who are obviously personifications of the sky and the earth, respectively. This divine pair produced diverse other deities and, too, the islands of Japan. Izanagi, the sky-father, begot the Sun Goddess (Amaterasu Ōmikami) and the Moon God (Tsukiyomi) when he washed his eyes (which calls to mind other mythologies that picture the sun and the moon as the two eyes of heaven). Further, when Izanagi washed his nose, the Storm God (Susano-o) came into being, indicating that the concept was current that winds and storms were caused by the breathing or snorting of the sky-father.

[1] W. G. Aston, *Shintō* (The Way of the Gods) (London: Longmans, Green and Co., 1905), pp. 8-9.

The Sun Goddess came to dominate the divine scene, and is to this day the most important figure in the national pantheon. She dispatched a grandson, Ninigi-no-Mikoto, to Japan to possess and rule the islands, he and his descendants, in perpetuity, saying: "This Reed-plain-1500-autumns-fair-rice-ear-land is the region which my descendants shall be lords of. Do thou, my August Grandchild, proceed thither and govern it. Go! and may prosperity attend thy dynasty, and may it, like Heaven and Earth, endure forever!"[2] A great grandson of Ninigi-no-Mikoto, called Jinmu, was eventually enthroned as the first emperor of Japan, and the imperial sovereignty has to this day remained in the dynasty established by Jinmu some two thousand or more years ago.

The foregoing divine basis for the imperial sovereignty was carefully provided in the compilation of two official histories of Japan, the *Kojiki* (712 A.D.) and the *Nihongi* (720 A.D.). These two histories sought to make the imperial position inviolable and eternal by investing it with the attributes of divine destiny.

In the early centuries of the Christian era, no distinction was made between religious and governmental ceremonies. The chief of a community (*uji*) acted as its spokesman or intermediary in spiritual as well as temporal matters, and the "emperor" was virtually the "high priest" for the whole people.

The *kami* were invoked in prayers of thanksgiving or of supplication for some measure of material blessing, such as good harvests, protection from natural calamities and evil spirits or forces, freedom from sickness, and the like. Concepts of moral wrongdoing or sin were barely being adumbrated, so that prayers were not for forgiveness of sins or spiritual blessedness, but for physical well-being and temporal prosperity.

The people feared and abhorred physical contamination, such as might result from contact with blood, sickness, death, or any form of natural disaster. Purification was effected by various forms of exorcism, lustration, ablution, or abstention. Notions of extramundane existence beyond the grave, whether in some celestial realm or in the lower regions, were attenuated at best, and there were no prayers for the deceased or for happiness in a future life.

[2] W. G. Aston, *Nihongi* (London: Kegan Paul, Trench, Trübner & Co., Ltd., 1924), reissue of original edition, Vol. I, p. 77.

With the arrival of that vast conglomeration of cults and faiths that Buddhism had become by the sixth century A.D., the indigenous faith of Japan took on the appellation "Shintō," or The Way of the Gods, to distinguish itself from "Butsudō," The Way of the Buddhas. As a vehicle of the culture of the continent, Buddhism effected epochal changes in Japan, and in point of doctrinal content there was great disparity between it and Shintō. The former found in the latter, however, a worthy and formidable adversary, inasmuch as the latter was inextricably identified with Japanese ethnocentrism, and, too, its temporal power as possessor of land and guardian of the imperial domain could not readily be wrested from it.

Several centuries elapsed before a measure of doctrinal assimilation was achieved, principally through the efforts of priests of the Tendai and Shingon sects of Buddhism. The former evolved what is generally referred to as Ichijitsu Shintō, or Single-verity Shintō, an expression derived from a passage in the *Saddharmapuṇḍarīka Sūtra*, reading, "All the Buddhas that come into the world are merely this one reality (*ichijitsu*)." The Tendai tenet that the multiform phenomena of the universe are but manifestations of, or emanations from, the all-embracing Absolute, the one Reality, the primordial Buddha, was now adduced to support the pronouncement that the divinities of the Shintō pantheon were all traceable ultimately to the same transcendent source, the one Reality. The syncretism is also interpreted as being based on the idea of *honchi suijaku*, or "source-manifest-traces," according to which every divine being of Shintō is an avatar of some Buddhist divinity, so that in the final analysis the two faiths can be equated, the one with the other.

The fusion movement was given great strength by Shingon thinkers who developed the *honchi suijaku* theory and produced the system of thought known as Ryōbu Shintō, or Dual Shintō. According to the proponents of this system, Shintō could well be translated in terms of Shingon metaphysics, which divided the universe into two cycles, phenomenal and noumenal. The infinite forms of matter were all, without exception, either direct or indirect emanations from the Absolute, Mahāvairochana (Dainichi Nyorai) while, on the other hand, all thought in the universe was encompassed by, and each thought in its partial way was identical with, the transcendent thought of the ultimate reality, Mahā-vairochana. Applied to Shintō, then, Shintō *kami* could be equated with "corresponding" Buddhist divinities, and Shintō thought could be regarded as being part of the omniscience of the Shingon Absolute, so that there was no inherent conflict between Buddhism and Shintō, according to Ryōbu Shintōists.

In an effort to restore Shintō to its pristine purity, and wrest it from its incorporation within Buddhist schemes of thought, several Neo-Shintō movements were started in medieval times, of which two may be mentioned here. The first is generally called Yui-itsu Shintō or One-only Shintō, and is closely associated with Urabe Kanetomo (1435-1511). Urabe substituted the *kami* for Buddhist equivalents of the Absolute or the Single Verity and sought to turn the tables on the Ryōbu Shintōists by arguing that Buddhist deities were the avatars (the *suijaku*) of Shintō *kami* (the *honchi*), rather than vice versa, as claimed by the Ryōbu Shintōists. And, under the sway of the ethnocentric imperatives of the indigenous faith, Urabe called attention to what he termed the peerless status of Japan as the Divine Country, and the matchless glory of the divinely de-scended Imperial Line.

Considerably more important as a movement than Yui-itsu Shintō was Fukko Shintō, or Return-to-antiquity Shintō, which developed in the eighteenth century with a succession of three dis-tinguished scholars as its leading exponents. First of these was Kamo-no-Mabuchi (1697-1769), scion of a long line of Shintō priests. He subscribed to Taoist naturalism in regarding careful observation of the processes of nature as invaluable for the de-termination of proper principles of human conduct. On the other hand he believed that the superior nature of the Japanese body politic was due to the intuitive apprehension and practice of natural principles of righteousness, on the part of both the divinely de-scended Emperors and their loyal subjects.

The amazing scholar Motoöri Norinaga, who succeeded Mabuchi as leader of this movement for the renascence of so-called Pure Shintō, spurned Taoism as being merely a way of nature whereas Shintō was the way of the gods. Elaborating the ethnocentric pre-suppositions of his predecessor, Motoöri lauded the unerring in-stinct for proper conduct which he claimed was possessed by the Japanese people by virtue of their direct genealogical kinship with the great divinities of the Shintō pantheon. He called on his compatriots to manifest unswerving and unquestioning fealty to their divinely descended imperial sovereigns, and wrote: "The superiority of Japan to all other countries is only natural, in view of the fact that the Mikados are descended directly from the *kami*. No other nation is worthy of parity with Japan, and all should render homage and pay tribute to the Japanese sovereign."

Further elaboration of these ethnocentric doctrines was provided by Motoöri's successor, Hirata Atsutane (1776-1843), according to whom the intimate divine connections of the Japanese people invested them with qualities and attributes superior to those of all other peoples. Hirata pointed with pride to the unbroken and matchless continuity of the divinely descended Imperial Line, which he believed was destined to extend its sway over the whole world.

The contribution of these ethnocentric pronouncements to the final collapse of the shogunate in Japan and the concomitant "restoration of the Imperial Sovereignty" (1867-1868) was potent, if subtle. Moreover, leaders of the reorganized imperial government, anxious to bolster the imperial position and to effect national solidarity, were impressed with the tremendous potentialities of the Neo-Shintō doctrines and hence actively fostered the propagation of these doctrines through such organs of modern nationalism as the school, the press, the armed services, and so on.

Today, Shintō is classified under two legal categories, Sectarian (*Shūha*) Shintō and State (*Kokka*) Shintō. In the former there are some thirteen officially recognized Shintō sects, the diversity of whose doctrinal content is similar to that of the various denominations of Protestant Christianity. Philosophical speculation of high order is to be found in a number of the contemporary Shintō sects, traceable in part to Buddhist, to Confucian, and to Western influences.

State Shintō preserves the mythological and ideological content of the earliest indigenous beliefs and the rituals of the ancient period, but adds to all this the doctrinal legacy of the Neo-Shintōists, albeit in modified or elaborated versions. It can hardly be denied that State Shintō has been effective in impregnating the national mind with concepts of a noble past rich in great traditions, a superior racial stock destined to endure as an eternal national family, and a matchless body politic headed by an unbroken, inviolable, divinely descended Imperial Dynasty.[8]

[8] The author wishes to commend to the reader three careful studies by Dr. D. C. Holtom: "The Political Philosophy of Modern Shintō," *Transactions of the Asiatic Society of Japan,* vol. XLIX, pt. II (Tokyo; The Asiatic Society of Japan, 1922) ; *The National Faith of Japan; A Study in Modern Shintō* (London: Kegan Paul, Trench, Trübner & Co., Ltd., 1938) ; *Modern Japan and Shinto Nationalism* (Chicago: The University of Chicago Press, 1943). The author gratefully acknowledges his indebtedness to Dr. Holtom's works for much of the material in the foregoing chapter.

CHAPTER VII

The Spirit of Oriental Philosophy

By Chan Wing-tsit

THE story of Oriental philosophy is a complicated one. To obtain a comprehensive view, it is necessary to have a proper angle of approach and a total perspective. In order to approach Oriental philosophy from the right direction, we must treat it as a philosophy in contradistinction to religion with which it has close historical but not necessarily philosophical connection.

THE NEED OF A TOTAL PERSPECTIVE

We may mention Taoism as an excellent example of the confusion between Oriental philosophy and Oriental religion. Unless we separate the naturalism of Taoist philosophy from the primitive and corrupt religion of nature worship, alchemy, and charms of all descriptions going by the name of Taoism, we cannot help getting a confused and distorted picture of Taoist philosophy. We need not go into the history of the way in which Taoist philosophy was utilized by the founder of a primitive cult in the first century A.D. to gain prestige and support, or how the Taoist religion developed more by imitation of Buddhism than by following the teachings of Lao Tzŭ. When we distinguish the Taoist religion from Taoist philosophy, we shall find that the belief in polytheism, meditation, transmigration, etc., belongs to Taoism as a religion and not as a philosophy. Similar procedure will reveal the fact that fantastic and abnormal "Yoga practices" do not represent the Yoga philosophy of dualistic, meditative intuitionism.[1]

Again, to approach Oriental philosophy from a proper angle, we must freely and generously use the literature in which it is embodied. English translations are still limited to a small fraction of Oriental philosophy, mostly ancient. For a comprehensive view of

[1] For the true function of Yoga practice, see S. N. Dasgupta, *Yoga as Philosophy and Religion* (London: Kegan Paul, 1924), Ch. XI.

Oriental philosophy, they are hopelessly inadequate. Take the philosophy of Mahāyāna Buddhism, for example. Only a few of the many basic works of the two most important Mahāyāna philosophies, namely the "Middle Doctrine" school and the "Mind-Only" school, are available in English. Indispensable texts such as the *Triṁśika* (Thirty Verses of the Mind-Only Doctrine),[2] *Vijñaptimātratāsiddhi* (The Completion of the Mind-Only Doctrine),[3] *Yogācārabhūmi* (The Stages of Perfection in Idealism), *Mahāyānasaṅgraha* (A Summary of Mahāyāna Philosophy), *Mādhyamika Śāstra* (A Treatise on the Middle Doctrine),[4] *Dvādaśadvāra Śāstra* (The Twelve "Gates" of the Middle Doctrine), etc., still await translation, not to mention the bible of the "totalistic" philosophy called *Avataṅsaka Sūtra*, the bible of the realistic school of Hīnayāna called *Abhidharmakośa Śāstra*,[5] or the bible of the nihilistic philosophy of Hīnayāna called *Satyasiddhi Śāstra* (The Completion of Truth). The list could be much further extended, but this is sufficient to show that only a small corner of the picture is visible in English.

This being the case, it is obviously impossible to have a total perspective of the Buddhist system, not to say Oriental philosophy as a whole. To have a total perspective of Oriental philosophy, we must survey comprehensively not only one or two major Oriental philosophies, but all Oriental philosophical schools. Too often has one prominent Oriental system been taken for the entire philosophy of the Orient. Both Hinduism and Buddhism have been taken separately as representative of "the" philosophy of "the" East. As we shall soon see, the philosophies of India and the philosophies of China actually form two groups, with as many, if not more, differences as similarities between them. We must remember that with the exception of Buddhism, Indian philosophies have not gone beyond the boundaries of their homeland.

[2] Available in French translation, by S. Lévi, *Matériaux pour l'étude du système vijñaptimātra* (Paris: Librairie Ancienne Honoré Champion, 1932).
[3] Available in French translation, by La Vallée Poussin, *Vijñaptimātratāsiddhi, La siddhi de Hiuan-tsang*, 2 vols. (Paris: Guethner, 1928 and 1929).
[4] Available in German translation, by Max Walleser, *Die Mittlere Lehre des Nāgārjuna* (Heidelberg: Carl Winter's Universitätsbuchhandlung, 1912).
[5] Available in French translation, by La Vallée Poussin, *L'Abhidharmakośa de Vasubandhu*, 6 vols. (Paris: Guethner, 1923-1925).

Buddhism has also been considered the representative philosophy of the Orient partly because it is the only Oriental philosophy that has covered India, China, and Japan, and partly because its concepts are so different from the philosophical tenor of the West that it presents a peculiar charm, a strong challenge, and some sharp contrasts. Consequently, Oriental philosophy as a whole has been described as advocating renunciation, escape, pessimism, negation, etc., simply because these tendencies exist in some schools of Buddhism. As a matter of fact, to what extent and in what sense these are true in Buddhism is not to be taken for granted, because the "realm of common truth" in Buddhism, which is of course lower than the "realm of higher truth," allows room for a reasonable and normal existence. But no Oriental, not even a Buddhist, would claim Buddhism to be the comprehensive philosophy of the East, for Buddhism has been a thing of the past in India for almost a thousand years. Even in the days of the Mahāsaṅghikas and Sarvāstivādins, and of Nāgārjuna, Asaṅga, and Vasubandhu, the days of its glory in India, it was regarded as a "heterodox" system. No reader of Indian Buddhist literature can help being impressed by the strenuous effort the Buddhist philosophers made to defend themselves from the attacks of the Nyāya, Sāṅkhya, Vedānta, and other Hindu philosophical schools. Equally heterodox was Buddhism in China. Although Chinese philosophy, especially Neo-Confucianism, was to some extent influenced by Buddhism, although China was the land in which the philosophies of Nāgārjuna and Vasubandhu came to maturity, and although China was the mother country of such Buddhist schools as Ch'an (Zen) and T'ien-t'ai, the fact remains that Buddhism as a philosophy existed only for a brief period in China and as a "perverse doctrine." Today Japan is called the land of Buddhism. From certain points of view this is permissible because it is in Japan that all the Mahāyāna Buddhist sects are found and that the best literature and traditions are preserved. Nevertheless, as a philosophy Buddhism in Japan has always been outshone by Neo-Confucianism; as a religion and a way of life it faces the keen competition of Shintō, the "Way of the Gods."

VARIETY AND CHANGE IN ORIENTAL PHILOSOPHY

Thus it is incorrect to take one Oriental philosophical system for Oriental philosophy as a whole. It is equally incorrect to take one period of Oriental philosophy for the entire course of its development. Because ancient Oriental philosophical texts are more easily available and therefore more familiar, medieval and modern Oriental philosophies have been considered, consciously or unconsciously, as footnotes to ancient Oriental philosophy. Nothing is further from the truth, however. If we go through the whole history of Oriental philosophy, we will find a great deal of variety and change, so that the ancient period, though a very important period, is by no means the whole story.

Perhaps the most striking example of the variety and change in Oriental philosophy is Buddhism. This may come as a surprise to those people to whom the term Buddhist philosophy connotes hardly anything more than the teachings of the Buddha. But the modification of the philosophy in the history of Buddhism is such that Gotama would have great difficulty in recognizing it. Take its basic doctrine the Middle Path, for instance. As taught by Gotama the Buddha, the Middle Path meant the middle ground between the extremes of hedonism and asceticism, a middle position formulated as the Noble Eightfold Path, namely, right views, right intention, right speech, right action, right livelihood, right effort, right mindfulness, and right concentration.[6] This developed into a metaphysical Middle Path in Hīnayāna, in the sense of the existence of the elements but nonexistence of the self.[7] When it came to the Mahāyāna, alteration became more varied and more radical. Practically every Mahāyāna school had its own interpretation of the Middle Path. To the Mādhyamika school it was nothing other than the Void,[8] and was identical with the Eightfold Negation, the total negation of production, extinction, annihilation, permanence, unity, diversity, coming, and departure.[9] The Yogācāra school, on the

[6] *Saṁyutta Nikāya,* V, 420. See E. J. Thomas, *Early Buddhist Scriptures* (London: Kegan Paul, 1935), pp. 29-30.

[7] It is true that the Buddha did suggest in the Middle Path neither the belief in nonbeing nor the belief in being. (*Saṁyutta Nikāya,* XXII, 90. See H. C. Warren, *Buddhism in Translations,* Cambridge, Mass., 1896, p. 165.) But the metaphysics was not developed until later. Even within the Hīnayāna, there was no general agreement about the Middle Path. The Satyasiddhi school, for example, took it to mean the denial of both the elements and the self.

[8] *Mādhyamika Śāstra,* Ch. XXIV, verse 18.

[9] Th. Stcherbatsky, *The Conception of Buddhist Nirvāṇa* (Leningrad: Academy of Sciences of USSR Press, 1927), p. 70.

other hand, opposed this totally negativistic position, and described the Middle Path as Thusness, the True State, which was to be realized by the highest state of consciousness, or consciousness "without impurity," stripped of any possible discrimination. According to this Middle Path "Neither is it asserted that all (the elements) are unreal (as held by the Mādhyamikas), nor are they all realities (as held by the Hīnayānists)."[10] "Thus the two extremes of affirmation and negation are avoided, the doctrine of Mere Ideation established, and the Middle Path confirmed."[11] Different from both these schools, the Avataṅsaka school interpreted the Middle Path on the basis of the "Universal Causation of the Realm of the Principle." Universal Causation involves both the One and the Many, both the universal and the particular, all of which combine in a "grand harmony without any obstacle."[12] The T'ien-t'ai school carried this doctrine of harmony further and culminated in the teaching that "There is not any color or fragrance that is not identical with the Middle Path."[13] This is to say that the truth of the Void (unreality of existence), the truth of temporariness (transitory existence), and the truth of the Mean (both non-existence and conditioned existence) are all identical, forming the "round and harmonious triple truth" or the "absolute triple truth."[14] From this rapid survey of a few Buddhist schools we can see the doctrine of the Middle Path has gone through many changes, changes that make the original almost unrecognizable.

A similar story can be told of Confucianism. The *Lun Yü* (*Analects*) of Confucius (551-479 B.C.) was the basis, but was only the beginning. The goal of the Confucian philosophy is Perfection, starting with the development of one's nature and ultimately cul-

[10] *Madhyāntavibhaṅga, Discourse on Discrimination between Middle and Extremes, ascribed to Bodhisattva Maitreya and Commented by Vasubandhu and Sthiramati*, tr. by Th. Stcherbatsky (Leningrad: Academy of Sciences of USSR Press, 1936), p. 24.

[11] *Vijñaptimātratāsiddhi, La siddhi de Hiuan-tsang*, tr. by La Vallée Poussin, p. 419.

[12] Fa-tsang, *Fa-chieh Yüan-ch'i Chang* (Chapter on the Universal Causation of the Realm of the Principle) and *Chin Shih-tzŭ Chang* (Chapter on the Golden Lion).

[13] Chih-k'ai, *Mo-ho Chih-kuan* (Concentration and Insight in the Mahāyāna), Ch. I.

[14] *Ibid.*, Ch. III.

minating in a well-ordered state and a peaceful world. This is *jên*, a word that has been variously translated as benevolence, love, goodness, and true manhood. To Confucius, *jên* meant simply human perfection, an essentially ethical concept. By the time of Mencius (371-289 B.C.), *jên* was defined as "that by which a man is to be a man." To the common-sense ethics of Confucius, Mencius added a psychological foundation by advocating the theory that human nature is good. Thus man not only *should* be perfect, but *must* be perfect. In other words, *jên* became a psychological necessity. In Neo-. Confucianism, *jên* was not only ethical and psychological, but also metaphysical. The incessant production and reproduction of the universe is an unalterable evidence of *jên*, and since man's original nature is identical with that of the Great Ultimate, man must strive to "fully exercise his mind" and "develop his nature to the utmost" so as to bring about a cosmic and moral order. Consequently a man must consider himself, other men, all things, and Heaven and Earth as forming one and the same entity.[15]

What is true of the Buddhist doctrine of the Middle Path and the Confucian concept of *jên* is true of many other ideas in Oriental philosophy. Even in the apparently most stagnant Oriental system, Taoism, variety and change is not wanting.[16] The tempo of change has been, of course, slower than that in the West, especially since the Renaissance. We want to bear in mind, however, that any general description such as traditionalism, stagnation, and conservatism must not be pushed too far.

We should not be misled into the belief of traditionalism, dogmatism, etc., by the peculiar Oriental love of quoting and referring to the ancients for authority. All the six orthodox Hindu schools claim that they get their authority from the Vedas and Upanishads. And yet from the spiritual monism of the Upanishads grew such systems as the logical atomism of Nyāya, the atomistic pluralism of Vaiśeshika, the realistic dualism of Sānkhya, the dualistic meditative intuitionism of Yoga, the realistic and ritualistic monism of Mīmāṁsā, and the idealistic monism of Vedānta. Furthermore,

---

[15] For details, see Ch. III, pp. 27 and 61. For further information on the change of the concept of *jên*, see my article "Jên," in *The Dictionary of Philosophy*, ed. by D. D. Runes (New York: Philosophical Library, 1942), p. 153.

[16] See Ch. III, pp. 33, 44, 49, and 51.

sharp differences existed within each school, as can best be illustrated by the absolute monism of the Vedānta of Śankara which considers multiplicity as illusion, and the "qualified monism" of the Vedānta of Rāmānuja which defends multiplicity as real.[17]

CHARACTERISTICS OF INDIAN AND CHINESE PHILOSOPHIES

When it is realized that neither all Oriental philosophies nor the different stages of an Oriental philosophy follow the same pattern, it becomes evident that any characterization of one system does not apply to the others. This does not mean that the different systems have no points of agreement. In the following discussions of specific characteristics, however, we must constantly bear in mind that similarities in Oriental philosophy are accompanied by differences, so that Oriental philosophy is not one, but many. In general, the philosophies of India and the philosophies of China and Japan form two different groups, as whatever general characteristics can be said of Indian philosophies are in most cases not applicable to the philosophies of China and Japan.

Where similarities and differences lie between these two groups in general and among the various philosophical systems in particular will be pointed out in later discussion. As to the general description of the two groups, let us resort to the opinions of outstanding native scholars.

Professor S. Radhakrishnan, in his *Indian Philosophy*, considers spirituality, dominance of interest in the subjective, monistic idealism, and intuition as general characteristics of Indian thought. By spirituality he means that there is a strong spiritual motive in Indian philosophy, and a keen recognition of the close relationship between

[17] The story is too long to be told here. For excellent accounts of the Six Systems of India, see S. C. Chatterjee and D. M. Datta, *An Introduction to Indian Philosophy* (Calcutta: University of Calcutta, 1939); S. N. Dasgupta, *A History of Indian Philosophy* (Cambridge: University Press, Vol. I, 1922, Vol. II, 1932, Vol. III, 1940); Āchārya Mādhava, *The Sarvadarśanasangraha, or Review of the Different Systems of Hindu Philosophy*, tr. by E. B. Cowell and A. E. Gough (London: Trübner, 1882); F. Max Müller, *The Six Systems of Indian Philosophy* (London and New York: Longmans, Green, 1899, new ed., 1903 and 1928); S. Radhakrishnan, *Indian Philosophy*, 2 vols. (London: Allen & Unwin, Vol. II, 1927, rev., 1931).

philosophy, religion, and life. This does not imply that Indian philosophy is dogmatic or nonintellectual. On the contrary, it is strongly intellectual, critical, and synthetic. Interest in the subjective comes from speculative synthesis, and is not opposed to science. Indian monistic idealism emphasizes that reality is self and that man must become reality. It is mystical in the sense of discipline of human nature leading to the realization of the spirit. Intuition, or rather *darśana,* includes perceptual observation, conceptual knowledge, intuitional experience, logical inquiry, and insight of the soul. Professor Radhakrishnan flatly denies the common charge against Indian philosophy that it is pessimistic, dogmatic, indifferent to ethics, and unprogressive.[18]

Another prominent and representative Indian scholar, Professor S. Dasgupta, considers the theory of *karma* and rebirth, the doctrine of emancipation (*mukti*), the doctrine of the soul (*ātman, purusha, jīva,* etc.), pessimism, and *sādhana* as "fundamental points of agreement" among Indian schools with the sole exception of the Chārvāka materialists. *Sādhana* denotes philosophical, religious, and ethical endeavor, including the control of one's passions, the avoidance of injury to life in any form, the restraint of all desires for pleasure, and the practice of the Yoga method of concentration.[19] Dasgupta explains that in Indian pessimism there is "absolute optimistic confidence in one's own self and the ultimate destiny and goal of emancipation."[20]

There has not been as much systematic appraisal of Chinese philosophy by native scholars as in India. Two aspects, however, have been given prominence by the eminent scholar, Dr. Hu Shih. In his *The Development of the Logical Method in Ancient China,* he emphasizes the fact that the logical method played an important role in both ancient and modern Chinese philosophy. In his article entitled "Religion and Philosophy in Chinese History," he stresses the fact that "philosophy, in China as well as elsewhere, has been a handmaiden, a defender, a critic, or an opponent, of religion."[21] Professor Fung Yu-lan thinks that Chinese philosophy is inferior to Western and Indian philosophies in demonstration and explana-

---

[18] S. Radhakrishnan, *Indian Philosophy,* Vol. I, pp. 24-53.
[19] S. N. Dasgupta, *A History of Indian Philosophy,* Vol. I, pp. 71-77.
[20] *Ibid.,* p. 77.
[21] Sophia Zen, ed., *Symposium on Chinese Culture* (Shanghai, 1931), p. 31.

tion; that Chinese philosophy emphasizes what man is and not what man has; that it does not attach much importance to epistemology; that it is not interested in knowledge for its own sake; that it does not contrast man and the universe; that it has not developed a system of logic; that it has subordinated metaphysics to human affairs; that it extensively and thoroughly discusses the problem of how to live; that it is not systematic in form but systematic in content; and that it is traditional only in name and is progressive.[22]

From their descriptions, it is clear that Indian and Chinese philosophies exhibit different characters. They agree, however, in one point, namely, the interest in man rather than nature or God.

MAN, THIS WORLD, IMMORTALITY, AND EVIL

Both the virtues and the vices of Oriental philosophy can be attributed to the central fact that it regards philosophy as a human problem. It is primarily devoted to the quest for the final solution of human problems. The ultimate goal is *Moksha* or emancipation for Hinduism and Jainism, Nirvāṇa for Buddhism, "long life and lasting vision" for Taoism, individual perfection and a harmonious social order for Confucianism and Neo-Confucianism, and general welfare for Mohism.[23] These are not set up as high and remote ideals incapable of realization. On the contrary, they are firmly believed to be attainable, and, what is even more significant, attainable in this world. Of course certain Oriental religions look for complete salvation in the next world, such as the higher stages of transmigration in Hinduism, the "Pure Land," "Paradise," and other versions of Nirvāṇa in certain Buddhist sects[24] and the "realm of immortals" in the Taoist cult. But these beliefs are departures from their respective philosophical systems, which insist that salvation takes place in this world. In all indigenous Chinese philosophies, the symbols of perfection, namely, the sage and the moral order, do not transcend this world. As Neo-Confucianists put it, reality "is right in front of our very eyes," and there is no such

[22] Fung Yu-lan, *The History of Chinese Philosophy*, Ch. I (cf. translation of Pt. I by D. Bodde, [Henri Vetch, Peiping, 1937], pp. 1-6).

[23] See Ch. III, pp. 25, 33, 38, and 54.

[24] Aside from the several essentially religious sects which advocate salvation on the "Other Shore," most of the Buddhist schools emphasize the necessity of "becoming a Buddha where you are."

ultimate principle as Reason or the Great Ultimate "beyond such daily matters as drinking and eating."[25] The main object of the Taoists is to "nourish our original nature" and to "preserve life" by letting it run its course naturally.[26] Even in apparently other-worldly Hinduism and Buddhism, freedom is gained whenever right and perfect knowledge is obtained, because the primary condition to *Moksha* and Nirvāṇa is the removal of ignorance, and this can happen at any moment during one's lifetime.

This does not mean that Oriental imagination goes no further than this mundane world. The Hindus, the Buddhists, and the Taoists who copied the Buddhists in a wholesale manner, have created more heavens and hells than all the rest of the world. But these are products of their religious fancy, and not the results of their philosophical speculation. In Hinduism, Buddhism, Taoism, and Confucianism as philosophies, the answer to the question of existence beyond this world has an entirely different color. In no Oriental system can the Western conception of personal immortality be found. The idea of the personal soul in the *Bhagavad Gītā* comes close to it, but the final stage of the soul in Hinduism is pure unity with Brahman, although that may not take place until after a long series of transmigrations.[27] The answer of Buddhism to the question of life after death is a unique one. Since Buddhism accepts no such thing as a permanent self, a specific life endures for no longer than a single moment, and at every moment a new life is born. For this reason, there can be no problem of immortality because there is no self to be immortal. If the wheel of rebirth is to be interpreted as immortality, that immortality is the immortality of creative and continuous rebirth, and not that of a person. Obviously Nirvāṇa cannot be interpreted as immortality, because Nirvāṇa is essentially the state where all specific entities disappear. Even the Absolute as an entity is extinguished; nothing but Suchness remains.[28]

[25] See Ch. III, pp. 54, 56, and 65.   [26] *Ibid.*, pp. 34 and 37.

[27] *Bhagavad Gītā*, II, 18-20; XI, 28-29; XII, 9.

[28] For Buddhist arguments against the self as a permanent entity, see the last chapter of the *Abhidharmakośa Śāstra* by Vasubandhu. French translation by Louis de La Vallée Poussin, *L'Abhidharmakośa de Vasubandhu*, 6 volumes (Paris: Paul Guethner, 1923), Vol. V, pp. 230-232; also *Vijñapti-mātratāsiddhi*, French translation by Louis de La Vallée Poussin, *La siddhi de Hiuan-tsang*, Librairie Orientaliste (Paris: Paul Guethner, 1928-1929), Ch. I.

All the indigenous philosophies in China and Shintō in Japan are completely at one in the theory that at death man's soul returns to the heavenly or active universal principle by which it was produced, and his spirit returns to the earthly or passive universal principle from which it came. This does not take place immediately after death, the individual retaining his identity for some time during which the active and passive elements in him are gradually dissipated. The length of the sojourn on this stage depends upon the amount of merits he has accumulated, which have a way of consolidating the universal forces in him. Confucius may be said to be still living as a spiritual being, while his fiftieth direct descendant might have ceased to be a spiritual entity. We may say, therefore, that the Chinese and Japanese generally believe in temporary immortality, if such an apparent contradiction in terms can be permitted.[29]

Although these three answers to the question of future life differ, they all point to a metaphysical position which is extremely important in the Orient and will engage our attention again and again in this chapter. This is the concept of the undifferentiated continuum, or, in the language of modern physics, the "field" to which all individual, particular, specific entities must finally be reduced. To the Orientals, this is the final abode of man, where his reality is identified with the One Reality. This identity may mean the loss of individual reality, as a drop of water in the ocean in the case of Hinduism. Or it may mean the absence of any difference between the individual and the universal, as a candle light in a bright room or a voice in a chorus, in the case of other Oriental systems. In any case, the undifferentiated continuum is the ultimate solution of the problem of immortality.

But Oriental philosophies in general are not much interested in the problem of life after death. They are busily occupied with problems of this world. Both the Buddha and Confucius refused to answer inquiries about the hereafter, the former explaining that a physician has no time to go into metaphysical discussion, and the

---

[29] See my article "Hun" in *The Dictionary of Philosophy*, ed. by D. D. Runes (New York: Philosophical Library, 1942), p. 132. This concept is set forth particularly in the writings of medieval Chinese philosophers, such as Huai-nan Tzŭ (d. 122 B.C.), Tung Chung-shu (177-104 B.C.), etc., and is upheld throughout modern Chinese philosophy.

latter saying that if we don't know life we cannot expect to know death.[30] Oriental philosophies are primarily concerned with man.

This deep interest in man led to the position in some Oriental philosophies, especially in Confucianism and Neo-Confucianism, that man is the proper means of study, not only of man, but also of the universe.[31] The Confucianists, whether ancient or modern, were unanimous in the assertion that when central harmony is established in man, it will also be established in the universe. Such a tendency was also noticeable in Buddhism, and culminated in the doctrine that one can see his nature and become Buddha by directly seeing into his own mind.[32] Taoism opposes nature to man. But the Tao, or the Way, of Heaven and Earth is to be discovered in the sage, or the "pure man," although Tao exists everywhere, even in such lowly things as the ant and the tare.

Such being the emphasis on the position of man in Oriental philosophy, it is to be expected that the question of human nature occupies a place of supreme importance. Practically all systems have gone into the question thoroughly and from many angles. There are many interesting discussions in the Upanishads on the creation of man, his soul, his nature, his four stages (bodily, empirical, transcendental, and absolute), and his relationship with Brahman.[33] It is in Confucianism, however, that one finds the keenest interest in the question, as there has never been a Confucian philosopher

[30] Lun Yü (The Analects), XI, 11; Majjhima Nikāya, suttas 63 and 72 (H. C. Warren, Buddhism in Translations, Harvard Oriental Series, Vol. III [Cambridge: Harvard University Press, 1922], pp. 117 and 123); Samyutta Nikāya, sutta 44.

[31] See Ch. III, pp. 25 and 54.   [32] Especially in the Zen School.

[33] The main problem of the Upanishads may be said to be the relationship between man as an individual spiritual entity and Brahman as the universal spiritual entity. See the Brihadāraṇyaka Upanishad, II, 5, 1; III, 4, 1; V, 5, 2; Chāndogya Upanishad, III, 13, 7; III, 14, 2-3; V, 11, 1; VIII, 8, 3; VIII, 14, 1; Taittirīya Upanishad, II, 8; III, 10; Muṇḍaka Upanishad, II, 1, 10; II, 2, 5 and 9; Aitareya Upanishad, V, 1-3; Śvetāśvatara Upanishad, I, 16. For the creation of man, see Ait., II, 2-4; Tait., II, 1. For the soul and its four stages, see Bri., IV, 3, 6; V, 6; Chānd., VIII, 3, 3; Kaṭha, III, 5; IV, 1-2; Maṇḍūkya, 3-7; Chānd., VIII, 3-12. Consult translation by R. E. Hume, The Thirteen Principal Upanishads (London, Oxford University Press, 1931). See also A. B. Keith, The Religion and Philosophy of the Veda and Upanishads, 2 vols. (Cambridge: Harvard Oriental Series, Harvard University Press, 1925), pp. 567-570.

who did not devote a great deal of attention to the problem of the nature of man.[34] While Oriental philosophy in general believes human nature to be originally good—for the source of man is Ātman, or Brahman as a personal principle in Hinduism, jīva in Jainism, Tao in Taoism, the Great Ultimate in Neo-Confucianism—each of which as ultimate reality is good—yet man's original nature has so degenerated because of ignorance, desires, or his beclouded mind that severe discipline is necessary to recover its original goodness. This is the main reason why in Oriental ethics severe discipline is advocated in order to recover the original virtue of man.

Herein lies the Oriental explanation of the emergence of evil. It is entirely the creation of man. Practically all the Indian systems, Buddhism included, and Taoism in China, trace the appearance of evil to man's ignorance, which gives rise to false knowledge and harmful desires. Confucianism in all its phases, Mohism, and other philosophical schools in China and Japan are more specific in their account of evil, and explain it in terms of selfishness, delusion, incapability, etc.[35] In other words, they do not maintain that there is one cause of evil; there are many reasons for man's downfall. But the significant point is that whether the cause of evil is simple or complicated, man himself must be responsible for his own misfortune. Even natural evil is believed to be caused by the gods as punishment for the evil conduct of man. How the absolutely good Brahman, Tao, or Great Ultimate can ever allow its own creation, man, to create evil, which is both novel and alien to its character, has never been satisfactorily explained. The theory, advocated by Hinduism, Buddhism, Taoism, and to some extent Neo-Confucianism, that the distinction of good and evil is foreign to the ultimate reality but is a human product, does not remove the difficulty, for

[34] A neat summary of the development of the Confucian theories of human nature is found in Andrew Chih-yi Chang's *Hsüntzu's Theory of Human Nature and its Influence on Chinese Thought* (Peiping, 1928). See my article "Hsing" (human nature) in *The Dictionary of Philosophy*, ed. by D. D. Runes (New York: Philosophical Library, 1942), p. 130.

[35] The question of ignorance and evil is discussed throughout the Six Indian Systems (especially the Vedānta School; see the *Vedānta Sūtra*, I, 1, 1-3, tr. by George Thibaut, *The Vedānta Sūtra with the Commentary of Śankara, The Sacred Books of the East* [The Clarendon Press, 1890 and 1896, Vol. XXXIV], pp. 3-19), the Buddhist Schools, Mencius (especially VI, I, 6), and the Neo-Confucianists (especially Chu Hsi and Wang Yang-ming).

this product must be taken as another instance of evil which can be traced back to the ultimate reality itself. One can find some consolation, however, in the fact that since man produces evil, he can also destroy it. Oriental philosophy insists on the possibility of man's transmuting evil himself. Probably this explains why in Oriental religions both the idea of original sin and the idea of forgiveness have been absent. Man causes his own downfall; he must, and can, work out his own salvation.

ORIENTAL PHILOSOPHY AND RELIGION

This is not to imply that Oriental philosophy is not religious. Oriental philosophy and Oriental religion have too often been confused as, for example, the superstitious Hindu cults are mistaken for Hindu philosophy and the corrupt Taoist nature worship is identified with the naturalistic, atheistic Taoism. But we cannot deny that the religious element is present in many Oriental systems, although not in all of them. Oriental philosophy is generally not religious in the sense of dependence on the supernatural for salvation or for knowledge. As has been said, man must work out his own salvation. As to knowledge, Oriental popular religions believe in revelation and dreams. In Oriental philosophies, however, revelation as a means of knowledge is found only in the case of the Vedas which are believed to have been revealed. Ever since the Upanishads, knowledge has depended not on direct revelation from a higher deity to man, but on man's study of the revealed Vedas, whether or not through a specially qualified teacher.

As to the belief in the existence of a deity, it is not as strong in Oriental philosophy as is generally understood. It is true that the Orient has the most thickly populated pantheons in the world. It is also true that the existence of supernatural beings is accepted in a number of Oriental philosophical systems. But ultimate reality in Hinduism, Jainism, and Buddhism is understood in terms of a universal principle, not a supernatural being. Confucius sometimes followed traditional religious observances but sometimes preferred to serve man first of all.[36] Most of the Neo-Confucianists and Taoists were quite skeptical about a divine sovereign. They said that

[36] *Lun Yü* (*The Analects*), XI, II.

if there were one, they had not found any clue to his existence.[37] It is true that Mohism openly defended the belief in spiritual beings, and Mo Tzŭ, but not Confucius or Lao Tzŭ, founded a religion in ancient China.[38] Yet we must remember that Mo Tzŭ encouraged the belief in spirits primarily because such belief contributed to the welfare of man. It is also true that the Yoga school in India found the twenty-five categories of the naturalistic and evolutionary Sāṅkhya school insufficient, and added Īśvara, a personal God.[39] But Īśvara and many others are mostly instrumental, that is, intended for psychological and aesthetic effect. The many gods of Vedic ancestry in the Mīmāṁsā school, for example, are more like the immortal characters in classical literature than existing personalities. They are types, ideals, symbols of universal forces, and aids to meditation. There are gods, such as Krishṇa in the *Bhagavad Gītā*, and God in Vedānta which possess all the qualities of divine beings. One will be surprised, however, to find how many systems in India tried to disprove God. The Jains, the Mīmāṁsā school, the Sāṅkhya school, and the Buddhists, presented argument after argument, all of which are deeply philosophical and highly critical, against his existence.[40] There is much more atheism in Oriental philosophy than one suspects.

But from another point of view, Oriental philosophy as a whole is deeply religious. Broadly speaking, it is religious because it affirms again and again the intimacy between man and reality. Constantly the note is struck in Oriental philosophy that man is a small self who partakes of the greater Self that is more real, more lasting, and more powerful than he. He must always stand in awe of this greater Self, sincerely and reverently, and even submissively. Here lies the basic reason why naturalistic Taoism, atheistic Buddhism,

---

[37] For example, *Chuang Tzŭ*, Ch. II; cf. translation by Fung Yu-lan, *Chuang Tzŭ, a new selected translation with an exposition of the philosophy of Kuo Hsiang* (Shanghai: The Commercial Press, 1933), p. 46.

[38] According to Hu Shih. See his *The Development of the Logical Method in Ancient China* (Shanghai: The Oriental Book Co., 1928), p. 57.

[39] The *Yoga Sūtra*, I, 23-29; II, 1, 45. See translation by J. H. Woods, *The Yoga-System of Patañjali*, Harvard Oriental Series, Vol. XVII (Cambridge: Harvard University Press, 1927).

[40] For example, the Sāṅkhya arguments in *The Aphorisms of Kapila*, translated by James R. Ballantyne (third edition; London: Trübner, 1885), I, 92-94; V, 2-12.

and humanistic Confucianism all developed a religion to run parallel with their philosophy. This is also why the Nyāya and Vaiśeshika schools of Hinduism greatly developed the idea of God which was but casually mentioned by their founders.[41] The Vedānta school, the most important of the Hindu schools, carried the idea of God to new heights, and reached the point of an Absolute in Śaṅkara and a personal deity in Rāmānuja.

This unusual phenomenon, the fact that some of the world's religions of the highest intensity grew out of nonreligious philosophies, may seem strange at first sight. But it is not so, because such development was, not only a social and a psychological necessity, but also a philosophical necessity. The fundamental character of Oriental philosophy demands it. All major philosophies of the Orient are unanimous in the belief that man and reality are common in essence. There exists a natural relationship between man and the cosmos that no man can fail to heed. To the Orientals this natural relationship is a harmonious one. Take the relationship between man and nature for instance. No hostile attitude is evident in Oriental philosophy, the Confucian philosopher, Hsün Tzŭ, being the sole exception who advocated that nature must be conquered and controlled. The general attitude toward the relationship between man and the universe is that of identity and correspondence. Since man and the universe are reducible to the same reality, whether it is called Ātman, *purusha, jīva,* Tao, Suchness, or the Great Ultimate, it follows that the only essential difference between them is in degree and not in kind.

The theory of correspondence between man and the universe has occupied a very important position in both India and China. A macrocosm-microcosm relationship is stressed so far in the Upanishads and in medieval Chinese philosophy as to be repulsive.[42] Different parts of man's body were held to correspond to different parts of heaven and earth, for no reason other than poetic imagination and outright superstition. This primitive fantasy was removed in modern Hindu and Chinese philosophies. In the Vedānta school, whether as represented by Śaṅkara or by Rāmānuja, the true rela-

[41] Udayana's *Kusumāñjali,* the classic statement of the Nyāya proofs for the existence of God, fully develops the idea of God casually mentioned in the *Nyāya Sūtra.*
[42] *Bri.,* I, 2, 3; *Isa,* 17; *Ait.,* I, 4; *Chānd.,* V, 12-18. See also Ch. III, p. 48.

tionship between man and the universe is a spiritual one, a relationship of the soul. The fundamental theme of the Upanishads was here solemnly restated. In Neo-Confucianism man is looked upon as a miniature universe. There is one Great Ultimate in the universe; there is also a Great Ultimate in each of the myriad things, including men.

THE ONE AND THE MANY

This leads us to the question of the relationship between the One and the Many, a question that is surrounded with a great deal of misunderstanding. Due to the Hindu idea, such as vigorously put forth in the Vedānta of Śaṅkara, that plurality is *māyā* or illusion, and also due to the Buddhist conception that Suchness or the Void admits no specific character, Oriental philosophy as a whole has been believed to allow no reality for the individual. The individual is nothing more than a drop of water in the ocean, it is believed. In the ultimate sense this is true in Hinduism, Taoism, and Buddhism. We should not, however, ignore the effort in the Vedānta school of Rāmānuja to reaffirm the reality of multiplicity. Rāmānuja's philosophy is called "qualified monism" primarily because he defended, without reservation, the world of multiplicity and refused to accept the world as *māyā*.[43] Nor should we ignore the fact that in the Sarvāstivāda school and the Abhidharmakośa school of Hīnayāna Buddhism, every particular thing is regarded as a separate entity. In Mahāyāna, too, particularly in the Avataṅsaka and the T'ien-t'ai schools, both the One and the Many are held to be equally real.[44] This, of course, does not seem to be consonant with the general Buddhist theory of non-ego. Buddhist philosophers explain this apparent inconsistency by referring to their equally important theory of the three grades of reality, namely, the illusory, the par-

[43] Radhakrishnan, *Indian Philosophy*, Vol. II, pp. 690 ff.; Dasgupta, *A History of Indian Philosophy*, Vol. III (1940), pp. 286 ff.

[44] The T'ien-t'ai School is very persistent in its theory of the true state of all *dharmas*, that is, all elements manifested are the elements in their own states (*sarvadharma svalakṣaṇatā*). It proclaims, "Everything, even the color or fragrance, is identical with the Middle Path, the Truth." Equally strong is the Avataṅsaka position of "All is One and One is All." See notes 12 and 13.

tial, and the absolute.[45] The rope is illusory when it is mistaken for a snake. As a rope, it has partial reality, since a rope is nothing but the effect of a number of causes such as hemp, space, etc. It has absolute reality when it is recognized as Suchness. The rope in itself is phenomenal, an extreme particular, whereas absolute reality has no such distinction as phenomenon and noumenon or the particular and the universal. This is the realm in which the One is the Many and the Many is the One. The ego, therefore, has partial reality and empirical efficacy, but no individuality in the ultimate sense. The main difference between Hinduism and Buddhism is that in Hinduism the individual is ultimately absorbed by the Absolute,[46] whereas in Buddhism neither the Absolute nor the individual swallows the other. Their distinction does not exist in the state of Suchness.

The position of Taoism comes close to that of Hinduism. Other schools in China and Japan, however, whether in Confucianism, Mohism, Neo-Confucianism, or Japanese philosophy in general, always stress the fact that *both* the particular *and* the universal are real. As a matter of fact, in Neo-Confucianism, which dominated Chinese thought in the last millennium and Japanese thought for many centuries, the reality of the one depends on the reality of the other. Without the vital force, the principle of differentiation, Reason or the universal principle cannot have any embodiment, cannot become concrete, and cannot operate. The One is discoverable only in the Many, just as the Many is discernible only in the One.[47]

Taking all Oriental philosophies together, however, there is undoubtedly the fact that the Many is definitely subordinated to the One on which it depends for its ultimate reality. In other words, Oriental philosophy is at bottom monistic, notwithstanding minor systems of dualism and pluralism in India. We are not unaware of the realistic pluralism of Jainism, the atomistic pluralism of Nyāya and Vaiśeshika, the realistic dualism of Sāṅkhya. But with the exception of Jainism, the duality and plurality in Hinduism ultimately

[45] As set forth in such work as *Madhyāntavibhaṅga, Discourse on Discrimination between Middle and Extremes, ascribed to Bodhisattva Maitreya and Commented by Vasubandhu and Sthiramati,* translated by Th. Stcherbatsky. Leningrad: *Bibliotheca Buddhica,* Vol. XXX, 1936.
[46] *Bri.,* IV, 3, 32; *Praśna,* IV, 7; *Tait.,* I, 4, 3.
[47] See Ch. III, p. 56.

resolve into the unity of Brahman. The Suchness of Buddhism allows no numerical qualification, and consequently it is impossible to determine whether Buddhism is monistic or pluralistic. Buddhist literature, however, is full of refutations of duality. The seventy-five *dharmas* or elements of existence of early Buddhism and the one hundred *dharmas* of later Buddhism are all to be transcended when Suchness is realized. In China and Japan neither dualism nor pluralism has found a place. The *yin* and *yang* tradition which maintains that all events in the universe are results of the inter-action of the universal principle of passivity, *yin*, and the universal principle of activity, *yang*, is not dualistic because these two forces are but different aspects of the one reality called the Great Ulti-mate. The suspected dualism of Reason (*Li*) and the vital force (*ch'i*) in Neo-Confucianism is not real, for they are finally synthe-sized in the Great Ultimate.

Whether the One in Oriental philosophy is determinate or in-determinate is a controversial matter. It is obviously indeterminate in the sense that it cannot be described in specific terms, such as the Void in Buddhism, and, to some extent, Tao in Taoism and Brahman in Hinduism. It is determinate in Confucianism, Neo-Confucianism, Jainism, several orthodox Hindu schools, Japanese philosophies and other minor Oriental systems, where ultimate real-ity can be understood in specific terms. It may be argued that these specific terms do not describe the One as noumenon, but the One as the "field" of the phenomenal world. In other words, the One in Ori-ental philosophy is intuited, but not postulated. There is no doubt that the monism of the Orient is built on a much less rational ground than that of the West. In systems like Hinduism, Taoism, and certain schools of Buddhism, where the world is regarded as phenomenal, the indeterminate character of the One is self-evident. In other systems, particularly in Neo-Confucianism and in certain Buddhist schools which refuse to distinguish the phenomenal from the noumenal, the specific character of the One is as clear as day.

The monistic emphasis has helped the Orient to avoid a great difficulty in philosophy, namely, that of the relationship between body and mind. Since they are never sharply contrasted and since they are, in the final analysis, identical, any difficulty arising out of the dualism of body and mind immediately disappears. The note of unity runs throughout Oriental philosophy as it does nowhere else in the world.

CHANCE AND FATE

The Oriental emphasis on unity should not be interpreted to mean a static universe. Unity involves what is and what is not. Reality consists of both Being and Non-Being, that is, Becoming. To the Buddhists, the Taoists, and the Confucianists reality is particularly dynamic. The momentariness of existence constitutes the basis of Buddhist philosophy. In Taoism, too, reality passes on "like a galloping horse." The Confucianists, especially the Neo-Confucianists, were also strongly impressed with the dynamic quality of the universe. Their philosophy is derived from the general Chinese tradition of transformation, which, according to the *I Ching* (*The Book of Changes*), takes place every moment, since every production involves the interaction of the two principles of *yin* and *yang*. Chinese philosophers since the eleventh century have spoken of things as "events," or "affairs," which have no "duration," even by Buddhist standards.[48]

The fleeting character of reality is a logical outcome of the Oriental conception of things as relations, a trait particularly prominent in Buddhism and Chinese philosophy. To Chinese philosophers, Confucianists and Taoists alike, a thing is produced by the Great Ultimate or Tao through the interaction of the universal principles of passivity and activity. These forces are never stagnated, but are in constant flow. To the Buddhists, any effect must have a number of causes or a number of elements coming into a peculiar relationship. This idea of relation is so deeply rooted in the Orient that human relationships become a main factor in Oriental ethics. It is also responsible for the gradation of reality found in most Oriental philosophies.

Oriental fatalism and pessimism which have attracted a great deal of attention in the West, can be traced to the Oriental conception of the transitoriness of reality. It has been pointed out that Oriental philosophy firmly believes in the possibility of salvation. But in a universe of universal and incessant transformation, and from the point of view of ultimate reality, man as an entity enjoys

[48] *Ibid.*, pp. 56 and 65.

no more permanence than a bubble or a shadow. For this reason, Chuang Tzǔ and most of the Taoists after him advocated spontaneous living, which means to let life take its course freely. Man should not work for riches and fame, nor should he worry about life and death. Nature has her own program which man can never hope to alter. In Buddhism and in Hinduism, the transitoriness of life is even identified with suffering. They consider the world as suffering simply on the ground that life and death succeed each other without end. They attempt to escape from this "wheel" of suffering, to terminate the round of rebirth. Why impermanence of life spells suffering has never been explained.[49] The Neo-Confucianists took incessant transformation more realistically. They looked upon it as a matter of duty for man to fit into the scheme of universal operation. He should not lament over the natural and necessary course of events. Instead, he should "establish his destiny," participating in and contributing to the universal law. They admitted that man has no control over life and death or wealth and poverty, but they insisted that it is sheer ignorance and folly, and even violation of the moral law, to stand by a wall which is about to crumble and count on one's luck. One must make full effort to understand things and to realize one's nature, for "the complete realization of the Reason of things, the full development of one's nature, and the establishment of destiny are simultaneous."[50] They allowed room for free will, although man, as an individual, must conform to the general pattern of the universe. The Buddhists, the Jains, and the Hindus all encourage the full exercise of the will, as only by serious endeavor can man hope to destroy ignorance.

THE MIND

Oriental philosophy has always attached immense importance to mental activity, although general respect for tradition and the weakness of the critical attitude seem to indicate otherwise. The critical spirit in Oriental philosophy, however, is stronger than is suspected, in spite of the fact that more rationalism is found in the West. The respect for tradition does not preclude that critical spirit. As a

[49] An interesting parallel can be drawn between the Indian idea of suffering and the Christian doctrine of original sin.
[50] *Ch'êng-shih I-shu* (Posthumous Works of the Ch'êng Brothers), Ch. II.

matter of fact, one of the chief defects of Oriental philosophy lies in its overemphasis on the creative ability of the mind.

No one can underestimate the place of the mind in Oriental philosophy. In a certain sense Oriental philosophy may be said to be predominantly idealistic, considering the importance of the mind not only in the idealistic schools of Hinduism, Buddhism, and Neo-Confucianism, but also in the naturalistic Taoism, totalistic Buddhism, and rationalistic Neo-Confucianism.[51] In Hinduism and certain schools of Buddhism, reality is conceived to be a principle of consciousness, whether it goes by the name of Ātman or Self, or Mind. One of the Buddhist schools and a Neo-Confucian school frankly labeled themselves as "Mind-Only school"[52] and "Mind-Philosophy"[53] respectively. In all cases of idealistic tendencies in Oriental philosophy, the mind is the universal mind, since the individual mind at bottom falls short of full reality. We are aware, of course, that neither Tao in Taoism nor Suchness in Buddhism can be reduced to mind, as Tao denotes the "Way" of nature, and Suchness admits no qualification, whether material or spiritual. Both Taoism and Buddhism as represented by certain schools are naturalistic. Nevertheless, the fact remains that the realization of Tao or Suchness depends on mental activity such as insight or enlightenment. We are also aware that the major philosophical system of China, Neo-Confucianism, is basically rationalistic, and that its Reason cannot be interpreted as consciousness. Yet the mind is considered the best starting point in the realization of Reason, since Reason is best embodied in the mind, although it is discoverable in all things. Materialism has had no notable place in the Orient, except the Chārvāka school in India and Hsün Tzŭ and Wang Ch'ung in China, all of which enjoyed only a short life.[54] It has been sug-

---

[51] Especially in India. See S. Dasgupta, *Indian Idealism* (Cambridge: University Press, 1933). Chinese philosophy does not go to the idealistic extreme. The Buddhist Mind-Only doctrine enjoyed but a short life in China. See Ch. III, p. 51.

[52] Vijñaptimātravāda (also called Yogācāra in Sanskrit, Fa-hsiang in Chinese, Hossō in Japanese, and Mere-Ideation in English). For literature of this school, see the *Viṁśatikā* by Vasubandhu, tr. by C. H. Hamilton, *Wei Shih Er Shih Lun* (New Haven: American Oriental Society, 1938); and also those referred to in notes 2 and 3.

[53] See Ch. III, p. 62.

[54] See Mādhava Āchārya, *The Sarvadarśanasaṅgraha, or, Review of the*

gested that the insignificance of materialism may be explained by the Oriental use of aesthetic intuition rather than concepts by postulation. Be that as it may, a philosophy deeply concerned with the realization of manhood and salvation of the human soul naturally refuses to accept matter as the quintessence of existence. Furthermore, ultimate reality in the Orient is not arrived at purely through intuition. Many volumes of books in the various schools stand as living testaments to the tremendous amount of speculation. It must be admitted, to be sure, that China and Japan lag far behind India in this respect, and the East, taken as a whole, does not measure up to the West in speculative activity. The point at issue, however, is that Oriental ultimate reality is not the result of intuition alone. If intuition alone were sufficient, the ultimate reality of Taoism and Buddhism, which employed intuition more than any other Oriental philosophical school, should have been idealistic. The Buddhist school that came out frankly with the doctrine of idealism, the Mind-Only or Vijñaptimātratā school, happens to be one of the most speculative schools, and its analysis of consciousness into three levels with its eight categories and fourfold function, offers something perfectly unique in the history of world philosophy. Its arguments and deliberations about the mind as the only reality compare favorably with any idealistic philosophy.[55] Buddhism has gone into the analysis of consciousness so extensively and so thoroughly that any suspicion of the complete dependence of Oriental philosophy on intuition should be dispelled.

INTUITION AND OTHER MEANS OF KNOWLEDGE

Of course, no one should underestimate the role intuition plays in Oriental philosophy as a whole. The fact remains, however, that, first of all, not all important schools employ it as the chief method of knowledge, and secondly, that those schools that use it as the main avenue to truth do so only with the aid of reasoning, observation, and other means of knowledge. Confucianism, Mohism, Neo-Mohism, Chinese medieval philosophy, Sophism, the several phases

Different Systems of Hindu Philosophy, tr. by E. B. Cowell and A. E. Gough (London: Trübner, 1882), Ch. I. Also see Ch. III, pp. 31 and 50.
[55] *Vijñaptimātratāsiddhi, La siddhi de Hiuan-tsang, op. cit.*

of Neo-Confucianism, Chārvāka, and indigenous Japanese philosophy regard all means of knowledge as trustworthy. If there is
any preference, it is with reasoning, surprising as this may sound.
The importance of reasoning is obvious in the logical schools of
Neo-Mohism and Sophism.[56] Confucius placed learning before any
method of knowledge, learning from the ancients, daily observation,
and serious thinking.[57] In the utilitarian philosophy of Mohism, we
find the famous Mohist threefold method of reasoning involving a
"basis," a "general survey," and a "practical application."[58] The
heaviest emphasis on intellectual deliberation, however, was laid in
the Neo-Confucian movement, otherwise generally called the "Reason" school, in which the surest way to discover the "Reason" or
Law of the universe is by "the extension of knowledge to the utmost" by way of "thorough investigation of things."[59] Unfortunately early Neo-Confucianists looked inward for such extension
and investigation, and in the second stage of Neo-Confucianism,
in Wang Yang-ming, it culminated in "inborn knowledge of the
good." However, in the third phase of Neo-Confucianism, that in
the last three centuries, reasoning, especially reasoning supported
by experience, is emphasized.

In most Oriental philosophical schools, intuition has its place,
of course. We do not forget—not for a moment—that while such
major Chinese systems as Confucianism, Mohism, and Neo-Confucianism (except Wang Yang-ming) emphasize experience and
reasoning, many Oriental philosophies rely ultimately on intuition.
What we intend to point out is that even in these schools, intuition
transcends, rather than excludes, other means of knowledge. Practically all of the six orthodox Hindu systems have their own theory
of knowledge which involves perception, inference, testimony, analogy, presumption, and synthesis. Hinduism, Jainism, Buddhism,
and Taoism have grades of knowledge which are distinguished as
"lower" and "higher" knowledge.[60] It is here that intuition begins

[56] See Ch. III, p. 38.
[57] *Lun Yü (The Analects)*, I, 1, 8, 14; II, 15; *Chung Yung (Central Harmony* or *The Doctrine of the Mean)*, XIX.
[58] See Ch. III, p. 39.   [59] *Ibid.*, p. 60.
[60] For the Hindu theories of knowledge, see Dasgupta, *A History of
Indian Philosophy*, Vol. I, pp. 261 ff.; 332 ff.; 382 ff.; 470 ff. For the Jain
theory of knowledge, see J. Jaini, *Outlines of Jainism*, Jain Literature Society
(Cambridge: Cambridge University Press, 1916), pp. 109-118. The Buddhist

to assume unusual importance, as it reduces all other ways of knowing to the position of an elementary or intermediate stage. Scholars
are quite justified in maintaining that while intuition occupies an
important position in Oriental philosophy, it comes only after a
series of vigorous intellectual efforts.

LOGIC

How vigorous these intellectual efforts are may be seen from
the significance that Oriental philosophy attaches to logic. From
the outset, we must declare that logic in Oriental philosophy does
not attain the prominence we find in Western philosophy. Early
writings of the East such as the Veda, the Upanishads, the *Tao-tê
Ching, The Analects*, etc., cannot fail to give the impression that
assertions are made and conclusions drawn without logical proof.
From this impression, people in the West have come to hold the
opinion that, first of all, Oriental thinkers do not reason logically;
secondly, that they do not reason at all; and thirdly, that they are
even illogical. No one can deny that the Orient has not developed
logic to the degree of subtlety reached in the West. But neither can
one deny that Oriental thinkers do reason, do reason logically, and
even reason by the use of logical syllogism. All Buddhist and Hindu
schools of philosophy very early perfected their elaborate systems
of logic. They reasoned in a way not at all different from that of
the West. For example:

1. Thesis   Sound is impermanent.
2. Reason   Because produced at will by an effort.
3. Example   Like a jar. Where an effort, there impermanence.
4. Application   Sound is produced at will by an effort.
5. Conclusion   It is impermanent.

Very often the five members of the syllogism were reduced to three,

doctrines of lower and higher knowledge are most vigorously set forth in the
Satyasiddhi Śāstra and the *Mādhyamika Śāstra* of which there are no English
translations. D. T. Suzuki gives an excellent general account of the Buddhist
doctrines of threefold knowledge and twofold knowledge in his *Studies in the
Laṅkāvatāra Sūtra* (London: Routledge, 1930), pp. 157-165. For the Taoist
idea of "great" and "small" knowledge, see *Chuang Tzŭ*, Ch. II; cf. Fung
Yu-lan, *op. cit.*, p. 45.

making it practically identical with that of the West, as the following example will show:

1. Where there is smoke, there is fire, as in the kitchen.
2. Here there is smoke.
3. There must be some fire.

Such an example may be found in any important philosophical treatise in the Hindu and the Buddhist schools. It is interesting to note that even in the three-member syllogism, an example is given, as Oriental logic insists that a concrete example must be cited in any legitimate process of deduction. Jainism, too, has its own system of logical reasoning, which is called the Doctrine of "May-be."[61] According to the Jains, there are seven forms of conditional predication:

A is.
A is not.
A is and is not.
A is unpredicable.
A is and is unpredicable.
A is not and is unpredicable.
A is, is not, and is unpredicable.

As a matter of fact, logic occupied such an important place in Oriental reasoning that some schools are called logical schools, such as Nyāya in Hinduism, Dignāga in Buddhism, and Neo-Mohism in Chinese philosophy. Oriental philosophies make use of all laws of thought. They use induction as well as deduction. For illustrations of the intricacies of Oriental logic, however, we must refer the reader to such books as the *Nyāya Sūtra*, Stcherbatsky's two-volume *Buddhist Logic*,[62] Vidyābhūshaṇa's *History of Indian Logic*,[63] and Hu Shih's *The Development of the Logical Method in Ancient China*. What is important to point out here is that where Oriental philosophers used syllogistic reasoning, they used it with reservation, and where they did not use syllogistic reasoning, they reasoned

61 Jaini, *op. cit.*, pp. 112-118.
62 Academy of Sciences of USSR Press (Leningrad, 1932; Cambridge, Mass., 1934).
63 M. S. C. Vidyābhūshaṇa, *A History of Indian Logic* (Calcutta: University of Calcutta, 1921).

no less clearly and distinctly. The first attitude is characteristic of Indian thought, while the second is characteristic of China.

The distrust of logical reasoning went so far that later in Zen there was not only a deliberate attempt to discard logic, but also to ridicule it. The dialogues between great Zen masters and their pupils must impress an uninitiated reader as nothing but nonsense. It is difficult to understand why, for example, when a pupil asked what the three Buddhist jewels were, the master should answer, "Rice, millet, and bean!" instead of the expected, "The Buddha, the Doctrine, and the Congregation"; or why, as an answer to the all-important question as to what constitutes the contents of the Buddhist canons, the master should merely raise his fist. There is nothing nonsensical in these. They represent a conscious effort to break down the habit of logical reasoning in order to create in the pupil's mind a unique mental attitude necessary to the apprehension of ultimate truth.

Chinese thinkers generally do not go to such an extreme. They believe in the efficacy of reasoning, although they do not for a single moment accept it as the exclusive way to truth. If they do not use the syllogism, it is only because they do not reason as methodically as Western philosophers, though none the less clearly and distinctly. There is no doubt that, compared with either the West or India, China lags far behind in systematic reasoning, in explanation, and in proof. Aside from the short-lived Neo-Mohist school of logic and the Buddhist logic that came in with Buddhist philosophy as a handmaid, there is hardly any formal system of logic in China. Even the Neo-Mohist school may not be called logical in the strict sense of the word, for, in spite of its definitions, explanations, and proofs, and in spite of its seven methods of argumentation, it is a question whether the school went beyond nominalism.[64] Nevertheless, any amount of familiarity with such thinkers as Wang Ch'ung (27-100 A.D.) and the Neo-Confucianists from the eleventh century onward will convince us that their minds were active and that their thinking processes were clear.[65]

[64] Paul Masson-Oursel, *Comparative Philosophy* (New York: Harcourt, Brace, 1926), pp. 119 ff.

[65] It seems to me that Professor Radhakrishnan has overstated the case of intuition in Oriental philosophy in his defense of intuition (summed up in C. E. M. Joad's *Counter Attack from the East, the Philosophy of Radhakrishnan* [London: Allen & Unwin, 1933], pp. 94-110).

SYNTHESIS AND NEGATION

We regret, however, that Oriental clear and distinct thinking has not emphasized logic more than it has, because the subordination of the intellect in the East has prevented the development of logic and natural science which in turn has retarded progress in metaphysics and epistemology on the one hand and industry and commerce on the other. We have just pointed out that logic has been, and still is, used in Oriental philosophy. But Oriental logic falls short in clear and definite description, in analysis, and in the use of postulates. Consequently, abstract science has not developed in the Orient, because abstract science is impossible without a well-established system of logic. This does not suggest in the least any incompatibility of Oriental philosophy with science, for so long as there exists unity of body and mind, any fundamental difficulty with science is avoided. But the intuitive method, even when supported by other means of knowledge and logic, tends to neglect science.

This sounds like a deplorable state of affairs. There is not wanting, however, an element of consolation. If Oriental intuition has underestimated analysis, it has emphasized the synthetic attitude. Since reality consists of both Being and Non-Being, both activity and inactivity, unity becomes the cardinal principle in the realm of nature as well as in the realm of man. Any absolute distinction, whether in facts or in ideas, is looked upon as a distortion of reality. Herein lies the secret of removing the difficulty of the dualism of body and mind. The Oriental mind almost instinctively looks for similarity rather than difference, and finds the subject-predicate proposition and the logical law of identity distasteful. It views with strong suspicion such a statement as "A is A and nothing else." It does not doubt for a moment that A is A, but it refuses to concede that the whole story can be told as simply as that. The universe is a network of close relationships, so that nothing can be reduced to a point in space or an instant in time. Ultimately, everything involves everything else, so that A is conceivably B. Absolute distinctions as indicated by the "either-or" point of view also do not meet the approval of the Oriental mind. Granting things individuality and particularity, most Oriental philosophies have insisted that things both stand by themselves and are related to others, that the universe is both One and Many, and a man is both an independent individual and his father's son. This "both-and" point of view is really the psychological foundation of the Taoist identification of contraries,[66] the Buddhist Middle Path and the Void as devoid of specific characters,[67] and the Hindu theory of the paradoxical nature of Brahman.[68] To some extent, it also explains the Confucian "central harmony," either in the sense of the golden mean or in the sense of a central and unalterable universal principle, since centrality implies the synthesis of the extremes.

Of course this synthetic approach sometimes has been carried so far as to be destructive. When unduly emphasized, it not only makes definition and analysis difficult, but any affirmation impossible. This is exactly what happened in an extreme tendency in Buddhism, namely, the nihilism or absolutism of Nāgārjuna. His fourfold negation of *ens, non-ens,* either *ens* or *non-ens,* and neither *ens* nor *non-ens* reduces reality to an absolute Void, which is "devoid" of all specific characters. While the Absolute is thus fully affirmed, the specific characters are altogether denied. The "Middle Doctrine" of Nāgārjuna, by the force of its own argument, left its "middle" position and became too extreme even for the ordinary Buddhist.[69]

Intuitive synthesis has been reduced to a process of negation. Although this form of intuition is extreme, the central purpose of that mental activity must not be overlooked. Intuition, whether as a result of negation or otherwise, demands nothing short of direct and immediate contact with the Absolute, the undifferentiated continuum, the "field."

MYSTICISM AND MEDITATION

Strictly speaking, such direct contact with reality is a form of mysticism. In this sense we may describe Oriental philosophy as mystical to an appreciable extent, bearing in mind that such a broad definition does not cover Confucianism, Neo-Confucianism, Mohism, Chārvāka, and other minor schools. In such systems as Bud-

[66] *Tao-tê Ching,* I, XLV, XXI, XL, etc.; *Chuang Tzŭ,* Ch. II.
[67] See p. 140 of this Chapter, and Ch. III, p. 51.
[68] *Bri.,* IV, 4, 5; III, 7, 3; *Isa,* V; *Katha,* II, 21; *Praśna,* II, 5; *Mund.,* II, 2, 1; *Tait.,* II, 6.
[69] Th. Stcherbatsky, *The Conception of Buddhist Nirvāṇa,* p. 70.

dhism, Hinduism, and Taoism where mysticism plays an important role, it is not the mysticism of communion, but rather that of identity, that is, pure unity with Brahman or Tao. In the case of Buddhism, mysticism is very difficult to define, since one neither comes into communion with the Buddha nor identifies oneself with the Buddha. In Nirvāṇa, one becomes Buddha, not as the Buddha or one of the many Buddhas, because no numerical distinction exists any longer. Thus Buddhist mysticism may be called the "mysticism of becoming," or, as Professor Takakusu puts it, the "mysticism of self-creation." Taoist philosophy really lies between Hinduism and Buddhism in this respect.

In the process of identification or "self-creation," the unique Oriental method of meditation plays an important part. The word "Oriental" is used here to indicate that meditation is important in the Orient, but not to mean that it is the general method of all Oriental philosophical schools. The topic of meditation is treated in another chapter of this volume. Suffice it to say here that in spite of its strangeness, its philosophical import should not be taken lightly. It is practiced in Hinduism, Jainism, and Buddhism. In both Taoism and certain phases of Neo-Confucianism, the unity and tranquillity of the mind are strongly emphasized. It would be a mistake, however, to identify this with meditation, because this is regarded as psychological preparation for a clear "insight" into, and "extensive knowledge" of, the existential world, whereas the method of meditation is an attempt to transcend existence. The meditation of Yoga and of Buddhism represents a conscious, active, and spiritual effort to transcend the world by the attainment of right knowledge, the achievement of moral perfection, and the discovery of ultimate reality.

ORIENTAL PHILOSOPHY AND ETHICS; A WORLD PHILOSOPHY

Here we have an excellent example of the affinity of Oriental metaphysics, epistemology, and ethics. They are interdependent, and one exists for, and leads to, another. The unity of knowledge and conduct in Oriental philosophy is almost proverbial. So is the insistence on the close relationship between the realization of human nature and the realization of reality. This explains the absence of knowledge for its own sake in the Orient. This also explains why philosophy and life in the Orient are closely related and why Oriental philosophy appears extremely ethical. Since the first and last problem of Oriental philosophy in general is human perfection and freedom, it is inevitable that ethics should be of paramount importance in Oriental philosophy. The problem of ethics is discussed in another chapter. Suffice it to say that in order to get a clear understanding of Oriental ethics, one must view it against the background of Oriental philosophy as a whole, metaphysics and epistemology included. Unless we remember that ultimate reality, to the minds of most Oriental philosophers, is amoral, we will find it difficult to understand why they insist that the distinction of right and wrong is acceptable and justified only for the empirical world. Again, unless we appreciate the relationship between the One and the Many in Oriental philosophy, we are likely to underestimate the proper significance which Oriental philosophy attaches to the individual.

Problems such as the status of the individual are forcing Western philosophy and Oriental philosophy to meet face to face. If the world is going to enjoy peace at all, the patterns of life of the various peoples must not be fundamentally incompatible. Therefore, as a united world is dictated by the progress of scientific inventions and cultural contact, a world philosophy must be evolved. We hope that the day of the emergence of a world philosophy is not far remote. There are already signs that the Orientals want their philosophy to be Westernized to some extent, to be more scientific, more rational, more positive and more affirmative with regard to the particular. At the same time, the Oriental emphasis on intuition, monism, the harmony between man and nature, the transmutation of evil by human effort, the tranquillity of mind, the ethics of simplicity, contentment, nonviolence, and noninjury, and above all, the concept of the undifferentiated continuum or the "field," may offer the West some food for thought. These Western and Oriental tendencies, in a properly balanced synthesis, may produce or constitute a world philosophy worthy of the name.

CHAPTER VIII

The Complementary Emphases of Eastern Intuitive and Western Scientific Philosophy

By Filmer S. C. Northrop

To DETERMINE the relation between diverse things it is necessary to express each in terms of a common denominator. One would not attempt to relate three-fifths to four-sevenths in mathematics without first reducing these two fractions to thirty-fifths. This is equally true of different philosophical theories, and especially so of systems which contrast as sharply as those of the East and the West. Before there can be a trustworthy comparative analysis of Oriental and Occidental philosophical doctrines there must be an unambiguous, commensurable terminology in which to express them. When such a terminology is provided, certain very interesting and important relationships appear.

THE NECESSITY OF A TECHNICAL TERMINOLOGY

This common denominator for international understanding is not given by the linguist's expert translation of the Sanskrit, Chinese or Japanese texts into the English language. This is necessary, but it is not sufficient. No one would suppose that the most competent translation of Professor Einstein's original paper on the Special Theory of Relativity from the German into English would provide a sufficient basis for comparing the theory of relativity with Newton's mechanics. A knowledge of physics would also be necessary. Similarly, the trustworthy student of comparative philosophy must be more than a mere linguist or possess more than trustworthy translations by linguists; in addition he must have a professional mastery of the problems, methods and theories of philosophy.

Additional difficulties remain. They arise from the nature of (a) the symbolism and (b) the subject-matter of philosophy.

At first sight the symbolism of philosophy seems easy to understand. Words of ordinary discourse are used. A little reading of philosophical treatises soon discloses, however, that these words are not used with their common-sense meanings. Ordinary words are given technical meanings. What is even more puzzling, the technical philosophical meaning which a common-sense term has in one philosophical system is usually different from what it has in another system.

The reason for this confusing condition may be appreciated if one considers the two alternatives open to anyone who desires to convey a precise technical meaning for which the conventional language is too ambiguous. One may choose a term with no previous meaning and assign the technical meaning to this otherwise meaningless mark. In short, one may resort to a novel technical terminology. Or one may select some well-known word with the common-sense meaning which is the nearest to the precise technical meaning that one desires to convey, and then either add a restricting definition or depend upon the diverse contexts in which the word is used to direct the reader's attention eventually to the exact meaning intended. Generally speaking, science takes the former alternative, philosophy the latter.

Each choice has its advantages and limitations. A technical terminology reduces to a minimum the chance of ambiguity, but automatically restricts the comprehension of the language to the expert with a professional technical training in the subject. Philosophy, partly because of the relevance of its problems for the layman as well as the expert, chooses ordinary discourse, thereby reaching a wider audience, but at the same time it has to depend upon lengthy contexts to convey its technical meaning. This is one reason why philosophical treatises tend to be longer than scientific ones. A language which uses contexts to convey meanings cannot be terse.

The difficulties for comparative philosophy which such a contextual symbolism presents now become evident.

One cannot compare whole treatises. If the inquiry is ever to get beyond the usual most banal generalities one must come down to chapters and paragraphs and sentences. One must take up specific doctrines and designate them by specific words. But to do this is to pull the sentences and words from their contexts, thereby losing their technical and philosophically important meaning.

The utter inadequacy of the expert linguist's translation of diverse philosophical systems into a common language also becomes evident. All that such translations can do is to give the dictionary renderings of the individual terms, but these provide only the common-sense, not the technical philosophical, meanings. Nor is the difficulty overcome if the expert translator is also an expert philosopher. As we have noted, the same common-sense word in the context of one philosophical theory has one technical meaning, in the context of a different philosophical theory a different meaning. This is especially true, as we shall see later, if one of the theories is from the East and the other from the West.

The point is that the terms of ordinary discourse are quite adequate, when developed at length systematically in various contexts, to convey the technical doctrine of a single philosopher or philosophical theory, but they are utterly inadequate to serve as the common denominator into which one translates diverse philosophical systems for the purpose of comparison. This is true of different Western as well as of Eastern systems. When philosophy becomes comparative, the character of its symbolism necessitates the introduction of a technical terminology.

The subject-matter of philosophy enforces the same conclusion. The total object of human inquiry embraces the entire range of experience. This is entirely too complex and extensive for any one discipline to investigate and comprehend. The task has to be broken up into its different portions, assigned to different specialists. Roughly speaking the special sciences treat restricted local factors in experience, such as living organisms or heavenly bodies, whereas philosophy has as its province the equally evident extensive factors of experience which are common to these more local details.

Because of its localized subject-matter, any special science attains precise determinate concreteness and intensive accuracy with respect to details, but only at the cost of leaving numerous equally important factors out of account, with the attendant risk of a loss of one's sense of proportions. Philosophy, on the other hand, because of its attention upon the more general extensive, but none the less factual, items in experience is able to keep technical details in their actual places, thereby preserving a sense of proportions, but only if it includes the data of the special sciences and of common sense in its own final extensive and systematic doctrine.

But to do this is to place the facts of common sense and technical science in a wider context. The difference between one philosophical theory and another is that this context is defined in different ways. Consequently, the philosophically important thing about any common-sense term as it enters into any philosophical theory is not its bare dictionary meaning, but the particular contextual meaning usually unique to the philosophical system in question. Philosophical materialists, idealists, dualists and neutral monists all admit the existence of what common sense denotes by the term "mind," yet there is all the difference in the world in the ways in which they analyze and conceive of this datum.

Hence, to learn from the expert linguist that the English literal equivalent of a certain Chinese or Sanskrit word is "mind" does not tell one very much that is significant for comparative philosophy. Such a translation provides us with the denotative associations of the common-sense symbol, but not with its technical philosophical, contextual connotative meaning. That which is directly apprehended is roughly the same in any philosophical system, but how it is analyzed and correlated with other factors, whether immediately given or postulated, is different; it is precisely these differences which concern us in comparative philosophy. Consequently, to reduce the diverse doctrines of Eastern and Western philosophy to the supposedly common denominator of the language of common sense is to be left with little more than denotative or dictionary meanings, and to lose the diverse technical contextual meanings unique to each system which are the important factors in any philosophical inquiry.

It is often said that Eastern philosophy is more "religious" or more "idealistic" than Western philosophy. Such statements, as we shall see, are very misleading and for the most part worthless, since they assume that the words "religious" and "ideal" have the same philosophical analysis and technical meanings in the East as in the West. We shall find, for example, that the Buddhist religion is atheistic and skeptical with respect to precisely those traits which the West regards as essential for belief in religion. Similarly, in ethics, many doctrines, such as the emphasis on the individual, which the West tends to regard as "good," the East tends to treat as "evil." Conversely, in the case of immediately apprehended factors, different philosophical systems in the East and the West often use different common-sense terms to denote precisely the same thing. Thus the same word in different philosophical systems often designates quite different and even opposite technical philosophical meanings, and different common-sense terms in different systems often denote the same meaning. Consequently, until we have a technical terminology for the commensurable expression of the precise philosophical meanings of diverse philosophical systems, attempts at comparative philosophy are likely to be more misleading than clarifying.

The terminology of common sense, when developed in various contexts throughout the many treatises of a single philosophical theory, may be reasonably adequate to guide one to the technical meaning of that particular doctrine, but, because of the nature of the symbolism and the subject-matter of philosophy, it is quite untrustworthy to serve as the common denominator for expressing and comparing different philosophical systems. Comparative philosophy must have a technical terminology.

A TECHNICAL TERMINOLOGY FOR COMPARATIVE PHILOSOPHY

A theory of any kind, whether scientific or philosophic, is a body of propositions, and a body of propositions is a set of concepts. Concepts fall into different types according to the different sources of their meaning. Consequently, the designation of the different possible major types of concepts should provide a technical terminology with the generality sufficient to include within itself as a special case any possible philosophical theory.

THE TWO MAJOR TYPES OF CONCEPTS

A concept is a term to which a meaning has been assigned. There are two major ways in which this assignment can be made. The otherwise meaningless term may be associated denotatively with some datum or set of data which is given immediately, or it may have its meaning proposed for it theoretically by the postulates of the deductive theory in which it occurs. We shall call these two basic types concepts by intuition and concepts by postulation respectively.

It is hoped that the terms "intuition" and "postulation" will guide the reader to the precise meanings intended. Since our aim, however, is to provide a technical terminology, it is important that this be not left to chance; hence, the following definitions:

A concept by intuition is one which denotes, and the complete meaning of which is given by, something which is immediately apprehended.

"Blue" in the sense of the sensed color is a concept by intuition. It is to be emphasized that in our terminology "intuition" refers to the direct opposite of what is given as a hunch; it is used to denote what is directly apprehended purely inductively. Were we concerned only with the West it might be better to call this type of concept a "concept by induction" rather than a "concept by intuition." Since we are concerned with the Orient, the latter terminology has advantages. Even so, the reader must keep our restricted use of the concept as prescribed in the above definition continuously in mind.

A concept by postulation is one the complete meaning of which is designated by the postulates of the deductive theory in which it occurs. Any concept which can be defined in terms of such concepts we shall also call a concept by postulation. "Blue" in the sense of the number of a wave-length in electromagnetic theory is a concept by postulation.

A deductive theory is a set of propositions which fall into two groups called postulates and theorems, such that the postulates formally imply the theorems by means of the logical relation of formal implication. Given the postulates, the theorems can be proved.

In considering any theory, proof must not be confused with truth. Proof is a relation between propositions, i.e., between those which are postulates and those which are theorems; whereas truth is a relation between propositions and immediately apprehended fact. The former is a purely formal relation which it is the business of pure mathematics and formal logic to define; the latter is an empirical relation which it is the task of empirical science and empirical logic to designate.

The relation of proof, defined by the formal logical relation of formal implication, is quite independent of the truth or falsity of the propositions it relates. The proofs of the theorems in Euclid's *Elements* hold irrespective of the empirical question of truth-value, concerning whether Euclidean geometry is that of the space of our actual universe. Newton's proof that the propositions in his *Principia* follow necessarily on logical grounds from the fundamental axioms of his mechanics is just as valid today as it was before the truth of this mechanics was brought into question by the Michelson-Morley experiment and Einstein's analysis. Hence, when the postulates of a deductive theory are defined as those propositions of the theory which are taken as unproved and used to prove the theorems, this must not be confused with the quite independent question of the truth or falsity of the postulates.

If what is meant by a postulate and a deductive theory is clear, one is prepared to understand a concept by postulation.

Our definition tells us that such a concept is one the complete meaning of which is designated by the postulates of the deductive theory in which it occurs. In other words the only meaning which such a concept has is that which it gains by virtue of the properties or relations assigned to it by the postulate or set of postulates within which it is a member term. It means what the postulates prescribe it to mean, nothing more, nothing less; apart from these postulates it is a meaningless mark.

When it is recalled that the proof of the theorems in a deductive theory can be carried through regardless of knowledge concerning the truth of either the theorems or the postulates, and when to this is added the fact that propositions can be proposed as postulates, in the construction of a deductive theory, irrespective of whether there is anything denotatively given in immediate apprehension which is identical with what the propositions propose, then it becomes evident that concepts which gain their meaning from such postulates may have meanings neither derived from, nor *directly* referable to, anything which is immediately apprehended. Such is the technical meaning of a concept by postulation. How theories formulated in terms of such concepts can be empirically verified will concern us later.

THE IMPORTANCE OF CONCEPTS BY POSTULATION

Concepts by postulation are especially important in the Western world. No serious attempt at a precise designation of the major difference between Western and Eastern philosophical systems can neglect them. This importance exhibits itself in three places: (a) Science, (b) Philosophy, and (c) Common-sense Beliefs. These merit consideration in turn.

Western Science

In modern science the first use of concepts by postulation and the first clear distinction between them and concepts by intuition was made by the man who formulated modern physics deductively —Sir Isaac Newton. At the beginning of his *Principia*,[1] Newton writes, "Hitherto I have laid down the definitions of such words as are less known, and explained the sense in which I would have them to be understood in the following discourse. I do not define time, space, place and motion as being well known to all. Only I must observe, that the common people conceive those quantities under no other notions but from the relation they bear to sensible objects. And thence arise certain prejudices, for the removing of which it will be convenient to distinguish them into absolute and relative, true and apparent, mathematical and common.

"I. Absolute, true, and mathematical time, of itself, and from its own nature, flows equably without relation to anything external, and by another name is called duration: relative, apparent, and common time, is some sensible and external (whether accurate or unequable) measure of duration by the means of motion. . . .

"II. Absolute space, in its own nature, without relation to anything external, remains always similar and immovable. Relative space is some movable dimension or measure of the absolute spaces; which our senses determine by its position to bodies; . . ."

In the more precise language of our technical terminology, what Newton is saying in his distinction between "mathematical" and "sensed" space is that there are two different types of concepts for

---

[1] Sir Isaac Newton, *Mathematical Principles of Natural Philosophy*, translated by Andrew Motte, revised by Florian Cajori (Berkeley: University of California Press, 1934), p. 6.

which the one term "space" is used. There is "space" in the sense of "mathematical space," which is a concept by postulation, and there is "space" in the sense of "sensed" or immediately apprehended space, which is a concept by intuition. These two concepts must not be confused, he notes, if "certain prejudices" are to be avoided. In the deductive theory of physics it is always space, time or motion in the sense of the proposed concept by postulation that is used. Put more concretely, this entails that if one wants to know what Newtonian physics means by a "physical object," one does not immediately apprehend the colored shapes of the table or chair of common sense; instead, one examines the postulates of Newton's *Principia*. Newton means by a physical object the kind of entity having the properties and behavior which his three laws of motion prescribe.

Between "physical object" in this postulationally prescribed meaning and "physical object" in the sense of a concept by intuition there is all the difference in the world. From "physical object" in the latter sense nothing whatever can be deduced. As Hume showed, the relation between one immediately apprehended factor and another is external and contingent. Newton's *Principia* demonstrates, however, that from "physical object" in the sense of his concept by postulation, the meaning of which is given by the "Axioms" of his mechanics, all the dozens upon dozens of propositions making up the major portion of his treatise can be deduced as necessary consequences. Among these deduced or proved propositions can be found Kepler's three laws of planetary motion and all the important empirically verified laws of the entire science of dynamics.

Recently, Einstein has replaced Newton's postulates for mechanics with a different set. But in Einstein's theory the same distinction exists between postulated time which flows "equably" and sensed time which flows nonuniformly.[2] Thus, contemporary as well as traditional modern physics distinguishes between concepts by intuition and concepts by postulation and formulates its theory in terms of the latter. Recently, Professor Whitehead and others, in an attack upon the "bifurcation of nature"[3] which the distinction

---

[2] See the writer's "Natural Science and the Critical Philosophy," *The Heritage of Kant* (Princeton: Princeton University Press, 1939), pp. 58-59.

[3] A. N. Whitehead, *The Concept of Nature* (Cambridge, England: University Press, 1920).

between concepts by intuition and concepts by postulation entails, have attempted to maintain that all scientific concepts are concepts by intuition gained from the immediately apprehended by "extensive abstraction." They have not to date, however, answered the evidence from science brought forward against this thesis by Professor Arthur O. Lovejoy.[4]

The presence of concepts by postulation shows more obviously perhaps in the case of the scientific concept of the electron, which was given precise meaning in the postulates of the generalized electromagnetic theory of Lorentz, several years before the existence of an entity possessing the properties designated by Lorentz's postulates was confirmed experimentally by Professor J. J. Thomson. Clearly, in this case, the concept was given a meaning postulationally before any denotatively given source for its meaning was present. Moreover, an electron is too small to be immediately apprehended. Its diameter is such, relative to the wave-length of light, that observation of it is not merely practically, but also theoretically, impossible.

This makes us aware of a second significance of concepts by postulation. It is by means of them that science is able to introduce unobservable entities and relations into its theory, and to predict the existence of scientific objects theoretically which are confirmed experimentally only later, and even then only indirectly.

Were there only concepts by intuition our scientific or philosophical theories could refer to nothing but the immediately apprehended. Our conception of the nature of things would be exhausted with the crude limits of our sense awareness and powers of immediate apprehension, and all Western scientific and philosophical knowledge would have the inexpressible ineffability which attaches to everything given with immediacy.

Western Philosophy

It is not an accident that the most distinguished Western philos-

---

[4] Arthur O. Lovejoy, *The Revolt Against Dualism* (New York: W. W. Norton & Company, 1930). See also the writer's chapter on "Whitehead's Philosophy of Science," *The Philosophy of Alfred North Whitehead* (Evanston: The Library of Living Philosophers, 1941). In the same volume Professor W. E. Hocking has also questioned the rejection of bifurcation even from the standpoint of the theory of mind.

ophers from Democritus, Plato and Aristotle through Albertus Magnus, Descartes, Leibnitz and Kant to Russell and Whitehead were mathematicians, physicists or biologists before they were philosophers. The verified science of a culture cannot use concepts referring to factors other than what is immediately apprehended without the effect upon epistemology and metaphysics becoming evident and inescapable. In fact, metaphysics, when unambiguously defined, is the thesis that there are concepts by postulation as well as concepts by intuition; positivism, conversely, is the thesis that there are only concepts by intuition. Curiously enough, as we shall show later, it is not to the science of the West, but to the philosophy and religion of the East, that one must go if one wants to observe what happens when positivism is taken seriously.

Concepts by postulation were first introduced into Western philosophy by Democritus because of the need for them in Greek physics and mathematics.[5] Plato merely continued what Democritus had initiated, analyzing the unobservable atoms of the Democritean theory into the intuitively given continuum which provided their "matter" and the ideal mathematical ratio which determined their geometrical form.[6] Democritus' and Plato's distinction between the "sense world" and the "real world"[7] is an example of our distinction between what is given to immediate apprehension as denoted by concepts by intuition and what is proposed by deductive scientific and philosophical theory as designated by concepts by postulation.

Aristotle, on the other hand, because of the breakdown of the postulates of the Democritean and Platonic theories in Greek mathematics, due to their incapacity to validate the Eudoxian method of exhaustion,[8] and because of his concern with biology, was forced to reject all postulated scientific objects such as the physical atoms of Democritus or the stereometrical atoms of Plato, and to admit into science and philosophy only concepts by intuition.[9] This led

[5] S. Luria, *"Die Infinitesimals Theorie der Antiken Atomisten"* in *Quellen u. Studien zur Geschichte der Mathematik*, Abt. B. Band II: 106-185 (Springer, Berlin, 1930).

[6] See the writer's "Mathematical Background and Content of Greek Philosophy," *Philosophical Essays for Alfred North Whitehead* (New York: Longmans, Green and Co., 1936), pp. 1-40.

[7] S. Luria. *Op. cit.*   [8] See footnote 6.

[9] To such concepts, the content of which is given empirically, he did, however, add a postulated immortality, due to their logical character.

him to deny any "bifurcation" between the real as given to the
senses in observation and the real as comprehended postulationally
in deductive theory; the former, when grasped in its logical character, exhausts reality. In his attack upon the "bifurcation" of traditional and contemporary modern science, Professor Whitehead has
returned recently to this Aristotelian thesis.

Contemporary students have tended to go astray in their interpretation of Plato and Aristotle because of the failure to distinguish
between concepts by postulation and concepts by intuition, not noting that "idea" for Plato is a pure concept by postulation, whereas
for Aristotle it is in part a concept by intuition. The distinction
in Plato's philosophy between "sensibles," "mathematicals" and
"ideas," to which Aristotle refers in the first book of the *Metaphysics* and which has been shown to possess specific scientific content in the mathematical and astronomical theories of Plato's day,[10]
also turns around our distinction between concepts by intuition and
concepts by postulation. A "sensible" is a concept by intuition the
meaning of which is given by immediate apprehension through sense
awareness. "Mathematicals" and "ideas" (i.e., ratios), on the other
hand, are concepts by postulation. The clarification of the distinction
between "mathematicals" and "ideas" must await the further development, in the sequel, of our technical terminology for comparative
philosophy, and in particular the classification of the different possible types of concepts by postulation.

When this is done, it will become evident also that a certain qualification must be placed upon the designation of the Aristotelian and
Whiteheadian theories of science and philosophy as ones which
use only concepts by intuition. This would be the case in the Aristotelian system were the "sensibles" taken only in their purely psychological character by the "passive intellect"; the moment, however, that one takes them in their logical character as a "positive
form," as one does in the transition from the "passive" to the "active intellect,"[11] then a slight element by postulation has been introduced. The change is not that one rejects denotatively given concepts by intuition from one's scientific theory, replacing them by

[10] See the writer's "The Mathematical Background and Content of Greek
Philosophy," *op. cit.*, and the investigations of Erich Frank, S. Luria,
O. Toeplitz, and J. Stenzel, designated therein.
[11] See Aristotle's *De Anima*.

purely theoretically designated concepts by postulation as do Democritus, Plato and the modern physicists, but that, retaining and using only concepts by intuition, one postulates of their intuitively given meanings a logical status and resultant immortal persistence beyond the brief spans during which they are actually sensed. In other words, one accepts only concepts by intuition and treats them, to use the language of Whitehead, as "eternal objects." What is meant is something given only by immediate apprehension. To this immediately apprehended content which is transitory as sensed, there is added by postulation merely an immortal logical status and persistence. It is precisely this slight element of postulation added to pure concepts by intuition which distinguishes obviously metaphysical theories like Aristotle's and Whitehead's from positivism.

It cannot be too strongly emphasized that Whitehead's "eternal objects" and Aristotle's "forms" are quite different from Plato's "ideas." An Aristotelian "idea," like a Whiteheadian "eternal object," is a Platonic "sensible" given an immortal persistence by postulation. A Platonic "idea," on the other hand, is not even in part a "sensible"; "ideas" and "sensibles" are totally different things. Plato agrees with the positivists and the philosophers of the East that "sensibles" are nominalistic and purely transitory. This is precisely why he says that the sense world is a world of becoming and not a world of being. It is only by giving up concepts by intuition (i.e., Platonic "sensibles") and formulating one's scientific and philosophical theory completely in terms of concepts by postulation (i.e., Platonic "ideas") that one can find the invariants obeying the principle of being which give "genuine knowledge" according to Plato.

Aristotle's and Whitehead's formation of "ideas" by giving "sensibles" an eternal status is a necessary consequence of their rejection of "bifurcation." Having repudiated all scientific objects or factors whose conservation is guaranteed by postulation, no meaning can be provided for the laws of science which hold, even when the scientist is not observing, except by smuggling into the transitory data of sense awareness an immortal persistence which they do not possess.

Plato forms "ideas" by rejecting concepts by intuition entirely in the formulation of the deductive theory of his science and philosophy and by using only concepts by postulation. Moreover, these concepts by postulation are given such meanings by the postulates of the deductive theory in which they occur that they designate nothing either sensible or imaginable. In the Sixth Book of the *Republic*, when describing the passage of dialectic from the "mathematicals" in the hypotheses of the sciences to the "ideas," Plato asserts that one "makes no use of images" (p. 510). It is not that one gives "sensibles" or "images" a logical immortal status; one does not use them at all. A Platonic "idea," with respect to its content as well as its immortality, is a quite different kind of concept.

But it is not merely Democritean and Platonic Greek philosophy and modern science which use concepts by postulation. This is true even of Western beliefs of common sense.

Common-sense Beliefs

Berkeley and Hume have shown that even our most ordinary beliefs, such as the supposition that there are public physical objects, or minds other than one's own, involve much more than mere observation or immediate apprehension can give. These beliefs, like the verified theories of modern science, are proposed by postulation and confirmed only indirectly by observation; they are not given completely, or guaranteed, by direct inspection alone. The errors in our perceptual judgments demonstrate this.

This presence of concepts by postulation in even the layman's ordinary beliefs is obscured by the fact that the postulates in question have been verified through their deductive consequences so many times in our daily experience that we have come to regard their trustworthiness as almost as secure as our belief in immediately apprehended factors such as colors and sounds.

In point of fact, however, there is a tremendous difference. The belief in the existence of colors is guaranteed solely by observation or mere immediate apprehension, and consequently involves only concepts by intuition. The belief in tables and chairs and other persons depends, however, on the postulation of more than is immediately apprehended and upon the checking of one's hypothesis by deducing logical consequences therefrom and confirming the deductions. Since what is postulated involves more than mere immediate observation provides, concepts by postulation are present.

When one passes from common-sense objects to the more deductively fertile and adequate postulated objects of science the amount of meaning introduced into Western theory by postulation increases, and what is meant diverges more and more from the meanings provided by concepts by intuition which restrict themselves completely to the immediately apprehended. As one of the most distinguished contemporary mathematical physicists has put the matter, "the modern physical developments have required a mathematics that continually shifts its foundations and gets more abstract." He adds, moreover, that "fundamental problems in theoretical physics awaiting solution" require further changes in our fundamental concepts of a character "so great that it will be beyond the power of human intelligence to get the necessary new ideas by direct attempts to formulate the experimental data in mathematical terms." In short, concepts by intuition are quite inadequate. Professor Dirac continues, "The theoretical worker in the future will therefore have to proceed in a more indirect way. The most powerful method of advance that can be suggested at present is to employ all the resources of pure mathematics in attempts to perfect and generalize the mathematical formalism that forms the existing basis of theoretical physics, and after each success in this direction, to try to interpret the new mathematical features in terms of physical entities."[12]

This presence of deductively formulated concepts by postulation in common sense and scientific theory has been indicated by Professor Albert Einstein in a paper concerning Clerk Maxwell. Professor Einstein writes, "The belief in an external world independent of the perceiving subject is the basis of all natural science. Since, however, sense perception only gives information of this external world or of 'physical reality' indirectly (i.e., through the deductive consequences of our scientific hypothesis)[13] we can only grasp the latter by speculative means (i.e., by postulating more than we immediately apprehend). It follows from this that our notions of physical reality can never be final. We must always be ready to change these notions—that is to say, the axiomatic substructure of physics (i.e., its concepts by postulation)—in order to do justice to perceived facts in the most logically perfect way. Actually a

[12] All quoted matter in this paragraph is from Professor P. A. M. Dirac, *Proceedings of the Royal Society of London,* Series A, Vol. 133, p. 60.

[13] The parentheses throughout this quotation include my terminology, not Einstein's.

glance at the development of physics shows that it has undergone far-reaching changes in the course of time."[14]

Since the belief in the external world is a belief of common sense as well as of natural science and hence is at best only an indirectly confirmed, highly probable hypothesis stated in terms of concepts by postulation rather than an immediately apprehended certainty denoted by concepts by intuition, this belief, too, need not be the only possible one for common sense. May there not be theories even for common sense other than those which the West uses? The answer must be in the affirmative. They are to be found in the East. A designation of the possible subtypes of concepts by postulation and concepts by intuition is necessary to make this clear.

POSSIBLE TYPES OF CONCEPTS BY POSTULATION

We can postulate entities or structures which we can imagine but cannot sense, and we can postulate factors which we can neither sense nor imagine. A concept by postulation which designates the former we shall term a concept by imagination, one which designates the latter a concept by intellection.

Centaurs, the atoms of Democritus, the Platonic regular solids of Book XIII of Euclid, and the atomic models of Bohr's and Rutherford's classical atomic physics are examples of concepts by postulation which are concepts by imagination. The many-dimensional structures of mathematical physics in those cases in which the dimensions are greater in number than three, are examples of concepts by postulation which are concepts by intellection. One cannot imagine more than three dimensions, yet by the use of concepts by postulation mathematical physicists have no difficulty in defining a space of any number of dimensions. The ratio ("idea") which defines the respect in which two similar geometrical figures ("mathematicals") in Platonic mathematics are identical, considered apart from the two sensed or imagined figures of different sizes in which the identical ratio is embodied, is another example. Thus, the Platonic distinction between "mathematicals" and "ideas" is, when unambiguously expressed in our technical terminology, the difference between a concept by postulation which is a concept by imagi-

[14] A. Einstein, *The World As I See It* (New York: Covici-Friede [now Crown Publishers], 1934), p. 60.

nation and a concept by postulation which is a concept by intellection. The deductive theories of the physics of the nineteenth century which required imaginable physical models used concepts by imagination. The deductive theories of contemporary physics which can only be expressed mathematically dispense with concepts by imagination and use only concepts by intellection.

Concepts by imagination and concepts by intellection each fall likewise into two groups, which we shall term pluralistic and monistic. Monistic concepts designate a single all-embracing factor; pluralistic concepts designate many externally related factors.

The kinetic atomic theory of Democritus or the kinetic theory of heat and gases of classical modern particle physics are examples of a pluralistic concept by imagination. The ether substance of prerelativistic field physics is an instance of a monistic concept by imagination. The four primitive ratios of the four atomic triangles of the Platonic mathematics exemplify a pluralistic concept by intellection. Einstein's tensor equation for gravitation, which designates the invariant metrical properties of four-dimensional space-time, illustrates a monistic concept by intellection.

In addition to concepts by imagination and concepts by intellection, there is a third major type of concept by postulation which our consideration of common-sense beliefs has indicated. Not merely atoms and tensor equations represent postulated factors, but ordinary external objects and other people's minds do also. Concepts designating those common-sense objects we shall term concepts by perception. Tables, chairs and the ordinary objects and persons of social discourse are examples. In designating such concepts as concepts by perception it is important to distinguish "perception" in this usage from immediate apprehension. As Berkeley and Hume have shown, and as we have previously indicated, "perceptual objects" are not immediately apprehended factors; they are postulates of common sense so thoroughly and frequently and unconsciously verified through their deductive consequences that only the critical realize them to be postulated rather than immediately apprehended.

Concepts by perception also fall into two groups, pluralistic and monistic. The many physical objects and people of ordinary discourse exemplify pluralistic concepts by perception. The single, publicly perceived space within which these pluralistic perceptual objects are located is an example of a monistic concept by perception.

Our consideration of the difference between Plato's "ideas," which are concepts by postulation that are concepts by intellection, and Aristotle's "ideas" or Whitehead's "eternal objects," which are concepts by intuition for which an immortal logical status has been postulated, indicates the possibility of a fourth, borderline type of concept by postulation. We shall call this fourth type logical concepts by intuition. They are concepts whose content is given by immediate apprehension and whose immortal persistence is proposed by postulation.

There are also pluralistic and monistic logical concepts by intuition. "Hot," in the sense of the immediately apprehended sensation functioning as a "form by privation"[15] in the physics of Aristotle, and the "eternal objects" of Whitehead in their relation of disjunction to each other are examples of the pluralistic case. The "Unmoved Mover" of Aristotle's theology, in which the pluralistic forms are treated as a hierarchical unity is a monistic example.

The following classification of Concepts by Postulation results:

I Concepts by Intellection = Concepts by postulation designating factors which can be neither imagined nor sensed.

   (a) Monistic. e.g., The space-time continuum of Einstein's field physics.

   (b) Pluralistic. e.g., Plato's atomic ratios.

II Concepts by Imagination = Concepts by postulation designating factors which can be imagined but cannot be sensed.

   (a) Monistic. e.g., The ether concept of classical pre-relativistic field physics.

   (b) Pluralistic. e.g., The atoms and molecules of classical particle physics.

III Concepts by Perception = Concepts by postulation designating factors which are in part sensed and in part imagined.

   (a) Monistic. e.g., The public space of daily life.

   (b) Pluralistic. e.g., Other persons, tables, chairs, and the spherical moon with its back side which we do not see as well as its presented side which we do see.

[15] Aristotle's *Physica*. Book I. 7. 190b25.

IV Logical Concepts by Intuition = Concepts designating factors, the content of which is given through the senses or by mere abstraction from the totality of sense awareness, and whose logical universality and immortality are given by postulation.

> (a) Monistic. e.g., The "Unmoved Mover" in Aristotle's metaphysics.
> (b) Pluralistic. e.g., Whitehead's "eternal objects," Santayana's "essences," or Aristotle's "ideas."

Since logical concepts by intuition are concepts by postulation merely so far as their immortality is concerned and are concepts by intuition with respect to their content, they provide a natural transition from the one generic type of concept to the other.

THE POSSIBLE CONCEPTS BY INTUITION

Since concepts by intuition gain their entire meaning from the immediately apprehended, it is necessary to consider its general character and the factors it contains in order to designate the possible types of such concepts.

We must start with the all-embracing immediacy from which any theory, Eastern or Western, takes its inception. This immediacy exhibits itself as a continuum or field which is differentiated. It would seem that all people could agree on this as a correct designation of what one immediately apprehends, however differently they might analyze it as inquiry proceeds. It will be well to have a name for this all-embracing, initial, immediately apprehended fact with which any attempt to arrive at a description of experience must begin. We shall call it the differentiated aesthetic continuum. The word "continuum" is used to denote the fact that what we immediately apprehend is an all-embracing field. The word "differentiated" is chosen to indicate that within this field there occur factors in one part different from those in another. We immediately apprehend a field which is white here and blue there. The adjective "aesthetic" is added to insure that it is the qualitatively ineffable, emotionally moving continuum of colors, sounds and feelings which the artist presents in its immediacy, not the logically defined continuum of mathematical physics which is a concept by postulation, that is indicated;[16] also only what Prall termed the "aesthetic surface" considered in and for itself is immediately apprehended; the common-sense external object which the aesthetic object sometimes symbolizes is a concept by postulation, not a concept by intuition. This initial, complex, denotatively given fact considered in its totality with nothing neglected is what we mean by the concept of the differentiated aesthetic continuum.

Since the differentiated aesthetic continuum with all its aesthetic and emotive immediacy includes everything that is immediately apprehended, all other concepts by intuition derive from it by abstraction. By "abstraction" we mean, throughout this chapter, the consideration of certain immediately apprehended factors apart from their immediately apprehended context; we do not mean the "abstract" in the sense of the postulated. It has been noted already that the differentiated aesthetic continuum contains two abstractable factors. There is (a) the field or continuum apart from the differentiations within it or the definite properties which characterize it, and there are (b) the differentiations or definite properties apart from the continuum which runs through them and embraces them. The former, (a), we shall call the indefinite or undifferentiated aesthetic continuum, the latter, (b), since they are many in number, the differentiations.

We arrive, therefore, at three major possible concepts by intuition. They are:

I The Concept of the Differentiated Aesthetic Continuum,
II The Concept of the Indefinite or Undifferentiated Aesthetic Continuum,
III The Concepts of the Differentiations. These, for reasons indicated later, we shall also term Concepts by Inspection.

It follows from the designations given above that the following relations hold:

$$I = II \text{ with } III;$$
$$II = I \text{ without } III;$$
$$III = I \text{ without } II.$$

[16] For this reason it is not to be confused with the field concept of field physics or the public space of common-sense perceptual objects, both of which, as we have previously indicated, are monistic concepts by postulation.

It is important to note that these relations do not define the meanings of these three concepts in the manner in which the postulates of a deductive theory prescribe the meaning of the concepts by postulation within the postulates. Concepts I, II, and III are concepts by intuition. Hence, the reader, to get their meaning, must find what they denote in immediate apprehension. Even then the full meaning can be gained only by contemplating what is apprehended.

The most difficult of these three concepts for the Westerner to appreciate is the second. This happens because of the influence of Berkeley and Hume. They insisted that all concepts are concepts by intuition but tended to regard the continuum as nothing but an aggregation of secondary and tertiary qualities. That this is false, an examination of what one immediately apprehends will indicate. We directly inspect not merely the white and the noise but also these in a field. The field is as immediately given as any specific quality, whether secondary or tertiary, within it. Moreover, most of the directly experienced field is vague and indefinite. Only at what William James termed its center is there specificity and definiteness. Thus it is evident that the indefinite, indeterminate, aesthetic continuum is as immediately apprehended as are the specific differentiations within it. Hence, the concept of the indefinite or undifferentiated continuum, gained by abstraction from the differentiated aesthetic continuum, is a concept by intuition, not a concept by postulation.

The concepts by intuition which are concepts of the differentiations fall into two groups. The differentiations which one immediately apprehends may be given (a) through the senses or (b) introspectively. The former we shall call concepts by sensation, the latter concepts by introspection. "Blue," in the sense of the immediately sensed color, is a concept by sensation. "Wants" and the images of phantasy are examples of concepts by introspection. We shall also call concepts by sensation or concepts by introspection, following Professor C. I. Lewis, "concepts by inspection." Concepts by inspection are, in our technical terminology, identical with concepts of the differentiations. The latter terminology is better in reminding us that sense data and tertiary qualities have no existence apart from the aesthetic continuum or field within which they appear and from which they are abstracted. Professor Lewis's terminology is better in providing a single concept for designating either concepts by sensation or concepts by introspection. We shall use whichever terminology is most suggestive at the time. No confusion will result provided the reader remembers that concepts of the differentiations and concepts by inspection denote, and hence mean, since they are concepts by intuition, precisely the same thing.

Professor George P. Conger has called my attention to an additional concept by intuition which is obtainable from the differentiated aesthetic continuum by abstraction. It is a specific inspected quality in the aesthetic continuum with all other differentiations, but not the continuum itself, neglected. Such a concept by intuition we shall term a field concept by inspection. A philosophy which takes this type of concept as basic and sufficient will be positivistic in that it admits only concepts by intuition but will differ from most modern Western positivism by holding a monistic rather than a pluralistic theory of the immediately apprehended. In this connection the philosophy of Bradley is suggestive, as is also Gestalt psychology.

We arrive at the following classification of the major possible concepts by intuition:

I The Concept of the Differentiated Aesthetic Continuum = The totality of the immediately apprehended with nothing abstracted away.

II The Concept of the Indefinite or Undifferentiated Continuum = The intuited continuum apart from all differentiations.

III The Concepts of the Differentiations = Concepts by Inspection = Atomic Concepts by Inspection = The specific inspected qualities or differentiations considered apart from the continuum.

    (a) Concepts by Sensation = III given through the senses.

    (b) Concepts by Introspection = III given introspectively.

IV Field Concepts by Inspection = any instance of III considered as inseparable from II.

This completes the classification of the different possible types of concepts from which any scientific or philosophical theory may be constructed. Since it exhausts the major possible ways of providing terms with meanings, our technical terminology for comparative philosophy may be regarded as provided.

Different philosophical doctrines can now be compared by noting which of the possible types of concepts they admit. By means of this terminology, also, diverse philosophical theories can be defined. Positivism, for example, is the thesis that there are only concepts by intuition. Western positivism has tended to maintain, in addition, that all concepts by intuition are definable in terms of or reducible to atomic concepts by inspection. A metaphysical theory, on the other hand, is one which maintains that there are also concepts by postulation. As we have indicated, the general tendency of Western science and philosophy has been to require concepts by postulation.

Only at those transitional periods in the development of Western thought, like the present, when the traditional concepts by postulation are breaking down and before the scientific ones which have replaced the old are made articulate philosophically does positivism and its attempt to restrict the whole of reality to the immediately apprehended appear in the West.

Concepts by intuition are especially and continuously important in the Orient. An examination of the major doctrines of Oriental philosophy and religion will make this clear.

In what follows it is to be emphasized that we are seeking for the common denominator of agreement underlying the very many differences in Oriental philosophy and religion, just as later we shall attempt to designate the common factor in the West which distinguishes Western from Eastern philosophy. This basic element of agreement in diverse Oriental systems does not prevent them in special instances from introducing additional assumptions which make certain of their positions in many respects similar to those in the West. Likewise, the major emphasis throughout Western thought which distinguishes us from the Orient does not prevent our philosophers and theologians at times from holding distinctly Oriental positions.

THE MAJOR ORIENTAL SYSTEMS

Brahmanism

It is a commonplace of Indian philosophy that it refers to the real as something which cannot be grasped by reasoning or by logical methods. Charles Johnston, in his commentary on the *Kena Upanishad*,[17] has summarized the attitude of the Hindu as follows: "all rationalistic philosophies end, and inevitably end, in agnosticism. This is the one logical conclusion to the search for knowledge in that way by that instrument . . . having been inspired and set in motion by intuition, . . . the rationalistic philosopher instantly turns his back upon intuition and commits the task to the lower mind, which is incapable of finding the answer. Having begun with intuition, he should go on with intuition." As the *Katha Upanishad* expressed it, "Nor is this mind to be gained by reasoning;[18] . . . It is to be apprehended . . . by direct experience."[19] This means that the concept or concepts which designate reality cannot be concepts by postulation and must be concepts by intuition. Our problem, therefore, is to determine which of the four major possible types of concept by intuition is used.

On the first page of the preface to his classical work on *The Philosophy of the Upanishads*[20] Paul Deussen writes that the "thoughts of the Vedānta . . . became for India a permanent and characteristic spiritual atmosphere. . . . To every Indian Brahman today the Upanishads are what the New Testament is to the Christian." In Chapter III, on "The Fundamental Conception of the Upanishads," he adds that "all the thoughts of the Upanishads move around two fundamental ideas. These are (1) the Brahman, and (2) the Ātman."[21] He then indicates that the Brahman "is identical with the Ātman," the former being the cosmical principle of the Universe, the latter being this same principle in its "psychical character."[22] If we concentrate attention, therefore, upon the con-

[17] *The Great Upanishads*, Vol. I (New York: The Quarterly Book Department, 1927), p. 83.
[18] Translated by Charles Johnston. *Ibid.*, p. 222.
[19] *Ibid.*, p. 232.
[20] Authorized English translation by Rev. A. S. Geden (Edinburgh: T. & T. Clark, 1906).
[21] *Ibid.*, p. 38.   [22] *Ibid.*, p. 39.

cept of the Brahman, we shall have the fundamental factor in the dominant system of Indian philosophy.

In Chapter V Deussen tells us what this concept means. "Brahman," he writes, "is that in men and in all objects of the universe which remains over when we abstract from them everything in them that is not-self, alien or different."[23] In other words, Brahman is what we immediately apprehend, with all the distinctions and differentiations within it abstracted away. If the reader turns back to our classification of the possible concepts by intuition, he will find that this is precisely how we characterized the concept of the indefinite or undifferentiated aesthetic continuum.

The Upanishads support this conclusion. The *Brihadāraṇyaka Upanishad* contains the following representative passage: "Has it not been established that the Brahman, the object of knowledge, is free from all differences, as before, behind, and the like, uniform, and, like the lump of salt of one taste?"[24] The reference to taste shows that we are dealing with a concept by intuition, and the freedom "from all differences" designates that the concept by intuition in question can be none other than the concept of the undifferentiated, or indefinite continuum.

The same Upanishad also adds explicitly that the primary concept is not a concept by intuition which is a concept by inspection. "That which the wise call the imperishable . . . is neither thick nor thin, neither short nor long, neither red (like fire) nor fluid (like water), neither shadowy nor dark, neither wind nor ether (space), not adhesive (like gum), without taste or smell, without eye or ear, without speech, without understanding, without vital force and without breath, without mouth or size, without inner or outer; never consuming anything, nor consumed by any."[25] In other words, the immediately apprehended fact denoted by Brahman is neither a secondary quality given to the senses nor a tertiary quality known introspectively. Since it is known by intuition rather than by reason

[23] *Ibid.*, p. 157. See also P. Deussen, *The System of the Vedānta.* Authorized translation by Charles Johnston (Chicago: Open Court Publishing Co., 1912), p. 94. Here Deussen writes that "the Brahman itself is free from all differences."

[24] As quoted by P. Deussen in *The System of the Vedānta* (Chicago: Open Court Publishing Co., 1912), p. 95.

[25] As quoted by P. Deussen and translated by A. S. Geden in *The Philosophy of the Upanishads*, p. 147.

or postulation, nothing remains for it but to be the indefinite or un-differentiated intuited continuum within which the transitory secondary and tertiary qualities appear.

The Hindu does not deny concepts by intuition which are concepts by inspection. The inspected differentiations within the intuited continuum exist. But they are transitory exactly as they are sensed. Having rejected reason and its concepts by postulation, there is no attribution of immortality to what is inspected as temporary, after the manner of the "forms" of Aristotle, the "essences" of Santayana or the "eternal objects" of Whitehead. The Hindu rejects all *logical* concepts by inspection. All concepts of the differentiations are pure concepts by intuition with no postulated logical character or immortality added. Upon this point, as upon all others, the Hindu is a thoroughgoing positivist. There are no concepts by postulation, only concepts by intuition.

Even with respect to Brahman nothing is postulated, all is immediately apprehended. In the discussion between Death and Nachiketas in The House of Death there is the following discourse:

> "Death: A mortal who has heard this and embraced it, who
> has *separated from it all qualities*, and has thus
> reached the subtle Being, rejoices, . . . The house
> of Brahman is open, I believe, O Nachiketas.
>
> "Nachiketas: That which thou seest as neither this nor that,
> as neither effect nor cause, as neither past nor
> future, tell me that."[26]

Clearly, the Brahman is that "from (which) all qualities" have been "separated." Also, it is not an unseen, imagined or thought postulated entity; it is "that which one seest"; it is immediately "open" to one. When one separates from the totality of the immediately apprehended all differentiations and distinguishable qualities, only the indefinite or undifferentiated intuited continuum remains.

Since what we immediately apprehend is a continuum embracing all that we apprehend, the undifferentiated continuum is "the cosmical principle" or Brahman. Since the immediately apprehended

[26] As translated in *The Bible of the World*. Edited by Robert O. Ballou, Friedrich Spiegelberg and Horace L. Friess (New York: The Viking Press, 1939), p. 47. The italics are mine.

self is the unlimited intuited continuum embracing the transitory, introspected local qualities and feelings and not the latter alone, the undifferentiated intuited continuum is "the psychical principle" or "self" or Ātman. Thus, as Deussen indicated, Brahman and Ātman are identical. In our technical terminology, the self is a field concept by intuition, not a mere transitory aggregate of atomic concepts by inspection.

The field character of Brahman, and of Ātman (the Self) which is identical with Brahman, is explicitly stated by the Hindu Scriptures. "An ocean is that one seer, without any duality; this is the Brahma-world." The self "knows nothing that is without, nothing that is within." Everything immediately apprehended is in the one continuum. "But there is then no second, nothing else different from him that he would see." Its "nature is like ether."[27]

The differentiations within the intuited continuum which is the self are transitory. The field, or intuited continuum itself, apart from the differentiations which come and go within it, is not transitory. This distinction between these two types of intuited factors making up the complex, differentiated, intuited self is the key to the doctrine of salvation in Oriental religion.

To understand this it is necessary to attempt to comprehend why the Hindus and, as we shall show, all the major Oriental philosophical and religious leaders regard immediate apprehension, without any recourse to the postulates of reason, to be capable of guaranteeing the immortal or nontransitory character of the immediately apprehended, undifferentiated continuum which is the "true" portion of the self. The reason is that the transitory is the temporal, and intuition alone informs us that time does not embrace the whole continuum, thereby making the latter transitory, but is instead intuited as but one dimension standing over against the distinguishable spatial dimensions. The entire continuum, involving spatial dimensions other than the temporal dimension, is more than and hence outside the temporal and thereby escapes the transitoriness of anything temporal. The temporal and transitory are within the continuum instead of the continuum being within time. Consequently, the field component of the complex, intuited self is not subject to the ravages of time.

[27] *The Bible of the World, op. cit.*, pp. 58, 57, 60.

Once this is realized, the philosophy and religion of the Upanishads become intelligible as a purely empirical thesis. There is no
reality except what is immediately apprehended. That which is
immediately apprehended is distinguishable into two factors—one,
the specific differentiations given through the senses or introspectively; the other, the immediately apprehended continuum which is
not given by any specific sense. The immediately inspected continuum, considered apart from its differentiations, is nontransitory.
The differentiations are all temporary and doomed to die. As the
Katha Upanishad asserts,

> "That which remains inaudible, intangible, invisible,
> Which can neither be tasted nor smelt, imperishable,
> That abides eternal, without beginning or end, greater
>   than the greatest,
> He who knows that has escaped the jaws of death."[28]

A Westerner may well wonder how the knowledge of that denoted by the concept of the indeterminate continuum will permit
one to escape the "jaws of death." This question also marks the
transition from Brahman to Ātman. The immediately apprehended
knower, considered as a determinate creature, is not primary and
irreducible. He, like the intuited determinate object of knowledge,
precisely because of his distinction from the object of knowledge, is
a differentiation in the otherwise undifferentiated intuited manifold. But to realize this is to become aware that the knower is the
indefinite intuited field common to his determinate self and all other
determinate intuited things as much as he is the determinate complex of transitory qualities which he inspects when he immediately
apprehends himself through the senses or introspectively. This
follows because, for the Hindu, all concepts by inspection are field
concepts by inspection. Since the indeterminate continuum is, by
virtue of its all-embracing field character, as indicated in the previous paragraph, outside time, the self in this sense "escapes the
jaws of death" also.

As the *Katha Upanishad* puts it, "The wise man, considering that
the activity of the powers of perception and action (the differentiated portion of the intuited self) is separate from his real being
(the undifferentiated field factor in the intuited self and in all in-

---

[28] As quoted by P. Deussen in *The Philosophy of the Upanishads*, p. 148.

tuited objects),[29] and that they have their rising and setting, as of activities arising apart from himself, grieves not."[30]

This quotation makes it clear that the introspected differentiations in the aesthetic continuum which constitute the empirical self are just as transitory as the sensed differentiations in the same continuum which constitute the empirical object. The determinate subject and the determinate object, being differentiations within the continuum common to both, are equally transitory. For this reason there is no immortality of the determinate personality in the Hindu religion. Only the indeterminate continuum which, since it embraces the distinction between subject and object,[31] is as much external cosmical principle (Brahman) as it is subjective psychical principle (Ātman) is immortal. The Hindu's identification of Brahman and Ātman and his doctrine of immortality are consequences of his observation that all concepts by inspection are field concepts by intuition. Every differentiation is a differentiation within one and the same intuited continuum.

The indeterminateness of the undifferentiated continuum is as important as its all-embracing intuited continuity. It is because of this indefiniteness that primary reality can never be positively described for the Oriental. As Dasgupta writes, "They found that by whatever means they tried to give a positive and definite content of the ultimate reality, the Brahman, they failed. Positive definitions were impossible."[32] This follows because any positive attribute gives a differentiation of the otherwise indeterminate continuum rather than the indeterminate continuum itself.

For this reason there is nothing in common between Brahman and ultimate reality as conceived by Democritus, Plato or Aristotle. The atoms of Democritus, the ideas of Plato and the forms of Aristotle were definite determinate things, the very antithesis of the unspecifiable Brahman. Also the Democritean atoms, the Platonic ideas and the Aristotelian Unmoved Mover were concepts by postulation, whereas Brahman, besides being indeterminate, is a concept by intuition.

---

[29] The remarks in parentheses are mine.
[30] Charles Johnston, *The Great Upanishads*, Vol. I, pp. 231-232.
[31] Cf. P. Deussen, *The System of the Vedānta*, p. 95.
[32] Surendranath Dasgupta, *A History of Indian Philosophy* (Cambridge: University Press, 1922), Vol. I, p. 44.

To find Brahman, no shift from what is immediately apprehended, to an unobserved postulated world, known only by the imagination or the intellect, is necessary. Having started with intuition, meaning thereby that given with immediacy, the Hindu remains with intuition. To the very end he is a thoroughgoing empiricist and positivist. He merely shifts his attention within the complex differentiated aesthetic continuum from the differentiations to the continuum of which they are the differentiations. Thereby, he learns to view conduct and life from the standpoint of the indeterminate manifold within one's determinate intuited self and all determinate intuited data and not merely from the standpoint of the determinate self considered as nothing but the transitory aggregate of successive impressions denoted solely by atomic concepts by inspection.

"If he has come to the knowledge of It (Brahman) in this present life, this is the supreme good. . . . Searching for, and discerning It in all things that are, sages, going forth from this world, become immortal."[33] As Charles Johnston, in his commentary upon this passage, has put it, "What is needed is the direction of attention to what is already there."[34] One does not leave the complex, differentiated manifold given in immediate apprehension by resorting to an unobservable reality designated by concepts by postulation; one merely neglects the differentiations while retaining the field and directs one's attention to this field in and by itself, much after the manner in which, upon sensing a colored shape, one might direct attention to the color while neglecting the shape or to the shape while neglecting the color.

In the Appendix to *The System of the Vedānta*,[35] Deussen points out that its Scripture "distinguishes two forms (*rūpa*) of Brahman: the higher, attributeless (*param, nirguṇam*) and the lower attribute-possessing (*aparam, saguṇam*) Brahman." He adds that "In the former case it is taught that Brahman is without any attributes (*guṇa*), differences (*viśesha*), forms (*ākāra*), and limitations (*upādhi*)—in the latter, for the purpose of worship many attributes, differences, forms, and limitations are ascribed to him."

Whether this compromise in the interest of practical expediency eventually corrupted and obscured the fundamental doctrine, need

---

[33] *The Great Upanishads, op. cit.*, p. 212.
[34] *Ibid.*, pp. 72-73.
[35] *Loc. cit.*, p. 456.

not concern us here. What is important is that the need for a new movement arose within India taking one back to the concept of an intuited irreducible manifold which is indeterminate and undifferentiated. This movement is Buddhism.

Buddhism

Buddhism is an interracial and international philosophy and religion. It arose in India, passed to Tibet, China and Korea, and exists today in remarkably pure form in Japan. An adequate treatment of it must deal, therefore, not merely with the original Sanskrit texts, but also with its development in diverse Chinese and Japanese texts and schools. It is not an exaggeration to say that the one scholar, perhaps above all others, who has investigated Buddhism in this all-comprehensive way is Dr. Junjirō Takakusu, Emeritus Professor of Sanskrit in the Imperial University of Tokyo. In our analysis of Buddhism we shall rest very heavily, therefore, upon the lectures and the mimeographed volume[36] written by Professor Takakusu for the members of his course on Buddhism in the 1939 Summer Session of the University of Hawaii, in connection with the East-West Conference of Philosophers.

The first thing which impresses one who examines Buddhism in the light of Professor Takakusu's systematic analysis is the large number of technical systems in which it is formulated. One finds theories developed with technical terms and distinctions as subtle, and formal, and intricate as those of the most abstract and sophisticated of Western philosophical theories. We shall consider the four major systems, as designated by Professor Takakusu, from which many other diverse systems stem. They are (1) Realistic Hīnayānistic, (2) Nihilistic Hīnayānistic, (3) Semi-Mahāyānistic and (4) Nihilistic Mahāyānistic Buddhism.

Systems (1) and (3) were formulated by Vasubandhu (420-500 A.D.) ; System (2) is the work of Harivarman (c. 250-350 A.D.), and System (4) is the creation of Nāgārjuna (c. 100-200 A.D.). Through these four systems as related by later thought there runs a dialectic of negation which culminates in the thoroughgoing Nihilism of the Mahāyānistic Buddhism (4) of Nāgārjuna. Only in the

[36] J. Takakusu, *Buddhist Philosophy and Philosophy of the Buddhist Religion.* 1939.

latter system does the logical method used in arriving at all four systems reach its final consequence.

An examination of the dates of the four systems reveals one very interesting point. The logical order of the dialectic is not the chronological order of the original formulation of the four theories. The final product of the dialectic of negation, the Nihilistic Mahā-yānistic Buddhism of Nāgārjuna, was the first system to be formulated chronologically. Thus the rationalistic dialectic of negation as developed by later scholars and applied to the four systems gave one nothing more than what one had initially before the dialectic was applied. This means that the product of the rationalistic dialectical method was actually discovered and hence must be knowable quite apart from the method. If what the dialectic leads to is something knowable by immediate apprehension as denoted by a concept by intuition, and if the function of the dialectic is not to present the truth directly but to eliminate error step by step, finally leaving what remains to be known by intuition, then the fact that what is last logically is first chronologically becomes intelligible. Such is the case.

The dialectic begins with the ordinary doctrine of common sense. According to the latter doctrine, the world is to be thought of as a system of (a) external physical objects in relation to (b) persistent persons who have (c) ideas about these objects and themselves.

System (1), Vasubandhu's Realistic Hīnayānistic Buddhism, is the result of applying the principle of negation to the common-sense doctrine of the persistent personal self. Its fundamental thesis is *pudgala-śūnyatā*, which, as translated by Professor Takakusu, means "personality-empty," i.e., the emptiness of the concept of the persistent determinate self. It is precisely the point which Hume makes with respect to Berkeley for Western philosophy. The thesis is that the notion of the personal self as a persistent substance designated by concepts by postulation which are concepts by perception does not designate anything real; there is, so far as the self is concerned, only the intuited manifold with its transitory succession of determinate factors denoted solely by concepts by intuition. In this manner the doctrine of the Sarva-asti school of Vasubandhu [System (1)], arises.

The important thing to note about this Buddhist doctrine is that it still retains the belief in the persistent determinate material object even though it has rejected the persistent determinate personal

REALISM	NEGATIVISM (1)	IDEALISM	NEGATIVISM (2)
Hinayānistic (Realism) *Sarva-asti school* (holding that everything exists)	Hinayānistic (Nihilism) *Satya-siddhi school* (holding that truth is attainable by antithetic negation)	Semi-Mahāyānistic *Vijñapti-mātra school* (holding that ideation alone exists)	Mahāyānistic (Nihilism) *Madhyamika school* (holding that truth is attainable by synthetic negation)
Pudgala-śūnyatā (denying individuality)	*Sarva-dharma-śūnyatā* (denying the reality of all—matter and mind)	*Bahya-artha-śūnyatā* (denying the reality of all outside things)	*Sarva-dharma-śūnyatā* (denying the reality of all—matter and mind and all attachments of living beings; thereby striving to reach the "highest" truth [Middle Path] which can be conceived only by negation or the negation of negation)
Middle Path as the ideal way in practical life; neither optimistic nor pessimistic.	Middle Path Truth attainable by the recognition of nonentity, admitting neither individuality (*Pudgala*) nor reality of matter and mind (*Dharma*). All end in Nirvāna (void). Nihilism as opposed to Realism.	Middle Path or Truth lies neither in recognizing the reality of all things because outer things do not exist, nor in recognizing the non-reality of all things because ideations do exist.	Middle Path attained by either reciprocal negation or repetitional negation; reciprocal negation being the eightfold denial of phenomena of being, and repetitional negation being the fourfold serial denial of the popular and the higher ideas.
Vasubandhu (420-500 A.D.)	Harivarman (c. 250-350 A.D.) Chinese translation 407 A.D.	Vasubandhu (420-500 A.D.)	Nāgārjuna (c. 100-200 A.D.)

THE FOUR MAJOR SYSTEMS OF BUDDHISM

From Professor Junjirō Takakusu's mimeographed outline of Buddhist philosophy, page 5.

self. Thus there is hardly a counterpart of this doctrine in the Western world. Modern Western philosophy lost confidence in the postulate of the existence of the persistent material object with Descartes and Berkeley, while retaining absolute confidence in the persistent self before it rejected the postulate of a persistent determinate self with Hume. Instead of beginning with the certainty of the self as does Modern Western philosophy with Descartes, Buddhism offers the example, in the Hīnayānistic school of Vasubandhu, of a philosophy which denies the persistent determinate self while it still retains belief in physical objects and the postulated external world.

The application of the principle of negation to the latter doctrine produces System (2), the Nihilistic Hīnayānistic Buddhism of Harivarman, represented by the Satyasiddhi school. The fundamental thesis of this school is *"Sarva-dharma-śūnyatā,"* which literally translated means "all-elements-emptiness." In other words, not merely the postulated selves, but even the postulated external objects of common sense are denied. There are neither determinate mental nor determinate material substances which are persistent. Concepts by postulation which are concepts by perception do not designate anything real.

To this negation of subjective, persistent, determinate, personal substances and of objective, persistent, material substances, it is possible to apply a second negation which gives, in addition to the negative doctrine concerning what does not exist, the positive thesis that ideas alone exist. This produced System (3), the Semi-Mahāyānistic Buddhism, Vasubandhu's second doctrine. This doctrine is attached to the Vijñaptimātra school, which literally translated means "the ideation-only" school. This is the Oriental equivalent of the philosophy of Hume and Mach.

To this doctrine it is possible to make one final application of the principle of negation. The result, in the words of Professor Takakusu, is "the fourfold serial denial of the popular and the higher ideas." Even the ideas of Hume considered by themselves without reference to the mind or to objects are denied to represent the primary factor. This is the thoroughgoing Nihilism of the Mahāyānistic Buddhism of Nāgārjuna. Here the dialectic of negation of Buddhistic logic reaches its final conclusion. The primary reality is not designatable by any determinate concepts whatever, neither concepts by postulation referring to persisting determinate selves and external objects, nor concepts by intuition which are concepts by inspection referring to mere determinate secondary or tertiary qualities.

Nevertheless, this thoroughgoing dialectic of negation takes one to the positive factor by showing what it is not; anything determinate, whether it be an immediately apprehended secondary or tertiary quality denoted by a concept by inspection or an unobserved common-sense or scientific object designated by a concept by postulation, is rejected as not giving trustworthy knowledge. What remains over is the positive factor. Since it is not designated by the logical method of dialectic it must be something immediately apprehended. Hence the concept which denotes it must be a concept by intuition. Since it is not a concept by intuition which is a concept of the differentiations (Type III), nothing remains for it but to be the concept by intuition of Type II, namely, the concept of the indeterminate aesthetic continuum. This is precisely what Nihilistic Mahāyānistic Buddhism designates it to be. The "highest truth" is "absolute emptiness";[37] that is, the differentiated field of immediate apprehension with the differentiations within it "blown" or "emptied" out.

By a rationalistic process of dialectical negation, historical Buddhism arrives at precisely the same intuitional concept of ultimate reality as Hinduism and Nāgārjuna reached by a more direct, purely empirical process of pure intuition and abstraction. The thesis that the basic concept of Brahmanism and Buddhism is the concept of the indeterminate manifold may be regarded, therefore, as established.

Before turning to the analysis of Taoism, two points with respect to Buddhism, often misrepresented, are to be noted.

First, Buddhism uses concepts by postulation as well as concepts by intuition in certain of its several formulations. The concept of the external world of the Realistic Hīnayānistic school of Vasubandhu is an example. But instead of using concepts by postulation as in the West, to designate the real, Buddhism uses them in conjunction with the logic of negation to establish the point that they do not designate the real. They merely guide one to what remains

[37] Cf. J. Takakusu. *Ibid.*

over when the rationalistic principle of negation is applied to the utmost limit.

Secondly, the dialectical logic of negation of Buddhism functions exactly oppositely to that of Hegel. When Hegel applies negation to a thesis and arrives at an antithesis, he then passes on to a more inclusive concept of the real which takes up within itself as synthesis the determinate distinguished thesis and antithesis. But when Buddhism applies negation to a thesis, that thesis is thrown away, and when it applies it again, the antithesis is thrown away also. For example, when Nihilistic Hīnayānistic Buddhism applies negation to mental and material substances, they are dropped, giving in the Semi-Mahāyānistic school the antithesis of ideas only, and when negation is again applied to the latter doctrine, the determinate ideas as designative of the real are dropped also. Thus the final reality arrived at by the Buddhistic dialectic of negation is what remains after everything determinate, whether mere determinate idea or postulated thing beyond idea, has been negated and rejected to the limit. There is no bringing together of the antithetical factors into a more inclusive absolute synthesis. It is quite erroneous, therefore, to identify Brahman or Nirvāṇa or the Buddha-nature of Hinduism and Buddhism with the absolute of Hegel. Hegel's absolute includes within itself all antithetical determinatenesses and differentiations. The ultimate reality as envisaged by the East is without specific properties: it is bare indeterminate experience designatable by no determinate concept, known only by intuition, and even then only after the differentiations, ordinarily apprehended along with it, are neglected.

When the unredeemed negativity, with respect to the determinate, of the Buddhist dialectic of negation is appreciated, one is prepared the better to understand the otherwise paradoxical character of Hindu and Buddhist writings. One comprehends the *Brihadāraṇyaka Upanishad* when it says that the Ātman "is not so, not so (*neti, neti*)"; nothing determinate designates the real. It is what remains when all specific factors, whether postulated or intuited, are denied or neglected. Since every definite property is a differentiation of the indefinite continuum one can correctly say that the latter is in all determinate intuited things while also denying that it is characterized by any specific predicate.

"That moves, That moves not;
That is far off, That is as if near.
That is within all this; That is outside all this."

In commenting upon such passages Charles Johnston points out[38] that "One finds exactly the same thing in the *Tao-tê Ching*, on page after page, when Lao Tzŭ seeks to indicate the Way. . . ."

Taoism[39]

Lao Tzŭ, as quoted by Johnston, says: "Therefore those of old said: Who has the light of the Way, seems wrapped in darkness; who has advanced along the Way, seems backward; who has mounted the Way, seems of low estate."

The first chapter of the *Tao-tê Ching*, as translated by Ch'u Ta-kao, describes this Way as follows:

"The Tao that can be expressed is not the eternal Tao;
The name that can be defined is not the unchanging name.
Non-existence is called the antecedent of Heaven and Earth;
Existence is the mother of all things.
From eternal non-existence, therefore, we serenely observe
   the mysterious beginning of the universe;
From external existence we clearly see the apparent dis-
   tinction.
These two are the same in source and become different when
   manifested.
This sameness is called profundity. Infinite profundity is
   the gate whence comes the beginning of all parts of the
   universe."

Again the primary factor is the indeterminate ineffable material of intuition from which come the differentiations which we grasp within it through the determinate senses and specific introspections.

In Chapter XVI, the *Tao-tê Ching* advises one to "attain to the goal of absolute vacuity." The identity of this with what Professor

[38] *Loc. cit.*, p. 27.
[39] In this and the subsequent analysis of Chinese philosophical doctrines I have drawn very heavily on the lectures and supporting source materials on Chinese Philosophy by Professor Chan Wing-tsit, given in the Summer Session of the University of Hawaii in 1939, and also in his voluminous mimeographed outline of Chinese Philosophy.

Takakusu designates as the "absolute emptiness," at which the final dialectic of negation of Buddhism arrives, is evident.

Two centuries later Chuang Tzŭ writes, "Only the truly intelligent understand this principle of the identity of all things. They do not view things as apprehended by themselves, subjectively; but transfer themselves into the position of the things viewed. And viewing them thus they are able to comprehend them, nay, to master them; and he who can master them is near. So it is that to place oneself in subjective relation with externals, without consciousness of their objectivity, this is Tao."[40]

What makes it possible for the self here to "transfer" itself into the thing there is that the self as immediately apprehended is the intuited continuum common to both, rather than merely the introspected qualities here which stand outside of and are other than the sensed qualities of the external thing there. Also it is because the external thing known is the aesthetic object in the intuited continuum rather than the postulated public object in postulated geometrical space that it is possible to "place oneself in subjective relation with externals, without consciousness of their objectivity." The reader will now appreciate why, in the original formulation of our technical terminology, we termed the continuum which is given by immediate apprehension the "aesthetic continuum."

Confucianism

Confucianism may be defined as the state of mind in which the concept of the indeterminate intuited manifold moves into the background of thought and the concrete differentiations in their relativistic, humanistic, transitory comings and goings form the content of philosophy. It is not that Confucianism has rejected the fundamental concept of the indeterminate manifold of Brahmanism, Buddhism and Taoism; always this concept is present to prevent the Confucian from making any of his concrete dicta too determinate and precise. But attention is centered more on the intuited determinatenesses of experience in their transitory and relativistic contexts with emphasis more on the humanistic than the naturalistic portion of the aesthetic continuum.

[40] *The Bible of the World*, p. 508. As translated by Herbert A. Giles in *Chuang Tzŭ, Mystic, Moralist, and Social Reformer* (London: Bernard Quaritch, 1889).

The Confucian writings illustrate this: "A gentleman is careful about three things: in his youth, when his blood is strong, he is careful about sex. When he is grown up, and his blood is full, he is careful about getting into a fight. When he is old and his blood is getting thinner, he is careful about money."[41] "There is pleasure in lying pillowed against a bent arm after a meal of simple vegetables with a drink of water. On the other hand, to enjoy wealth and favor without coming by it through the right means is to me like so many floating clouds."[42] The concern with immediately apprehended, naturalistic human experience, and the use of the concrete imagery of the aesthetic experience are obvious.

Again, "Confucius said, 'If you have the wisdom to perceive a truth, but have not the manhood to keep it, you will lose it again, though you have discovered it. If you have wisdom to perceive a truth, and the true manhood to keep it, and fail to observe decorum in your public appearance, you will not gain the people's respect for authority. If you have the wisdom to perceive a truth, the manhood to keep it, and have decorum of appearance, but fail to be imbued with the spirit of *li* (or social discipline) in your actions or conduct, it is also not satisfactory."[43] ... "Women and the uneducated people are difficult to deal with. When you are familiar with them they become cheeky, and when you ignore them they resent it."[44]

There is nothing transcendental about this ethics. It is grounded in a naturalistic, long-range, shrewd observation of the consequences of different forms of immediately apprehended human conduct. At most only the concept by postulation of common sense is used. Clearly, it is an ethics of this world. In it, to be sure, there are value judgments which pure intuitive empiricism does not give, but these are defined by the norms set by tradition as revealed to Confucius through his insistent study of the classics. As he put it, "If you do not study the classics, you have no guide to your conduct."[45] Mere empirical naturalism is not enough. "I'm not born a wise man. I'm merely one in love with ancient studies and work very hard to learn them,"[46] he writes.

[41] *The Analects*, XVI, 7. *The Wisdom of Confucius*. Edited and translated by Lin Yutang (New York: Random House, 1938), p. 193.
[42] *Ibid.*, VII, 15, p. 162.   [43] *Ibid.*, XV, 32, pp. 201-202.
[44] *Ibid.*, XVII, 25, p. 197.   [45] *Ibid.*, XVI, 13.
[46] *Ibid.*, VII, 19.

It is clear that Confucius took his normative theory of good conduct for granted as provided for him by the traditional ceremonies.
"These were the things Confucius often talked about: Poetry, history and the performance of ceremonies."[47]
Concerning the relativity of purely naturalistically given forms of
conduct, apart from the "guide" of the classics, Confucius is specific.
"I am different from all of them. There is no course of action which
is necessarily agreeable with me, and there is no course of action
which is necessarily disagreeable with me."[48] As Mencius put it,
"When it was proper to go into office, then to go into it; when it
was proper to keep retired from office, then to keep retired from
it; when it was proper to continue in it long, then to continue in it
long; when it was proper to withdraw from it quickly, then to withdraw from it quickly: That was the way of Confucius."[49] With
the word "proper" left on such a purely intuitive and undefined
basis, such tautological pronouncements do not tell us much unless
it be that intuitional empiricism in ethics, apart from the norm set
by the ceremonies of tradition, is rather barren.

The shifting of attention from the indefinite aesthetic continuum
of Brahmanism, Buddhism and Taoism to the transitory differentiations alone, in their relativistic contexts, with emphasis upon
those concrete factors exhibiting themselves in human conduct,
seems complete in Confucianism. Nevertheless, Confucianism is
characteristically Eastern.

First, the real is designated in terms of concepts by intuition,
not in terms of concepts by postulation.[50] Even the intuited determinatenesses are taken with all the relativity and transitoriness
which characterize them as exhibited to immediate apprehension.
No immortal persistence beyond the time when they are sensed is
postulated for them, as was done by Aristotle in the West in developing a natural history philosophy otherwise somewhat similar to

---

[47] *Ibid.*, VII, 17.   [48] *Ibid.*, XXIII, 8.
[49] *The Works of Mencius*, II, I, 2. Translated in *The Four Books*, by
James Legge (Shanghai: The China Book Co. [no date given]).

[50] To be sure, concepts by postulation which are concepts by perception are
also used, but the common-sense objects are taken more in the aesthetic sense
in which they impress the observer than as external objects considered in and
for themselves. For this predominantly aesthetic emphasis of Confucianism as
it has exhibited itself in Korean culture, see *The Grass Roof* by Younghill
Kang (New York: Charles Scribner's Sons, 1939).

Confucianism. This restriction to concepts by intuition, notwithstanding the Confucian emphasis upon the concrete, is asserted explicitly even by Mo Tzŭ, who criticized Confucius because of the latter's failure to develop a logical method. Mo Tzŭ writes, "My views of the existence or the nonexistence of anything are based on what the actual experience of the eyes and ears of the people hold to be existent or nonexistent. What has been seen or heard, I call existent. What has never been seen or heard, I call nonexistent."[51] The rejection or neglect of all concepts by postulation is evident.

Secondly, notwithstanding this emphasis in both the Confucian and the Mohistic schools upon the concrete which is immediately apprehended, the concept of the intuited indeterminate manifold is none the less present implicitly in the background. It was largely because of their implicit confidence in the underlying persisting monistic indeterminate manifold so explicit in early Taoistic and Buddhist Chinese thought and ceremonies that the later Confucianists, Mohists and Neo-Confucianists were so willing to acquiesce in the intuited relativity and transitoriness of all things determinate. A consideration of the primitive ideas of the Confucian philosophy in their relation to the fundamental concept of the indeterminate continuum in the Taoism of Lao Tzŭ, as indicated by Dr. Hu Shih in his *The Development of the Logical Method in Ancient China,* will make this clear.

Dr. Hu begins his account of Lao Tzŭ as follows: "He was a philosophical nihilist. He held that 'All things come from being; and being comes from non-being.' This non-being was identified with empty space. . . . This non-being is conceived as the beginning of all things: 'Before heaven and Earth it was. Alone it stands and changes not; . . . it may be called the Mother of the World.' "[52] By nonbeing Lao Tzŭ clearly means that which is not determinate being or what we, using the suggestion of empty space, as does Lao Tzŭ, have called the undifferentiated aesthetic continuum.

Dr. Hu's quotation from Lao Tzŭ proceeds, "The five colors blind the human eye; the five notes (of music) deafen the human ear; the five tastes spoil the human mouth; racing and hunting madden the

[51] Hu Shih, *The Development of the Logical Method in Ancient China* (Shanghai: The Oriental Book Company, 1928), p. 73.
[52] *Ibid.,* p. 14.

human mind; the highly prized treasures degrade human conduct."[53]
The point is not merely that the undifferentiated continuum is real
and immortal, but that the intuited differentiations within it, being
transitory, do not provide anything more than a transitory ephem-
eral basis for human conduct. Extreme as this doctrine may seem,
it has never lost its influence on Chinese character and conduct even
unto the present day. It makes many Chinese who have not fallen
under the spell of Western doctrines suspicious of causes which
propose uncompromising reform or action and of ways of life which
require that a man should lay down his life for some determinate
principle. All things determinate are relative and transitory. No
determinate theory of man can be taken as an unqualified principle
for moral action holding under all circumstances. Only the indeterminate underlying intuited background can be counted on always.
To this indeterminate factor Lao Tzŭ advises one to attach oneself
and to beware of all determinate forms of experience or conduct as
a permanent basis for living. "Act non-action; undertake no undertaking; taste the tasteless," the *Tao-tê Ching* advises.[54]

At first sight it would seem that Confucius went to the other extreme, emphasizing the concrete differentiations rather than the indeterminate continuum. As Dr. Hu suggests: "Lao-Tze, as we have
seen, carried this idea too far by insisting on the non-existent as
still superior to the simple and easy, and on the possibility and
desirability of returning to the truly original state of non-action.
Confucius was a positivist and contented himself with the simple
and easy as the starting point."[55]

Dr. Hu adds, however, that Confucius, following *The Book of
Changes*, said, "There is the Grand Terminus (—), which generates the Primeval Pair (— and - -). The Primeval Pair produces
the Forms (= ⚎ ⚏ ⚍), from which are derived the Eight *Kwas*.
The Eight *Kwas* (may be used to) determine all good and evil, and
therefrom arises the great complexity of life."[56] This suggests that
all the different determinate things in the world reduce to two principles, here called the Primeval Pair, at other times in Chinese
philosophy termed the *yin* and *yang*, and that this dualism is derived
from an underlying monism, the Grand Terminus or the Great

[53] *Ibid.*
[55] Hu Shih, *op. cit.*, p. 33.
[54] *The Bible of the World, loc. cit.*, p. 497.
[56] *Ibid.*, p. 32.

Ultimate, which is the indefinite continuum of Taoism. It becomes clear, therefore, that even in Confucianism and Mohism with their concentration of attention on the differentiated and the concrete, the fundamental indeterminate aesthetic continuum of Brahmanism, Buddhism and Taoism is still in the background, at the basis of all things and all conduct.

As Professor Chan Wing-tsit has said, "Oriental philosophy is overwhelmingly monistic, nothwithstanding minor systems of dualism and pluralism. . . . In Confucianism, Neo-Confucianism, Shintō, Jainism, Mohism, certain schools of Buddhism, certain trends in Taoism, and some Hindu systems, the Many (are) fully real as components of the One."[57] Even the dualistic principles are mere transitory differentiations in the all-embracing indefinite continuum. This holds true even in modern Neo-Confucianism.

Neo-Confucianism

Chou Lien-hsi (1017-1073), who was one of the first of the Neo-Confucianists, in eulogizing and expounding *The Book of Changes*, writes as follows: "The *T'ai Chi* (Great Ultimate) comes from the infinite. The *T'ai Chi* by its energy produces the *yang*. Energy having reached its limit, inertia ensues. By inertia, the *T'ai Chi* produces *yin*. By the transformation of *yang* and the union therewith of *yin*, Water, Fire, Wood, Metal and Earth are produced."[58] And out of the latter the many determinate things which we observe are derived. Throughout Neo-Confucianism this derivation from the underlying indefinite field of the differentiations which we sense and introspect within it is present.

Even as late a philosopher as Wang Yang-ming (1473-1529) writes as follows: "The adult is an all-pervading unity (one substance) with heaven, earth and things. He views the earth as one family. . . . If he sees plants destroyed, he surely feels sympathetic. This implies that his benevolence includes plants. . . . When he sees tiles and stones being broken, he surely will have regard for them. This implies that his benevolence is one with inanimate things. They

[57] This is from a paper in outline mimeographed form entitled *The Spirit of Oriental Philosophy*, presented at the above-mentioned Conference.

[58] From Chan Wing-tsit, *loc. cit.* Cf. J. P. Bruce, *Chu Hsi and His Masters* (London: Probsthain & Co., 1923), pp. 128-131.

are all the benevolence of the same body."[59] To a Westerner this seems somewhat strange, yet if one recalls that what Wang means by "things" are immediately apprehended aesthetic objects given by concepts by intuition, not postulated, material, external objects designated by concepts by postulation, and notes that all immediately apprehended aesthetic factors, whether those constituting intuited man the knower or those composing intuited plants and inanimate things, are differentiations within the indeterminate continuum common to both, then the statement loses its strangeness.

In any event, the thesis seems established that the intuitively given concept of the indefinite continuum is the primary concept of Oriental philosophy, not merely for Brahmanism, Buddhism, Taoism and traditional Confucianism, but also for Neo-Confucianism and as late a Chinese philosopher as Wang Yang-ming. Confucianism and Neo-Confucianism differ from the orthodox schools of Brahmanism, Buddhism and Taoism in emphasizing the reality of the concrete differentiations taken just as they are intuited as transitory, but in doing so the Confucianist and Neo-Confucianist never desert the untransitory indeterminate continuum from which the determinations arise and into which they fade. Always the indefinite continuum, which only indeterminate immediate intuition can apprehend, is primary, and it runs through the specific differentiations, insuring for the concrete Chinese mind an element of uncertainty and indefiniteness even in the most precise of experiences.

It appears, therefore, that in the major systems of the Orient, the real is always conceived as something denotable only by concepts by intuition and in particular by that one which we have termed the concept of the undifferentiated aesthetic continuum.

IDENTITIES AND DIFFERENCES
BETWEEN EASTERN AND WESTERN DOCTRINES

Positivism

Positivism may be defined as the thesis that there are only concepts by intuition. According to this doctrine nothing exists but what is immediately apprehended. This thesis has appeared only intermittently in the West during those periods, such as the present

[59] F. G. Henke, *The Philosophy of Wang Yang-ming* (Chicago: Open Court Publishing Co., 1916), pp. 204-205.

one, when the traditional scientific, philosophical and religious beliefs formulated in terms of concepts by postulation are breaking down and before the new ones are put in their place. In the Orient, however, it is the persistent doctrine. Consequently, if one wants to see what happens when positivism is taken seriously, it is not to Western science but to the intuitive philosophy and religion of the East that one should turn.

When this is done, several interesting consequences appear. First, there is very little science beyond the most obvious and elementary information of the natural history type. The Indians did initiate mathematics but never pursued its modern Western developments. This is not an accident. As we have indicated earlier, Western philosophy introduces and requires concepts by postulation. A culture which admits only concepts by intuition is automatically prevented from developing science of the Western type beyond the most elementary, inductive, natural history stage.

Second, the emphasis upon the ineffable and the mystical is inescapable. It is a surprising but true fact that the things which are ineffable in the sense of being indescribable and unconveyable to anyone who has not experienced them immediately are the directly observed factors. This is obscured to us in the West because our confidence in postulated scientific objects and the postulated perceptual objects of common sense is so secure, due to the power of our logical and experimental methods for checking such immediately unobservable factors through their deductive consequences, that those of us who have not read Berkeley and Hume carefully, suppose that we immediately observe these postulated entities. Berkeley and Hume, however, remind us that all that are immediately observed, apart from postulated inference indirectly rather than directly confirmed, are the deliverances of our senses and introspections. These are not public tables and chairs and persons but colors and odors and sounds and pains and pleasures. Every one of these immediately apprehended items is indescribable and incommunicable to anyone who has not immediately experienced it. No amount of discourse or of expertness in postulational technique can convey the color blue to Helen Keller. If positivism is correct, everything is mystically indescribable and ineffable. The real cannot be said. Words merely direct attention to it; it must be intuited and then contemplated. To be sure, Western positivism tends to emphasize only the inspected secondary and tertiary qualities, whereas the East concentrates attention on the equally evident aesthetic continuum within which these appear. But the latter emphasis is merely a difference of direction of attention within the realm of the positivistically intuited and not a departure from positivism.

Also, if positivism be accepted, there is no need of reason and logic except as a negative method, since the goal of all knowledge is present by pure induction and immediate apprehension. Logical positivism strictly speaking is a contradiction in terms. To accept positivism, therefore, is to be forced to all these consequences which the East has so unequivocally confirmed.

Conversely, if concepts by postulation are introduced, then the methods of logic and the deductive systematic formulation of scientific, philosophical and religious doctrines which is the unique achievement of the West is inescapable. Since concepts by postulation refer to factors which are not immediately apprehended, the methods of observation and contemplation alone are quite inadequate to test the correctness of theories using such concepts. The only way yet known to man by which unobservable scientific objects can be handled scientifically is by designating their properties and relations with precision in a set of postulates, then applying formal logic to these postulates to determine what else must be the case if they are true, and then checking these deduced consequences by direct inspection in a crucial controlled experiment. Precisely because Western science is metaphysical, due to its introduction of scientific objects and processes designated by concepts by postulation, logical and mathematical methods are a positive tool absolutely necessary for trustworthy knowledge rather than purely negative, as is the case for the most part in the Orient.

This shows in the major treatises of the West. The intuitive poetry of the Upanishads or the *Tao-tê Ching* or the intuitive discursive wisdom of the disconnected sayings of Confucius are not enough. Euclid's *Elements,* Aristotle's *Metaphysics,* St. Thomas's *Summa,* Newton's *Principia,* Spinoza's *Ethics,* Maxwell's *Equations,* and Russell and Whitehead's *Principia Mathematica* are also required. Bare observation, followed by the contemplation of its items, is not sufficient. There must also be primitive ideas and postulates pressed by rigorous, formal deduction to their logical consequences, then to be checked indirectly against the bare inspected data under experimentally controlled conditions.

In emphasizing this use of concepts by postulation and their attendant deductively formulated and indirectly and experimentally verified theory in Western science, philosophy and religion, it must not be overlooked that the West also uses concepts by intuition. This is inescapable since one can verify the existence of the postulated even by the indirect methods of Western science only by inspecting the immediately apprehended. Also, before even Western science can pass to the stage of deductively formulated, experimentally verified scientific theory, it must go through a preliminary natural history stage in which intuition, description and classification predominate. In this stage concepts by intuition are used, although concepts by postulation which are concepts by perception also creep in. A robin, for example, is described as a bird with a red breast. In this description the word "red" refers not to the wavelength in electromagnetic theory, which is a concept by postulation, but to the immediately sensed color; hence, it is a concept by intuition.

To be sure, concepts by postulation are also present. The Western student of natural history refers the "red" to the "breast" of the robin. By the "robin's breast" he means not the mere aesthetic surface in the immediately apprehended aesthetic continuum, but the lower, curved portion of a three-dimensional, public, biological object in external space. The latter, as we have previously noted, is not denoted immediately by a concept by intuition, but is instead designated only indirectly by a concept by postulation which is a concept by perception. Thus even in the preliminary natural history stage of its development Western science is not completely positivistic; the postulated public objects of common sense are introduced as the subjects which the immediately sensed qualities (the redness) qualify.[60]

---

[60] This has appeared in an amusing way in the development of the contemporary, supposedly positivistic program of the Vienna Circle. This movement began with an attempt to derive the technical concepts of mathematical physics from nothing but concepts by intuition which are concepts by inspection together with logical constants defined as truth functions of truth possibilities, according to the theory of Professor Wittgenstein. Thus in its aim it was genuinely as well as nominally positivistic. When Professor Carnap attempted,

In certain deductively formulated Western philosophical doctrines a basic concept by intuition has been present along with equally basic concepts by postulation. The "indeterminate dyad" in Plato's philosophy and "prime matter" in Aristotle's science and philosophy are examples. Neither is a concept by postulation; each has a purely denotatively given meaning. In fact, although they bear different names they are identical; each denotes the immediately apprehended continuum with all differentiations and definite characteristics abstracted away. Translated into our technical terminology, Plato's "indeterminate dyad," like Aristotle's "prime matter" and the basic concept by intuition of the major systems of the Orient, is the undifferentiated aesthetic continuum. It is very likely that this intuitive component of these systems was not original with Plato and Aristotle but came to them by way of Anaximander's ἄπειρον (Boundless) from the Orient.

The Originality of the West

What was original with Parmenides, Democritus, Plato and Aristotle, and with the deductive formulation of science which arose in conjunction with them, was the discovery of an entirely new component of reality beyond the reach of positivistic immediate apprehension and contemplation, which required the introduction of concepts by postulation to supplement the Oriental concepts by intuition, and necessitated the development of the formal methods

however, to carry this program through in his book *Der Logische Aufbau der Welt*, the difficulty indicated previously by Berkeley, of providing meaning for the *public* world of physical apparatus, operations and physical processes without recourse to concepts by postulation, became evident. Consequently, the "logical positivists" found it necessary to shift to the "physicalism" of Dr. Neurath. When this occurred positivism had been rejected. By thing (*Ding*) they mean not the purely positivistic, immediately apprehended aesthetic object which is private to an individual consciousness, but the public, external, material object of common sense. As Professor Einstein indicated in our previous quotation from him, this common-sense public object, to say nothing about the more subtle scientific objects of current physics, is not given purely positivistically by mere observation but depends instead upon a postulate which is confirmed only indirectly through its deductive consequences. In short, the "Ding Sprache" is not the positivistic language of concepts by intuition which are concepts by inspection, but the metaphysical language of concepts by postulation which are the concepts by perception of common-sense beliefs.

of logic and mathematics combined at the end with crucial experimentation to secure trustworthy knowledge.

This new scientific method brought with it a new theory of knowledge. Forthwith, concepts by postulation were used not negatively as in the Orient to indicate what the real is not, but positively to designate what the real is. The rationalistic methods of the logician and the mathematician when combined by the new scientific method with observation and experimentation became not the snare and the delusion which they were to the Oriental but the major if not the only means to genuine knowledge. What the concepts by postulation designated, when properly controlled and tested by this new Western scientific method, was taken as the real. Thus it was bluntly announced that there is an entirely new component of reality designated by the postulated in addition to that which the Oriental had emphasized and restricted to the immediately intuited.

With Democritus, Plato and Aristotle this new scientific concept of knowledge and reality was made articulate as a philosophy. From this philosophy was born a new religion, the Christianity of the Christ of the Fourth Gospel, of St. Paul, of St. Augustine and of St. Thomas Aquinas, which identified the divine factor in the nature of things not with the immediately intuited undifferentiated continuum termed Brahman or Nirvāṇa and denoted by a concept by intuition, but with the unseen principle, termed God the Father, and designated only by a concept by postulation.

The Fourth Gospel does not open with the statement "In the beginning was the indeterminate dyad," as it would have done were it continuing in the Oriental tradition; instead, it reads, "In the beginning was the λόγος and the λόγος was God." This was a shockingly new announcement in the history of world religion. It literally proclaimed a new God, a divine factor in the nature of things which not only is not immediately apprehended, but also is determinate (a limit rather than the indefinite unlimited) and at the same time immortal. To the Oriental this is incomprehensible; everything that is determinate and specific is transitory; only the indeterminate continuum with the transitory differentiation neglected can claim immortality. But to the Westerner this new thesis is not nonsense for there are concepts by postulation as well as concepts by intuition and there is a trustworthy scientific method involving a combination of formal logical and mathematical symbolic and deductive instruments with controlled experimentation which indicates whether what is postulated is confirmed experimentally to exist or not.

"My kingdom is not of this world," says Christ to Pilate. "We look not at the things which are seen, but at the things which are eternal," writes St. Paul to the Corinthians, "for the (determinate) things which are seen are temporal," exactly as the Oriental affirms, "but the things which are not seen (those given by the postulates of a scientific theory which places no temporal limitation on the existence of the primary factors which are postulated) are eternal." Such is the character of the new world religion which arose in the West when its science, philosophy and theology supplemented concepts by intuition with concepts by postulation, and which, because of the effectiveness of the new scientific method devised to control and verify concepts by postulation, concluded that the unobserved component of the nature of things designated by concepts by postulation gives even more important and trustworthy knowledge than the seen or immediately apprehended component denoted by concepts by intuition. Only when we put Western religion in contrast with that of the East do we realize fully the extent to which Western science, philosophy and religion, notwithstanding their internal conflicts, are all of one piece. The key to the novelty, importance and success of all three is the use of concepts by postulation to designate trustworthy positive knowledge.

It appears also that the supposed agreement between Eastern and Western religions, as suggested especially by the translation of Oriental texts by mere linguists, has its basis solely in the use of common-sense terms in comparative philosophy to convey the technical meanings of diverse doctrines. When the technical philosophical and religious meanings of specific Eastern and Western systems are reduced to a common denominator to make commensurable comparison possible by means of our technical terminology for comparative philosophy, the supposed identities are replaced by a clear-cut opposition.

This opposition between Western and Eastern religion centers not merely in the distinction between the metaphysically postulated and the positivistically intuited but also in the distinction between the intuited indefinite or undifferentiated continuum and the specific or determinate, whether the latter be intuited or postulated. For example, the God the Father of the Fourth Gospel and the male principle in Plato's *Timaeus* are identified with the λόγος concept of Greek Platonic, mathematical science and philosophy. This is both a concept by postulation and a concept of something definite and determinate. The same is true of Aristotle's "Unmoved Mover," which defines the concept of God the Father in the Catholic Christianity of St. Thomas Aquinas. In short, the "religious," according to the traditional Western Christian conception, is designated by a definite doctrine or a determinate thesis. This is why an irreligious person in the West is called an atheist.

The Difference between Eastern and Western Religion

Now it is precisely such atheism—such a denial that any determinate factor or thesis of any kind designates the real or the religious—which the major religions of the East affirm. Professor Takakusu in his exposition of *The Principle of True Reality* in the Buddhist religion writes as follows: "It is natural for people first to seek an innermost essence among the outward appearance of all things or to attain an unchanging fact among many changing things. Failing in this, people would try to distinguish the unknowable from the knowable, the real from the apparent, or the thing-in-itself from the thing for us. This effort, too, will end in failure, for what they select as the real or the thing-in-itself is utterly beyond human knowledge. Such efforts may be called the search after the world principle or that after the life principle. The method of search is also various. Some are monistic or pantheistic, while others are dualistic or pluralistic. Against all these views Buddhism stands aloof by itself. Buddhism is atheistic—there is no doubt about it."[61] No definite characteristic whatever, whether intuited or postulated, designates the real or the religious. Wisdom and bliss are to be found instead, Professor Takakusu adds, in "the state without a specific reality," or in other words in "bare indeterminate" immediacy without any specific property or differentiation.

The religion of the East has often been compared with the God of Spinoza. Nothing could be further from the truth. They are at

---

[61] *Loc. cit.*, p. 56. Also, in his *The Pilgrimage of Buddhism* Professor J. B. Pratt writes (p. 19), "For the Buddha there is no God in the Jewish or Christian sense."

opposite poles from each other. The God of Spinoza had an infinite number of determinate attributes, the religious and philosophical ultimate of the East has no determinate attribute whatever. This is why it can be only intuited and contemplated and cannot be positively described.

Transcendence

The Easterner and the Westerner often speak of the real as "transcending" what the senses convey. For this reason it has been supposed by many, again misled by the use of a common-sense terminology in comparative philosophy, that the Easterner and the Westerner are saying precisely the same thing. Our technical terminology indicates the error. When the Easterner says that the real transcends the sensible, he means the concept of the indeterminate aesthetic manifold as opposed to concepts by inspection. It is an opposition wholly within positivistic concepts by intuition between the monistic indeterminate manifold and its pluralistic differentiations. When a Westerner, on the other hand, refers, as does Democritus or Plato or Newton, to the "real, true, or mathematical" as being other than or transcending the "apparent, relative and sensible," he means thereby that which is designated by a concept by postulation as opposed to that which is denoted by a concept by intuition, irrespective of whether the latter type of concept refers to the indeterminate manifold or to the differentiations.

The Realism of the East

Once this fundamental difference with respect to the concept of transcendence is grasped the utter positivism and pure empiricism of the philosophy and religion of the East become evident. No other religion in the world so completely resigns itself to the immediately apprehended transitoriness of everything determinate, including even the determinate human personality. All determinate things are observed to die. Faced with this fact the West tends to admit it but to say that this is true only of the empirical self and to add that there is another self given by postulation which is determinate and immortal. And even Western materialists who deny this immortality of the self postulate an immortality for scientific factors in the laws of the conservation of matter and energy in physics. But the East, in its rejection of all concepts by postulation as designative of the real, has no such recourse. It takes the intuited, completely transitory, determinate, empirical self as the only determinate self which exists. "As to the life-principle," Professor Takakusu writes in his exposition of Buddhism, the Buddha "denied the existence of ego or soul or any kind of (definite) thing which one may call the real self."[62]

From this, the initial and basic principle of the Buddhist religion, "the principle of suffering," follows. Man in his natural state immediately apprehends himself and those he loves as specific definite creatures; he observes also that all determinate things are transitory and doomed to pass and die. From this there is no escape to a "more real and immortal and determinate self" given by postulation. Consequently, man is doomed to suffer. Never was there such a thoroughly empirical and positivistic religion as the religion of the East.

None the less, within all this realism and pure empiricism there is a way of salvation.

The Eastern Concept of Salvation

The Westerner gains salvation by what he calls the "Word," meaning thereby a determinate doctrine designated by concepts by postulation. He is saved not by intuition and contemplation but by the doctrine—the faith. Even the hard-boiled modern materialist in the West believes this also. The postulated scientific objects, and the laws of physics and chemistry concerning them, define his concept of salvation. By means of these indirectly verified doctrines he orders his industrial processes, builds his bridges, expresses the good life in activity in applied science and hopes to master more and more of the natural processes which determine his pains and pleasures, his health and his disease, and the forms even of his art and literature. But the Easterner has no such concepts by postulation to which to appeal; denying the significance for conduct or for one's concept of reality of all concepts by postulation, salvation must come, if it is to come at all for him, in another way.

The fundamental concept of the undifferentiated continuum, which we have shown to underlie the major doctrines of the East, defines this "Way." By giving up all cherishing of the determinate, transitory empirical self and of determinate transitory intuited

[62] *Ibid.*

things, and by relapsing passively, by indeterminate but none the less purely empirical immediate intuition or apprehension, into the indefinite intuited continuum within oneself and common to all other intuited things, one gains salvation. Time is a differentiation within the all-embracing aesthetic continuum and hence presupposes the latter for its own existence. Hence, instead of the undifferentiated continuum being subject to time and the "ravages of death" which destroy all things temporal, the temporal is subject to and secondary to the indefinite continuum. Consequently, by acquiescing in this immediately apprehended indeterminate field portion of oneself and all things and by intuiting and contemplating its ineffable, indescribable, unspeakable depth and richness, thereby "blowing out" all specific desires either for the differentiated portion of the introspectively given complex self or for the determinate portion of immediately sensed complex things, so that indeterminate immediately apprehended experience alone remains as cherished, one attains salvation.

Taking the standpoint of the undifferentiated continuum which is as much oneself as is the transitory collocation of tertiary and secondary qualities given introspectively or through the specific senses, one acquires the capacity to give up the latter temporal and, mortal portion of the empirical self without regret.

The Difference between Eastern and Western Morality

One tends also to look upon the performances of Westerners, as they turn transitory definite theses into immortal moral issues, thereby destroying all chance for compromise short of vigorous wars to the death, as the overenthusiastic sophomoric conceit of those who lack wisdom concerning the transitory character of definite items and specific personal theses. Such at heart was the standpoint of the older Chinese, the Indian who was not a Moslem and the Buddhistic Japanese before the advent of Western nationalism, Occidental science and Christian missionaries.

Today, with Japan dominated by the tribal nationalistic religion of Shintō, which was revived at the time of Perry's visit to Yokohama, rather than by the nonnationalistic, nondifferentiating religion of Buddhism and with the New China stemming from the Christianity of Sun Yat-sen with its determinate thesis that a man is not a man unless he lays down his life for some determinate, restricted principle, the spirit of compromise has gone out of the East and its people also are at last able to enter into healthy bloody wars to the death just like good Westerners.[63] Western religion and morality have their liabilities as well as their assets.

The first glimmering of light with respect to the ills of the contemporary world will come when mankind awakens to realize that one of the basic sources of its trouble is neither the evil nature of men nor their incapacity to live up to their ideals but the partiality and resultant inadequacy of those ideals themselves.

When this awakening occurs man will see that the major task of our time is a revision of our concept of the good. Toward this end the comparative analysis of Eastern and Western doctrines which we have been making is important since it shows how this concept of the good is identified with and determined by one's philosophical conception of the nature of things. The old East, locating primary reality in the indefinite aesthetic continuum has one theory of the good life; the traditional West, identifying the real with something determinate which possesses a postulated immortality, has a correspondingly different theory of that of which ideal conduct consists.

There are reasons for believing that each side of the world—the East with its emphasis upon the indefinite and the aesthetically immediate, the West with its insistence on the definite and the scientifically postulated—has an essential element of permanent truth. The constructive task of our time is to bring them together, being guided, however, not merely by comparative philosophy but also by the fresh description and analysis of the differentiated aesthetic continuum which contemporary empirical philosophy and impressionistic art is making and by the profound reconstruction of our concept of the postulated in which mathematical physics is now engaged.

A consideration of method in the Orient and the Occident will indicate the direction likely to be taken.

[63] An excellent portrayal of this difference between the old Eastern and the traditional Western concept of the good is to be found in the warm debate between the old Chinese father and his Westernized, nationalized and Christianized son in Vicki Baum's novel *Shanghai '37*, pp. 511-521.

Intuition and Logic in Philosophical Method

Formal reasoning and deductive science are not necessary if only concepts by intuition are used in a given culture. If what science and philosophy attempt to designate is immediately apprehended, then obviously all that one has to do in order to know it is to observe and contemplate it. The methods of intuition and contemplation become the sole trustworthy modes of inquiry. It is precisely this which the East affirms and precisely why its science has never progressed for long beyond the initial natural history stage of development to which concepts by intuition restrict one.

The method of the East is, however, slightly more complicated than this. This complication arises because the main factor to be known is not everything which intuition gives but primarily the indeterminateness and continuity of the aesthetic continuum with the differentiations which it contains omitted or neglected.

Although this indeterminate factor is exactly as immediately and empirically apprehended as the determinate items given through the distinctive senses and by introspection, the intuition of it, in and for itself, is not given by a specific sense and is by no means easy. Consequently, it was natural that methods should be devised to facilitate this difficult achievement.

The Yoga is precisely such a practical method. The dialectic of negation of Buddhism by which one rationalistically rejects all determinate factors whether postulated or intuited until only the bare indeterminate manifold remains is another. The practice of the early Indian sages of sitting on their haunches in the heart of an Indian forest, so overwhelmed with the diversity and complexity of its tropical foliage that the mind loses all capacity to distinguish differentiations and is left to contemplate the unfathomable and ineffable intensity and the inexpressible immediacy of indeterminate experience itself, is a third.

If, on the other hand, that which knowledge is attempting to determine is designated by concepts by postulation which propose scientific, philosophical and theological objects and structures quite other than the ineffable aesthetic material which mere immediate apprehension reveals, it is evident that the Eastern methods of observation, intuition and contemplation, while necessary, are quite insufficient.

The question immediately arises, therefore, in the West, how trustworthy postulated factors can be distinguished from spurious ones. Without logic and deductive reasoning this is impossible. Only by applying formal logic or mathematical computation to what is postulated to deduce from it consequences which can be put to an empirical test in a crucial experiment can the proposal of a crank be distinguished from that of a Newton or an Einstein. This is the reason why the West in its science and philosophy, having introduced concepts by postulation, is necessarily forced to maintain that mathematics and formal logical reasoning, and not merely intuition and empirical apprehension and contemplation, are absolutely necessary to gain trustworthy knowledge.

The precise method involves four parts: (1) The postulational formulation of various hypotheses concerning unobserved entities and structures, (2) the application of formal logic to the postulates stated in terms of concepts by postulation to deduce theorems stated in terms of the same kind of concepts, (3) the designation of what the writer elsewhere[64] has termed "epistemic correlations" which relate the concepts by postulation in the deduced theorems to corresponding concepts by intuition which are usually concepts by sensation, thereby bridging the gulf between the postulated and the empirically intuited in order to make empirical verification or falsification possible, and (4) the immediate inspection of fact to note whether it is what the concepts by intuition designated in (3) prescribe. When the latter is the case, the postulated entities, for example, electrons, atoms or electromagnetic propagations, are said to exist; when it is not the case, the postulated factors are said not to exist. In this manner false theories in terms of concepts by postulation are distinguished from trustworthy ones.

The important point to note, for our present purposes, is that this distinction between false and trustworthy knowledge is not possible without the deductive formulation of theory involved in steps (1) and (2) and the attendant inescapable use of precise definitions and formal logic. This is the reason why the West has tended to insist on mathematics and logic in its criterion of genuine knowledge, and why even its ethical, philosophical and theological trea-

[64] *The Journal of Unified Science*, Vol. IX, pp. 125-128. See also "The Method and Theories of Physical Science in Their Bearing on Biological Organization," *Growth Supplement* (1940), pp. 127-154.

tises have had the systematic technical, logical form of Spinoza's
Ethics, Aristotle's *Metaphysics*, Kant's *Critique of Pure Reason*,
St. Thomas's *Summa* and Whitehead's *Process and Reality* rather
than the intuitive, informal, poetic temper of the Upanishads or
the *Analects* of Confucius.

Stages (3) and (4) in the foregoing analysis of Western scientific and philosophic method make it equally evident, however, that
the West, notwithstanding its insistence upon concepts by postulation as designative of real knowledge, also uses concepts by intuition. Without the latter the bridge cannot be made through the
epistemic correlations from the postulated to the positivistically
and aesthetically intuited, which is essential if verification or falsification is to be attained. The charge often made by Easterners
that the West entirely neglects intuition cannot, therefore, be maintained. It may be doubted whether anyone in the East has ever
intuited and contemplated all the fine distinctions in the different
species of observed plants and animals to the degree to which this
is true of a Western naturalist such as Linnaeus. The West has its
natural history science as well as its more mature deductively formulated science and philosophy, and even in the case of the verification
of the latter, as well as almost exclusively in even the statement
of the former, concepts by intuition and the Eastern methods appropriate thereto are used.

Consequently, there is a very definite sense in which the dominant
philosophy of the West is more inclusive than that of the major
systems of the Orient. Whereas the latter tend to rule out logical
methods and concepts by postulation as positively designative of
anything ultimately real or important in knowledge, the West in
its insistence upon concepts by postulation and their attendant formal logical method as essential for real knowledge of what exists
nevertheless also uses concepts by intuition.

For this reason the East, if it is to gain an understanding of the
aspect of reality grasped by the West, must accept as positive factors the concepts by postulation and the formal methods to which
the sages of the Orient have at most given only a negative value.
The West, however, in order to include within its outlook the basic
insight of the East, needs merely to begin with its present concepts
by intuition which tend to be restricted to those which are concepts

by inspection[65] and to note their apprehension not as atomic simples but as transitory differentiations of the equally intuited manifold. When this manifold is considered in abstraction by itself, apart from the differentiations, as indeterminate, the West will have the basic concept by intuition of the East.

Even so the West has much further to go before it has comprehended the full import of this which the East has to teach it. For the tendency of the West when confronted with the immediately apprehended is either to confuse it and corrupt it with the postulated or to use it merely as a sign of the presence of the postulated and forthwith to neglect it, as Plato and the West's other metaphysical philosophers have tended to do. Thus the West, even in its occasional brief intervals of positivism or in the case of those of its philosophers, like Bergson, who have emphasized intuition, has never learned fully to appreciate the immediately apprehended in and for itself. As a consequence, the Westerner has tended to become emotionally and spiritually starved. He has been saved in theory but unsatisfied in spirit. What must be grasped is the fundamental insight of the Orient that the intuited is quite other than the scientifically, philosophically and theologically postulated and yet is nevertheless an ultimate and essential component of reality worthy of attention and contemplation in and for itself.

Contemporary Western art, which is breaking the immediately apprehended aesthetic materials free from their epistemic correlation with the old postulated common-sense and theological symbolic references, is a development in this new direction.[66] There are other evidences that this movement by the East and the West toward an all-inclusive world philosophy is already under way.

The World Philosophy of Tomorrow

One has but to talk to any contemporary leader in China or Japan or to observe what these countries are now doing to realize that the major factor which they propose to learn from the West is its

[65] There are exceptions to this in certain post-Kantian doctrines such as that of Schopenhauer and in the philosophy of Bergson, also in Gestalt psychology.

[66] For a further development of this point see the writer's "The Functions and Future of Poetry" in *Furioso*, Vol. I, No. 4 (New Haven, Conn., 1941), pp. 71-82.

technology. Their contemporary military adventurers are making this all the more necessary. With respect to religion, art and humanistic as opposed to scientific philosophy many important Orientals regard the West as having little to teach them.

To use Western technology effectively, the Oriental must master the Western scientific theories from which it stems. These scientific theories have already made the Oriental aware of the positive significance of concepts by postulation and of the necessity of the formal, logical and mathematical methods of the West upon which their trustworthy usage depends. In this manner the East is being forced to enlarge its concept of the nature of things to include the postulated component of reality discovered by the West. Consequently, the philosophy of tomorrow, even in the more passive, contemplative portion of the Orient, as well as in the busy, active technical West, is going to be a philosophy of natural science. It is not from mere fancy, but because of a profound understanding of the basic task of his own culture that Professor Junjirō Takakusu, at the age of seventy-two, after spending his entire life upon the study of the Sanskrit and other historical sources of the Buddhist religion, turned the major portion of his thought and time to the study of the philosophy of natural science.

The Easterner's own intuitive philosophy will also be retained. Such a believer in Western science as Dr. Hu Shih has made this clear. In the Introduction to his *The Development of the Logical Method in Ancient China,* he writes as follows: "It would surely be a great loss to mankind if the acceptance of this new civilization (of the West) should take the form of abrupt displacement instead of organic assimilation."[67] To this end he proposes a return to the ancient Chinese classics where the beginnings of Western scientific methods were suggested but never pursued. One result of such a return may well be the rediscovery of the intuitive concept of the indeterminate continuum which is at the basis of Confucianism, as we have previously indicated, and the retention of this along with the concepts by postulation from Western science. Between these two factors there is no conflict whatever. In this manner, the basic doctrine of the East and the unique use of concepts by postulation from the West can be combined.

[67] Page 7.

There is a converse movement in the West already taking it to the same position. This movement has its origin in the intense analysis of the method of deductive, empirical science which is now going on. This analysis centers around the question concerning how theories about unobserved scientific objects designated by concepts by postulation can be verified. The epistemic correlations, referred to previously, answer this question. They also make it evident, however, that any complete and adequate philosophy of science must have an irreducible concept by intuition as well as irreducible concepts by postulation. Otherwise theories formulated in terms of the latter concepts could never be verified, and there would be only the theoretically conceived and no directly intuitable world with all its moving aesthetic immediacy to apprehend and contemplate. In this manner the analysis of the method of verifying scientific objects designated by concepts by postulation is driving the West to the acceptance of a concept by intuition as essential also.

One other development in the West is enforcing the same conclusion. Its modern philosophy began with Descartes' conviction of the indubitable certainty of the existence of his own self as a mental substance. It is significant that Descartes justified this conclusion not on the empirical grounds of intuition and contemplation but on the rationalistic ground that it was logically presupposed in the introspected fact of his own doubting. Only the doubting, not the doubter, was given by immediate apprehension. Thus Descartes' mental substance was a concept by postulation. His concepts of God and matter were of the same kind.

This is true also of Locke's mental and material substances. They arose as a result of the necessary attempt to clarify the relation between the postulated atoms in Newton's physics and the directly inspected colors and sounds and odors given to the senses. As Newton emphasized, only the latter were concepts by intuition.

It was an essential point in the theories of Descartes and Locke that colors, sounds and all other immediately apprehended aesthetic impressions had their basis solely in the action of the material substances on the mental substances. In short, modern Western philosophy has been reared upon the attempt to define the intuited away in terms of an interaction of the postulated.

The history of modern philosophy is the story of the failure of this attempt. Berkeley and Hume showed that upon such a basis the knower could never get the meanings requisite to formulate even the notion of a substance, whether it be mental or material. Modern psychology and psychobiology have confirmed Berkeley's and Hume's analysis. All attempts to clarify the manner in which the atoms of physics and their emissions of energy act upon the mental substance to cause the latter to project the supposedly phenomenal continuum of colors and sounds have been unproductive. The theory has now turned out to be a deductively futile scientific hypothesis. The results in epistemology have been similar. All attempts of modern philosophers subsequent to Descartes and Locke to resolve the epistemological difficulties, into which this modern Western attempt to reduce the intuited to the postulated lands one, have ended in failure.

The reason is very simple. It has been obscured, because of the neglect of the distinction between concepts by intuition and concepts by postulation. Colors and sounds being immediately apprehended things are factors denoted by concepts by intuition. Persistent mental and material substances being unobserved postulated factors are entities designated by concepts by postulation. Since these two types of concepts get their meanings in different ways they refer to different worlds of discourse. The logical methods of definition and deduction can move within a given world of discourse, but they cannot move from one world of discourse to an entirely different one. This is the reason why no amount of logical manipulation by means of definition or deduction can take one from the wave-length for "blue" which is a concept by postulation to the immediately sensed "blue" which is a concept by intuition. Yet it is precisely this which the modern attempt to derive the aesthetically immediate factors which we directly apprehend from the interaction of postulated mental and material factors has tried to do. Modern philosophy has ended in failure because its basic thesis, that the aesthetically immediate is a secondary, purely phenomenal factor derived from the postulated, attempts what is logically impossible, namely the logical derivation or deduction of concepts by intuition from concepts by postulation.

Consequently, modern Western epistemologists are being gradually forced to the same position to which modern logicians have been led as a consequence of their analysis of the relation between empirical intuited and postulated theoretical factors in scientific method, the conclusion namely that there must be an irreducible concept by intuition as well as irreducible concepts by postulation. But to admit this is to accept the fundamental thesis of the Orient that the aesthetically immediate known solely by intuition and contemplation represents something scientifically and philosophically irreducible and ultimate.

The psychological, epistemological, religious and cultural consequences of this, when its full implications are grasped, will be tremendous. A veritable revolution will have occurred in Western thought. Instead of defining the aesthetically immediate away as a mere phenomenal projection resulting from the interaction of mind and body, body and mind and the medium joining them will be defined, each in turn and all together, in terms of the relation between the aesthetically immediate denoted by concepts by intuition and the theoretically ontological designated by concepts by postulation. In short, instead of defining aesthetics and logic, including mathematics, in terms of a relation between psychology and physics, psychology and physics will be derived from a more primary aesthetics and logic. Put more concisely, this means that instead of regarding consciousness as a faculty or property of a knower by means of which he takes hold of and is aware of purely subjective projected aesthetic materials such as colors and sounds, a knower will be thought of as conscious because he is composed of irreducible, ineffable, aesthetic materials. It is the primacy of the aesthetic and the ineffability of anything known with immediacy which is the source of the so-called consciousness of the individual and not the consciousness of the individual which is the source of the aesthetic materials. Thus aesthetics and logic, including a mathematics defined in terms of logic, become the primary subjects, the one as irreducible, fundamental and important as the other, and psychology, physics and even religion will be derived from them—a complete reversal of the basic assumptions of modern Western thought.

Just as his importation of Western technology is forcing the Oriental to supplement his traditional insistence upon the primacy and irreducibility of the intuited with an equal status for the postulated, so recent developments in Western empirical logic and epistemology are driving the Occidental to supplement his traditional emphasis upon the primacy of the postulated with a similar recognition of the importance of the intuited.

The question immediately arises: Which concept by intuition must the West take as primary? Two considerations, the one arising from the contemporary analysis of scientific method and having to do with (a) the status of the epistemic correlations, the other dictated by (b) the principle of parsimony, indicate the answer.

The Status of Epistemic Correlations

The necessity of these relations in connecting concepts by postulation in scientific theory to concepts by intuition and thereby making verification possible has been indicated. The question arises: Are these correlations merely arbitrary conventions or do they signify something in the character of the world which the scientist is investigating? Since the scientific objects designated by concepts by postulation are said by scientists to exist, when, by recourse to these correlations, their postulated existence is verified, it is difficult to escape the conclusion that in some sense these epistemic correlations must exist also. In what can this "existence" consist?

Consider what epistemic correlations relate. They join intuited reality to postulated reality. Or, to put the matter more concretely, they join anything as known by immediate apprehension to what is in some sense that same thing as known by postulated, systematically formulated theory which is verified indirectly and experimentally through its deductive consequences. What character of the intuited might define such a relation to the postulated? An answer is: The symbolic character of the immediately apprehended— its capacity to point beyond itself to the postulated.

That this symbolic character of the intuited exists no one can deny. It is impossible for any one of us to inspect a given visual image without being forced on by that immediately apprehended datum to pass judgment on whether it is the sensuous sign of a postulated object such as a table or chair in public space.

It is precisely because of this symbolic character of the intuited to direct attention away from itself to the postulated that we in the West, in our concern with the postulated, have become emotionally starved because of our neglect of the intuited in and for itself. It is for the same reason, also, that the East has had to devise specific methods such as Yoga and the negative dialectic of Buddhism in order to restrain the human mind into remaining with the immediately apprehended long enough to secure the emotional, aesthetic and spiritual sustenance which it provides, so great is the symbolic power of the intuited to direct attention away from itself to the postulated.

The result of any purely inductive observation of the differentiated aesthetic continuum is to suggest to the common-sense and scientific mind the postulated. Only in this way can we arrive, instinctively, without conscious, deliberate thought, as we do when infants, at a public world of external objects. This the intuited can accomplish for us only if in itself, apart from our conscious minds and wills, it has a symbolic character. We are led, therefore, to this theory of the status of epistemic correlations: They are not mere conventions but have their basis in the symbolic character of the immediately apprehended qualities of the differentiated aesthetic continuum.

The East never pursued the latter materials to the discovery and verification of the postulated and the attendant highly developed science of the West because either, as in Hinduism, Buddhism and Taoism, it neglected the differentiations in the aesthetic continuum in order to direct attention upon the indefinite continuum itself or, as in Confucianism, it considered concepts by inspection solely in their relative transitory relations to each other. Epistemic correlations exist in science and represent a symbolic reference in the nature of things because the determinately intuited symbolizes a definite postulated factor beyond itself, and because the truly (i.e., deductively and experimentally verified) postulated only actualizes itself analogically in the empirically intuited sufficiently to distinguish itself from the merely hypothetically possible by introducing differentiations into the intuited and otherwise indefinite and undifferentiated aesthetic continuum.

It appears, therefore, that the postulated component of reality of the West and the intuited or aesthetic component of the Orient are both ultimate and in part at least irreducible, the one being the symbolic complement of the other.

The Prescription of the Principle of Parsimony

The principle of parsimony reminds us that we must not multiply our primitive concepts, either those by intuition or those by postulation, beyond necessity. It should guide us, therefore, to the concept or concepts by intuition which we in the West must take as primary.

In pursuing this topic some ten years ago in connection with an attempt to clarify the relation between aesthetic and scientific elements in Western science and philosophy, the writer discovered that it is not necessary to take all four concepts in our classification of the four possible major types of concepts by intuition as primitive. It is sufficient to select as the sole indefinable and irreducible concept by intuition the concept of the indefinite or undifferentiated continuum, or as it was then termed,[68] and what amounts to the same thing, "bare indeterminate experienced quality, . . . the determinable of all determinables." In terms of the undifferentiated aesthetic continuum and the primitive concepts by postulation, together with the notion of the epistemic correlates, the other three concepts by intuition can be defined.

The function of the intuited primitive—the undifferentiated aesthetic continuum—is to ensure an intuited reality which is a single manifold of immediate experience. It has the additional merit of keeping the sensed colors of the aesthetic sky in the aesthetic continuum where they are actually observed instead of locating them in the mind of the observer where traditional modern Western science and philosophy were forced to place them. The function of the postulated primitive is to ensure a determinate, persistent, immediately unobserved, theoretically conceived reality. But these two, the intuitional and the postulational components of reality, are not in isolation. Because of the symbolic relation between them defined by the epistemic correlations, they are combined to generate the specific symbolic differentiations denoted by atomic concepts by inspection and that totality of immediately apprehended fact which is the differentiated aesthetic continuum. Thus, given the concept of the undifferentiated continuum and the undefined concepts by postulation as primitive, together with the epistemic correlations, all other concepts can be derived as defined concepts.

In this manner, guided solely by the need for clarifying the relation between inductive and theoretical factors in Western science and philosophy, without any thought of Oriental philosophy, the writer was led to the very concept by intuition as irreducible and hence ultimate which the present study has shown to be the basic

[68] *Science and First Principles* (New York and Cambridge, England: University Press, 1931), pp. 256-261.

conception of the five major philosophical and religious systems of the Orient.

It appears that by independent developments in the East and in the West a new and more comprehensive philosophy is being made articulate in which the basic intuited factor discovered long ago in the Orient is being combined with the newly conceived postulated component of the nature of things, necessitated by the recent revolutionary scientific discoveries of the West. This new philosophy, by enlarging the outlook and values of each part of the world to include those of the other, may well serve as a trustworthy criterion of the good for a truly cosmopolitan and international world order, in which the diverse basic conceptions and resultant valuations of two great cultures are combined into a single world civilization, the richer and better because it includes in complementary harmony with balanced emphasis the most profound and mature insights of each.

CHAPTER IX

Eastern and Western Metaphysics

By George P. Conger

IF ANY apology is needed for metaphysics, let us say that the term is here used to mean the study of the chief general characteristics of the universe. In spite of many traditions, the metaphysical is not and need not be merely the metempirical; any metaphysics should cover the empirical data, whether or not it attempts to push its explorations further. When we come to think of it, metaphysics is a good deal like gravitation; we are somehow inextricably involved in it, and any alleged or attempted contravention of it serves only to show its strength in a fresh manifestation. The danger, particularly for some sections of contemporary thought, is not so much that there will be no metaphysics as that one or another method of obtaining knowledge, about which plenty of merely methodological questions may still be asked, will be magnified into a metaphysics and regarded as an answer to the problem of the universe and man's status in it.

A study of Eastern and Western metaphysics is of no small importance; it should serve to indicate whether or not there is yet available any framework for a planetary philosophy. It is the kind of study in which one could spend a lifetime over a preface, but let us proceed at once to the essentials.

The terms "Eastern" and "Western" are to be taken with some of their usual looseness. The former means India, China, and Japan; the latter for special reasons is made to include Arabia and Palestine as well as Europe and the Americas. The boundary line or region appears to be in the neighborhood of the Persian Gulf, but indigenous contributions from Australia and Africa (except for Ikhnaton) can be dismissed as primitive.

It is noticeable at once that East and West as here taken are in several respects not evenly balanced. The Eastern cultures are older. They arise in territories which are more thickly populated. In the

West the known history of philosophy is correlated much more closely with economic pioneering, political organization, and scientific advance. These differences have had their effect upon the respective metaphysics; to traverse all the ground involved, a metaphysical generalization, like an airplane route, must be high, with a broad outlook.

Of all generalizations, that afforded by the abstractions of number is here most serviceable. Systems of metaphysics differ according to the number of general characteristics, or entities, which are regarded as essential to the world. In monistic systems it is held that everything is essentially one kind of thing; in dualistic systems, two kinds; and in pluralistic systems, many kinds. It should be said at once that there is no absolutely sharp distinction between such systems, and that in most cases each sooner or later involves something of the others. Nevertheless, when Eastern and Western systems of metaphysics are classified in these ways, their most significant features begin to appear; and other generalizations in terms of substance, causality, etc., can be adapted to the arrangement.

We proceed to an analysis of monistic systems, with a series of cross-classifications shown in the table.

In the first column of the table, the monisms are grouped according to their descriptions of the One Reality in terms more or less concrete, and correspondingly less or more abstract. Attempts to define "concrete" and "abstract" are like attempts to define "north" and "south"; they depend upon whatever standpoint is presupposed. When we take for granted some actual situation, anything said to be concrete is relatively more contentful. It is less analytical and less remote. It takes into account or includes more qualities actually found in the given situation as a whole. "Concrete" describes the way we really live, here and now; "abstract" describes the way we think and theorize. As the terms are used here, "concrete" refers more or less completely to the range of personal qualities, properties, or processes, such as volition, purposiveness, intelligence, sentiments, emotions, consciousness. Anything abstract has fewer of these qualities, etc., or has them in a lesser degree.

When their descriptions of the One Reality are thus regarded as relatively more or less concrete, the monisms may be arranged, as in the first column, in a kind of spectrum, beginning with descriptions all-inclusive as to qualities and properties and extending in

MONISTIC SYSTEMS

1. The One Reality described with various degrees of concreteness (and corresponding degrees of abstraction) in terms	2. The One Reality described as known, realized, or attained	3. The One Reality described as being sought by
pantheistic		perception (sometimes called "intuition," but see below)
personalistic	actually	
spiritualistic		
idealistic		
panpsychist		reason, more or less critical or dialectical
	proximately	
naturalistic		
materialistic	ultimately	will, with more or less voluntary discipline
mechanistic		emotion
mathematical		meditation
neutral		intuition (in the more usual sense of this term)
or		
referred to merely as "one," otherwise not described		
or		
regarded as ineffable.	or in some combination of these ways.	or by some combination of these procedures.

more or less definite gradations through a long range to mere references which tend to keep the described or ascribed qualities at a minimum. The word "spiritualistic" is used in its philosophical rather than its popular sense; it is not to be confused with "spiritistic." It must be emphasized that all along the range it is hard to fix any clear lines of demarcation; the terms are used by various authors with different shades of meaning, and even when a meaning is pretty well fixed it tends to shade off into some of the others.

In the second column the words "known, realized, or attained" refer to procedures listed in the third column, and the monisms are classified as actual, proximate, ultimate, or some combination of these. If a monism is known, realized, or attained actually, no further procedures are necessary to establish it for the person who experiences it. If it is known proximately, procedures of reasoning, training or discipline may be necessary before the person comes to the ultimate realization. The ultimate monisms, as we shall see, may be said to include some if not all of the so-called dualisms.

In the third column, the classification singles out various procedures and methods which are used in attempts to know or realize that Reality is One. First we list perception, although few would hold that any ultimate monism is apprehended by mere perception, or that it alone is important. The word "intuition" is sometimes used for immediate perception, but suggests so many components, particularly emotional, that it is better to retain the term for a more nearly integral experience, as below. Very frequent in the literature of monism is the appeal to argument, to reason. Sometimes this has been quite naive, but often also it has been critical and elaborate, with ponderous statements and subtle dialectic. According to many writers and schools, the ultimate unity of the world is to be apprehended by the exercise of will, or by more or less unrestrained emotional responses, or by the disciplines of meditation, or by direct, immediate intuition integrating and fusing all the resources of the human organism and personality.

The monisms as thus analyzed may be reassembled in a large number of permutations and combinations. Some of them, perhaps, have not been tried, even in the long history of philosophy, but many others are readily recognizable, especially when allowances are made for minor qualifications.

Turning to the great Eastern systems, we find that the central philosophy of the Upanishads and the Vedānta, often said to be pantheistic, is more accurately described as spiritualistic monism. A better example of pantheism is afforded by Spinoza's God with an infinite number of attributes. In the Advaita Vedānta the one Brahman is characterized by *sat* (being), *cit* (intelligence), and *ānanda* (bliss), rather than by the whole range of personal attributes; Rāmānuja's modifications of the Advaitist doctrine ascribe richer personal qualities to Brahman, but by that development move in the direction of a personalism rather than a pantheism. In either version of the Vedānta, Brahman is attained by the individual who comes to understand his own identity with that One Reality. Such knowledge, realization, or attainment is actual or ultimate, according to the interpretation of *avidyā*, ignorance, and the degree of difficulty which the condition of ignorance imposes. The knowledge of one's identity with the One comes proximately by reason, as well as by disciplines borrowed from or reflected in Yoga, but the consummation of the whole process is an ineffable intuition. It is toward such intuition that the argument of reason points, and upon it that the argument ultimately rests.

The Tao, or Way, of Taoism is an ultimate goal or state. It is referred to by the use of a singular term, and must be given its place among the monisms. Specific descriptions of it are reduced to a minimum, but since in the face of religious sentiments it is only with great difficulty that any high abstraction can be sustained, a few clues are offered to the seeker. Some of the clues never get clear of paradox, but on the whole their meaning is plain. Taoism with all its vagueness offers a kind of cosmic discipline. For Lao Tzŭ as for Chuang Tzŭ there is one ground for all things. Seen through Chinese, rather than through some foreign eyes, the Tao is more naturalistic and less spiritualistic than the Brahman of Vedānta. One does not become identical with the Tao, although he may identify himself with it. There is little speculation and comparatively little mysticism about it; the Tao is adumbrated by reason, but is to be attained by the quiet observances of a simple life which refuses to be perturbed by evils which are superficial, because it is able to see them in the perspective of remote ideals.

The characteristic Chinese inclination toward "both-and" philosophies appears when any attempt is made to classify Confucianism. The system is humanistic and practical, but still there is an ultimate moral order with which man is to find union. True knowledge is achieved in quite matter-of-fact fashion "by the investigation of things." Neo-Confucianism is at least monistic in its account of beginnings; a *T'ai Chi* (Great Ultimate) gives rise to a dyad, thus initiating the cosmic process, which is permeated by *Li*, the principle of reason; but again humanistic interests supervene upon metaphysical theories and all but obscure them. Here, as in Taoism, the One Reality can hardly be called spiritual or psychical; if it has any qualities they seem to be qualities familiar to us in nature.

Buddhism is so varied that the combinations which it exhibits are difficult to trace, to say nothing of harmonizing them. It is primarily a personal discipline in which reason, often by the use of very subtle dialectic, helps to find the way to an ultimate reality. If we are to understand the Buddhist systems, we must not be deterred by ordinary difficulties. Buddhist negations and nihilism, for example, mean, not that the Buddhist denies everything and has nothing to say, but that he thinks he has penetrated beyond the range of ordinary experience and has found something there which cannot be said. In any case, the word "nothing" is always a term of reference, used for an object considered as having a minimum of specific qualities. It does not mean absence of everything; it means presence of something merely referred to and otherwise left undescribed.

Buddhism typically points to an ultimate (e.g., Suchness, Nirvāna, *Dharmadhātu*) which is "not void, but devoid" of specific qualities; in these phases it belongs with the other monisms of reference which we have considered. In other phases, for example in Aśvaghosha's doctrine of the ideation-store, in the later work of Vasubandhu and in the Yogācāra school where the tradition takes an idealistic turn, Buddhism runs close to familiar monisms. The Mādhyamika negativism, too, is thorough enough to be monistic; it is a kind of mirror image of a positive monism, attained by dialectic treatment of alternatives in which none of the successive steps is quite ultimate but each is related to the others somewhat as are the classes of classes in a theory of types. Nāgārjuna's usual negativism is best understood as a kind of theory of negative types; in one of his works he stated his monism more affirmatively.

In the realism of the Sarvāstivādin and the Vaibhāshika schools of Buddhism, as in the Sānkhya, the monism is more difficult to see. The world is essentially independent of us. We do not absorb it, nor become identical with it; we get free from it and let it go. The world which we let go presumably does not cease to exist, but it is at most quite worthless, and we may say that these realisms issue in a practical or valuational monism, although theoretically they belong with the dualisms.

The West, as we shall see, has made monotheism more characteristic of its thought than monism; where monisms have appeared they have been the views of minorities. Western mystics have always echoed or rivaled Eastern mystics in their half-articulate accounts of the One Reality; they have tended to picture their relationship with it as communion rather than union, but have advocated the latter often enough to make it familiar in their part of the world.

The Western thinker who has been perhaps most Oriental in his view of the ultimate Reality quite likely came to it under Indian influences. Plotinus, with his doctrine that all things emanate from the ineffable First Being and that we at length by reason, will, emotion and intuition gain reabsorption into that source, belongs among the ultimate monists. His emphasis is there, on the goal rather than the course, although the adaptation of his views to meet the needs of Christian theology makes him look like a dualist.

After Plotinus the next monistic mountain is Spinoza. We noted that Spinoza in his pantheism ascribed to God an infinite number of attributes (of which only two, thinking and extension, were specified or regarded as knowable by us). But pantheism, like Spinoza himself, has never been quite at home in the West—the light and shadow of theism have been too strong. It has been difficult for the personalists, too, to achieve monism. The higher personal qualities seem to thrive best upon contrast; they need to be etched on a background, and not merged with it.

Hegel's recurring syntheses of theses and antitheses place him among the ultimate idealistic monists, for whom the real is the rational and our self-realization is the self-realization of the Absolute. The systems of Bradley, Bosanquet, and Royce differ in their descriptions of the One Absolute Reality, but in their arguments to substantiate it seek to remain steadfastly on monistic ground. Fichte's voluntarism, as well as Schopenhauer's, issues in idealistic monism, and in many ways anticipates the later pragmatism without letting itself be shattered into pluralistic fragments.

Bergson's creative evolutionism is not as dualistic as sometimes

interpreted: it is panvitalism (rather than panpsychism), unless the
mystic's vision of God is to be understood as superseding all other
theories and principles. Other recent evolutionisms, notably those
of S. Alexander and R. W. Sellars, have been more naturalistic;
they are metaphysical versions of monistic trends in the sciences,
where the increasing tendency to express everything in mathematical form makes for a monism formal and abstract. Except by
Eddington and a few like him, any nonmathematical or nonmetrical
aspects of the world are likely to be denied, neglected, or minimized.

DUALISTIC SYSTEMS

We noted that the line between monistic and dualistic systems
is not precisely drawn and that all the latter tend ultimately to pass
into the former. There is perhaps no ultimate dualism, but the view
most characteristic of Western philosophy is so much more conspicuous in its dualistic than in its monistic features that it may be
set in contrast to the systems we have considered. This view is
monotheism, the doctrine that there is one personal God, distinct
from the universe of nature. Here metaphysics merges with philosophy of religion, and even with those institutionally sanctioned
forms of philosophy of religion which are theologies. Throughout
many centuries monotheism has dominated Western philosophy;
practically always it has been the ethical monotheism of the Semitic
religions, the doctrine of the righteous, just, but also compassionate
God of Judaism, Christianity, and Islam.

This statement about the dominance of monotheism in Western
thought is made in the face of three qualifications which are important, but remain secondary.

First, the great Greeks were hardly monotheists, at any rate in
the full sense. Plato sometimes speaks of God in the singular, but
usually he is more consistently a Platonist. Aristotle may be called
a monotheist, but almost for lack of a more accurate term; he introduces his Prime Mover from logical and ontological, rather than
theological or religious reasons. But the Greeks, and with them Plotinus, were just close enough to the Semitic monotheisms to be useful. In particular, Christianity came out of Palestine into the Medi-
terranean world with great religious dynamic but with only a naive
and overpicturesque metaphysics—a morally refined but intellectu-

ally simple supernaturalism. It went where Greek thought had brought more intellectual maturity but less moral influence. Of the Semitic and Greek traditions, each had what the other lacked; the result was that Christianity, Judaism, and Islam, all availed themselves of the resources of Greek metaphysics. Greek ideas were incorporated so thoroughly into Christianity that generations of scholars hardly noticed them. Incidentally, this was mainly what secured the preservation and transmission of the Platonic and Aristotelian literature: Plato, Aristotle, and Plotinus were more useful to the Christians than was, for example, Democritus. So the very fact that we have the Greek documents, with all their variations from Semitic monotheism, testifies to the influence of the latter. It was weak enough to need them, but powerful enough to absorb or obscure their differences.

The second qualification is that, as we have noted, none of the three Semitic monotheisms has been quite free from decidedly monistic views. Judaism has had its Spinoza, Christianity its Hegel, and even Islam its Sufi mystics.

A third qualification is due to the fact that much contemporary thought is breaking with supernaturalism and monotheism altogether. If only contemporary thinkers are considered, it is not at all plain that monotheism now dominates Western thought. Recent revivals of supernaturalism (Roman Catholic Neo-scholasticism, Protestant Fundamentalism, Barthianism, Buchmanism, and whatever may come out of the war) represent reactions rather than advances. Their new ways of insisting on old philosophies bear witness to the force of recent attacks. The modern scientific and social-economic conflict with monotheism is too recent for its value to be judged or its course forecast; but it is at all events recent, a matter of two or three centuries, and the statement must stand that historically monotheism has dominated Western thought. Augustine, Thomas Aquinas, Descartes, and Leibnitz, not to mention Kant, are too strong to be gainsaid. In our own day Whitehead's virtual panpsychism is offset by his theism (as well as by his Platonism), so he may be counted among the dualists.

With these historical facts in view, the major contrast between Eastern and Western metaphysics becomes evident: it is the contrast between a predominant ultimate monism on the one hand and a predominant monotheism, shading ultimately into a monism, on the other. For Indian thought, the ordinary world tends to melt away. Distinctions matter little; the individual man and the gods alike eventually disappear. In China there is much more concern about ordinary human relationships; the monism is decidedly in the background, but it abides there. In India and China alike there is probably more ease and composure of ethical adjustment. Whether due to climate, density of population, superior insight, or all three, the ideal is to be *content* with life rather than, like the West, all the time *intent* upon changing it. In the West we have monotheism's sharp contrast between God and the world, as well as between good and evil. Where in the East all differentiations tend to disappear in the One Reality, in the West they tend to be guaranteed, both here and hereafter, by the one good God. Those who envisage these contrasts in geographical or racial terms find, curiously if not significantly enough, that on the border line between East and West, in the region of the Persian Gulf, Zoroastrianism appears, with its ultimate monism but its proximate dualism of the principles of light and darkness, good and evil.

With the chief point fixed it must by all means be added that along with such monisms and monotheisms we find in the East, too, prominent systems which are dualistic, but at most only indifferently theistic. Besides the Zoroastrian border case, the East shows this tendency in the Sāṅkhya philosophy of India and in the doctrines of *yin* and *yang* which permeate Chinese thought. In the West, Plato with his realm of ideas could, as we have indicated, properly enough be counted among the dualists, and Aristotle, if accorded only a formal monotheism, is still dualistic, much like his master.

No account of the dualisms is complete without passing from metaphysics to epistemology, where the "bifurcation of nature" into the subjective and objective components has been a typical procedure, and where "epistemological dualism" has provided material for many controversies. If the process of knowing is to be emphasized, it is bound to stand out in contrast to something else. In the Hindu Sāṅkhya, Nyāya, and Vaiśeṣika, in the Buddhist Sarvāstivādin school and in typical Western realisms the soul, self, or mind is contrasted with the ordinary objective world from which, if it succeeds in winning salvation, it must somehow escape. In the

more critical Western epistemologies there is more emphasis upon
the mind's contribution to some objective raw material which in one
way or another (according as one follows Locke, Hume, or Kant)
is worked up to constitute the world which we know. Fichte's doctrine of the non-ego as a postulate of the ego brings the critical
epistemologies back to an ultimate monism.

The epistemological dualisms of mind and world cross and re-
cross the lines of the metaphysical dualisms of spirit and matter.
Thus our minds are sometimes regarded as spiritual, and contrasted, as in Berkeley, with a higher spiritual Reality. Again, our
minds are regarded as not much more than material, and contrasted,
as in neosupernaturalism, with an utterly transcendent Deity. The
lines, Eastern and Western, are so confused by agelong controversies that it is probably difficult to pick up anything of real value;
the conviction deepens that whatever is found will be found along
the avenues of metaphysics rather than the bypaths of epistemology.

PLURALISTIC SYSTEMS

Pluralistic systems, if there really are any such, can be treated
briefly; usually the pluralistic features are combined with some
form of monism or dualism. Qualitative pluralisms are more important than quantitative, but either kind has difficulty in maintaining itself against the drift to other views. As things now stand,
pluralism is not much more than an invitation to philosophy; it is
a question to which monism or dualism attempts to supply the answer.

If the foregoing adequately describes the traditions and the situation, what, we may ask, are the prospects for a planetary metaphysics? A century ago the issue would have been along time-honored
lines, between Eastern monisms and Western monotheisms. The
fact that even then the former were affiliated with various poly-
theisms and the latter with an occasional pantheism was significant; each had enough of the main emphasis of the other to prevent
any complete break and even to suggest a possible bridge between
them. In the nineteenth century some of the Hegelians, in particular, thought that they saw and possessed the way to understanding
and synthesis. If the philosophical landscape had not changed, the

question might have been answered—first, by a fusion of Eastern and Western idealisms (which might not have required much more than verbal and methodological adjustments) and, second, by composing the differences between both these monisms and the monotheisms so as to allow each view to dissolve into the other as the mind or the world was turned this way or that. This was the dream of some, and should have been the dream of all, idealists.

Since the nineteenth century, however, new influences have made themselves increasingly felt and have begun in their own ways to rewrite the prolegomena to any future metaphysics. One of these is empirical science, which, although only gradually freeing itself from epistemological swaddling clothes, and not even yet beyond the reach of the principle of indeterminacy's argument from ignorance, is pointing unmistakably in the direction of naturalism. Another is power machinery, which, although in some parts of the world slow in effecting its transformations, and in contemporary pragmatism misinterpreted to give man an exaggerated sense of his importance, is gradually transforming man's attitudes and thus his ideas of the nature of things. A third is the approaching exhaustion of the areas where economic pioneering can be carried on—an influence which tends to crowd men back to facts and make them reestimate some too hastily discarded ideas about the natural world. These factors together, in their action and reaction upon one another, are slowly recasting men's philosophies. The question is not whether the traditional monisms and monotheisms are compatible with one another, but in what form any of them may persist in the realism and naturalism of the future.[1]

---

[1] In order not to close without indicating some possibilities for a constructive theory, let us add that if some mutual concessions are made, naturalism may not be so dark as it is painted, nor so forbidding to the values associated with monistic idealism and monotheism. First in the way of concession, the monisms, especially the idealisms, should not insist that the world must be infinite or absolute; if these words are used, let them signify merely our refusal to set limits or to impose certain specific qualifications upon nature. The monisms should concede that any world of which we think is a selected world against a neglected background; any monism carries an implicit duality. Second, the naturalisms should subject the data of evolution to detailed study, to see whether it is not true that matter, life, and mind resemble one another in their structures and processes so much that man is not merely apical but also in a way typical of the universe—that, as countless Eastern and Western philoso-

phies have maintained, man when studied empirically is a microcosm of the whole and thus of special significance within it. Finally, the supernaturalisms and theisms should concede that spirit and matter are by no means necessarily opposites; that in nature and history together some good has evolved in contrast to whatever is evil; and that this developing good is capable of recognition as the object of religious devotion. The empirically detected resemblances in the structures and processes of matter, life, and mind, showing that man is in certain specific respects a microcosm, will then be available to interpret this good with reference to personal qualities which in monotheisms have been ascribed to God. In this way the widespread Eastern and Western theories of man as a microcosm may furnish a basis for understanding, even if contemporary idealisms, naturalisms, and supernaturalisms fail to do so.

CHAPTER X

Comparative Philosophies of Life[1]

By Charles A. Moore

THE most fruitful view of the relation of Eastern and Western philosophy—metaphysical, ethical, etc.—is that the one supplements the other, each providing or stressing the concepts which the other lacks or tends to minimize. This interpretation holds, further, that these two disparate sides of human thought can and should be brought together into a synthesis that would lead us closer to a world philosophy[2]—to a philosophy worthy of the name by truly fitting the nature of philosophy as "total perspective." Neither East nor West is faultless in its perspective; both need correctives that are not sufficiently forthcoming from within their own prejudiced perspectives. The wisdom of the East and the wisdom of the West must be merged to give man the advantage of the wisdom of mankind.

This, in general, is the essential attitude to be adopted in any comparative study of the philosophies of East and West, and yet there are dangers in adopting this attitude too uncritically. First, such an interpretation seems to imply that the East and the West stand at opposite poles in matters of philosophical concepts, theories, and methods, and this implication, besides being inaccurate, is apt to destroy rather than foster interest in comparative philosophy, for, practically speaking, neither East nor West is ready to look for correctives from a culture, a tradition, or a perspective that is alien

[1] This chapter presupposes knowledge of all preceding chapters. The material of those chapters is applied here to the comparative study of East and West. In order to avoid extensive repetition, specific reference to such ideas will be omitted.

[2] The possibility of such a single world philosophy of life—in all details— is questionable, of course, since geographical, economic, and other conditions are significant factors in determining the problems and attitudes of peoples. What we are seeking, however, is a philosophy of life for *man* over and above less significant differences among places, nations, and races.

to its own. A second implication is that the philosophy of the East and that of the West are, each, simple, clear-cut, of one pattern, such that the two can be set over against each other. To see the situation in that light is to do manifest injustice not only to the West but also to the East by overlooking a rich variety of thought that defies any such categorization.

Our immediate problem arises out of this complex situation. Two points are to be stressed: first, the variety and complexity of Oriental ethical thought must be specifically noted and, second, some effort must be made to determine exactly those special phases of Oriental ethical philosophy which may be synthesized most advantageously with the main tendencies of Western ethics. A third factor, namely, the equally important problem of the Western ideas that may serve as corrective complements to the Oriental trends, will be treated only briefly, being left largely to the subsequent thought of the reader.

THE VARIETY, COMPLEXITY, AND RICHNESS OF ORIENTAL ETHICAL THOUGHT

Needless to say—in view of earlier descriptive chapters—there is an almost infinite variety of philosophies of life, systems of ethics, and interesting and significant ethical ideas in the Orient. This is true no matter what approach one employs in analyzing the philosophical situation of the East, whether one be interested primarily in the definition of the *Summum Bonum*, in the rules of moral conduct, in the status of ethics itself (as well as the distinctions of good and bad), in the ways of reaching the *Summum Bonum*, in the status of the individual moral agent, or in the status of worldly activity. There is no unanimity of opinion among even the greatest of the Oriental systems on these phases of ethical philosophy.

Such an observation may appear thoroughly fatuous on the ground that no one who is at all interested in the philosophy of the East would be so naive as to think otherwise. The fact of the matter is, however, that such a naive interpretation is not uncommon in the West, where it is frequently held that there is such an attitude as "*the* Oriental philosophy" or "the Oriental tradition." This misunderstanding is the result of the hasty generalization that, *in effect*, all of the Oriental philosophies are at one in spirit and in essential teachings, regardless of differences of opinion on unessential details. A statement of the variety of systems and ideas in Oriental ethical philosophy, then—even if it be merely a brief recapitulation—will serve the double purpose, first, of indicating the richness and possible fruitfulness of Oriental thought and, second, of denying any oversimplification which would of necessity produce a serious misunderstanding of and lack of appreciation for Oriental ethical philosophy.[3]

[3] Since the original purpose of this study was the more humble task of pointing out the fallacious nature of some of the more prominent Western misinterpretations of Oriental philosophies of life it may be permissible to indicate one such interpretation—extreme in nature, to be sure, but not untypical of the West.

"In the Eastern tradition," writes W. C. Bell in his *If a Man Die* (Mrs. Anne Lee Laird, ed. [New York and London: Charles Scribner's Sons, 1939], pp. 96-98), "man's inborn will-to-live as an individual found itself confronted early in its history by a religious philosophy which tended to cancel rather than to direct and fulfill it. The Vedānta philosophy found that the final Reality and highest form of Being in the Universe is Brahma [Brahman], which is understood as an impersonal, inactive Being of whom no definite qualities can be affirmed, the placid lake whose bosom no storms ever ruffle. Since the changelessness of Brahma [Brahman] is the real and highest fact of the world it follows that all active, personal living is a huge mistake, and salvation is rescue into the eternal placidity. 'We must strive to be freed from all striving.' It follows, too, that personality is a low form of life, and that the individual will-to-live is a disease. One must cut the strands that bind one to life by an ascetic renunciation of the world, empty the soul of emotion and desire, inhibit the action of the will. So will active, individual living come to an end. The actual goal is variously conceived—Nirvāṇa has meant different degrees of non-being to different people. To Buddha there seems little doubt that it meant annihilation. 'The flame that is blown upon by the wind,' he says, 'goes out and cannot be rekindled.' To others this has meant the permanent anaesthesia which empties life of the dreams of pain and sorrow; to others still, a heaven of immortal life. But this last view is taken only by contradicting the philosophy that produced the conception, for the final verdict of the highest wisdom of this tradition is that personal, active living is life at its lowest, that the ambition to live is an unworthy ambition.

"In this system of thought there still remains, of course, a certain ambition. By ceasing from all thinking, feeling, and willing, one will reach the highest state of existence in union with Buddha; and that highest state is Being, not Doing. The vision which holds the East is the vision of a state of eternal inertia which is blessed because it is free from pain. The conviction which underlies that vision is the conviction that life is not worth living. Therefore

In philosophy proper, in its essential search for the truth, it is imperative that we pay strict attention to all suggestions that may have something to contribute to the whole truth. We must then, in our study of East-West philosophy, concern ourselves with all of the Oriental philosophies and with their multitudinous attitudes and ideas, if we would see what the East has to contribute to philosophy as such, as well as to the West specifically. This attitude of giving due consideration to all of the many philosophies of the Orient must be adopted in spite of the fact that some of them did not have equal success and no longer remain as dominant strains of thought. We intend first to note the richness of the Oriental picture and then to indicate the dominant strains or tendencies that seem to have proved their right to prominence through philosophical and practical competition with other systems. At the moment it is our purpose to show that the East—*if* it has any dominant tendencies in ethics— has reached these attitudes not because of any dearth of ideas or any lack of critical methods but by an agelong process of selection from a vast array of almost all possible attitudes.

The ethical views of the East range from complete materialism and hedonism to absolute monistic spiritualism and extreme asceticism. There is represented every form and degree, so to speak, of negativism and activism, of asceticism and indulgence or worldliness, of monism and individualism, of religious interest and atheism or agnosticism.[4] Furthermore, on the question of the very status of ethics itself and of the validity of any ethical judgments there is a similar absence of agreement. Thus the East has not lacked imagination or ingenuity in this, its most significant interest in the field of philosophy. There is no such attitude as *the* Oriental philosophy of life, just as there is no single or definitive attitude in the West.

Before passing on to a more detailed statement of these varieties of attitudes let us look briefly at certain general or broader differences, for these, too, are indicative of the variety of basic attitudes

the Eastern ascetic can write of life with contempt and of Nirvāṇa in terms of religious enthusiasm."

[4] "A striking characteristic of Indian thought is its richness and variety. There is practically no shade of speculation which it does not include." M. Hiriyanna, *Outlines of Indian Philosophy* (New York, 1932), p. 16. By permission of The Macmillan Co., Publishers.

in the East and yet they have been generally ignored by the West in its tendency to oversimplify the Oriental picture.

First, with reference to the *sections or countries*[5] of the East, there are rather remarkable differences of philosophical perspective, tendency, and specific attitudes among the major countries under discussion, namely, India, China, and Japan.[6]

For example, it is not at all accurate to offer analyses of "the Oriental tradition," of "the essentials of Eastern philosophy" or of some similar topic and consider merely the philosophy or philosophies of India. China cannot be considered "an exception" and forthwith ignored. In some senses, in basic senses, India and China are "worlds apart"—in many ways direct opposites—in their attitudes toward life and activity in the here-and-now and toward the values involved in such activity. It may well be that India's primary concerns are essentially "religious," that its methods are essentially "negativistic," that escape from life or from rebirth is the chief good, that India's attention is directed primarily toward the ultimate state and destiny of man. If so, China's predominant ideas, as found especially in Confucianism, are at considerable variance with those of India. Schweitzer's contrast of India as essentially "world-and-life-denying" with China which is "world-and-life-affirming"[7] is too facile but there is much in the systems of the two countries to justify that contrast—within limits.

China's philosophical attitudes[8] consist of humanism, common-sense practical living, a rather constant emphasis on morality and character as the supreme good, moderation in nearly all things but

[5] For further discussions of Oriental ethics in a similar way see K. Saunders, *The Ideals of East and West* (Cambridge, England: University Press, 1934), and H. N. Spalding, *Civilization in East and West* (London: Oxford University Press, 1939).

[6] This is not to deny that there is *an* "East" as a unit. Certain conditions tend to give India, China, and Japan a similar perspective, certainly as compared with the West: the influence of Buddhism, vast populations, similar social conditions, similar economic conditions, and a general non-mechanical culture.

[7] Albert Schweitzer, *Indian Thought and its Development*, translated by Mrs. C. E. B. Russell (London: Hodder and Stoughton, 1936), p. 1.

[8] See also Professor Chan's description in this volume, Ch. III, and Fung Yu-lan, *A History of Chinese Philosophy*, Eng. translation by D. Bodde (Peiping: Henri Vetch, 1937), pp. 2-3.

also at times—certainly in Mencius and in much of Neo-Confucianism if not in Confucius—full self-expression or full living. There is a natural love of life. There is the ideal of the "inner sage and the outer king," i.e., the combination of inner virtue and outer accomplishments. Such an attitude hardly corresponds to the spirit of Indian ethical philosophy.[9] Taoism and Buddhism are both significant parts of the Chinese philosophical complex, to be sure, but as we saw in Professor Chan's description Taoism is much more in tune with China's spirit of moderation than we in the West had suspected and Buddhism, in its struggle for existence in China, was either modified to fit the Chinese temper or was criticized and rejected because of its negativistic tendencies.

In contrasting the Indians and the Chinese Professor D. T. Suzuki indicates how little the two peoples have in common. "The Chinese people," he writes, "love life most intensely; they do not take it so pessimistically as the Indians; they have no special desire to escape it." The Chinese, he continues, "are preëminently practical, moral, and historically minded," as contrasted with the Indians who are "altogether too metaphysical, transcendental and above all worldly things." The Chinese, further, "are industrious and bent on increasing their economic efficiency"; and have been "pursuers from the beginning of their history of the three desires: Bliss, Prosperity, and Longevity."[10] The contrast is seen also in the fact that in Chinese philosophy there is "no soul-stirring religious emotion," where-

---

[9] See Surendranath Dasgupta, *A History of Indian Philosophy.* (Cambridge, England: University Press, V. I, 1922, V. II, 1932, V. III, 1940). Fundamental points of agreement among Indian systems, excepting Chārvāka, are: the theory of *karma* and rebirth, the doctrine of *mukti* or emancipation, the doctrine of the existence of the Soul—Buddhism excepted—a pessimistic attitude toward the world and an optimistic faith in the end and certain general principles of ethical conduct such as control of passions, noninjury, etc. (See I, 71-77). See also S. Radhakrishnan, *Indian Philosophy,* 2 vols. (London: George Allen & Unwin Ltd., V. I, revised edition, 1929, V. II, revised edition, 1931.) See I, 24-53.

[10] Introduction, by D. T. Suzuki, to Beatrice Lane Suzuki's *Mahāyāna Buddhism* (London: Buddhist Lodge, 1938), pp. xv ff. See also Bingham Dai, "Some Chinese Fears," in *Asia and the Americas,* XLIII, No. 11, Nov. 1943, p. 617: "The Chinese on the whole are hopelessly mundane and have a love of this life that their material conditions sometimes do not justify; but to be less so would mean to stop being Chinese."

as in India "every doctrine is turned into a passionate conviction, stirring the heart of man and quickening his breath."[11]

Japan represents still a third major attitude since its point (or points) of view cannot be identified with those of either India or China—despite the fact that most of its philosophy has come from one or both of these sources. Japan has little of India's pessimism and indifference toward life in the here-and-now and little, if any, conscious desire to escape life. Like China—and unlike India (in general)—Japan is definitely "world-and-life-affirming," but has expressed this affirmation in such a way and to such a degree that she seems to have gone far beyond Confucian China. With China, Japan is often said to participate in the Far Eastern ideal of the Middle Path but the actual content of the attitude varies significantly between the two countries.

Unlike China and India, Japan has long emphasized what amounts to the soldier or military class. The prominence of the *bushi* and the *samurai* (warriors), the *daimyō* (head of a feudal province), and the *shōgun* (military head of the nation), is uniquely characteristic of Japan as distinct from both India and China. For all her imitation, Japan is Japanese in life and in philosophy. What she has adopted she has also adapted to her own use. So different is this philosophy that one wonders how, as part of the Orient, Japan could have arrived at such a view.

The philosophy of Japan is a composite of elements from Confucianism, Neo-Confucianism, and Buddhism in a synthesis with indigenous elements derived from ancient Shintō and an attitude of the feudal ages, later termed "bushidō," the "way of the Knight (or warrior)." This combination produces a philosophy of duty and loyalty of a most compelling sort, beginning with an extreme sense of filial piety, and culminating in absolute duty to country and to Emperor. *This characteristic Japanese sentiment of loyalty— whether of religious or merely social origin and basis—has from very early days been the chief virtue of the Japanese and as such has always transcended in the scale of virtues all other virtues.* It is a nationalism and a racial point of view that calls not only for obedience to superiors but also for the spirit of activity to a degree that seems to be wanting in the rest of the Orient. Nor is there justifica-

---

[11] Radhakrishnan, *Indian Philosophy*, I, 27. By permission of The Macmillan Co., Publishers.

tion or any necessity for identifying this with mere imitation of the West. This attitude is at least as old as the fifth century A.D. At that time, even under conditions of a primarily agricultural and, on the whole, a peaceful society we read of the clansmen, hereditary escorts of the Sovereign, who boasted: "We will not die peacefully, we will die by the side of our king. If we go to the sea our bodies shall steep in the water. If we go to the hills, our corpses shall lie under the grass." Confucianism and Buddhism had their day in Japan, but throughout the ages—with certain nonconforming intervals—there has been the predominance of this essentially native Japanese way of life.

"The soil of the Japanese spirit," says Professor Takakusu,[12] "... is no other than the sacred message of the Imperial Ancestress" which declared that Japan "was the land where the line of her Imperial Family should reign, and that the fortunes of the throne would be eternal with the heaven and the earth." This Japanese spirit is further explained as consisting of four elements: "the strong spirit (as an expression of bravery), the quiet spirit (an expression of benevolence), the active spirit (an expression of intelligence) which is the origin of economic activities, and the mysterious spirit (an expression of wisdom) which is the origin of personal idealism."[13] The three characteristic virtues, namely, intellect, benevolence and courage—symbolized by the Three Treasures of Shintō tradition (the Mirror, the Jewels and the Sword)—are the same virtues as are praised by Confucius and recognized by Buddhism but, as interpreted in Japan, there seems to be a distinctively Japanese emphasis. As Professor Takakusu continues, "After all, the Japanese spirit has grown up on the soil of the Imperial message, has manifested its forms of activities in the four spirits, and has had its roots firmly in the spirit of the sacred treasures. It is the age-old inheritance of ours, the common ideal of all the Japanese with the background of over 2600 years, ever living in the hearts of the people."[14]

There is, in the spirit of Japan—we are still following Professor Takakusu's interpretation—a consciousness of the "Culture of the

[12] *The New Japanism and the Buddhist View on Nationality*, translated by Kiyoshi Maekawa and Eiichi Kiyooka (Tokyo: Hokuseido Press, 1938), p. 9.
[13] *Ibid.*, p. 10.   [14] *Ibid.*, p. 14.

Blood." "The Imperial Japan has its own land, state structure and people who are conscious of the Culture of the Blood."[15] Also, as in contrast even with the Germans—who also have a consciousness of the "Culture of the Blood"—the Japanese have a distinct Ideal, handed down to them literally.

Add to this—and here we see how Japan has assimilated doctrines from foreign sources but has molded them to fit her native perspective—the Confucian doctrine of loyalty and the Buddhist doctrine of "totalism"[16] or oneness of all things and beings. These doctrines, applied in senses or in degrees that hardly seem consonant with their originals, have served to increase the intensity of the indigenous Japanese spirit and the feeling of a divine Destiny. As Dr. Kenneth Saunders says, "Confucius would have been surprised" if he had seen how the Japanese had adapted his virtue of loyalty to the "glorification of warriors and feudal chieftains, over scholars and philosophers."[17] Similarly, while Buddhism seems to be a doctrine of peace and pacifism,[18] nevertheless, the doctrine of "totalism" and other cardinal virtues of Buddhism, such as compassion and meditation, have been made to serve the purposes of the Japanese attitude. Totalism, to the Japanese, seems to mean the ideal of a completely united world, and this ideal, when viewed through the perspective of Shintō, assumes a rather obvious form. Compassion, meditation (zen), and the attitude which recognizes the transiency of this world have all been molded into the Japanese picture. Zen is the practical side of the Totalistic metaphysics and serves as a complementary technique not only for searchers after salvation, but also for soldiers, as a new basis for courage, that courage which, along with loyalty, seems to be the paramount Japanese virtue.

[15] Ibid., pp. 14-16.

[16] Ibid., pp. 16-22. There is also the positive and active doctrine of Love which is characteristic of Mahāyāna Buddhism which is the type of Buddhism accepted in Japan. As Schweitzer says, Japan "with magnificent ingenuousness [sic] simply reinterpreted Buddhism in its own sense. . . . Thus Japanese world and life affirmation transforms Buddhism and makes it harmonize with its own spirit." Op. cit., p. 153.

[17] The Ideals of East and West (Cambridge, England: University Press, 1934), p. 88.

[18] See Junjirō Takakusu, Buddhism, the Fountain Head of Intellect (Tokyo: International Buddhist Society, 1938), pp. 67-68.

This analysis,[19] while doing justice to one phase of the variety of Oriental ethical thought, tends to do injustice to others. In pointing to the variety of philosophies *by countries*, we have tended to ignore: (1) vast varieties of systems within each of the countries, (2) varied interpretations within all of the more important systems, leading, in effect, to new sets of systems that express significantly different ethical attitudes, (3) the variations within countries, systems, and subsystems (as well as in the interpretations of specific ideas and principles) resulting from the changing historical perspective, and (4) an almost exhaustive variety of attitudes in answer to every one of the basic problems of ethical theory and practice.[20]

To illustrate: within the philosophical complex of India, for example, we find, not only Hinduism, but also Chārvāka, Jainism, and Buddhism; within Hinduism we find, not only Vedānta, but also Sāṅkhya, Yoga, Mīmāṁsā, Nyāya, and Vaiśeshika (not to mention the *Bhagavad Gītā* and numerous more specifically religious attitudes); within Vedānta itself we find the differing views of Bādarāyaṇa, Śaṅkara, and Rāmānuja, etc.; and finally, within Buddhism we find metaphysical realism, relativism, idealism, and nihilism, as well as a corresponding lack of agreement in ethics, and such contrasting major systems as Hīnayāna and Mahāyāna. China presents a similar picture, with Confucianism (Confucius, Mencius, Hsün Tzŭ, and others), Taoism (Lao Tzŭ, Chuang Tzŭ, Yang Chu, and others), Mohism, Hedonism (in Yang Chu or some unidentifiable author), and Neo-Confucianism (Chu Hsi, Wang Yang-ming, Tai Tung-yüan, and others)—not to mention the significant developments and modifications of Buddhism and the almost innumerable synthetic philosophies of the medieval period.

In order to justify and to explain these general observations concerning the variety of views within Oriental ethical philosophy and to indicate more specifically the complexity of that philosophy, let

[19] In such an analysis by *countries* or *sections* of the East, perhaps we should mention also the lands of Zoroastrianism and Islam. In contrast to several of the more important Oriental doctrines, neither of these philosophies is pessimistic—even initially—or world-and-life-denying. Both call for active living, the recognition of human and worldly values and personal immortality.

[20] These several points of view will be indicated briefly in the pages to follow, but for fuller explanations see descriptive chapters, this volume, II-VII.

us note briefly—in the form of a summary and recapitulation—the specific doctrines of the major systems.

HINDUISM[21]:

The performance of the duties of one's position in society through the four stages of life, culminating in the final period of asceticism and ultimate renunciation of all worldly attachments. *Moksha* (release, emancipation) possible in and during life through the attitude of *Karmayoga* (the spirit of nonattachment *in work*). Salvation ultimately only by means of knowledge of Brahman but with morality and dutiful activities as essential preliminaries. Morality is transcended in the ultimate state of man. Salvation consists of separation of independent soul from bodily attachments and thus from rebirth and suffering; it also involves some form or degree of nonseparation from Brahman. *Ahiṁsā* (noninjury to living beings) is basic practical virtue.

RIG VEDA:

Polytheism, later monotheism, and finally monism. Rather complete absorption in the everyday values of life. Hymns and prayers to nature-gods for assistance in enriching life. Some vague belief in individual immortality.

UPANISHADS:

Great variety of attitudes. Tendency toward monism and asceticism. Common-sense morality and acceptance of social philosophy of *karma*, rebirth, and stages of life. Salvation consists of some form of return to Brahman and release of soul from body and the world.

BHAGAVAD GĪTĀ:

A philosophy of action, of the performance of one's dutiful activities regardless of all else. Main theme is "duty done with singleness of eye and sincere attachment to God." Doctrine of *Karmayoga*. Paradoxical virtues of renunciation, compassion, simplicity, and humility on the one hand, and activity, energy, fearlessness, and courage on the other. Many roads to salvation: action, knowledge, devotion to and love of God, morality, faith. Salvation interpreted in two ways: either as individual immortality of the soul in the presence of God, or as some form of absorption into Brahman.

[21] In addition to primary sources, see Dasgupta, *A History of Indian Philosophy*; Radhakrishnan, *Indian Philosophy* and *Eastern Religions and Western Thought* (London: Oxford University Press, 1939); E. W. Hopkins, *Ethics of India* (New Haven: Yale University Press, 1924); J. McKenzie, *Hindu Ethics* (Oxford University Press, 1922); S. K. Maitra, *Ethics of the Hindus* (Calcutta University Press, 1925), and Albert Schweitzer, *Indian Thought and Its Development* (Eng. tr.) (New York: Henry Holt & Co., 1936).

SĀṄKHYA:

Summum Bonum consists of release from bondage, suffering, and rebirth. Release is obtained when the *puruṣha* (soul) is freed from its apparent bondage to the body and returns to its original pure state, which is above both pleasure and pain. *Moksha* is gained ultimately only by knowledge. Moral activities and Yoga practices are partial and preliminary aids. Pluralistic—both in the here-and-now and in *Moksha*.

YOGA:

State of bondage, cause of bondage (ignorance) and *Summum Bonum* essentially the same as in Sāṅkhya. Devotion to God and practical discipline emphasized as essential aids to the obtaining of *Moksha*. Knowledge is ultimate method, but knowledge alone is not sufficient. Tendency to pluralism in the here-and-now and in *Moksha*. Occasional reference is made to realization of some form of unity with God.

VAIŚEṢHIKA:

Summum Bonum consists of *Moksha* or release from rebirth and thus from bondage and suffering. Ignorance is the cause of bondage and thus knowledge is the primary means of escape. Moral discipline is recognized as an aid to knowledge and to the attainment of *Moksha*. Definitely pluralistic, but there is also the ideal of some form or degree of nonseparation from Brahman. Differences of opinion among authors and commentators as to exact nature of *Moksha*—whether it be a state of pure existence above pleasure and pain (which seems to be the general view) or a state of positive bliss.

NYĀYA:

Companion system of Vaiśeṣhika. Accepts main principles of Vaiśeṣhika in ethics and metaphysics. More positive in its conception of the nature of *Moksha* as a state of bliss. Knowledge (jñāna) is primary means to salvation.

MĪMĀMSĀ:

Salvation through *karma* or action in contrast to other orthodox systems. Knowledge of injunctions in Vedic texts and correct performance of these obligations and sacrifices lead to *Summum Bonum*, consisting of eternal joy in heaven. Unquestionable doctrine of plurality of souls. More "negativistic" later, adopting the theory of *Moksha* as a state beyond pleasure as well as pain.

VEDĀNTA:

(a) Śaṅkara—*Summum Bonum* consists in *Moksha*, a state of bliss—or rather, a state of pure existence, in absolute identity with Brahman. All plurality, all activity, all qualities are transcended, even moral distinctions.

Bondage and suffering are due to ignorance and thus are avoidable by knowledge alone. Empirical world is relatively real and therefore moral life, activity, and distinctions are real and valid—to that extent. In sum, *Moksha*, Jñāna, and absolute monism.

(b) Rāmānuja—Qualified monism. World is real; souls are real; soul and Brahman have characteristics. Knowledge is the essential way to *Moksha*, moral activity is significant and moral distinctions valid, but *Moksha* consists, *not* of identity with or absorption into Brahman, but of some kind of nonseparation from Brahman. Eternal plurality of souls. Theistic emphasis.

CHĀRVĀKA[22]:

Unqualified materialism and egoistic hedonism.

JAINISM[23]:

A *Moksha* philosophy; *Summum Bonum* is escape from suffering of the world, and consists in liberation of *jīva* (soul) from *ajīva* (non-soul). The soul, after liberation, lives in a state of perfect wisdom, perfect power, etc. Pluralistic. Liberation is attainable by the threefold method of right faith, right knowledge, and right conduct. Tendency toward asceticism for all, but much more so for devotees than for "householders." Fivefold vow of abstention from injury, falsehood, theft, unchastity, and worldly attachment. *Ahiṁsā* as greatest of these.

BUDDHISM[24]:

Many schools and many philosophies. Essentially a Middle Path doctrine (of various types) except for ultimate attitude of *Śūnyatā* (Emptiness or Void), involving the transcendence of all distinctions and particularity— but without absorption into an Absolute. Distinction between Hīnayāna (small vehicle), a rigorous individualistic philosophy of escape from suffering, and Mahāyāna (great vehicle), a more moderate and more uni-

[22] See *Sarvadarśanasaṅgraha*, translated by E. B. Cowell and A. E. Gough (London: Kegan Paul, 1904), pp. 2-11.

[23] For source material see *The Sacred Books of the Jains* (Lucknow, India: Central Jaina Pub. House, V. I, *Dravyasaṅgraha*, 1917, V. II, *Tattvārthādhigama Sūtra*, 1920, V. III, *Pañchāstikāyasāra*, 1920). For studies of Jain ethics, see J. Jaini, *Outlines of Jainism* (Cambridge, England: University Press, 1916), and Mrs. S. T. Stevenson, *The Heart of Jainism* (Oxford University Press, 1915).

[24] For studies of Buddhist ethics, see Louis de La Vallée Poussin, *La Morale Bouddhique* (Paris: Nouvelle Librairie Nationale, 1927); S. Tachibana, *The Ethics of Buddhism* (Oxford University Press, 1926); Mrs. C. A. F. Rhys Davids, *Buddhism: A Study of the Buddhist Norm* (London: Williams and Norgate, 1912); A. B. Keith, *Buddhist Philosophy in India and Ceylon* (Oxford: Clarendon Press, 1923); E. W. Hopkins, *Ethics of India*; and J. B. Pratt, *The Pilgrimage of Buddhism* (New York: Macmillan, 1928).

versalistic philosophy, characterized by the virtues of wisdom and love. In the former, Nirvāṇa means the cessation of desire and therefore of all pain and in the latter, the attainment of Buddhahood. Two levels of morality, a rigorous code for the monk and a moderate one for the layman. Effort to avoid pain of life through avoidance of rebirth. Suffering is due to ignorance; knowledge, aided by moral activity, is the means to Nirvāṇa. Doctrine of *anātman* (no self) in contrast with Hinduism, but this doctrine is open to numerous interpretations. Nirvāṇa is attainable in life through achievement of attitude of nonattachment and the overcoming of hatred, lust, and ignorance.

CONFUCIANISM[25]:

Confucius: Humanism, the effort to establish an ideal society by human effort and moral improvement, but also the union or continuity of the "State of Nature" and the "State of Art" (Fung, *A Comparative Study of Life Ideals*, p. 162). Requirement of society, state, education, wealth, and morality for the welfare of man. Primary virtue is *jên* or true manhood. *Chung yung* in the sense of being true to the principle of one's nature and applying this principle in one's relations with others. "Universal virtues" of wisdom, benevolence, and courage. Following Destiny. Activity, propriety and moderation (*chung yung*) stressed. Morality is supreme value. Personal rectitude, family harmony, social orderliness, and world peace as Ideals (in *The Great Learning*, Introduction).

Mencius: Goodness of human nature. Follow way of heaven by knowing our own mind and by "full exercise of one's mind." Ideal is an "unperturbed mind." *Jên* (love or benevolence or "that by which a man is to be a man"), loyalty to parents, and the "four fundamental virtues" of benevolence, righteousness, propriety, and wisdom. Emphasis on human relationships. Practical program of governmental activity for welfare of people. Democratic tendency.

Hsün Tzŭ: Man evil by nature. Consequent necessity of education and training and rules of propriety as means to improvement and goodness of men. Natural desires to be gratified but under moderating control of propriety. Extreme humanism—control of nature rather than intellectual interest therein. Ideal of simple life, tranquillity or equilibrium of mind. Rectitude of mind is basic virtue.

Chung Yung (*The Doctrine of the Mean*) : Harmony (*chung yung*) of man and nature grounded in metaphysics (knowledge of heaven necessary), with resulting sense of moral obligation. Five universal duties (as in Mencius) between sovereign and minister, father and son, husband and wife, elder brother and younger, and friends. Basic virtues of benevolence, wisdom and

[25] For discussions of Chinese ethics see Fung Yu-lan, *A Comparative Study of Life Ideals* (Shanghai: Commercial Press, 1924) ; F. Rawlinson, *Chinese Ethical Ideals* (Peiping: College of Chinese Studies, 1934) ; and P. C. Hsu, *Ethical Realism in Neo-Confucian Thought* (Peiping, 1933).

courage. Requirement of unceasing activity and full development of one's nature, but with universal harmony among men.

"NEO-CONFUCIANISM":

Li (law or reason) is central principle. Harmony is result of *Li* both in universe and in society. Proper conduct involves harmony (*chung yung*) of activity and passivity which are both moral and cosmic principles. Rational or Moral order is a social order, allowing no escape from social living (in contrast with Buddhism). Equal emphasis on all aspects of threefold doctrine of (1) "investigation of the reason of things to the utmost," (2) "full development of one's nature" by and in full development of others, and (3) fulfillment of Destiny. Virtue of all-comprehensive love (*jên*) not only as understood in early Confucianism but also in the sense of absolute impartiality toward *all things*—the Unity of Man and Nature. Sincerity (being true to one's nature and also in harmony with the Truth) and Seriousness ("unity of mind" or "absolute equanimity and absolute steadfastness"), as well as the three "Universal Virtues" and the four "Fundamental Virtues" of earlier Confucianism, are basic virtues.

TAOISM:

Lao Tzŭ: Naturalism as opposed to Confucian humanism and moralism. Naturalness and spontaneity as essence of conformity with Tao. Criticism of all artificiality. Simple living. Ideal of a state of quietude, harmony, and insight, not "inaction" but nonstriving. In a sense, the Middle Path doctrine—it is the cloudburst or the whirlwind that does not outlast the morning. Naturalism, but *never* in Nietzschean or Thrasymachean sense.

(A different interpretation is that adopted by Hu Shih in his *The Development of the Logical Method in Ancient China*, Shanghai: The Oriental Book Co., 1928—pp. 13 ff.—in which Lao Tzŭ is called the "greatest of the Sophists" and a "philosophical nihilist" whose "criticism was always destructive and iconoclastic," and "who held to a doctrine of the 'exaltation of the Non-being.'" He attacked the Confucian ideal society as, "foolishly civilized and refined and artificial.")

Yang Chu: A follower of nature, mainly interested in passing life and keeping the essence of one's being intact—not to injure our material existence with things. Let life run its course freely. Ignore not only riches and fame but also life and death.

Chuang Tzŭ: Primitivism, mysticism, quietism, fatalism, pessimism. Primitivism to the last degree; extreme naturalism; extreme position of abandonment. Rejection of all benevolence, righteousness, rites and music (of Confucianism). No name, no fame, no accomplishment. "Make an excursion into the void." "In a word, be empty." Moral relativity and, in a sense, no moral distinctions whatsoever.

(For less extreme interpretations, see Hu, *ibid.*, pp. 137 ff., and Fung, *Chuang Tzŭ* [Shanghai: Commercial Press, 1933], Introduction, and *A Comparative Study of Life Ideals*, Ch. II.)

HEDONISM (Chinese):

Lieh Tzŭ, Ch. VII (the Chapter entitled "Yang Chu"). Pessimism, fatalism, self-interest, avoidance of pain and the enjoyment of immediate and sensuous pleasures. Futility and artificiality of benevolence and righteousness. (This attitude was especially prominent among the libertines of the fourth to seventh centuries A.D.)

MOHISM:

Utilitarian humanism. "Promote the general welfare and remove evil," general welfare consisting essentially of wealth and population. Doctrine of universal love, based on principle of utilitarianism and on religious sanction. Criticism of ritualism and formalism of Confucianism, also of its determinism and its doctrine of gradation of love; opposition to any form of luxury, to the fine arts, to war—to anything that works against general welfare.

LEGALISM:

Rules of social conduct not applicable solely as rites but must be enforced by legalistic methods. Acceptance of basic principles of Confucianism. Rejection of intellectualism.

SHINTŌ[26]:

Ancient interest in physical well-being and temporal prosperity. "Reflect truth as a mirror; be clean within and without." Virtues of intellect, benevolence and courage. Feeling of national destiny and extreme concept of loyalty or duty. Purity and cleanliness as practical and spiritual ideals. Loyalty to the sovereign, reverence for ancestral memory, filial piety. Discipline, duty to parents, elders, superiors, country, and Emperor. Simplicity, sincerity, purity.

"BUSHIDŌ":

Loyalty, personal honor (in comparison with which life itself is cheap), rectitude or justice, courage or the spirit of daring, benevolence, politeness and modesty, veracity, self-control, education, suicide or redress, and "the Sword, the Soul of the Samurai."[27]

[26] See D. C. Holtom, *The National Faith of Japan* (London: Kegan Paul, 1938); Genchi Katō, *A Study of Shintō* (Tokyo: Maruzen Co., 1935), esp. Chs. XV and XVI; W. G. Aston, *Shintō* (London: Longmans Green & Co., 1905), esp. Ch. XI; K. Saunders, *Ideals of East and West*; and E. Kaibara, *The Way of Contentment*, translated by G. K. Hoshino (London: J. Murray, 1913).

[27] This list comprises the chapter headings of Inazo Nitobe, *Bushidō, the Soul of Japan*. Twentieth edition (Tokyo: Tuki Publishing Co., 1914).

ZOROASTRIANISM:

"A religion of life in the noblest sense of the word." "The ideal of re-nunciation has no fascination for the intensely practical mind of the Zoro-astrians." No mysticism, no attempt to fathom the deeper and darker shad-ows of life, no flight to the transcendental. Reality of the individual soul and its capacity for activity. Vigor in life and an earnestness in moral liv-ing. Duty of man is to enlist himself on the side of good in opposition to the powers of evil, to further all the vital forces and to retard all the forces of death. Recognition of physical values and of the duty of striving for them—at the expense of intellectual pursuits. Not mere utility or world-liness. "A vivid appreciation of the higher and finer possibilities of the human soul." Basic ideals of truth, righteousness and purity, and horror of contaminations.[28]

ISLAM:

Monotheism, individual immortality, salvation in eternal heaven of hap-piness (of worldly sort). (*Koran*, LVI, Sale's translation, pp. 435-436.) Basic commands: absolute obedience to God and to Him alone, kindness to parents, kindred, orphans, and the poor, constancy at prayer, and alms-giving. (II, p. 11; IV, pp. 65-66; XXI, p. 273; XLII, p. 491.) Other vir-tues: moderation (VII, p. 118), patience (II, p. 18), truthfulness (LXX, p. 465), beneficence and mercy (III, p. 51), justice (LX, p. 447; XVI, p. 221), willingness to fight for the religion (II, pp. 22-23); opposition to iniquity, oppression (XVI, p. 221), pride, covetousness (IV, p. 63) and hypocrisy (IX, p. 157).

So great, then, has been the philosophical subtlety, ingenuity, insight, and variety of views, so intense and real has been the com-petition among systems, that the variety and suggestiveness of Oriental ethical philosophy truly seem to be inexhaustible. We in the West have barely "scratched the surface" of this vast storehouse of ideas and ways of life. True, any study of Eastern philosophy involves, along the way, much disappointing contact with strange and seemingly ridiculous doctrines; the essential truths often lie hidden beneath a surface of unessential and unacceptable attitudes. These, however, are not the essence of the matter, and to ignore the worthwhile because of the worthless is not only unjust to the best that Oriental philosophy has to offer but it is also unproductive for the West which is so badly in need of new insights and new perspectives.

[28] See M. A. Buch, *Zoroastrian Ethics*, published, with an Introduction, by A. G. Widgery, the College, Baroda (1919), Gaekwad Studies in Religion and Philosophy, IV. See also, M. N. Dhalla, *History of Zoroastrianism* (New York: Oxford University Press, 1938).

THE "SPIRIT" OF ORIENTAL ETHICAL PHILOSOPHY
—ITS EMPHASES

Such is the variety of Oriental ethical thought—as we have just seen—that it is impossible to determine any "Spirit" of Oriental ethical philosophy unless one ignores or minimizes significant phases of that philosophy. And yet that, in a sense, is the very task with which we are faced, for a comparative study must attempt at least to indicate those general contrasts that are prominent between East and West.

A striking and suggestive parallel presents itself in the effort of Oriental scholars to do for the West what we are here attempting in reference to the East. Dr. Shastri, in his *The Essentials of Eastern Philosophy*,[29] points to "the spirit of activity, which appeals to the Western mind as forming the very essence of life," and further generalizes to the effect that "Western civilization is, in fact, the deification of desire," is "soulless, irreligious, and artificial," and is given to "an over-emphasis on the individual." We in the West are in the paradoxical position of being forced to admit and at the same time deny that description. Certainly it has within it more than an element of truth. On the contrary, however, the facility of the description betrays it; it is too simple to be accurate. Nevertheless, especially if we are comparing East and West, the elements of Western civilization which are indicated by Dr. Shastri are the very ones which the investigator must choose for emphasis, for, *despite numerous directly contrasting views* in the course of the history of Western thought and civilization, these ideas and attitudes do, to a great extent, constitute the "Spirit" of the West. Surely they are at least the basic contrasting emphases of the West and are therefore the chief contributions which Western ethical thought can offer to the East or to any philosophy that would comprehend both East and West.

The attitude of this study is exactly that same attitude: we are to look in vain for any single "spirit" of Eastern ethical philosophy, but we may be able, by noticing *emphases*, to call attention to significant differences in tendency and thus to single out for special consideration those attitudes which will be most important for the

[29] P. D. Shastri, *The Essentials of Eastern Philosophy* (New York, 1928), Lecture I. By permission of The Macmillan Co., Publishers.

West and for any world philosophy that mankind may be able to attain by virtue of a world perspective.

The East—like the West—has known nearly all varieties of philosophies of life, positive and negative, hedonistic and ascetic, worldly and otherworldly, religious and nonreligious, monistic and pluralistic. In the East—as in the West—some attitudes have "caught on" while others have not. In the East, Hinduism (especially Vedānta as formulated by Śaṅkara), Buddhism, and Confucianism have assumed prominence as systems while the others, relatively, have lost significance. Some systems have survived, have enjoyed general acceptance, have exerted a strong influence upon the mind and life of the East; while others have either disappeared altogether as significant factors in the living of the East or have been outstripped in philosophical and practical competition with other systems, or finally, have been so modified as to bear little resemblance to the original ideas.[30]

In other words, the East has found some attitudes to be logically and practically satisfactory and others to be logically and practically wanting. As a result of this process of choice and elimination certain significant Oriental emphases have emerged, while many attitudes—including some of the West's most prominent theories—have been generally repudiated or have been found to represent mere approximations to the truth. Our immediate concern is with those attitudes which the Orient has tended to accept.

The Priority of the Practical Over the Theoretical

In only one respect has the entire East reached unanimity of opinion within the field of our study. This is the view that all philosophy is ultimately for practical purposes, that ethics or the philosophy of life is the essential phase of philosophy, that the theoretical finds its sole justification in its service as a guide for the practical.

Paradoxical as it may seem, Oriental philosophy is thoroughly "practical" in spirit and in fact whereas Western philosophy as a rule is not. From the point of view of the Orient, philosophy must

[30] For example, the extreme system of Vedānta of Śaṅkara as the outgrowth of the much less extreme Upanishads. Also, Mahāyāna as related to Hīnayāna—such that even Mrs. Suzuki can entertain the question as to whether Mahāyāna is Buddhism. See Preface to *Mahāyāna Buddhism*, pp. x-xi.

be intimately related to life and its problems; seldom, if ever, does philosophy adopt the role of an academic or purely theoretical exercise. The determination of the correct way of life constitutes the supreme object underlying—and *consciously* underlying—the search for the truth. If there is any generalization that is applicable to all of the great philosophies of the East it is this fact.

In sharp contrast, Western philosophy had its rise and has found its incentive, from the days of the early Greeks, largely in human curiosity, in the sense of wonder, and in the desire to know simply for the sake of knowing.[31] The result has been a long history of philosophical speculation that has been branded by Orientals[32] (and by the "man in the street" even in the West) as a theoretical, academic exercise with little or no relation to life.[33] This is not meant to imply that there has been no theoretical philosophy in the East,[34] but merely that philosophy in the East has never become divorced from life. The great Oriental philosophers, whether they be the originators of the great philosophies or their more theoretical followers and system-builders, wish above all else to solve the practical problems of life, its meaning, its values, the destiny of man, etc. Curiosity has never been the primary impelling incentive behind Oriental philosophy. Almost every basic philosophy (metaphysical

[31] Cf. Plato, *Theaetetus*, 155 D, and *Republic*, 475c; Aristotle, *Metaphysics*, 980a; R. B. Perry, *The Defense of Philosophy* (Cambridge, Mass.: Harvard University Press, 1931), p. 16: "the philosopher is impelled primarily by curiosity of a peculiarly dogged and exaggerated sort." However, Perry defines the business of philosophy thus: "to discover the nature of the universe and to apply it to the meaning of life" (pp. 3-4).

[32] See Shastri, *op. cit.*, pp. 12-14.

[33] This statement and the point of the argument cannot be nullified by the twofold observation (1) that Western *religions* are thoroughly "practical" in interest and (2) that the Oriental philosophies either are religious in fact or are Eastern equivalents of religion. In many cases the Oriental systems are accepted with conviction and lived with enthusiasm, but the Oriental philosophies are not religious in the usual sense. See Professor Chan's distinction between Religion and Philosophy in the East (this volume, Ch. VII), and also note differences between the religion and the philosophy in Hinduism, Buddhism, Taoism and Confucianism, where the two developments are quite distinct.

[34] See F. Thilly, *History of Philosophy* (New York: Henry Holt & Co., 1914), p. 3. "The doctrines of Oriental peoples . . . consist, in the main, of mythological and ethical doctrines, and are not thoroughgoing systems of thought."

and ethical) known to man has been developed in the East but *in every case* the metaphysical attitude has been reached as the solution of practical problems or it has had practical consequences which were consciously emphasized as the essential feature of the system.

Buddhism, the only philosophy which has exerted an influence upon the entire East, is an apt illustration. The prevalence, if not the universality, of suffering as expressed in the first of the Four Noble Truths constitutes the starting point and the problem of the philosophy. Said the Buddha:

"Birth is misery; old age is misery; disease is misery; death is misery; sorrow, lamentation, misery, grief, and despair are misery; to wish for what we cannot have is misery; in short, all the five attachment-groups are misery."[35]

This, then, is the initial problem. The remaining three Noble Truths in a way constitute the essence of the remainder of Buddhist thought; namely, the discovery of the cause of suffering, the discovery of the cause of the cessation of suffering, and the discovery of a way to reach that cessation of suffering. These involve the psychological, metaphysical, and moral analyses that are designed to provide a solution of the original practical problem. Without that problem there would have been no Buddhist philosophy; but with that problem the speculation that was necessary to its solution was inevitable. Such is the beginning of Buddhist philosophy which, in the course of its long history, has become elaborate in every sense of the word and in every phase of philosophical study but has never lost sight of its initial problem and of the fact that all philosophy has its *raison d'être* in its effort to solve that problem.[36] The Buddha himself often refused to discuss questions of metaphysics since they "profit not."

Hinduism too, including the Vedas, the Upanishads, the *Bhagavad Gītā*, and all of the Six Systems have had a similar practical interest. Except for the Vedas, which are joyous and utilitarian in tone, this same sense of pain and suffering in the ordinary life of

[35] H. C. Warren, *Buddhism in Translations* (Cambridge, Mass.: Harvard University Press, 1896, 8th issue, 1922), p. 368. For other Noble Truths, see pp. 370, 372, and 373.

[36] *Majjhima*, LXIII. For a discussion of the Buddha's attitude on this question, see J. B. Pratt, *The Pilgrimage of Buddhism*, pp. 89-91; also pp. 71, 76, 82-84.

the here-and-now—or at least the feeling that this life is incomplete
—constitutes the problem from the Upanishads through the Six
Systems as well as in heterodox Jainism.[37] Furthermore, all of the
philosophical systems—including elaborate metaphysical and logical
exposition—follow almost exactly the pattern set forth in Buddhism. As an example let us take the system that might be least
expected to be interested primarily in the practical problems,
namely, the Logical School of Nyāya:

"Pain, birth, activity, fault, misapprehension—on the successive
annihilation of these in the reverse order, there follows release.

". . . Release, which consists in the soul's getting rid of the world,
is the condition of supreme felicity marked by perfect tranquility
and not tainted by any defilement. A person, by the true knowledge
of the sixteen categories, is able to remove his misapprehensions."[38]

In other words, the problem is the practical one of reaching "supreme felicity" or "release," and the method is by knowing the
nature of reality, which in this particular system consists of the
sixteen categories. The remainder of the book of *sūtras* explains a
complex logical-metaphysical system, but this entire elaboration is
for the sole purpose of explaining the truth whereby one reaches
a solution of his practical problem. Nyāya, in its method of stating
the issue or problem and the solution, is typical of all Indian systems.[39] In Sāṅkhya and Vaiśeṣika the literal beginnings of the
sūtras establish the problem of pain to be overcome.[40] In Vedānta

---

[37] Jainism, finding the world—in which the soul is in bondage to the body—
to be full of suffering, sets as its main problem the liberation of the soul
from the body. See *Pañchāstikāyagāthā*, 28 and 172.

Chārvāka also recognizes the suffering of the world. It advises not escape
but the search for whatever pleasure is obtainable in such a world.

[38] *Nyāya Sūtras*, I, 1, 2 with commentary. *Sacred Books of the Hindus,*
VIII, translated by M. S. C. Vidyābhūshaṇa (Allahabad City: L. M. Basu,
1930).

[39] As Professors S. C. Chatterjee and D. M. Datta say, "The most striking
and fundamental point of agreement [of all Indian systems] is that all the
systems regard philosophy as a practical necessity and cultivate it in order
to understand how life can be best led. The aim of philosophical wisdom
is not merely the satisfaction of intellectual curiosity but mainly an enlightened life led with farsight, foresight and insight." *An Introduction to Indian
Philosophy* (Calcutta: University of Calcutta Press, 1939), pp. 14-15.

[40] *Sāṅkhya Kārikā*, I-II; *Sāṅkhya Aphorisms*, I, 1. Śaṅkara Miśra's Introduction to *Vaiśeṣika Sūtras* and *sūtra* I, 1, 4. *Sacred Books of the
Hindus*, VI.

it is the knowledge of Brahman that is stated as the object of the search but it is immediately explained that "The Infinite (Brahman) is bliss" and that "there is no bliss in anything definite,"[41] thus indicating that the underlying quest is for bliss or at least that there is the initial consciousness that knowledge of Brahman will bring such bliss. In the *Yoga Sūtras* the initial problem is the definition of *yoga* but the purpose of such a definition—as "concentration"—is to point to this as a means of escape from pain, for "all is pain to the discriminating."[42] Finally, in the Pūrva Mīmāṁsā the originating problem is the determination of the nature of *dharma* (duty) and the point is that by following the true *dharma* one will win salvation.[43]

This practical motive and interest is even more pronounced perhaps among the Chinese philosophies. This is not true in the sense— often the sense in which Westerners think of Chinese philosophy— that there is no philosophy in China except ethical and political thought. It is true, however, in the sense that practically all of the philosophy of China, possibly from *The Book of Changes* through modern classical Chinese philosophy, has had a primary interest in practical matters and has been applied thereto often at a very serious cost to metaphysics, logic and epistemology as well as to the scientific spirit in general.[44]

Dr. Hu Shih, in *The Development of the Logical Method in Ancient China*, explodes the theory of the lack of logical, metaphysical and even scientific philosophy among the ancient Chinese thinkers. His thesis is that the logical and scientific methods of the West "are not totally alien to the Chinese mind, and that on the contrary, they are the instruments by means of which and in the light of which much of the lost treasures of Chinese philosophy can be recovered."

[41] *Vedānta Sūtras of Bādarāyaṇa*, I, 1, 1, with commentary. *Sacred Books of the Hindus*, V. See also *Vedānta Sūtra*, I, 1, 4 with commentary by Śaṅkara. *The Sacred Books of the East*, XXXIV (Oxford: The Clarendon Press, 1897), p. 25.

[42] *Yoga Sūtras*, I, 1 and II, 15. *Sacred Books of the Hindus*, IV.

[43] *Mīmāṁsā Sūtras*, I, 1, 1-2. *Sacred Books of the Hindus*, XXVIII.

[44] See Fung, *A History of Chinese Philosophy*, I, 1-2; also Hu, *The Development of the Logical Method in Ancient China* (the entire volume). All future quotations from Dr. Hu will be from this book unless another source is noted.

He continues: "The emphasis on experience as against dogmatism and rationalism, the highly developed scientific method in all its phases of operation, and the historical or evolutionary view of truth and morality,—these which I consider as the most important contributions of modern philosophy of the Western World, can all find their remote but highly developed precursors in those great non-Confucian schools of the fifth, fourth, and third centuries B.C."[45]

These theories are not in themselves theories of the practical nor is their significance limited to the solution of practical problems. Nevertheless, as Dr. Hu indicates, in all of these cases the theory in question had its rise in a practical problem or was interpreted so as to apply almost exclusively to practical interests; or was neglected and undeveloped—the latter because of the theory's impracticality, the superior practical applicability of Confucianism, or the authoritarian position which practical Confucianism achieved among Chinese thinkers and over Chinese culture generally. It is not our purpose here to study the variety of views originated and developed by the great thinkers of China's Golden Age, but it is to the point perhaps to survey this development briefly for the purpose of demonstrating the fact that Chinese philosophy is typically Oriental in being practical rather than theoretical in interest.

To begin with, the very rise of philosophy as something beyond the level of the Poets and the early Sophists lay in the need for a solution of the practical problem of the age, namely, the problem of "intellectual anarchy" and chaotic living conditions—"perverse doctrines and violent deeds."[46] "Even in this seething torrent of intellectual anarchy," writes Dr. Hu, "there were signs which heralded the arrival of a new age, the age of constructive thinking. Philosophy was already in the field, and was busying herself with the conditions and problems of the age. She was searching for the *tao*—a word which has been unnecessarily mystified by amateurish translators but which simply means a way or method, a way of individual life, of social contact, of public activity and government, etc. In short, philosophy had set out in quest of a way or method of ordering the world, of understanding it, and bettering it."[47]

[45] Introduction, p. 9.
[46] See *The Works of Mencius*, III, II, 9.
[47] Pages 16-17.

Another approach to our problem is found in the observation that Confucianism has rather completely dominated Chinese philosophy and that the spirit of Confucianism has always been the practical motive. Confucius and later Confucians were by no means merely ethical thinkers—Confucius, for example, approached sound scientific methods in several of his doctrines—but "he was too deeply interested in human institutions and relations to fully develop this scientific aspect of his system."[48] He was too much of a reformer, a politician and a statesman, in his philosophical attitudes and in life—and too much of a humanist—to allow his purely speculative theories to carry his attention away from man and his problems. He seemed to deny all interest in speculation beyond the level of man.[49] His follower Hsün Tzŭ, the "Moulder of Confucianism," even more emphatically believed in conquering and utilizing nature for man's welfare—instead of merely studying her in a disinterested way.[50]

Even the more logical and scientific theories of Confucius were applied to, or interpreted for, humanistic situations, as for example when he allows his logical doctrine of the "rectification of names" to take the form of a theory of social organization and betterment by putting upon it a thoroughly practical and social emphasis. As Dr. Hu says, "the logical outcome of such a rectification, as Confucius conceived it, would be an ideal society in which every member of the community would faithfully discharge the duty proper to his or her 'calling' or status."[51] The practical application of this doctrine may be seen from the words of Confucius: "When the father is father, the son is son, the elder brother is elder brother, the husband is husband, and the wife is wife,—then the family is in proper order. When all families are in proper order, all will be right with the world."[52] We might well say of all of the doctrines of Confucius what Dr. Hu says of his doctrine of *hsiang* or "ideas": "Behind all the fantastic imaginings, behind all its almost occult appearances, we must not fail to recognize *the practical and human-*

[48] Hu, p. 39. See the whole of Part II for an exposition of the many-sided Confucian logic.
[49] *The Analects*, XI, 11; also VII, 20 and VII, 24.
[50] *Hsün Tzŭ*, Chs. VIII, XII, and XVII.
[51] Pages 26-27.
[52] Cited by Hu, p. 27; see also *The Analects*, XIII, 3.

istic ideal which animates the whole Confucian philosophy."[53] To sum up the attitude of Confucius, which continued to dominate Chinese philosophy through the work of his followers, "it was natural that the central problem of Confucius should be the reform of society. The task of philosophy was conceived as that of social and political regeneration. He too was in quest of the *tao*, of a way of ordering the world."[54]

This typically Confucian attitude of humanism and practicality not only dominated the followers of the Master in the early ages of Chinese philosophy but continued on through the whole of modern philosophy. The dominating text, a Confucian text, of the great modern philosophers in the Sung (960-1279) and Ming (1368-1644) periods was the following from the Introduction to *The Great Learning* (Hu's translation) :

"When things are thoroughly investigated, knowledge will be extended to the utmost. When knowledge is extended to the utmost, our ideas will be made true. When our ideas are made true, our minds will be rectified. When our minds are rectified, our individual character will be improved. When our individual character is improved, our family will be well ordered. When the families are well ordered, the state will be well governed. When the states are well governed, the whole world will be in peace."

This passage serves as the keynote of modern Chinese philosophy and determines its method. The passage itself and the way it was interpreted by modern Chinese philosophers indicate unmistakably the continuance of the typically Confucian practical and humanistic attitude. First, there is the potential fruitfulness of the passage for a sound philosophical approach to things not limited to the problems of man and society. Yet this fruitfulness was not developed because the great thinkers who adopted this passage as the basis of their systems chose, in true Confucian fashion, to interpret the word "things" as "affairs." Accordingly, as Dr. Hu says, "this humanistic interpretation of one word has determined the whole nature and scope of modern Chinese philosophy. It has limited philosophy to the realm of human 'affairs' and relations."[55] It might be pointed out also that in the passage the practical ideal of world peace is directly the goal of the "investigation of things" and of the "extension of knowledge."

[53] Page 39; italics mine.   [54] *Ibid.*, p. 22.   [55] Pages 4-5.

The customary description of ancient Chinese philosophy recognizes six main schools: Confucianism, Taoism, Mohism, Yin Yang, Sophists, and Legalists. In all of these schools the main interest has been almost exclusively the practical. Let us note briefly the practical basis of the non-Confucian schools.

Taoism is the most metaphysical of all the schools, but the universal quest among the variations within the system is for the *tao* as a way of life through knowledge of the Tao which is the variously interpreted cosmic principle. The very name of the school, *Tao*ism, serves sufficiently to indicate its essentially practical motive.

Like Confucianism, Taoism had its rise within the matrix of the age of intellectual anarchy and chaotic living conditions. Whatever the interpretation put upon Lao Tzŭ's teachings,[56] there is no doubt that he was interested primarily in the practical problems of the individual man and of society. His task was to find a solution for the troubles of the time and his particular solution took the form of a philosophy of "following Nature" (Tao), an attitude that was critical of the Confucian solution by rules of propriety and strict moral standards. His was a plea for a "return to Nature" or to naturalness. Such was his problem and his solution although he was forced to employ metaphysical speculation and mystical insight before he could find a basis for this way of life.[57]

Later Taoists retained Lao Tzŭ's basic concept of Tao and its ethical parallel but modified in one way or another the meaning of Tao and the way of life which was in conformity therewith. They also retained the practical motive and interest. Yang Chu agreed with Lao Tzŭ on metaphysical principles but adopted a significantly different interpretation of this metaphysics in its application to the practical problem. He offered a theory of semi-hedonism; and again it is the way of life that stands out above the metaphysical theory as the dominating interest. Chuang Tzŭ developed a rather extreme form of mysticism and a corresponding logical theory of the relativity of all concepts—thus going considerably beyond his master in the fields of metaphysics and logic—but from his master he inherited the practical problem, as is evidenced from the tenor of the

[56] Compare interpretations of Chan Wing-tsit, this volume, Ch. III, and Hu, pp. 14 ff.
[57] See *Tao-tê Ching*, Chs. I, XI, XII, XIX, XLVIII, LVII, LXXX.

entire text of the basic seven chapters of his work.[58] And so, on the basis of his new metaphysics and logic, Chuang Tzŭ offered a new practical solution. It consisted of a correspondingly more extreme philosophy of life than Lao Tzŭ's (discarding altogether the Confucian and orthodox distinctions of right and wrong) and in a more extreme form of negativism or escapism.[59]

The other main schools of Chinese philosophy were so practical in spirit that there is little reason for an extensive consideration of them. Certain facts must be noted, however:

(1) Mohism was exclusively practical-minded and practical in fact, with its doctrines of universal love and of wealth and population as the supreme goods of society and with its definitely pragmatic and utilitarian methods, involving criticism even of Confucianism for its lack of practicality in that the latter failed to test its doctrines by the criterion of their practical effect upon the people.

(2) Even the doctrine of the Sophists which to all appearances is utterly divorced from any interest in practical matters was also motivated by practical interest. For example, the ten famous Paradoxes of Hui Shih reached their climax in the final paradox: "Love all things equally; the universe is one." In other words, this logical construction is subject to interpretation as a metaphysical and logical demonstration of the validity of ethical monism, the doctrine of universal love as enunciated by Mo Tzŭ. (Professor Chan presents in Chapter III a radically different interpretation of the motives of this school.)

(3) The Yin Yang school was also practical in its significance since it was relatively unimportant as a school of philosophy except as a method of divination. To be sure, there was an extensive development of cosmological speculation and study of the correspondence of man and nature but this merely provided the development of this potentially significant philosophical doctrine along lines of divination, magic, etc.[60]

[58] See such chapter titles as "The Happy Excursion," "The Fundamentals for the Cultivation of Life," and "The Philosopher-King."

[59] Chuang Tzŭ's philosophy is open to differing interpretations: compare Chan Wing-tsit, this volume, Ch. III, and Fung, *Chuang Tzŭ*, introduction, esp. pp. 6-11.

[60] These remarks are made with much hesitation, since the doctrine of *yin yang* in early Chinese thought was probably much more significant—

(4) The practical motive of the Legalist school is rather patent from the very name of the school. It too had its "logic,"[61] but the motive of the school was the practical ordering of society by legalistic methods. The new idea of this philosophy was the addition of "ways and means" of enforcing and generalizing the application of the laws to all the people, thus modifying the orthodox Confucian solution in the direction of practical enforcement and in the extent of the application of rules and regulations. This movement was so practical in interest that it was directly instrumental in bringing about the famous incident of the Burning of Books in 213 B.C., an event which was one of the main causes of the near absence of disinterested speculation for centuries thereafter. The Burning of Books was justified by the Legalists on the practical grounds that:

"What is now called wisdom consists of subtle and speculative theories which even the wisest men do not understand. . . . When you have not even coarse rice to eat, think not of wine and meat. When you have not even rags to wear, think not of silk and embroidered garments. And in ordering a state, when the most urgent needs are not met, one has no business to undertake things which have no immediate bearing on the needs of the time. Nothing is more detrimental to good government than to encourage what even the wisest do not quite understand, when the actual need is common sense. Therefore subtle and speculative theories are no business of the people."[62]

The philosophies of Japan also fit the general Oriental pattern of interest in the practical side of philosophy. The dominant philosophies of Japan are (or have been) Confucianism in its several forms, Buddhism, Shintō, and Bushidō, or some synthetic or eclectic combination of principles from these. We have already recognized the practical as the dominant motive in Confucianism and Buddhism but it is worthy of special note that Buddhism has in many cases taken a definitely religious form in Japan whenever the philosophy itself became too abstract to serve as a ready guide for practical living. As for Shintō and Bushidō, the very names indicate their practical nature for the last syllable of each is comparable to *tao*

metaphysically and scientifically—than is indicated here. See Fung, *A History of Chinese Philosophy*, I, Chs. III and VII, Sec. 7.

[61] See Hu, pp. 170-184.

[62] *Han Fei Tzŭ*, Bk. 46, as cited by Hu, pp. 183-184.

as described above, so that Shintō provides the "way of the gods" as a guide to life, while Bushidō inculcates the "way of the *Bushi*" or of the *samurai*, the knight or warrior.[63]

The intimate relation of philosophy and life in the Orient is not limited to the East's primary interest in life's problems and the determination of a way of life as distinct from the disinterested search for the Truth. This common Oriental tendency is often expressed or exhibited differently. "To those who realize the true kinship between life and theory," writes Radhakrishnan in explaining the common characteristics of Indian thought, "philosophy becomes a way of life, an approach to spiritual realization. There has been no teaching . . . which remained a word of mouth or dogma of schools. Every doctrine is turned into a passionate conviction, stirring the heart of man and quickening his breath."[64] With some qualifications the same may be said of the systems, or at least of the "spirit," of Chinese and Japanese philosophy, to the extent that philosophy is not for the intellectual few but for the many—to be *lived*. The many know and live the philosophies although they might not understand them completely. Furthermore, even the philosopher must live morally[65] and comprehend life more than in an intellectual sense before he can understand his own philosophy; or rather, before he can understand the Reality approached in his philosophy. The intellectual and the practical are one; one does not know the truth until one lives it.

Objection to the thesis that Oriental philosophy is "practical" comes from many sides. Among these are (1) the view that Oriental philosophy in both India and China had its originating incentive not in practical matters but, as in the West, in curiosity and

---

[63] In the philosophies of Persia and Arabia (primarily Zoroastrianism and Islam) as well as in those of India, China, and Japan, there is also a predominant "practical" motive in the sense that purely intellectual or theoretical speculation is subordinate or instrumental to ethics. For example, the Zoroastrian *Avesta* consists almost entirely of rules of conduct. So, too, the *Koran*. In all cases, whether it be in the less mystical and ascetic original forms of these philosophies or in their more mystical developments, the search for salvation and the doing of good are primary considerations.

[64] *Indian Philosophy*, I, 26-27. By permission of The Macmillan Co., Publishers.

[65] This is true especially in the Indian systems.

the disinterested desire to solve the riddle of Reality;[66] (2) the view that Indian philosophy not only transcends but actually minimizes or ignores ethics and the practical side of life, making knowledge the only "royal road" to salvation;[67] and (3) the view that the very word "practical" is completely out of harmony with the nature and spirit of Oriental philosophy.

We cannot examine all of these criticisms but let us look at the final one because that seems most significant for the West. The contention is that Oriental philosophy is characterized by its "remoteness from practice," by its otherworldliness and asceticism, whereas the term "practical" must imply primary interest in every-

[66] Possibly *The Book of Changes* and the doctrine of *yin yang* were disinterested efforts of early Chinese to understand and describe reality—although such a contention is extremely doubtful. Perhaps also, as Radhakrishnan suggests (*Indian Philosophy*, I, 22), the beginning of Indian philosophy was preceded by "the security of life, the wealth of natural resources, the freedom from worry, the detachment from the cares of existence, and the absence of a tyrannous practical interest," which "stimulated the higher life with the result that we find from the beginnings an impatience of spirit, a love of wisdom, and a passion for the saner pursuits of the mind." (See also, *ibid.*, I, 72 and 93-94.) By permission of The Macmillan Co., Publishers.

In China, however, all philosophy was turned into practical channels or discarded as insignificant, and in India practically the same spirit prevailed. Even in the most philosophical of the Vedas (the Hymn to the Unknown God, *Rig Veda*, 121) the quest is for knowledge of the God "*to whom we shall sacrifice.*" Further, the "aim of the Upanishads" is described by Radhakrishnan himself as "not so much to reach philosophical truth as to bring peace and freedom to the anxious human spirit" (I, 138). As for the Six Systems, "All the systems have for their ideal complete mental poise and freedom from the discords and uncertainties, sorrows and sufferings of life" (I, 126). By permission of The Macmillan Co., Publishers.

[67] Ultimately, much of Indian philosophy and Buddhism does hold to the transcendence of moral distinctions, although, as pointed out repeatedly, all such philosophies recognize the significance of morality in the here-and-now. Morality is not considered as an end in itself but only as a means to ultimate salvation; once that goal—or perfection—has been achieved, morality is no longer necessary. (See Radhakrishnan, *ibid.*, II, 625 ff., and 633-634.)

Furthermore, the same philosophies *do* recognize knowledge as the ultimate road to salvation—which, as a matter of fact, may be a more philosophical attitude than the recognition of action as the primary method—but by "knowledge" or wisdom (*jñāna*) the Oriental means a complicated process including mental and physical discipline and moral living, as well as theoretical knowledge.

day activities and values; certainly to be "practical" means to be interested in "life" and "living," not in escape or liberation therefrom.

The contention that the East is not practical in this sense is obviously correct with reference to much of the Orient. Perhaps the choice of term—"practical"—was unfortunate for it has paved the way for much confusion of meaning. The entire Orient *is* "practical" in the sense of having a primary interest in the practical rather than the theoretical side of philosophy—the problem of the true way of life is universally the basic problem of the East. But the Orient is *not* universally practical in the sense intended in the criticism now under discussion. While it is true and to be emphasized that China and perhaps the whole of the Far East (not to mention Zoroastrianism) are predominantly interested in the more practical and utilitarian values of the here-and-now, nevertheless Hinduism, Buddhism, and Jainism—which constitute the major philosophical genius of India—are not practical in any similar sense. The Indian philosophy of life is not predominantly a philosophy of "living" in the narrow Western sense. Most of its philosophy is not practical if that characterization denies the ultimate transcendence of the here-and-now and implies the absence of renunciation.

Nevertheless, let us examine this thesis that Indian philosophy is not practical. "All Hindu philosophy," says Professor Franklin Edgerton, "has a practical aim. It seeks the truth but not the truth for its own sake. It is truth as a means of human salvation that is the object." And, he continues, "all Hindu philosophy is religious in basis. To the Hindu mind, 'the truth shall make you free.' Otherwise there is no truth in it."[68] The question that comes to mind is, Isn't Indian philosophy really practical in two senses, both as to interest and as to actual content? A further point is that there are two conceptions of the content of the practical. "In one sense," as Professor Schaub so aptly describes it, "its associations are with utility, with particular ends to be attained, with the relations of objects and instruments to needs and desires, and to specific purposes realizable through courses of action; in the other, it refers to the satisfaction of a religious and spiritual yearning, to an experience of the Absolute, to the attainment of a salvation that puts to

[68] *Bhagavad Gītā* (Chicago: Open Court Publishing Co., 1925), p. 6.

rest the restless questioning of the intellect and the passionate urge of desire."[69]

It is in something like this latter sense that much of Indian philosophy is practical; that is, as a means to salvation, to a religious and spiritual experience, often in relation to an Absolute. The accuracy of this interpretation and the validity of this use of the term "practical" must be emphasized. To deny this use of the term is to beg the question as to the true nature of the practical. To miss the distinction of these two senses is to miss, also, the significance of much of Oriental philosophy for the West. One of the ideas that the West can derive from the East is this very notion that ultimate values—and even ultimate salvation—are the essence of the truly practical.

By contrast—as we shall have occasion to see later—the West's "practicality" is a narrow concept. It often reduces to "busyness," to activity and doing, to complete submergence in the immediate and the here-and-now, usually without any studied sense of direction or of ultimate value. India has the long view of "practicality" while the West tends to be dominated by the short view. In this respect, as in so many phases of our general problem, China—and possibly the whole Far East—seems to have reached the sounder position of the true Middle Path, avoiding the extreme tendencies of both India and the West. The Chinese are not especially concerned with salvation or a transcendental religious experience, but neither are they enslaved by the immediate and the worldly.

The first and most universally approved way in which Oriental ethical thought may supplement that of the West is, then, this many-sided emphasis upon the practical aspect and function of philosophy. Without this practical import philosophy would never have come into being or developed in the Orient and, despite differences of opinion as to the exact nature of the practical function and meaning of philosophy, this general characteristic of all Oriental philosophy stands as one of the East's major contrasts to the West which has tended to lose sight of this attitude in favor of the more disinterested and theoretical search for the truth. Both views are

[69] Edward L. Schaub, "Indian Philosophy in its Divergence from the Spirit of the Contemporary West," *The Open Court* (Chicago: Open Court Publishing Co., October 1930), Pt. II, p. 592.

narrow and therefore unsound; the East *and* the West stand in need of correctives, but in synthesis they point the way to an easy and sound solution.

No other attitudes are universally accepted in the East: neither monism, nor negativism, nor pessimism, nor otherworldliness, nor religious interest, nor transcendence of the distinctions of morality, nor any of the other commonly accepted descriptions of the thought of the Orient. However, certain of these attitudes are the very ones which, when properly understood and properly related to their Western parallels or counterparts, constitute the basic emphases or tendencies of the East. Let us choose for special consideration, descriptive and evaluational, those which seem to be most significant. In addition to (1) the practical interpretation of philosophy, these are: (2) the attitude of *Ultimate Perspective*; (3) the attitude of *Dual Perspective*, involving the theory of "two levels" in metaphysics and in ethics and the accompanying doctrine of "initial pessimism"; (4) *Negativism* (a dangerous word and one that comprehends many attitudes, but one which, when properly understood, is as good as any substitute); (5) *Monism*; (6) *Spiritual-mindedness* and the definite rejection of typical Western attitudes to the contrary such as Hedonism, Naturalism, and Materialism in every sense.

Ultimate Perspective

One of the most striking marks of much of Oriental philosophy (Hinduism as a whole, Buddhism, Jainism, and possibly Taoism) is its interest in the ultimate state and status of man. The perspective which recognizes only the present (and the things thereof) as significant—Shastri's way of describing the attitude of the West[70] —or any view which allows for pettiness, selfishness, attachment, or worldliness is denounced as being out of accord with the ultimate nature of things. It is the relation of the self to the universe, the ultimate condition of man, that is the only real concern of the Indian and the Buddhist. Ethically, nothing short of ultimate salvation— regardless of differences as to the exact nature or content of salvation—is good or *the* good. This is indicated by the fact that *Moksha,* the state of ultimate release, is the constant goal of all Hinduism and Jainism while Nirvāṇa is the only true goal of Buddhism.

70 *The Essentials of Eastern Philosophy,* pp. 7-8.

If we look at the more significant systems of Oriental philosophy, and if we concentrate on the ultimate principles of these systems, it is manifest not only that conformity with the ultimate state of reality is the real goal but also that there is a marked uniformity of interpretation as to the specific nature of this ultimate state of man and of things. As is pointed out by Professor Northrop in an earlier chapter,[71] if we concern ourselves only with the basic concepts of the most significant Oriental systems we find that the theory of the "undifferentiated continuum" (to use his expressive terminology) represents the ultimate metaphysical truth in all of them. There is no disputing the validity of this interpretation with reference to the Vedānta of Śaṅkara (and possibly also with reference to the spirit of the Upanishads), to Buddhism with its ultimate concept of śūnyatā, and even to Taoism in its more metaphysical or more mystical phases.

Furthermore, there can be no mistaking the implications of such a metaphysical view for ethics. If this metaphysics of the "undifferentiated continuum" is *the* truth, then many of the usual Western descriptions of the philosophy of life of the East are apparently sound, at least *in so far as they refer to the ultimate principles of the systems*; for it follows that the ethical situation should then consist essentially of monism, otherworldliness, negativism and renunciation, the transcendence of all moral distinctions, and the reduction of all worldly activity to the status of insignificance— all of which would of necessity involve pessimism in so far as the values of the here-and-now are concerned.[72] Accordingly, it is these very ideas that we must study for they are emphatic tendencies in the East. Paradoxically, they constitute the most vital of the Oriental attitudes;[73] but at the same time, *when misunderstood*, they have jeopardized the significance and influence of Oriental ethical philosophy beyond the limited borders of its origin.

[71] Ch. VIII.

[72] Many of these attitudes are also present in Jainism which has no Absolute or "undifferentiated continuum."

[73] For example, see (1) Shastri's defense of renunciation, *op. cit.*, pp. 17-18; and (2) the defense of the attitude of transcending worldly distinctions, such as those of morality: Shastri, pp. 7-8; Radhakrishnan, *Indian Philosophy*, II, 621, 633-634; and Chatterjee and Datta, *Introduction to Indian Philosophy*, pp. 25-26.

All of these doctrines, even in their extreme forms, are recognizable in these Oriental philosophies but there are two circumstances that must be noted before we proceed to study them in detail. First—even if it be sheer repetition—there are, in addition to these systems, many others and, in fact, within each of these systems themselves there is significant opposition to this extreme interpretation. This being true, *the* East must not be defined in terms of these attitudes. Second, these attitudes, *in the extreme form in which they have been known by most of the West*, do not represent the whole truth even of these systems themselves. As doubtful as the statement may appear to be, there is no system of philosophy in the East which holds to these views exclusively in their extreme sense. In every system every one of these ideas is qualified or moderated. That this *seems* to be an inconsistency[74] with the systems' ultimate metaphysical view is obvious; that it *is* inconsistent is denied in view of considerations to follow.

(The fact that this attitude of what I have called "Ultimate Perspective" is one of the supremely important doctrines of much of Oriental ethical thought is well known. The West is quite well acquainted with this aspect of Oriental ethical thought—thus obviating the necessity for further elaboration here—but it is not so well aware of the doctrine's qualifications and of more moderate teachings and interpretations that serve to render it less extreme. The most important consequences of the doctrine, namely Monism and Negativism will be examined in detail later; at the moment, it is intended to correct certain misunderstandings of Oriental ethical philosophy by suggesting some important qualifications and limitations of this basic, but extreme, doctrine of "Ultimate Perspective.")

Dual Perspective: The Doctrine of "Two Levels"

There are two most important attitudes, be they implicit or explicit in these systems, that constitute the sum and substance of the Oriental's answer to such an extreme interpretation of his philosophies. They are: first, the concept of "two levels"—call them

---

[74] See W. C. Bell, *If A Man Die*, quoted above, p. 250 n.; also Albert Schweitzer, *Indian Thought and its Development* (Eng. tr.), pp. 7, 111, 179, and 54 ff. For a detailed answer to this charge, see S. Radhakrishnan, *Eastern Religions and Western Thought*, pp. 64 ff.

"opinion and knowledge," "reality and appearance," "noumena and phenomena" or what you will—in metaphysics and in ethics; and second, the attitude of *karmayoga* which demands the performance of one's social and moral duties but always without attachment thereby to the less real aspect of things. These doctrines are explicit in Buddhism, Hinduism and Jainism.[75] As for Taoism, the doctrine of "levels" (of knowledge) is explicitly accepted[76] and the attitude of *karmayoga* is accepted in spirit in Taoism's philosophy of naturalness or spontaneity devoid of striving. Even Confucianism approaches the attitude of *karmayoga* in Confucius' doctrine of activity for its own sake rather than for the results of action; and it specifically recognizes levels of knowledge and of moral action.[77]

If the "undifferentiated continuum" or its equivalent were the exclusive sum-total of reality so that all else were unreality, then it would follow that morality, activity, individuality and all that goes therewith would be unreality, and that complete renunciation and pessimism would constitute the essence of the good life. It would also follow that any recognition of a way of life which would accept the here-and-now as significant would constitute an inconsistency. If, to repeat, the "undifferentiated continuum" were the only reality, living in the here-and-now would lose all significance.

But, says Radhakrishnan, voicing the opinion of Eastern *and* Western critics of such an extreme view, "if we have to play the game of life, we cannot do so with the conviction that the play is a show and all the prizes in it mere blanks."[78] The point is, however, that our world is not unreal. We cannot indulge here in an analysis of Oriental metaphysics. Suffice it to say that, in one sense or another, all of the systems now under special consideration hold to a metaphysics which ascribes at least empirical reality to the everyday world, with man and man's activities as parts thereof. In Śaṅkara alone is there a decided tendency to carry the notion of the

[75] See below, footnotes 80, 82, and 83; also section on "Negativism" par. (c).
[76] See *Chuang Tzŭ*, Ch. II; *Tao-tê Ching*, LXXVII and LXXXI.
[77] See *The Doctrine of the Mean*, Ch. IV, and Fung, *A Comparative Study of Life Ideals*, pp. 176 ff.; *The Works of Mencius*, I, I, 7, and *Analects*, VIII, 9.
[78] *Indian Philosophy*, II, 463. By permission of The Macmillan Co., Publishers.

ultimate undifferentiated Brahman to extremes that make for the
unreality of all else, and even in this case there is the explicit acceptance of the empirical reality of this world and the demand for moral
activity therein.[79] Except in Śankara's occasionally extreme interpretation Vedānta agrees with Buddhism in holding to a threefold
division of reality, such that only the first is wholly real, the second
(our ordinary world, Kant's "phenomena," Plato's Being-and-Non-
Being) is conditional reality, and only the third is illusory.[80] In
Taoism, except in the extreme view of Chuang Tzŭ, there is little
effort to demonstrate the unreality of the world, of man, and of
man's activity; instead, all of these acquire reality by virtue of the
presence of Tao therein; what is denied is the artificiality or un-
naturalness of certain man-made things and deeds that violate Tao.

The question that the Oriental might put to his Western critic
would be this: What inconsistency or contradiction is there in the
doctrine of an ultimate reality *and* an accompanying empirical reality? Is it not almost inevitable that any metaphysics except the
theory of pure naturalism should entertain such a distinction? Is it
not almost necessarily true that, unless this world be the ultimate
reality, it must be, not wholly unreal, but relatively real? That is
the Oriental point of view and it nullifies the extreme and critical
interpretation which would make the Oriental system—be it Vedānta, Buddhism, Jainism, or Taoism—take the either/or position
of either accepting worldly activity, morality, etc., as the sum and
substance of things, or of denying to these all reality whatsoever.

This metaphysical doctrine of levels of reality is applied within
the field of ethics in two important senses: first, as a justification
for ethical and other activity in the here-and-now even if the only
ultimate reality does transcend all distinctions including those of
morality; and second, as a principle of distinction between the moral
life of the avowed seeker after salvation on the one hand and that
of the layman on the other. This latter attitude of accepting two
codes of morality is a highly significant feature of Hinduism, Jainism, and Buddhism.[81] Through it even the most extreme systems

---

[79] See Radhakrishnan, *ibid.*, II, Ch. VIII, Sec. XL.

[80] In Vedānta, see *Vedānta Sūtra*, I, i, i, with commentary of Rāmānuja,
The Sacred Books of the East (Oxford: The Clarendon Press, 1904),
XLVIII, pp. 38-47. In Buddhism, see *Laṅkāvatāra Sūtra*, Ch. VI.

[81] See below, footnotes 82 and 83.

avoid the practices (and the critic's charges) of universal and extreme asceticism, inaction, etc. It is only the religionist, the extremist, the one who is excessively and exclusively interested in salvation who must adopt the life of extreme renunciation.

Despite its basis in the metaphysics of "levels of Reality," this theory, in permitting significant activity in the here-and-now (which is not ultimately real), has lent itself to the charge of inconsistency. The unsoundness of that charge is now apparent. It is answered also in a nonmetaphysical way through the doctrine that, despite the recognition of activity on the lower level, it is only the ascetic or devotee who can actually reach ultimate salvation. The Buddha praised the moral man, the follower of the lower code of morality, outside the Order;[82] the *Bhagavad Gītā*, as representative of Hinduism, emphasizes everyday duties and activities; and Jainism sets up an elaborate code of moral conduct for the "householder." But in all cases such morality—like the degree of reality with which it is associated—is admittedly of only secondary importance and efficacy; it cannot lead all the way to *Moksha* or Nirvāṇa. This does not mean, however, that all the systems are ascetic, for there is almost universal recognition of the lower level of morality as a preliminary, often as an absolutely indispensable preliminary, to the true and final path of renunciation and knowledge.[83]

If the theory of two levels of morality seems peculiar to Western minds or strikes one as self-contradictory, it may not be amiss to recall that the same doctrine is to be found in some of the West's most profound and influential thinkers and systems although it has failed to receive the serious consideration it deserves. It is definitely propounded in Plato's *Republic*[84] and in Aristotle's *Nicomachean Ethics*[85] where the content of the theory seems quite similar to the

[82] *Majjhima*, II; *Digha*, III.

[83] E.g., see Radhakrishnan, *Indian Philosophy*, II, pp. 615-616, for a discussion of this problem in Śaṅkara, the most extreme of all Oriental monists and transcendentalists. Compare *Vedānta Sūtras of Bādarāyaṇa*, III, 4, 35-43, *Sacred Books of the Hindus*, V, where the thorough devotee is said to be superior to such activity.

[84] See the levels of knowledge, Bks. V-VI; also levels of morality, that of Philosopher-King (who alone is truly moral because he alone knows The Good) and that of the people generally. Compare also the differing types of life suggested in the *Phaedo* and the *Republic*.

[85] Cf. Bk. VI on Practical Wisdom, and Bk. X on the "higher" ("higher

underlying ideas of the East. In Christianity, too, we find the distinction between certain "Counsels of Perfection" and the Commandments that are necessary for salvation. This distinction, then, like that on the metaphysical level, is quite intelligible even to the Western mind; in fact, some such distinction in the realm of conduct, as in the realm of metaphysics, seems inevitable and necessary if either realm is to be made really intelligible. The only alternatives are absolute Transcendentalism or absolute Naturalism, neither of which is philosophically defensible.

If it be granted that the Oriental has not lost all sight or sense of the life, the activity, and the world of the ordinary individual man, despite the tendency to Transcendentalism, let us return to a fuller discussion of the ethical implications of this latter doctrine; for these constitute—as emphases at least—important contributions of the East to the West. *Now that we have noted that these extreme views are not the whole story* we may proceed to their exposition without fear of misunderstanding, without fear that we shall fall back into the errors of the past and interpret *the* East in terms of these extreme doctrines.

"Negativism"[86]*—by Western Definition*

The first implication of this sort of metaphysics ("undifferentiated continuum") and of the general attitude which we have called "ultimate perspective" is a many-sided doctrine of, let us say, "nega-

than mere human nature") life of Contemplation. If the Oriental is unable to explain the relation of these two completely, so is Aristotle. "The relation of it [the higher life] to the lower, is left somewhat obscure." J. S. Smith, Introduction to Everyman Edition (New York: E. P. Dutton & Co., 1911), p. xxiii. See also Radhakrishnan, *Indian Philosophy*, II, p. 625, for similarities between Aristotle and Indian attitudes.

[86] This is perhaps the most common but also the most questionable (and objectionable, to the Oriental) characterization applied generally to Oriental philosophies of life. Among the best replies are: Radhakrishnan, *Indian Philosophy* and *Eastern Religion and Western Thought;* M. Hiriyanna, *Outlines of Indian Philosophy*; S. C. Chatterjee and D. M. Datta, *Introduction to Indian Philosophy*; Carus, *The Gospel of Buddha* (Chicago: Open Court Publishing Co., 1921), introduction and appendix, and *The Canon of Reason and Virtue* (Chicago: Open Court Publishing Co., 1913), introduction and comments; S. Yamakami, *Schools of Buddhist Thought* (Calcutta: University of Calcutta, 1912); Fung, *A Comparative Study of Life Ideals*; J. B. Pratt, *The Pilgrimage of Buddhism*; and F. Rawlinson, *Chinese Ethical Ideals*.

tivism." Furthermore, such an attitude in one form or another is not exclusively dependent upon the metaphysical theory of an ultimate undifferentiated monism; it is prevalent almost throughout the Orient—in one form or another, in some degree—in Absolutist Vedānta, in non-Absolutist Nyāya, Vaiśeshika, Sāṅkhya and Yoga, in later Mīmāṁsā, in heterodox Jainism and Buddhism, in Taoism, and *in a special sense* possibly even in Confucianism.

In what sense can there be such a strong tendency toward negativism in the Orient that it is to be singled out as one of the basic attitudes? What, exactly, do we mean by "negative"? It is impossible to give a direct or simple answer. *The attitude of the East is never considered negative by the East itself*; it is always the renunciation of something of lower value for something of greater reality and higher value. However, in such a comparative study and only in such a study, it is permissible to state what the West means when it applies the term "negative" to this attitude. It is only from the point of view of what the West tends to call "positive" that we may describe certain doctrines of the East as negative—and even then it is largely a matter of degree. If some attitude like that exemplified in the statement, "life is real, life is earnest"—saying a full "yea" to life—expresses the essence of a positive philosophy, if "positive" refers to the acceptance of life (and all therein), to be lived seriously and *as fully as possible* and in a sense for itself,[87] then the Oriental attitudes under discussion, with the exception of Confucianism, may properly be called "negative."[88]

[87] Schweitzer describes the competing philosophies as "world and life affirmation" and "world and life negation." *Op. cit.*, pp. 1-10.

[88] Most Indian views take their beginnings from an attitude of initial pessimism, the feeling of dissatisfaction with the world, and therefore seek escape. For example, see S. Dasgupta, *A History of Indian Philosophy*, I, 74-76:

". . . if we could divest ourselves of all such emotions, ideas, or desires as lead us to action, we should find within us the actionless self which neither suffers nor enjoys, neither works nor undergoes rebirth. When the Indians, worried by the endless bustle and turmoil of worldly events, sought for and believed that somewhere a peaceful goal could be found, they generally hit upon the self of man. The belief that the soul could be realized in some stage as being permanently divested of all action, feeling or ideas, led logically to the conclusion that the connection of the soul with these worldly elements was extraneous, artificial or even illusory. In its true nature the soul is untouched by the impurities of our ordinary life, and it is through ignorance

It is not a simple "negative" that we may properly apply to any attitude of the East, however. There are many forms and degrees of this generally negative point of view. Few of the systems agree in detail but most are of one mind in *moderating or denouncing* worldly activity as an end in itself and, with few exceptions, reject any effort to define the *Summum Bonum* in terms of worldly accomplishment or perfection, be it hedonistic, naturalistic or idealistic. Let us examine some of the various ways and degrees in which Oriental ethical philosophy is "negative"—*for each of these has a special significance for the West.*

(a) On the basis of the definition we have adopted, Buddhism, Hinduism, and possibly Taoism in strict metaphysical accuracy and consistency are, *from the point of ultimate truth*, negative ethical theories.[89] Ultimate salvation involves the loss of all individuality and of all differentiations and distinctions; and as for method, salvation is attainable only by discarding, through any degree of renunciation necessary, all that is differentiated. This is the philosophy of renunciation which is so strong in Buddhism (throughout the Orient) and in all major Indian systems. It finds its parallel also—though to a much lesser degree—in the "fatalistic resignation" or "passive endurance" of Chinese life and thought, and specifically in the Taoist search for ultimate peace or quietude.[90] All of

and passion as inherited from the cycle of karma from beginningless time that we connect it with these. . . .

"Though the belief that the world is full of sorrow has not been equally prominently emphasized in all systems, yet it may be considered as being shared by all of them. . . . All our experiences are essentially sorrowful and ultimately sorrow-begetting. Sorrow is the ultimate truth of this process of the world . . . through the highest moral elevation a man may attain absolute dispassion towards world experiences and retire in body, mind, and speech from all worldly concerns. . . . There was never the slightest tendency to shirk the duties of this life, but to rise above them through right performance and right knowledge. It is only when a man rises to the highest pinnacle of moral glory that he is fit for aspiring to that realization of selfhood in comparison with which all worldly things or even the joys of Heaven would not only shrink into insignificance, but appear in their true character as sorrowful and loathsome."

[89] See Professor Northrop's analysis of the basic metaphysical principles of the great Oriental systems, Ch. VIII.

[90] See Fung, *Chuang Tzǔ*, Introduction, for a discussion of the similarity of Spinoza and Chuang Tzǔ in this respect.

Hinduism joins Vedānta and Buddhism in this general interpretation of the ultimate, not in the sense of complete monistic extinction
of the individual and of all differentiations, but unquestionably in
the sense of terminating the process of rebirth. *Moksha* or "release" and the cessation of rebirth (and thereby the cessation of
pain) constitute the *Summum Bonum*. This, under our definition,
is negative and "world-and-life-denying"—ultimately and ideally—
and so is the method thereto.

(b) Strictly speaking, even the more moderate theory of the two
levels of reality implies a negativistic attitude toward the everyday
world. The world and the events therein do not constitute reality
itself and so the *Summum Bonum* cannot be found there; they are
relatively real only, possibly a necessary stepping stone from the
finite to the infinite, but still *at most* only a means to a more ultimate
end. In keeping with all of these attitudes is that which the Indians
call "initial pessimism," a dissatisfaction with the world which all
the Hindu system-builders as well as the Buddha found to be full
of pain. That such pessimism is merely "initial" and not complete
or final, since there is an ultimate way of escape, does not change
the picture materially with reference to the world, for *as a rule* the
reaction of these systems does not take the form of a positive effort
to improve the conditions of the world but merely to change the
state of mind of the sufferer by inculcating attitudes of detachment
and by pointing to the goal of ultimate release. Like "Reality," the
Summum Bonum transcends the here-and-now and all its meanings
and values; the latter are accepted only as partially significant.

(c) This negativism in its more moderate sense may be summed
up as the essence of the doctrine of *karmayoga*. This is a composite
of two attitudes that seem contradictory until they are synthesized.
There is, first, the attitude of *karma*, work or deeds or action to be
done; and second, the attitude of *yoga* or control, primarily of one's
mind, so as not to become in any way attached to that action or to
any possible benefits therefrom. It is the attitude of doing one's
duty as one's duty and since it is one's duty, the purely disinterested
performance of duty. *Karmayoga* does not advocate inaction or
negation; the work is to be done and it is done. However, the attitude one adopts toward that work is negative for it consists of an
absolute rejection of all attachment to things worldly. It is well expressed and its manifold significance is implied in the summary

statement that "there are two kinds of action, one that is done under the influence of attachment, hatred, infatuation, another that is done without these. It is only the first that strengthens our desire to cling to the world and generates the seeds of *karma* causing rebirth."[91]

Such is the spirit of *karmayoga* which, better than any other single doctrine, constitutes the spirit of a great portion of the Orient.[92] It is the essential principle of the working philosophy of the Hindu, the Buddhist and the Jain. In a sense it seems also to express the true attitude of the Taoist whose spontaneous action is characterized by a similar lack of striving to do something or to accomplish, and the practice of "doing work but not taking pride in it." *Karmayoga* in a sense, also expresses the spirit of the Japanese way of life which is a composite of the activism of Confucianism, Shintō and Bushidō and the detachment, discipline, control of desires, meditation, etc., that come from Buddhism. The resultant mode of living is strikingly similar to *karmayoga*, the doing of one's worldly duty but with a sense of detachment or serenity which gives both to Arjuna in the *Bhagavad Gītā* and to the Japanese *bushi* or *samurai* (or even the present-day warrior) a soul-inspiring courage.[93]

The doctrine of *karmayoga* cannot be overemphasized. In spirit it is present in the major philosophies of all of the countries we are discussing. It might easily be accepted as the most significant discovery of the East. It is second only to the theory of the practical basis and function of philosophy as the most nearly universal attitude of the Orient. *Karmayoga* is in large measure the spirit of the East and stands in sharp contrast to the spirit of the West. There is something here that reminds one of Kant's philosophy of "duty for duty's sake." Generally speaking, the West, in contrast

[91] Chatterjee and Datta, *op. cit.*, p. 142.

[92] As we have seen, attachment is one of the chief vices in Buddhism and is rejected completely in the fivefold vow of Jainism, while detachment is the essential point of the entire *Bhagavad Gītā*. *Karmayoga* is also implied in every orthodox Hindu system. (See Radhakrishnan, *Indian Philosophy*, I, pp. 215 ff.; II, pp. 163, 222-223, 309, 619, 625, 631-633, 629, 704.) The Buddha and Śaṅkara, active but unattached after their attainment of wisdom, were living embodiments of *karmayoga*. Representing modern India, see R. Tagore, *Sādhanā, The Realization of Life* (New York: The Macmillan Co., 1914), esp. Ch. VI.

[93] Even Confucianism has the germs of this attitude in the doctrines of "activity for the sake of activity" and "the union of tranquillity and activity." (Cf. Fung, *A Comparative Study of Life Ideals*, pp. 176 ff., and 221-222.)

to the East, has "deified" activity. More important is the contrast of the *motive* of activity; in the West there is no spirit of *yoga* or control, no sense of detachment or disinterestedness in activity. In the West one acts primarily for the sake of the immediate result of the action, or because of love of activity as such, and this is not only the very opposite of *karmayoga*, but also perhaps, the secret of the West's bondage to the world and its values.

Karmayoga represents the spirit of the Orient in action and the Lotus flower symbolizes this spirit. It could hardly symbolize the spirit of the West. The Lotus symbolizes the East because, although it comes to birth, lives, and grows in contact with the world and with the mud and often with the filth of the world, it is completely undefiled by that mud or filth and is not even stained by the water that touches it. Thus it is not so much detachment or world-denial that the Oriental demands but rather the absolute denial of attachment in the sense of *undue* love of the temporary and relatively insignificant things of the here-and-now.

Were it not for the dominant idea of obtaining eternal life in heaven, Christianity—although it too is Eastern in origin—would link the West with this basic Oriental attitude. Such "interested" action, so intimately related to the gaining of a desired goal, is specifically rejected by the *karmayoga* philosophies. Nevertheless, in its attitude toward the world and the things thereof, Christianity is in harmony with *karmayoga*. The Buddha or even Śaṅkara, as well as St. Paul, might have said that it is the *love* of money that is the root of all evil. Essentially, Christianity shows here something of the spirit of the East; and the Orient, despite Western and Christian critics, has the true spirit of Christianity *in this respect*. Attachment to the worldly (to anything that can distract one's interest from the real and the ultimate) is evil—in Buddhism, in Hinduism, in Jainism, in Taoism, and in Christianity. In none of these is the world to be rejected in any complete sense, nor are the normal functions of living to be denied. In all, however, there is to be no attachment to the temporary, the transient, the relatively unreal.

(d) Another phase of the negativism of the East is the attitude of the Middle Path, the Golden Mean, or Moderation. This attitude was defined and evaluated very significantly by the late Professor C. R. Lanman who described it as "simple living and moderate desires," and called that *the* essential lesson that the East could teach the West. Such a description of the East and such an evaluation must seem strange indeed to the West which is not accustomed to think of the Orient as a land of moderation. Moderation is an essential attitude of much of the East, however, from Persia to Japan. The East is not a land of extremes—of asceticism or indulgence. There are asceticisms in all Oriental lands and they are prominent. There have been hedonisms, too. But moderation is explicitly one of the basic virtues of Buddhism[94] and Zoroastrianism,[95] and in the specific senses just mentioned ("two levels" and *karmayoga*) it is basic also in Hinduism and Jainism as well as Buddhism. There is also strong evidence of the influence of moderation even in Japan where the more activistic philosophies of Shintō, Bushidō, and Confucianism are blended with the more negativistic spirit of Buddhism.

The attitude of moderation is more clearly and more specifically a Chinese contribution, however. Not only is it a fundamental virtue of Confucius (*chung yung*) and Confucianism, but it is present even in Taoism, although the latter is much more negativistic in general tone than Confucianism. Aside from specific systems, China *as a whole*, more than any other part of the East and of the world, is the land of "simple living and moderate desires"—as is almost inevitable where the dominant attitude is a synthesis of Confucianism, Taoism, and Buddhism.

One illustration from Chinese philosophy may prove enlightening. Lao Tzŭ makes the statement that "when a tree has grown strong it is doomed."[96] Consider this in connection with his other statements that "it is better to adhere to the central principle (middle path),"[97] that "he who knows content's content is always content,"[98] and that he "who is content incurs no humiliation, who knows when to stop risks no vitiation,"[99] and the meaning is clear.[100]

[94] The Sermon of Benares (*Mahāvagga*, I, 6, Secs. 10-47 and *Buddhacaritakāvya Sūtra*, 1217-1279).
[95] *Dinkard*, Bk. VI, x, 11-12; XII, 56; *Menuk-i Khrat*, 47. (Cited by M. A. Buch, *Zoroastrian Ethics*.)
[96] *Tao-tê Ching*, LXXVI, 4; or, as Chuang Tzŭ would say: "It [the tree] is useless and good for nothing. Therefore it has attained to so great an age." (*Chuang Tzŭ*, Ch. IV.) The even more extreme negativism of Chuang Tzŭ's more famous illustration and of his philosophy in general induces one to follow Lao Tzŭ in the present discussion.
[97] Lao Tzŭ, *op. cit.*, V, 3.   [98] *Ibid.*, XLVI, 3.   [99] *Ibid.*, XLIV, 3.
[100] See also, *ibid.*, XLIV, 3; XXIX, 3; XXXII, 3; XIX, 4.

Though the general tendency in Taoism is in the direction of negativism, it is no philosophy of inaction or nothingness; it is rather
a philosophy of "simple living," a negation only of striving, extravagance and artificiality. It is unquestionably a philosophy of "simplicity," and that is almost synonymous with the present meaning
of the term "moderation." At all events, the tree that does not try,
as it were, to wax strong, to develop to its fullest capacity, is permitted by the woodsman to live an untroubled if undeveloped existence; it is given "long life."

This illustration is merely a particular case, but its significance
goes far beyond that because it describes the spirit of the general
Chinese way of life. Confucius and Confucianists generally would
agree in spirit on this major point of moderation although they most
certainly would not agree as to the actual content of life (as we shall
see later). "To go beyond is as wrong as to fall short,"[101] says
Confucius. "Extravagance leads to insubordination, and parsimony
to meanness."[102] "Perfect is the virtue which is according to the
Constant Mean (*chung yung*)."[103] The Confucian, unlike the Taoist, never seeks mere contentment or long life; and, furthermore,
the later Confucian doctrine of the "exhaustion" of one's nature,
or the "full exercise of one's mind,"[104] seems to contradict the principle of moderation—and it most certainly does indicate a deviation
from simple moderation—but actually Confucianism never lost the
spirit of *chung yung*. Mencius, for example, urges us to "make the
desires few,"[105] to practice the Middle Path,[106] and to seek as our
goal an unperturbed mind[107] and tranquillity.[108] Hsün Tzŭ contended that man's natural desires should be gratified but always under the moderating control of propriety.[109] Rites and music, essentials of all social living, have for their specific purpose the
moderation of man's desires, sentiments and passions.[110] In fact,
the spirit of all Confucianism is that of harmony in all things and
with all things, and in such a philosophy there is no place for ex-

---

[101] *The Analects*, XI, 14.   [102] *Ibid.*, VII, 36.   [103] *Ibid.*, VI, 27.
[104] *The Doctrine of the Mean*, XIII, 3; XXII; XXV. See also Tai Tung-
yüan: "When a man does not develop his capabilities to the utmost, it is due
to two evils, namely, selfishness and delusion."
[105] *Mencius*, Bk. VII, II, 35.   [106] *Ibid.*, V, II, 4.   [107] *Ibid.*, II, I, 2.
[108] *Ibid.*, IV, I, 11.   [109] *Hsün Tzŭ*, Ch. XIX.
[110] *Li Chi*, Bk. XX, Sec. 4 and Bk. VII, Sec. I, Chs. 10 and 19, as cited by
Fung, *A Comparative Study of Life Ideals*, pp. 167-168.

tremes. Even in later and Neo-Confucianism the search is for tranquillity and equilibrium of mind,[111] for "rational happiness,"[112] which is found in not making one's happiness depend upon the external success of one's actions, and for "absolute calm," which is "the union of tranquillity and activity,"[113] "the highest and best state of mind."[114]

Lao Tzŭ's statement (about the tree) indicates how this Oriental type of moderation (or "simplicity") of activity is in sharp contrast to the theory of the West, and especially—paradoxically—to the view of Aristotle.[115] To put the point briefly, it is highly doubtful if Plato or Aristotle or St. Thomas or any other major Western advocate of moderation would make the statement quoted from Lao Tzŭ or accept its implications. In essence Lao Tzŭ is advising one not to live fully but long and contentedly. He is urging that the best life is one of contentment and that the best means thereto is to avoid anything that can bring discontent. Negatively, he is opposing what the West would call "perfectionism."[116]

[111] *The Works of Wang Yang-ming*, Bk. I.

[112] See Fung, *op. cit.*, pp. 179 ff.

[113] China, especially Confucian China, could never really go beyond this synthesis—of activity and passivity—in either direction. Despite considerations and complications to be noticed later, it could never attain the West's exaggerated explicit emphasis on the purely positive or active. China, that is, must always keep in mind the basic dualism of *yang* and *yin*, neither of which may be explicitly or implicitly ignored. A compromise or a harmony of these two essential forces and attitudes is almost inevitable.

[114] Fung, *op. cit.*, p. 221.

[115] Aristotle always calls for intense activity and "work," never for "rest" or "mere life"—for the "flute-player, statuary, or artisan of any kind," or for that superior person, if any, who can live the life of Contemplation which consists of ceaseless intellectual activity. "The work of a harp-player is to play the harp, and of a good harp-player to play it well . . . in fact everything is finished off well in the way of the excellences which peculiarly belong to it: if all this is so, then the Good of Man comes to be 'a working of the soul in the way of its Excellence,' or, if Excellence admits of degrees, in the way of the best and most perfect Excellence." *Nicomachean Ethics,* 1097b-1098a (Everyman Edition). See also 1177b-1178a. Plato has a similar view, of course. See *Republic,* 352-354. Recall also Socrates' refusal to accept "mere life" in the *Apology* and *Crito.*

[116] This is not to be interpreted to mean that Chinese philosophers such as Lao Tzŭ and Confucius advocated moderate morality or that they opposed moral perfection. On the contrary, both *demanded* moral perfection—though in different senses of the term.

If[117] moderation in this sense is indicative of the spirit of the Chinese philosophy of life, a most important contrast between a great part of the East and the West becomes manifest. The West has tended strongly to follow Plato (especially of the *Republic*) and Aristotle in their attitude of living fully, of development, of perfectionism or self-realization in the sense of the *full* actualization of one's potentialities. "Living" is the primary requisite. Living fully is the ideal. The attitude of sacrificing fullness of life for mere contentment is not unknown in the West,[118] but it is not prominent in the main stream of Western philosophy, where it has arisen occasionally but has been rejected. The relative insignificance of such negativistic ethical philosophies as those of the Stoics, Epicurus, the Neo-Platonists, and Schopenhauer—as factors either in Western life or as influences upon the development of Western thought in the negative direction—is a clear indication of the West's domination by a more positive point of view. Most important of all, perhaps, is the clear-cut case of Christianity, in which the negative and otherworldly tendency of the early period was progressively modified in the direction of a much more positive attitude toward life and activity in the here-and-now. At this point, then, the East offers a strong contrast and protest to the West's dominant philosophy of life, the philosophy of unlimited striving for perfection in whatever direction one chooses (hedonistic, naturalistic, idealistic), often, or rather, inevitably, at the expense of contentment.

This Oriental view must not be misunderstood or it will be attacked—as it has been so often—as worthless. It is not fatalism,[119] indifference, or an attitude of inactivity. It is not a running away

[117] It is possible that this account overestimates the importance of moderation of activity and the search for contentment as parts of the total Chinese philosophy of life. Confucianism, which is decidedly the predominating factor—though not the only one—in China's synthetic philosophy admittedly stresses more positive methods of living and more positive goals of human conduct. We shall return to this latter point shortly.

[118] The Stoics and Epicurus, as examples, and even Socrates in the *Gorgias*.

[119] Despite the fatalistic tendency in Taoism and Confucianism and the appearance of determinism implied in the Indian and Buddhist doctrine of *karma*, every Oriental system modifies this theory by calling for personal moral effort and for personal responsibility.

from life in any extreme sense. To one who is dominated by the attitude of striving on and on toward some unattainable goal, this Oriental philosophy of moderation seems "weak" and "cowardly."[120] It is none of these. It simply avoids excess in the direction of striving for a goal which is always beyond one's reach. Contentment, for the Oriental, does not mean contentment with anything; it does not involve any deadening lack of activity; it does not exclude moderate effort; nor does it mean blind acceptance of Fate. As lived and as formulated into theory, the philosophy of moderation and contentment is merely a common-sense protest against the inevitably unsuccessful philosophy of life which seeks, but cannot find, happiness or man's *Summum Bonum* in continual and excessive striving, the striving for perfection in some worldly sense, of course. It consists essentially in the recognition of the futility of a philosophy that is doomed to insatiability. The philosophy of perfectionism, of relentless striving without knowing "when to stop," of never being content with what one has but always being dominated by the urge to be or have more, has produced what we in the West call progress; but it has also produced competition, destruction, uncertainty, insecurity, and the complete absence of "peace of mind." The Orient rejects that philosophy of life.

(e) This dominant philosophy of the West is rejected because it fails to lead to the one supreme goal of mankind: peace of mind, or spiritual peace. When the Hindu and the Jain seek *Moksha* and when the Buddhist seeks Nirvāṇa, these philosophies are "negative" in the sense of rejecting (ultimately) the world of the here-and-now. They are excessive in their denunciation of things worldly and in the price they pay for "peace." They stand at the opposite pole in relation to the West, for the latter, even in its religious philosophies, can never reject the meanings and values of this life, but must have them preserved in some way, even in the ultimate, in the hereafter—a view which the Oriental considers just as antagonistic to reason as the West finds the Indian philosophy of *moksha* or Nirvāṇa. Be that as it may, the Chinese have still a third philosophy to suggest: the seeking of peace of mind or general contentment through moderation and simple living. This is also a middle path between the excesses of the Indian philosophies of re-

---

[120] It may be "unprogressive," but that criticism depends, partly at least, upon a question-begging definition of progress.

nunciation and the Western philosophies of perfectionism. Here, then, seems to be a clue to the synthesis we must seek between East and West.

[This and similar observations in the present phase of our study are not to be mistaken for (1) the conviction that happiness (or, specifically, peace of mind) rather than moral character is the ultimate good, or (2) the contention that Oriental philosophy maintains this thesis. The former question is not under discussion here. The latter, a frequent misunderstanding of much of Oriental philosophy, has been discussed to some extent and will be examined further in a later section on Hedonism.]

The West is apt to consider this philosophy of "peace," "quietude," and "contentment," as negative just as it habitually ascribes such descriptions to the more extreme philosophies. These less extreme goals, so positive to the Oriental, are negative and objectionable to the Westerner because he considers activity, self-realization, success, fame, accomplishment, possessions, and even excitement and risk as the true goals of man. To the typical Westerner "unrest is divine." We have deified activity. The East questions the truth of a philosophy which finds these values to be the constituents of the "good life." What is man seeking, after all? Is it not whatever can provide him with lasting satisfaction, real contentment, or peace of mind? Is desire really desirable? That is the question that so many Orientals have answered in the negative. Struggling, the ambition to go on and on, the endless striving for activity and improvement, has become the dominating spirit of the West. But has this attitude been adequately demonstrated or even adequately challenged? Can lasting satisfaction be derived from such a way of life? To be sure, we all—East and West—like excitement and risk, but is that reasonable when, as is almost universally the case, such pursuits jeopardize our real goal which is contentment? And can one really be happy without contentment? Perhaps Callicles[121] was right in saying that a contented man is like a stone—dead—but so, perhaps, was Schopenhauer when he noted that the ceaseless driving of the Will led to only momentary satisfaction along with almost continuous dissatisfaction. Perhaps Nietzsche too was right when he noted the implications of his philosophy of the

[121] See Plato's *Gorgias* for a pointed debate on this question—with Socrates defending the philosophy of contentment.

"will to power," for he saw clearly what we apparently fail to see; namely, that the continual striving to push ahead involves competition, ruthlessness, and the destruction of those not capable of surviving. Few, if any, in that state of affairs achieve contentment or happiness.

Our typical Western way of living is not so extreme as that of Nietzsche, but neither is the Chinese philosophy of contentment the equivalent of Callicles' stone or of Schopenhauer's "denial of the will." The Chinese think and live by common sense,[122] and it is common sense to be moderate, to be contented short of achievement of greatness or wealth, of "name, fame and accomplishment." The suggestion is merely the innocuous one that the West, for all its prowess, for all its mechanical achievements, has not achieved either contentment or happiness. The philosophy of "perfectionism" (in the sense described herein) is essentially the philosophy of life of the West, and its worth and soundness have been overestimated by the West. One need not be a defeatist, a fatalist, or a pessimist to recognize that. The East—especially China—suggests a solution, a common-sense solution: moderate desires and simple living.

This may not be the full or exclusive meaning of any single ethical system of China—Confucianism, Taoism, or Buddhism—but it is the spirit of the characteristic Chinese synthesis of these several philosophies. Such an analysis must not lead to any misunderstanding of these several systems that contribute to the total Chinese attitude. For example, as suggested above, Confucianism, especially later Confucianism, is a philosophy of "Perfectionism" and Self-Realization. Although Confucianism never loses sight of the virtue of the Golden Mean, it is neither an attitude of modera-

---

[122] For an interesting and nontechnical description, see Lin Yutang, *My Country and My People* (1935), and *The Importance of Living* (1937). New York: The John Day Co. See also Bingham Dai, "Some Chinese Fears," in *Asia and the Americas*, XLIII, No. 11, Nov. 1943, p. 619: "If one stops to reflect on the facts of Chinese cultural history, . . . one cannot help observing a note of nonaggressiveness or nonassertiveness running through them all. Nor can one help asking whether underneath there is not a basic Chinese character or personality structure that is essentially noncombative, one that is characterized by no great urge toward perfection or absolute mastery or undisputed success but by a highly developed sensitiveness to human feelings and a very great concern about personal relations."

tion *in activity* nor a search for mere contentment. It is this aspect of Chinese philosophy that distinguishes it so clearly from the more negativistic philosophy of India. To begin with, the very basic concept of *chung yung* is open to several interpretations; it need not mean mere moderation—in fact, it seldom means only that. A more accurate translation is "central principle," so that Confucianism is not so much a philosophy of moderation or the golden mean as it is a philosophy of following the central principle, of doing the "just right." This latter interpretation requires exact and full performance of one's duty and the fulfillment of one's nature—nothing "half-way," even in the name of contentment, is acceptable. For example, as early as *The Analects* of Confucius and the doctrine of the "rectification of names," the prince is to be prince, the minister is to be minister, the father is to be father, and the son is to be son (XII, 11). That is self-realization.

But even this is not sufficient. Such self-realization and the activity involved therein are to be carried out to the limit of one's capacity. Herein lies much of the contrast between Taoism and Confucianism. Confucius speaks, for example, of serving one's parents with one's utmost strength (I, 7), and of the fullest observance of all rules of propriety in serving one's prince (III, 18). Mencius says that he who would be a ruler or a minister must "to the fullest extent" fulfill the way of a ruler or minister (IV, I, 2), and speaks of the ideal of "exhausting one's heart or mind" (VII, I, 1). The *Chung Yung* advises one to "realize one's nature to the fullest extent" (XXII), while *The Great Learning* calls for the "utmost endeavour" (II) and urges one to "rest in the highest good" (I). Similarly, the *Li Chi* demands that one "follow the way to the fullest extent" (XXVI, 10) and, specifically, "in the matter of respect go to the fullest extent of respect" (XXV, 12).

That general attitude is "Perfectionism" and as such represents the spirit of Confucianism as a whole. In this sense, then, "Perfectionism"—not mere contentment—is the ideal of Confucian China (and China, of course, has been primarily Confucian throughout most of its history). Nevertheless, *Confucian China has been modified, and not insignificantly, by Taoism and Buddhism.* The above description which emphasized moderation as a central principle of the Chinese way of life, was an attempt to portray the

Chinese attitude which results from the practical and theoretical merging of these three philosophies.

Here—to return to the point—is possibly the most important single contrast of East and West. Disregarding for the moment the fallacy of oversimplification, it is clear that the West is a world of activity, of doing and getting; it has a positive philosophy in that sense, whereas the East generally tends to denounce or at least to moderate activity in the name of such goals as peace, harmony, contentment. Stated baldly, the West has a positive philosophy of action, but has little comprehension of any ultimate goal of action. It too often forgets that action is only a means to an end. The East, on the other hand, has concentrated its attention on the goal but has often lost sight of the means of better living (although it has not lost sight of the means to "salvation"). The result of these opposite tendencies, for the West, is that its unbridled activity or "busyness," especially since it is directed toward no clearly defined goal acceptable to thinking men, has led to frightful consequences; to interminable confusion, disorder, unrest; and even to war as one of its inevitable results—without any possibility of peace, contentment, or lasting satisfaction.

The proof of this is the ever-recurring destructiveness and the insatiability of Western civilization despite its recognized genius for production. The airplane, for example, was invented, theoretically, for the betterment or convenience of mankind. But since production, action, doing, grew apace without due consideration of the goal to which all of this might lead, this product of human intelligence is now used for the very opposite purpose. Making and doing are not the essence of the good life; they must be guided and, if need be, curtailed in view of a rationally and practically acceptable comprehension of the meaning of life and of the ultimate values thereof.

It is no answer to say that activity in itself is its own reward— even Confucianism says this at times—for this is at least questionable; it becomes almost unintelligible if such activity is blind, if it has no goal to which it is directed. It is with the greatest difficulty that one can accept the thesis that activity, endless striving, or excitement—without goal or direction—is the supreme good of man. Action is almost unquestionably only a means to some end. The means and the end of life are not identical and must not be confused as in the West; nor should either be discarded in the name of the other, as seems to be the practice in both East and West. The good life consists, not in action or power alone, nor in their elimination, but in the directing of man's activities toward an acceptable human goal. The great contribution of the East in this respect is not only its insistence that the West must not, in its busy life of doing, lose sight of the goal of its activity, but also its suggestion that the goal of man, the only goal that does not lead to chaos, confusion, or dissatisfaction, is spiritual peace or contentment. This goal of Peace is of two kinds, the more ultimate spiritual peace which is characteristic of Hinduism and Buddhism, and the more commonplace peace or contentment which is characteristic of the Chinese point of view. The weakness of Western philosophy—and living—is that it has failed to emphasize and to provide either of these.

Monism

Another of the ways in which the philosophy of the Orient can supplement that of the West is through its famous and widespread tendency to monism as contrasted with the West's "overemphasis on the individual."[123] The West has had its monistic philosophies, from Plato to our day, but in emphasis and in living—especially since Christianity's insistence on the infinite value of the individual—there is little question that the West has tended in the opposite direction. Oriental philosophy varies greatly on this question, from absolute monism to absolute pluralism.[124] This is not the place to discuss the extent of the monism of the philosophies of the East, except to indicate the various types of monism as reflected in their ethical applications—for *each* of these has a distinct significance for the West.

(a) There is extreme monism—for example in Vedānta, the most significant philosophy of India—although only Vedānta (of Śaṅkara) of all the major philosophies of the East is completely monistic. On the other hand, to the extent that several of the Oriental

[123] For a more extensive comparative discussion of this problem of the status of the individual, see E. R. Hughes (ed.), *The Individual in East and West* (Oxford, 1937).

[124] See previous descriptive chapters and summary outlines of systems in the present chapter.

philosophies hold to the theory of the "undifferentiated continuum" as the ultimate reality—and this is significantly prominent throughout the East—so far are they monistic *from the ultimate point of view*. Rejecting all finite differentiation, these philosophies reject also all particularity as being ultimately unreal or insignificant. These Orientals see things from the point of view of an ultimate perspective and from this perspective the individual as such loses all status. The place of man in the universe is the real interest of these more monistic systems in clear contrast to the West's individualism. In the more extreme of these Oriental philosophies all mundane meanings and values are transcended and the individual is absorbed in or reunited with the One. This has been the tendency in Hinduism from the Upanishads to Vedānta and it has been criticized by the West as an unacceptable philosophy since it does injustice to the individual, the person. For the Hindu, however—and this is the significance of the attitude for the West—it is not a case of losing reality but of gaining infinity of Being; it is not loss of self or of self-realization but the identification of the self with the Absolute. It is the infinite expansion of self. The self which can become identical with the very Absolute is the truly "expanding self" rather than that self of the West's "centrifugal philosophy of the 'expanding will' which, at its best, centers about the perfecting of society and the world."[125] *Tat tvam asi* (that art thou) does not mean annihilation but realization.[126]

This extreme monism is rare even in India. Buddhism is difficult to describe but in the large it seems to conform, ultimately, with the general implications of the philosophy of the undifferentiated continuum. In that sense—*ultimately*—Buddhism is nonindividualistic. Furthermore, the consciousness of self is frequently described as the source of all evil or suffering. (Selfishness in any form is rejected universally in the great Oriental philosophies.) However, there are phases of Buddhism which deny any extreme interpretation. The spirit of Buddhism is universal altruism and the rejection

---

[125] Edward L. Schaub, "Indian Philosophy in its Divergence from the Spirit of the West," *The Open Court* (Chicago: Open Court Publishing Co., 1930), Sec. II, p. 598.

[126] The answer to this question of the ultimate status of the individual depends, of course, upon metaphysical considerations; thus the Oriental tendency cannot be condemned except on the basis of metaphysical disproof.

of all self-interest. The spirit of the Bodhisattva (would-be Buddha) who will not even accept Nirvāṇa until all have been saved is the essence of Buddhism. The status of the individual when all have been "saved" is open to question; but beyond all question this ultimate state of man is not one of personal immortality in any form similar to the usual Western meaning of that concept. Furthermore, as in much of Hinduism, in this ultimate state of salvation not only is the individual transcended but so also are all of the particular interests and values of the individual—the worldly meanings and values and interests. This brings to our attention one observation that must be made with reference to *any* philosophy which believes in "salvation" of the transcendental sort. Hinduism and Buddhism suggest that such salvation must consist in the transcendence of things worldly since these are only partially real. Consequently, they further suggest that the individual, the private self, must also be transcended for the private self is the self of these worldly interests. This suggests that *any* such philosophy must accept also these implications. What justification is there for demanding, as the West does almost universally, the preservation of the meanings and values of the here-and-now? Owing to its close tie with the world of the here-and-now the West has often said, in effect, that if one cannot "live" and "do things" even in the hereafter one cannot find the hereafter desirable. The Hindu and the Buddhist consider this attitude unintelligible philosophically; and, practically, as the root of all evil, for it is significantly indicative of the West's bondage to this life and to the things of this life—with the further indication of the lack of ultimate perspective. By comparison, then, the West is narrow-sighted—it thinks excessively in terms of the many and the here-and-now.

(b) There are still further—though less extreme—phases of the monistic tendency of the Orient that are significant for the West— and they all agree on one point, namely, the rejection of any view which places ultimate value upon the individual as such. In all there is a higher principle. One of these is the Taoist tendency to monism. Tao, the only real, is one. It produced the many but these, essentially, are only appearances. As in Plato, the many, the appearances, gain what reality they have by virtue of their participation in the One. Tao is the universal principle of all things, the essence of reality. It transcends finite particularity; it cannot be defined. In the more mystical interpretation Tao is conceived of as something similar to Brahman, but Tao is primarily the *way*, the essential or underlying law or principle of reality, like, say, the *Logos* of Heracleitus or the Idea of the Good of Plato (though not identical in specific nature). In this sense, Taoism represents a different type of monism from that of Hinduism (and Buddhism). The ideal in Taoism is conformity with the law of reality, whether that be interpreted as a purely natural law or as a supernatural principle. All types of metaphysical pluralism are rejected since the many do not constitute reality, but, at the same time, there is no absorption of the many into the One. True, there is no individual immortality but in another sense Taoism demands individuality or differentiation. The way in which any particular thing can best conform to Tao is actually to conform absolutely to its own *tê*, its own "virtue" or its own specific nature,[127] for the universal law of Tao is exemplified in the natural functionings of the many particular kinds of things. It is doubtful if Tao has any meaning apart from the various *tê* of the many. The many were created by the One, to be sure, but they are not therefore unreal; they are most real, however, only when they conform absolutely to Tao, to the way of things, just as in Plato the world would be at its best and would be most real if and when all things conformed to the Idea of the Good.

Here is monism of a significant kind. Obviously it is not unknown to the West, but it becomes more significant when seen in the context of the whole Oriental picture where *some* form of monism is found to be necessary. The spirit of Taoism, though unlike that of Hinduism and Buddhism which are much more monistic in their extreme forms, is still unmistakably monistic. Each thing, by conforming to its own *tê*, conforms also to the universal Tao, and in this way the universe runs smoothly. It is a philosophy of the harmony of things with each other and of all things with Nature or

[127] "Tao produces a thing: *Tê* maintains it." *Tao-tê Ching*, Ch. LI. "The duck's legs are short, but if we try to lengthen them, the duck will feel pain. The crane's legs are long, but if we try to cut off a portion of them, the crane will feel grief. We are not to amputate what is by nature long, nor to lengthen what is by nature short." *Chuang Tzŭ*, Ch. VIII. "Act according to your will within the limit of your nature, but have nothing to do with what is beyond it." Kuo Hsiang, Comments to Ch. IV. (Fung's translations, in *Chuang Tzŭ*, Introduction.)

with the inner principle of Nature. Practically speaking, it is opposed to any philosophy of competition or the effort to expand oneself beyond the natural limits of one's nature. In these senses Taoism is monistic. Its contrast with the spirit of the West is that its naturalism or its philosophy of self-realization (if it may be called such) is directed toward and achieves a decidedly different result from that of Western Naturalism or Western philosophies of self-realization. The contrast may be stated simply as that between harmony and competition. The spirit of harmony is very largely the spirit of the East while competition is the spirit of the West. Perhaps neither is exclusively acceptable but a more serious synthesis than the West has yet achieved seems essential.

(c) The metaphysical side of Confucianism as developed in Neo-Confucianism and the ethical implications of that metaphysical theory produce another phase of the Orient's tendency to monism.

Confucianism, from Confucius through its modern formulations, holds that the form of a thing's activity is to be guided or determined by that thing's essential nature and the sum-total of all such activity (as in the social organization advocated by Confucius) is to take the form of a harmonious and cooperative complex of activity.[128] In this form of Confucianism there are the germs of a more extreme type of metaphysical monism such as would nullify the significance of individuality. The seeds of this interpretation are to be found in the fact that Confucianism also has its ultimate One, the Great Ultimate from which all things are supposed to have originated. As Professor Chan has so well explained, however, in Neo-Confucian metaphysics there is an essential harmony and an interdependence between the One and the many, the *Li* and the *ch'i*. The ideal is a harmony or unity of man and Nature and of each man with all men and with all things. The Confucian does not "overemphasize" either the individual or the more monistic Great Ultimate of all reality; the individual is not "swallowed up into" any Absolute—but neither is he personally immortal.[129]

---

[128] "All things live together without injuring one another. All courses are passed without collision with one another." *The Doctrine of the Mean*, Ch. XXX. (Fung's translation in *A Comparative Study of Life Ideals*, p. 183.)

[129] For a discussion of the question of immortality in Confucianism, see F. Rawlinson, *Chinese Ethical Ideals* (Peiping: California College in China, 1934), pp. 104 ff.

(d) From the less metaphysical point of view, too, the Oriental has found that a more monistic form of life and society is the best. The caste system of India, the clan-family system of China and Japan, the nationalism of Japan, and the concept of duty (perhaps better described as loyalty in Japan and possibly also in China) are well-known Oriental attitudes which, from the purely practical point of view, make the individual primarily a part of a larger whole and deny to him any degree of complete significance in himself. This point need not be labored except to state what is obvious to the modern West—perhaps chiefly to the American—that one of the weaknesses of democracy and individualism as we know them, with their insistence on the rights of the individual, has been the inability to instill in that individual any *adequate* sense of the reality of society as a whole or of the individual's obligation to society. Great social, political, and philosophical writers from Plato's day to this have indicated the significance of the group above the individual, or rather, as supplementary to the individual's rights. But it has taken war and devastation to bring us to our senses. The Orient, on the other hand, has seldom thought of individual man as individual and nothing more; in its philosophy and in its living the individual is considered from a wider point of view. Although the East has not sufficiently appreciated the personality of the individual man, it has recognized the other side of man, man the member of the family, of society, of the universe. The East has centered its attention on making the individual more than an individual. The West has been too much interested in his personal individuality. Again, neither East nor West is true to the real or full nature of man; again, a synthesis is the wiser course.

In sum, then, whether it be the thoroughly metaphysical attitude of the Vedāntin or the more down-to-earth social philosophy of Confucius, the Orient has tended to put man in his place in some larger context. In general, harmony among men has been the intended and the actual result. Along with this social harmony has gone harmony of man with Nature or with the universe, rather than the spirit of otherness which more or less prevails in the West. The East has adopted such monistic trends, because of both metaphysical speculation and practical wisdom. The net result—barring contemporary exceptions—has been a world at peace with itself and with others. "Above all nations is mankind." Perhaps the Oriental's tendency to look away from the individual and his private interests may join the Christian doctrine of the brotherhood of man to convince the world that such an ideal is truly worth while.

"Spiritual"-minded vs. Materialistic

One final way of contrasting East and West must be mentioned so as to indicate again the need for supplementation of East by West and of West by East. Positively, it may be said—with many qualifications that will not be drawn forth here—that the East is more spiritually minded, that it is more religious in tendency, than the West. This is the contrast that Shastri had in mind in the quotation previously cited to the effect that the West is soulless, unspiritual, irreligious. At least one way of interpreting this contrast is permissible without qualification; namely, that the East is more spiritually minded if by that one intends to say that the East is primarily more interested in the meaning, the value, the significance of things and even of life than in the things themselves or in life.[130] The West, on the other hand, has been *living* more than it has been *thinking about* life.

A more definite formulation of this contrast may be made negatively, by indicating that the East, in the past and in the present,[131] has in the large rejected as unsound several of the most prominent specific attitudes of the West. It seems significant for us in the West where these theories or ways of life are accepted—explicitly or implicitly—to be reminded of their inadequacy in the eyes of that vast part of mankind known as the Orient. It was said before that in the East certain theories of life "caught on" in the competition of systems through the long ages of Oriental history. It is now time to note the theories that failed to win out, for, *strikingly*, these are in large measure the predominant theories of the West. All of these attitudes have been developed in the East but the emphasis has been almost exclusively in other directions. It is not the absence

[130] This general attitude has differing meanings in the Orient. In India it refers to the predominant interest in man's ultimate status as contrasted with his worldly welfare and also to the dominance of the doctrine of "tendance of the *soul*." In China it refers largely to the interest in culture and beauty rather than physical welfare and efficiency.

[131] For example, the work of Gandhi and Tagore. The modern reaction apparently has not been so strong in China nor, more especially, in Japan.

of the theories but their almost universal and complete *rejection* that is to be noted. In other words, both the positive emphases and, conversely, the rejected attitudes of East and West stand in rather constant and complete contrast. The three major attitudes in mind here are: (1) Hedonism, (2) Naturalism in the Western sense of Thrasymachus, Callicles, Nietzsche, etc.—the philosophy of "might makes right"; and (3) what, for want of a better name, may be called Materialism.

(1) In a sense, and in contradiction to our thesis, the entire East may be described as hedonistic. Strangely enough, this interpretation is not based upon the prominence of specific hedonistic systems, for these—Chārvāka in India and that of "Yang Chu" (as described in the chapter by the same name in *Lieh Tzŭ*) in China— became the least significant philosophies in their homelands and are now without philosophical status. It is based primarily, however, upon unmistakable tendencies within India and China and in all the major philosophies of both. For example, Hinduism seeks escape from the suffering of this world and sets up a *Summum Bonum* which consists either of *Moksha* (release from pain) or Bliss in Brahman; it does not seem to be interested directly in morality or moral conduct except as a means to this so-called hedonistic goal.[132] Jainism has the same problem and the same general perspective (without the concept of Brahman).[133] Buddhism also conforms (with the same qualification), for the problem of Buddhism is to escape the suffering of the world and to reach Nirvāṇa which in this respect is comparable to *Moksha*.[134] All such views seem to qualify at least as "negative hedonism." China also fits the pattern, for the entire philosophy of "simple living and moderate desires," the philosophy of contentment—characteristic of the whole of China—is nothing but moderate or common-sense hedonism. Furthermore, there is no serious opposition to the enjoyment of life[135]—within limits—or any rejection of the satisfac-

[132] See earlier references in this chapter (pp. 268-270) to statements which tend to justify this interpretation.

[133] See pp. 260 and 269 n., this chapter.

[134] See Pratt, *The Pilgrimage of Buddhism,* p. 20, for an interpretation of Buddhism as "altruistic hedonism." Bishop Copleston, in his *Buddhism* charges that Buddhism is completely selfish. See S. Yamakami, *Systems of Buddhist Thought,* pp. 55 ff. for the Buddhist's reply.

[135] See *The Analects,* VII, 26, XVI, 5; *Li Chi,* Bk. VII, Sec. I, Ch. 19.

tion of desires in either Confucianism or Taoism. As Fung says, "Like hedonistic Taoism, Confucianism was in favor of the expression of passion and the satisfaction of desires. . . . Like hedonistic Taoism, Confucianism was in favor of enjoyment of the present and disregard of the future."[136]

Be that as it may, the hedonistic interpretation either exaggerates or misinterprets tendencies within the several systems; or, which is worse, fails completely to comprehend their deeper meanings. To identify Hinduism, Buddhism and Jainism with hedonism is clearly to oversimplify these systems, to think only in terms of their more primitive concepts or problems, and to miss the point of their deeper spiritual meaning. *Moksha*—which is a state of the soul's "natural integrity," beyond both pleasure and pain, or a state of Bliss which (in Hinduism) comes from living in the presence of Brahman or from identification with Brahman—is not to be compared with the spirit of hedonism.[137] *Moksha* and Nirvāṇa are not merely the escape from pain but also from all limitations and differentiations of the relatively unreal; they are the achievement of a state of conformity with reality—and that is not hedonism. Furthermore, inner purity of soul and morality of thought, word, and deed is an almost universal demand.

"Hedonism" in the moderate sense *is* a very real part of the Chinese way of life but even this cannot be compared in any comprehensive way with the philosophical hedonism of the West. China does not know Western hedonism—either in philosophy or in life. In the first place, Taoism transcends hedonism, unless we are to miss the deeper meaning of the system—as in the cases of Hinduism and Buddhism. Conformity with Tao is the *Summum Bonum*. It will lead to peace as well as to "accomplishment" and "happiness," but the important fact is that Tao is the essence of reality—that is why men should "follow Tao."

Perhaps, however, the philosophy of contentment does qualify as hedonism, as *moderate* hedonism, and as such is a necessary part of any sound philosophy or way of living. But hedonism as it is known in the history of Western philosophy—and we intend no

[136] *A Comparative Study of Life Ideals*, pp. 183-184.

[137] If these are to be called hedonistic, so also are the lives of the Christian and the martyr (Christian or otherwise) ; obviously such an interpretation is an oversimplification, to say the least.

exaggeration or caricature of Western hedonism—is an ethical theory which establishes pleasure (exclusively) as the *Summum Bonum*, and defines moral conduct in terms of the pleasure produced, thus denying the rejection or moderation of pleasure in terms of any other or higher value. Such hedonism does not fit the Chinese picture. In Chinese philosophy and living the pursuit of pleasure is always held in check by other and obviously higher standards. One's pleasure seeking is disciplined by one's duty to parents and to family. It is held in check by the universal demand for moderation. Finally, and most important, it is to be determined absolutely in terms of moral principles which, therefore, are not determined in terms of pleasure. For example, both Confucius and Mencius place morality above even life itself[138] and Mencius' greatest dread seems to be that "the principles of Yang Chu and Mo Tzŭ" will not be stopped, for they stand in opposition to "the principles of Confucius . . . (namely) benevolence and righteousness."[139] In other words, China does not recognize philosophical—strict and uncompromising—hedonism as a true way of life. Confucianism condemns it, and Confucianism is not only the basic *philosophy* of China but also the primary guiding principle of Chinese living.

(2) Naturalism in its etymological sense is present throughout the East, for the Oriental has always insisted that one's way of life conform to the nature of things. Naturalism in the narrower Western sense of "natural justice," of "might makes right," of "the survival of the fittest," of "the will to power," has never been a prominent philosophy of the East; it has never been known to the Orient as a basic formulated philosophical system.[140] This is true

[138] *The Works of Mencius*, VI, I, 10; *The Analects*, XV, 8.
[139] Bk. III, II, 9.
[140] It may be contended that there are implications of Naturalism—to some extent at least—in several aspects of Indian philosophy, literature, and living: (1) Kauṭilya's *Arthaśāstra*, a treatise on realistic politics (*c.* 300 B.C.), (2) the *Bhagavad Gītā*, with its apparent approval of war and of the duty of the warrior, and (3) the *Mahābhārata* or Great Epic as a whole, as well as the Code of Manu, both of which recognize the warrior class and demand the fulfillment of its duty. In reply, suffice it to say that orthodox Hindu morality, with its emphasis upon realization of one's social function, but also with its fundamental ideal of noninjury (the very opposite of Naturalism) and its ultimate goal of *Moksha*, is maintained in all of the sources mentioned. This is true even in the case of Kauṭilya, although his emphasis is unques-

despite the fact that the East has had theories of evolution that closely parallel our Western scientific theories which have provided a scientific basis for such ethical doctrines.[141] The inconceivability of such a doctrine to the Oriental seems distinctly significant. Naturalism, in the competitive and even in the aggressive sense, has been prominent throughout the history of Western philosophy. Like hedonism it retains a prominent place both in ethical theory and in practice and from time to time regains a dominant position. Yet the East has never developed a thoroughgoing Naturalism of this type. Why?

Possibly this is explained by the fact that Naturalism would conflict with so many of the basic tenets of Oriental thought and culture generally.[142] There is, for example, the almost universal Indian tendency to find its *Summum Bonum* beyond this world where there is so much suffering. There is also the equally universal Indian doctrine of *ahiṁsā* (noninjury to living creatures). In China, Naturalism would face the contrasting philosophy of contentment as well as the doctrine of harmony. Clearly, Western "Naturalism" has had little chance of success in India where the tendency is to look beyond the world for the chief good and where, in this world, there is the basic attitude of noninjury. The same is true in China where contentment, rather than aggression and power seeking, is universal and where the doctrine of harmony, which dates back to the pre-Confucian effort to harmonize the opposing forces of *yang* and *yin*, stands opposed to any doctrine that calls for conflict as the best way of life. The ideal of all Chinese philosophy is peace and order and harmony. Even the Confucian ideal of individual self-realization and "exhaustion" of one's nature must be actualized under conditions of peace and harmony. "Naturalism," then, by its very nature, is alien to the spirit of India and China.

But what of Japan in this opposition to Naturalism? Modern Japan—since 1868—certainly seems to adhere to a policy of "might

tionably on the practical and the "here-and-now." (See English translation by R. Shamasastry, Mysore, India, 1923.)

[141] See Hu, *The Development of the Logical Method in Ancient China,* Pt. IV.

[142] Another significant consideration here is that for the Oriental "Nature" has seldom meant Nature in the narrower Western sense, so that "following Nature" has not been interpreted in the sense of Western "Naturalism."

makes right," and to a program of aggressive conflict to gain her ends. The picture is further complicated by the fact that *present-day Japan is not a wholly new Japan*, but the older Japan in modern dress. Even feudalistic Japan with its "bushidō" and the *samurai* was much the same[143] essentially. It would be easy—too easy—to fall back upon the theory of the "invented religion"[144] to explain present-day Japan, or to recognize *merely* the influence of the more naturalistic West.[145] Both of these theories undoubtedly have much truth, but the dynamic spirit is as old as Shintō itself, and so is the dominant spirit of absolute loyalty and devotion to country. Japan has learned from the West, primarily its "ways and means," its methods, rather than its philosophies.

The place of Japan in the philosophical picture of the Orient is a serious obstacle to *any* clear-cut description of the East. Japan is in the East and of the East and yet, looked at today, it seems so different. One point is essential, however; namely, that we must not judge the Japanese or Japanese philosophy entirely by the events of recent years. Throughout the ages Japan has been dominated by a mixture of Confucianism, Buddhism and its own Shintō. That combination need not produce "Naturalism" except under extraor-

[143] See J. Takakusu, *The New Japanism*, where it is shown that basic principles of Shintō, Buddhism and Confucianism are still supreme. See also B. H. Chamberlain, *Things Japanese*, 5th edition, revised (London: John Murray, 1905), pp. 7-8: "... so is it abundantly clear to those who have dived beneath the surface of the modern Japanese upheaval that more of the past has been retained than has been let go ... the national character persists intact, manifesting no change in essentials. Circumstances have deflected it into new channels, that is all."

[144] See B. H. Chamberlain, *The Invention of a New Religion* (London, 1912). This article appears in *Things Japanese*, 5th edition, reprinted with two appendices. (London: Kegan Paul, 1927.) The revival of pure Shintō in the late eighteenth and early nineteenth centuries by Motoöri, Mabuchi, and Hirata is clear evidence that the Japanese were highly conscious of this indigenous nationalism and racialism long before the Restoration of 1868.

[145] The West has had great influence upon Japan with its exceptional capacity for imitation and adaptation of alien ideas. The philosophies of Spencer and Mill, the general attitude of American civilization (through the extremely influential writings of Yukichi Fukuzawa), and the industrial methods of the West have all played significant roles in redirecting the modern Japanese mind.

dinary circumstances. Japanese culture is activistic but so is Confucianism (which has served Japan so long) activistic—within the framework of harmony, however, rather than naturalistic aggressiveness. The indigenous activistic spirit of Japan has been molded along naturalistic lines by many forces—some of them emanating from the West and others from the military minority that has held political control—but the modern *naturalistic* Japan is not traditional Japan and thus is not our primary concern—*except* (as we shall see later) *to the extent that it brings to light the thoroughly naturalistic implications of the traditional Japanese philosophy.*

Furthermore, the Japanese have not developed—even in view of modern trends—any formulated doctrine of Naturalism. The so-called Naturalism of modern Japan does not qualify as one of the significant philosophies of the East. In fact, even present-day Japan has repeatedly repudiated philosophical Naturalism, justifying its actions on moral grounds at all times and thinking of recent events in China as "incidents" or "punitive expeditions" (justified in Confucianism),[146] but never as naturalistic acts of aggression. The events of and since December 7, 1941, contradict such explanations and justification of past actions, of course, and reveal the true explanation.

In sum, paradoxical—though not contradictory—as it may seem, the Japan of today is neither traditional Japan nor a new Japan. Even the naturalistic unprincipled present-day warring Japan is not really new. The spirit of the *samurai* and the *bushi* is not new. Nor is the spirit of unflinching devotion to country. Nor are the *basic* virtues of absolute loyalty, obedience to duty, and bravery. These—though they have not necessarily led to naturalistic activities and a naturalistic code of ethics in the past—have prepared the

[146] *The Analects*, XVI, 2. See also Kamazo Mizoguchi, "Orientation in the Study of Shintoism," in *A Guide to Japanese Studies* (Tokyo: Kokusai Bunka Shinkokai, 1937), p. 148: ". . . whether Shintoism is a religion or an ethical code, it ought to promote world peace for the Japanese are not a warlike people as some outsiders might suspect. . . . the Goddess [Amaterasu Ōmikami] . . . did not like warfare. Further back, in the *Nihonshoki* and *Kojiki*, the gods are represented as hating war. . . . But even war-haters would rise on the occasion when national peace and culture were at stake. In this attitude is seen something of the Japanese spirit. Our history proves that we have never declared war against foreign countries; we have fought only to protect our peace and security against the violence of foreign forces."

way for recent events. The philosophy of traditional Japan has long called for a high standard of honor and other recognized moral values—so much so that one can understand recent events only with the greatest difficulty. Actually, however, there is nothing insurmountably difficult in the situation. Honor, sympathy, modesty, politeness, benevolence, etc., have long been fundamental virtues of the Japanese, but above all of these and above all standards whatsoever there has always stood the keystone of the arch: namely, loyalty and duty to ruler, country, and race. In deference to this absolutely supreme standard all else shrinks into insignificance. Not explicitly stated, but implicitly embodied in the general situation, is the undeniable fact that *whatever* is deemed consonant with or essential to loyalty to ruler and country will be accepted—regardless of conflict with other (and lesser) standards. The end justifies the means—and apparently *any* means. The unscrupulous actions of present-day Japan seem to be at variance with the high standards of the *samurai* and with bushidō in general but these actions are not really contrary to the basic principle of Japanese morality. Japan has been *potentially* naturalistic all the while. The militarists of Japan have forced this implicit Naturalism to become explicit and to reveal itself as the essential or ultimate ethical principle *underlying* many commendable but actually relatively superficial virtuous traits of the Japanese people—*as a nation*.

(3) The third of the prominent Western attitudes which has been generally rejected by the East is the complex and indescribable attitude of materialism-mechanicalism-"scientificism." Efficiency, mechanical production and progress, mechanical devices for the comfort of men, material possessions, and the dependence upon economic and scientific enterprise for the solution of man's problems and to provide him with the *Summum Bonum* of all living— that is the spirit of the West, especially the modern West.[147] It has never constituted the spirit of the East—although that general attitude is becoming more significant in the Orient today (except in

[147] Few Easterners but many Westerners would say with Dr. H. M. Kallen: "Wherever salvation is sought chiefly by the means of science and by the technologies based on science, men are freer, healthier, better fed, happier, more peaceable, and live longer." *The Bertrand Russell Case*, ed. by John Dewey and Horace M. Kallen (New York: The Viking Press, 1941), pp. 35-36.

India, however, where the leaders of thought are still insistent upon the validity of the traditional idealistic philosophies).[148]

To say that such has been the philosophy of the West may give the impression that we too are guilty of interpreting a culture by its latest stage alone. That is not the case, however, for the West, almost throughout the history of its thought, has been science-minded[149] and economic-and-power conscious,[150] and has centered its attention on the search for worldly goods as the goal of man's actions. The point need not be labored or examined extensively. Strictly speaking there are numerous exceptions to the view that the West has been dominated by this general attitude but, practically speaking, there is little doubt that this is true.

In contrast to these Western tendencies which the East has rejected, much of the Orient has adopted some form of what is often called "Idealistic Self-Realizationism" or "Idealistic Perfectionism."[151] In the West this philosophy calls for the recognition of the supreme worth of the Person—often in the individualistic sense—and also sets up perfection as the ideal. It demands, further, the full realization of the many-sided nature of man, the complete energizing of his excellences, but always in the service of the highest, the idealistic, side of his being. There are major tendencies in the East that do not conform to these demands, as we have seen. In criticism of these Oriental tendencies it may be said that here— from the West's point of view—lies the seat of the East's (especially India's) greatest narrowness of view: namely, its blindness to the *full* nature of man resulting from its excessive recognition of his ultimate nature and status in relation to the universe. Its attitude of ultimate perspective, its view of man as a part of the uni-

[148] See S. Radhakrishnan, ed., *Contemporary Indian Philosophy* (London: Allen and Unwin, 1936). See also A. K. Coomaraswamy, "Eastern Wisdom and Western Knowledge," *Isis*, XXXIV, 1943, p. 360: ". . . as Guénon says, 'what the people of the West call "rising" would be called by some "sinking"; that is what all true Orientals think.' "

[149] See, for example, John Burnet, *Greek Philosophy*, Part I, Thales to Plato (London: Macmillan and Co., 1920). See Introduction.

[150] The Middle Ages are an exception, of course, and so is that element or degree of Western thought and civilization that derives from Christianity or other religions.

[151] For a statement of the essentials of this theory, see W. M. Urban, *Fundamentals of Ethics* (New York: Henry Holt & Co.), Chs. VI-VIII.

verse, has stood in the way of an adequate recognition of man as *man.*

However, in contrast to all worldly and more materialistic philosophies, the East does conform to the doctrine of Idealistic Self-Realization. Negatively, it is idealistic by virtue of its rejection of all nonidealistic attitudes, and positively, by virtue of its insistence upon some form of *Summum Bonum* or Self-Realization above the level of the material or bodily. This idealism, in one form or another, is characteristic of the main trends of ethical thought throughout the East.[152] "The East has never been seduced by matter."

CONCLUSION

Such, then, are the major phases of Oriental ethical thought which, *as emphases,* are in contrast to the major *tendencies* of Western philosophy and Western civilization: (1) the recognition of the "practical" aspect of philosophy, (2) the attitude of "Ultimate Perspective," (3) the attitude of "Dual Perspective," (4) the tendency toward some form of "Negativism," (5) Monism or the tendency to see individual man in some larger perspective, and (6) Idealism in some general meaning of that term.[153]

These emphases constitute the more important ways in which the ethical thought of the East may supplement the ethical perspective of the West. The West has not failed to discover these various attitudes, to be sure, but it is unquestionable that its trend has been in other or opposite directions and that these emphases of Oriental philosophies of life have, relatively, been neglected. The converse is true in the case of the East. Each, that is, has found certain

---

[152] This statement is based, in general on the prevalence of some doctrine of "tendance of soul" in all major Indian philosophies and on Confucian China's primary concern with moral rectitude as the supreme value—even above life itself. Even the Japanese, as Professor Karl Löwith recently wrote in *Fortune Magazine* (Dec. 1943), "despise our civilization for its materialism, the care for life and comfort, for individual happiness, health, and wealth."

[153] Many other ideas and practices of Oriental ethics—such as *ahiṁsā, Karma, yoga,* etc.—are also worthy of extensive consideration as provocative suggestions to the West. These have been briefly explained in earlier descriptive chapters or here, but no adequate study of all such ideas could be attempted. Special attention is called to the doctrines of *ahiṁsā* and *karma* for these have been called the most significant ideas of Indian philosophy by competent authorities.

attitudes more acceptable practically and philosophically. Such tendencies have won out so thoroughly in the competition of ways of life that their opposites have lost status generally. This has been the mistake of both East and West. This tragedy, philosophically and practically, can be overcome. The obvious suggestion is that a sounder philosophy of life—a world philosophy—might be found in a synthesis of these major contrasting points of view.

The emphasis in this analysis, as in the entire volume, has been consciously directed toward calling the attention of the West to those ideas and attitudes of the East which seem most significant as possible correctives or supplements to the tendencies in Western ethical thought. The emphasis, further, has been in the direction of interpreting these attitudes in their best—that is, their proper—light so as to counteract the much more frequent critical interpretation. No distortion of meanings has been indulged in. The attempt has been made simply to present the ideas as the Oriental understands his own theories but also in such a way as to indicate their special significance for the West, with its particular problems and interests. This form of presentation may have given the impression that the Oriental ideas are superior to those of the West. That was not the intention. The underlying thesis has been that both East and West are faulty in their analysis of the ethical situation and in their philosophies of life and consequently that both need correctives. It happens that the East and the West do, in their emphases, offer rather clear-cut antitheses on certain main points, so much so that a synthesis readily suggests itself. Such a synthesis, however, must be a real one, based upon adequate, sincere, and sympathetic study of East by West and of West by East. The search for such a synthesis has actually been begun by the East—which has advanced considerably toward a proper understanding and appreciation of the philosophies of the West[154]—but has not been seriously attempted by the West.

In this study the main effort has been directed toward the deficiencies of Western thought in connection with each of the main points considered. The deficiencies of the contrasting Eastern attitudes

[154] The text and the index of almost any recent work on Oriental or comparative philosophy written by an Oriental provide ample evidence of the accuracy of this statement. Contrast histories of philosophy written by Westerners.

have been rather manifest, of course, to the Western reader—it is easy to see the defects of an alien culture—and it has been the intention to leave this side of the picture to the reader's own consideration. While each of the main attitudes presented as Oriental contributions to ethical thought is significant, *not one of them* is sufficiently comprehensive to be acceptable as the final answer to the problem in question. Nevertheless, these bits of the wisdom of the Orient, being based upon keen intellectual insight and proved in theory and in practice by ages of criticism and of trial as actual guides to the living of a great part of the human race, cannot be ignored or even minimized if we would attain to a philosophy that is worthy of the name. It is not enough—it is not even logical—to say that these ideas do not fit our Western tradition. Perhaps our tradition itself is in need of some remolding. Be that as it may, philosophy as philosophy is not searching for concepts that fit certain traditions; it is seeking the meaning of life and the essence of the good life. In this quest the wisdom of the East must not be overlooked for it has significant ideas to suggest. They may not displace the traditional attitudes of the West but our vastly younger Western civilization—and philosophy—may benefit in untold ways from the wisdom of the East, which in many of its attitudes seems to have matured far beyond anything yet achieved in the West.

Let us conclude on a note of specific suggestiveness and hope, an idea that comes to us from the former Ambassador to the United States from China, Dr. Hu Shih,[155] one of the most prominent figures in recent Chinese philosophy. He opposes the usual interpretation that the Orient is more spiritual (in the broader sense) than the West—at least potentially. His point is that the East can hardly indulge fully in the more spiritual side of life because of the urgency of the very process of living; the problems of satisfying the actual needs of life are so great that the more spiritual side of life must perforce be neglected. In the West, on the other hand, where the mechanics of providing for the actual needs of life have been perfected, there are the prime requisites for the spiritual side of life: the nonurgency of the practical problem of living and

[155] See his "Our Attitude Towards Modern Western Civilization" (originally published in Chinese in 1926), in his *Hu Shih Wen-ts'un* (Collected Essays) (Shanghai: Commercial Press), Third Series, V. I, 1930, especially p. 8.

the accompanying leisure which is so necessary before the spiritual side of life can be appreciated. Here then is a specific suggestion for a synthesis: The West should turn to the more spiritual aspect of life, to a more serious concern with the meaning and true goal of life, since it has mastered its practical side; the East should learn from the West, not necessarily its interpretation of the meaning of life, but its practical machinery, its methods for supplying the needs of life. In that way both East and West may finally experience real and complete human living.[156]

[156] Another specific suggestion—relating India and the West—comes from Kenneth Saunders (*The Ideals of East and West*, p. 25) : "Indian acceptance of the fundamental law of *karma* has its weakness: personality is merged in the mass and its nerve is too often cut—a fatalistic attitude being very usual. And the pantheistic soil of India is not good for those virtues most valued in the more individualistic West—energy, initiative, and determination to harness nature in the service of man." On the other hand, "every Hindu frankly confesses that in social service the West has set a new and creative standard; and many own that even *ahiṁsā* and detachment need the control of logic and a sane scale of values. Can India retain her gentleness and add energy, preserve her devotion to God in serving men, practise detachment in acquiring zeal? If so, she can help to cure us of the worship of the machine and can work out with us a more humane order of society."

Who's Who of Contributors

CHAN WING-TSIT. Professor of Chinese Philosophy and Institutions, University of Hawaii. Similar post at Dartmouth College since 1942. Recent writings include "Living Philosophies of China" in *Twentieth Century Philosophy*, and articles on Chinese Philosophy in *Dictionary of Philosophy* and *Encyclopedia of Religion*. A.B. Lingnan, A.M. and Ph.D. Harvard.

GEORGE P. CONGER. Professor of Philosophy, University of Minnesota. With YMCA in Siberia in World War I. Sabbatical study in India, 1933-1934. *The Horizons of Thought* and *The Ideologies of Religion* are latest books. A.B. Cornell, B.D. Union Theological Seminary, Ph.D. Columbia.

WILLIAM ERNEST HOCKING. Widely known Professor of Philosophy at Harvard University. Now Alford Professor Emeritus. A.B., A.M., Ph.D. Harvard. Honorary degrees from Williams, Chicago, Glasgow, and Oberlin. Trustee Lingnan University, China. Author of many books, among them being: *Spirit of World Politics* and *Living Religions and a World Faith*.

CHARLES A. MOORE. Chairman, Department of Philosophy, University of Hawaii. Formerly instructor in Philosophy, Yale University. Sometime Acting Director, Oriental Institute, University of Hawaii. Chairman, East-West Philosophers' Conference. A.B. and Ph.D. Yale.

FILMER S. C. NORTHROP. Professor of Philosophy and Master of Silliman College in Yale University. Author of *Science and First Principles* and numerous articles in the philosophy of science. Member, International Committee, YMCA, Hong Kong, 1919-1920. A.B. Beloit, A.M. Yale, A.M. and Ph.D. Harvard.

SHUNZŌ SAKAMAKI. Assistant Professor of History, University of Hawaii. Author of *Japan and the United States, 1790-1853*. A.B. and A.M. University of Hawaii, Ph.D. Columbia.

DAISETZ (DAISETSU) TEITARŌ SUZUKI. Professor of Zen Buddhism, Otani University, Kyoto, Japan. Prolific author and translator in field of Buddhism and Far Eastern Philosophy. Among his writings are: *Essays in Zen Buddhism* (three series) and *Buddhist Philosophy and its Effect on the Life and Thought of the Japanese People*. Editor, *The Eastern Buddhist*.

JUNJIRŌ TAKAKUSU. Emeritus Professor, Tokyo Imperial University. Member, Imperial Academy of Japan. Author, translator, and editor of many works on Buddhism and Indian philosophy. Editor, *Dictionary of Buddhism*. Graduate, Kyoto Imperial University; Oxford, 1890-1894. Honorary D.Litt. Heidelberg, D.Litt. Oxford.

Index

Oriental religion, *see* Religion
Otherworldliness, 10-11, 19, 282. *See also* Negativism
Otto, Rudolf, 124

Pañchāstikāyagāthā, 269n
Pañchāstikāyasāra, 260n
Pantheism, 237, 239, 241, 320n
Parmenides, 215
Patañjali, 17
Paul, St., 292
Payne, Richarda C., 125n
Peace, 35, 38-39, 273, 298, 302, 312, 314
Perfectionism, *see* Self-Realization
Perry, R. B., 267n
Persia, 277, 293
Pessimism, 19, 46-47, 144, 156-157, 253n, 262-263, 288n, 290
Phaedo, 286n
Philosophies of life, comparative, 248-320
Philosophy, complementary emphases of Eastern and Western, 168-234
Physica, 185n
Plato, 178-181, 183-185, 196, 215-216, 218-219, 226, 242-244, 267n, 285-286, 295n, 296n, 298n, 302, 304-305, 307. *See also Apology; Crito; Gorgias; Phaedo; Republic; and Theaetetus*
Plotinus, 241, 243
Pluralism, 16-17, 142, 153-156, 245, 259-260
Polytheism, 13, 21, 130-135, 258
Positivism, in West, 5, 178, 180, 189, 226; in East, 15, 39, 193, 197, 209, 219; as category of comparison of East and West, 211-214
Postulation, *see* Concepts, by postulation
Poussin, La Vallée, 138n, 141n, 146n, 260n
Prabhākara, 18
Pragmatism, 11
Prakriti (Material Principle), 17, 72
Praśastapāda, 16
Praśna Upanishad, 154n
Pratt, J. B., 218n, 260n, 268n, 287n, 309n
Propriety (*li*), 27, 32, 206, 294
Purusha, see Soul

Pūrva Mīmāṁsā (Mīmāṅsā), *see* Mīmāṁsā

Quietism, 36-37, 54. *See also* Negativism

Radhakrishnan, S., 143, 144n, 153n, 253n, 254n, 258n, 277, 278n, 282n, 283n, 284, 285n, 286n, 287n, 291n, 316n
Rāmānuja, 18, 143, 152-153, 239, 260, 285n. *See also* Vedānta
Rawlinson, F., 261n, 287n, 306n
Realism, 16, 72, 97-99, 199-202, 219-220
Reality, descriptions of, in East, 14, 58-62, 69-72, 83, 113, 119, 150, 155-157, 164, 191, 203, 207, 211, 290; levels of, 153-154, 167, 283-287 (*see also* Dual Perspective); defined in terms of East and West, 232
Reason and Reasoning, in West, 224-225. *See also* East, science, logic, and reason in; Logic; Knowledge; *and* Science
Rebirth, 15, 81, 144, 146, 258-259, 290-291
Rectification of names, 6, 29, 32, 272, 300
Release, 14-18, 258-259. *See also* Emancipation *and* Moksha
Religion, in East, 11, 21, 25-26, 41, 118, 144-145, 279; contrast of, in East and West, 171, 217, 219. *See also* Atheism *and* East, relation of philosophy and religion in
Republic, The, 181, 286n, 295n, 296
Revelation, as means of knowledge in East, 150
Rhys Davids, C. A. F., 260n
Rig Veda, see Vedas
Rinzai, 115-117
Royce, Josiah, 241
Runes, D. D., 68n, 142n, 147n, 149n
Russell, Bertrand, 213
Rutherford, Sir Ernest, 183

Saccidānandam, 69-70
Sacred Books of the East, The, 270n, 285n
Sacred Books of the Hindus, The, 269n, 270n, 286n

334 INDEX

Value of East for West, 1-2, 4-8, 10-11, 20-23, 178, 230, 265, 280-281, 289-298, 302-303
Value of West for East, 11, 213, 215-219
Vasubandhu, 72, 109, 198-202, 240
Vātsyāyana, 15
Vedānta, 9, 16, 21, 142-143, 151-153, 191, 239, 250n, 257, 266, 269, 282, 285, 288, 290, 302-303, 307; basic doctrines of, 18, 72, 259-260. *See also* Hinduism; Rāmānuja; *and* Śaṅkara
Vedānta Sūtras, 18, 149n, 270n, 285n, 286n
Vedas, 12-15, 18, 71, 142, 150-151, 161, 259, 268, 278n; *Rig Veda*, 13, 20, 258, 278n; *Sāma Veda*, 13; *Yajur Veda*, 13; *Atharva Veda*, 13, 71
Vidyābhūshaṇa, M. S. C., 162n, 269n
Vienna Circle, 214n
Vijñāna Bhikshu, 16
Vijñaptimātratā school, *see* Buddhist systems and schools
Vijñaptimātratāsiddhi, 138, 141n, 146n, 159n
Viṁśatikā (Viṅśatika), 158n
Visuddhimagga, 103
Void (*Śūnyatā*), 52, 55, 57-58, 85-87, 99, 119, 140, 153, 155, 165, 240, 260, 282. *See also* Suchness *and* Thusness

Waley, Arthur, 25n, 33n, 34n
Walleser, M., 138n
Wang Ch'ung, 48-51, 158, 163
Wang Yang-ming, 62-65, 160, 210-211
Warren, H. C., 140n, 148n, 268n
West, 5, 67-68, 181-183, 216-219, 224-225, 230, 241-245, 280, 286-287; basic doctrines of, 4-5, 10-11, 171-172, 190, 241-242, 265, 301, 315. *See also* Contrasts; Criticisms; Misunderstanding; Similarities;

Value of East for West; *and* Value of West for East
Western Philosophy, *see* West
Whitehead, A. N., 176n, 177n, 178n, 179-180, 185, 193, 213, 225, 243
Widgery, A. G., 264n
Will, freedom of, 157. *See also* Destiny; Determinism; *and* Fatalism
Wittgenstein, L., 214n
Woods, J. H., 151n
Wu wei, 35-37, 46-48. *See also* Taoism

Yājñavalkya, 14, 69
Yajur Veda, see Vedas
Yamakami, S., 287n, 309n
Yang Chu, 33-34, 262, 274, 309, 311
Yengo, 117-119
Yin yang, 48-50, 52, 56-60, 155, 209, 244, 275n, 278n, 295n, 312
Yin Yang school, 24, 44, 48, 275
Yoga, 17-18, 72, 137, 142, 151, 166, 223, 231, 239, 259, 270, 288, 317n; basic doctrines of, 17-18, 259-260. *See also* Hinduism
Yoga Sūtras, 17, 151n, 270n
Yogācāra school, *see* Buddhist systems and schools
Yogācārabhūmi, 138
Yü Lei (Sayings [of Chu Hsi] *Arranged by Topics)*, 55n, 57n, 58n, 59n, 60n
Yüan Shan (An Inquiry into Goodness), 66n, 67n

Zen (Ch'an, Meditation) Buddhism, 53-54, 72, 102-107, 109-129, 163, 256; relation of, to Japanese life, 107, 109; uniqueness of, 117, 119-120, 129; relation of, to mysticism, 120-127. *See also* Buddhism *and* Buddhist systems and schools
Zen, Sophia, 144n
Zoroastrianism, 244, 257n, 264, 277n, 279, 293